# BLADE
## OF THE IMMORTAL

# The Gathering

publisher
# Mike Richardson

series editor
# Mike Hansen

collection editor
# Chris Warner

collection designer
# Amy Arendts

**English-language version produced by Studio Proteus for Dark Horse Comics, Inc.**

This book collects issues forty-three through
forty-nine of the Dark Horse comic-book series,
*Blade of the Immortal.*

Published by
Dark Horse Comics, Inc.
10956 SE Main Street
Milwaukie, OR 97222

www.darkhorse.com

To find a comics shop in your area, call the
Comic Shop Locator Service toll-free at 1-888-266-4226.

First edition: August 2001
ISBN: 1-56971-546-7

1 3 5 7 9 10 8 6 4 2

Printed in Canada

# BLADE
## OF THE IMMORTAL

art and story
# HIROAKI SAMURA

translation
## Dana Lewis & Toren Smith

lettering and retouch
## Tomoko Saito

# The Gathering

**DARK HORSE COMICS®**

# ABOUT THE TRANSLATION

## The Swastika

The main character in *Blade of the Immortal*, Manji, has taken the "crux gammata" as both his name and his personal symbol. This symbol is also known as the *swastika*, a name derived from the Sanskrit *svastika* (meaning "welfare," from *su* — "well" + *asti* "he is"). As a symbol of prosperity and good fortune, the swastika was widely used throughout the ancient world (for example, appearing often on Mesopotamian coinage), including North and South America and has been used in Japan as a symbol of Buddhism since ancient times. To be precise, the symbol generally used by Japanese Buddhists is the *sauvastika*, which moves in a counterclockwise direction, and is called the *manji* in Japanese. The arms of the *swastika*, which point in a clockwise direction, are generally considered a solar symbol. It was this version (the *hakenkreuz*) that was perverted by the Nazis. The *sauvastika* generally stands for night, and often for magical practices. It is important that readers understand that the swastika has ancient and honorable origins, and it is those that apply to this story, which takes place in the 18th century [ca. 1782–3]. *There is no anti-Semitic or pro-Nazi meaning behind the* use of the symbol in this story. Those meanings did not exist until 1910.

## The Artwork

The creator of *Blade of the Immortal* requested that we make an effort to avoid mirror-imaging his artwork. Normally, all of our manga are first copied in a mirror-image in order to facilitate the left-to-right reading of the pages. However, Mr. Samura decided that he would rather see his pages reversed via the technique of cutting up the panels and re-pasting them in reverse order. While we feel that this often leads to problems in panel-to-panel continuity, we place primary importance on the wishes of the creator. Therefore, most of *Blade of the Immortal* has been produced using the "cut and paste" technique. There are, of course, some sequences where it was impossible to do this, and mirror-imaged panels or pages were used.

## The Sound Effects & Dialogue

Since some of Mr. Samura's sound effects are integral parts of the illustrations, we decided to leave those in their original Japanese. We hope readers will view the unretouched sound effects as essential portions of Mr. Samura's extraordinary artwork. In addition, Mr. Samura's treatment of dialogue is quite different from that featured in typical samurai manga and is considered to be one of the features that has made *Blade* such a hit in Japan. Mr. Samura has mixed a variety of linguistic styles in this fantasy story, with some characters speaking in the mannered style of old Japan while others speak as if they were street-corner punks from a bad area of modern-day Tokyo. The anachronistic slang used by some of the characters in the English translation reflects the unusual mix of speech patterns from the original Japanese text.

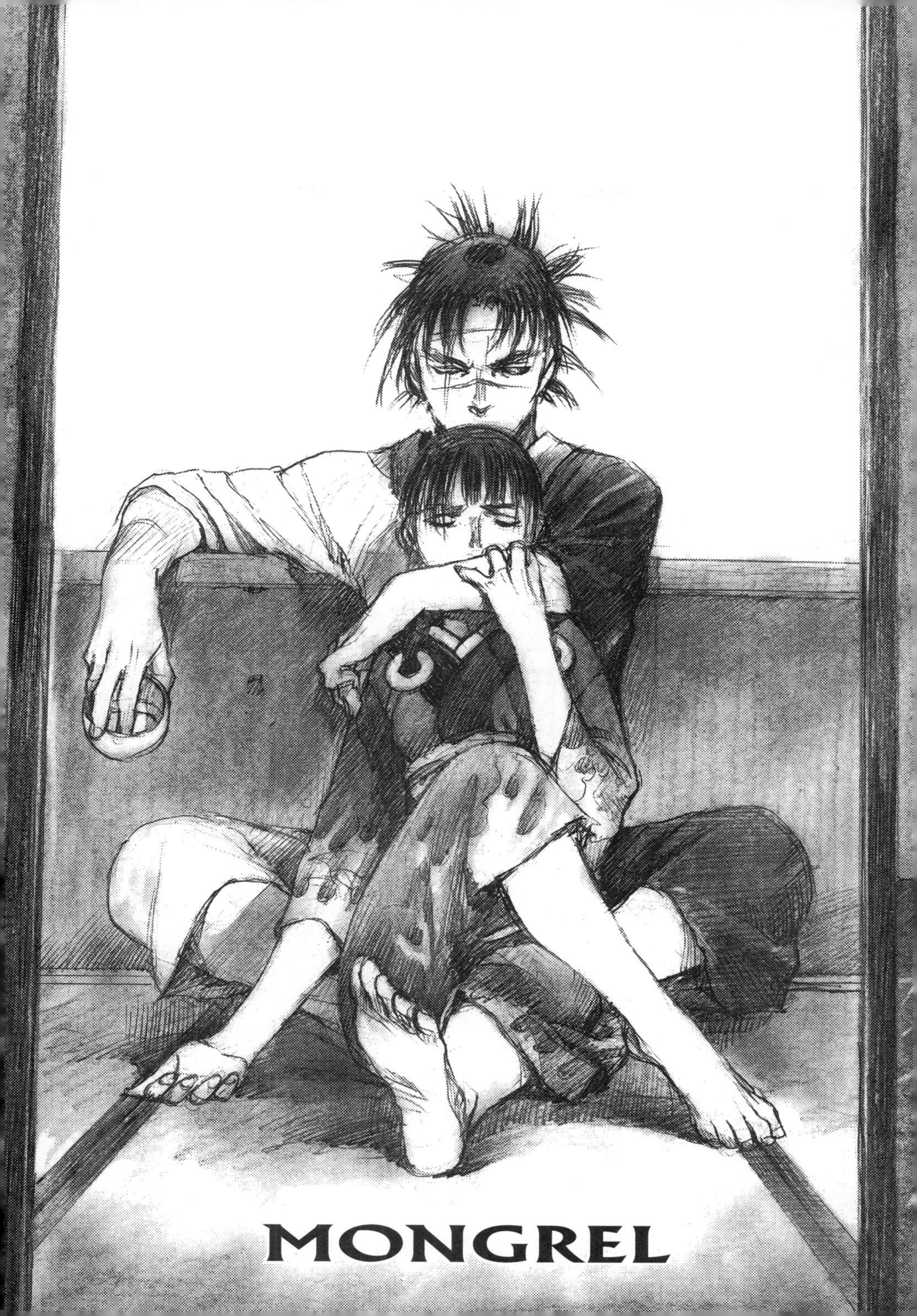

# MONGREL

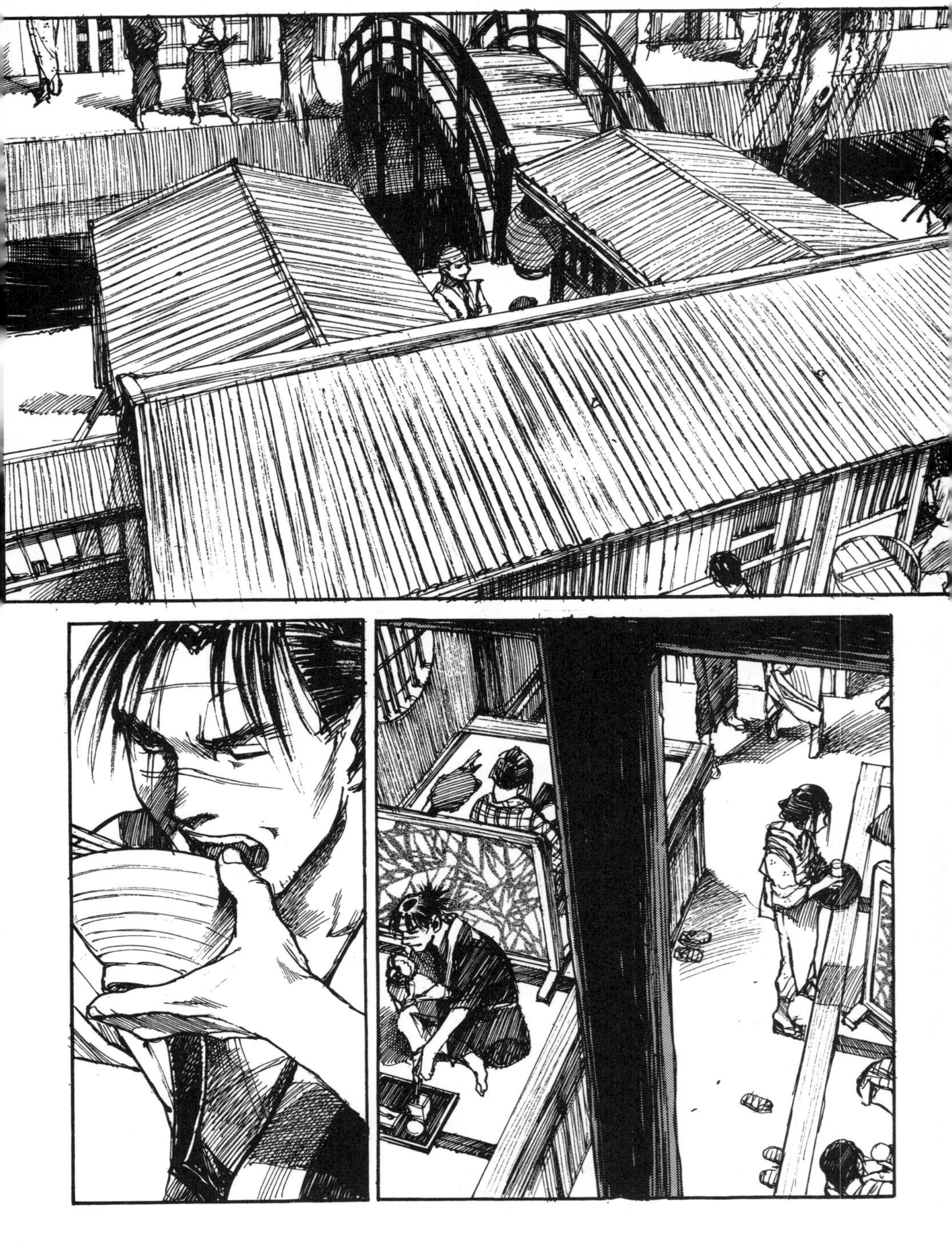

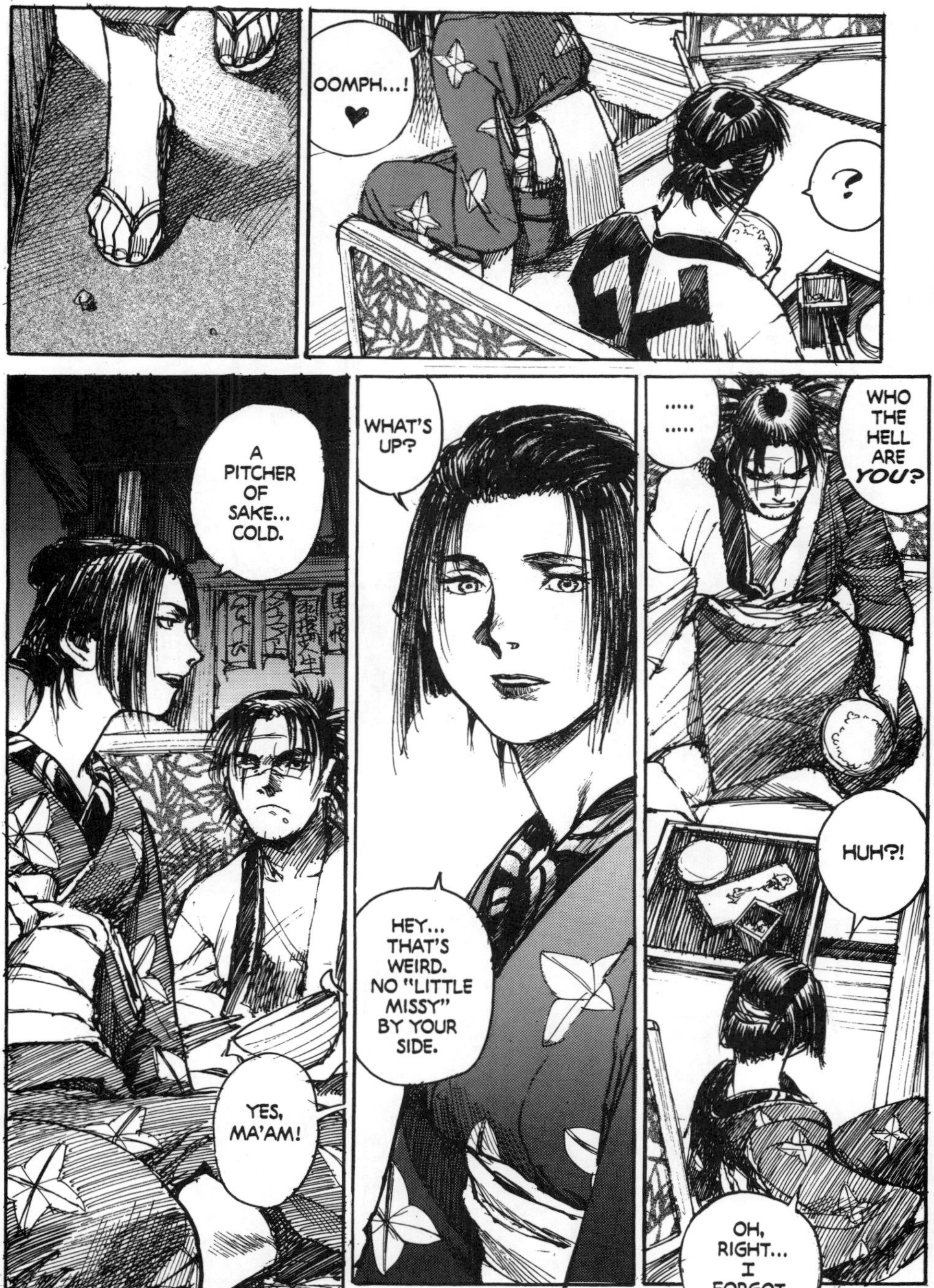
OOMPH...! ♥
?
A PITCHER OF SAKE... COLD.
YES, MA'AM!
WHAT'S UP?
HEY... THAT'S WEIRD. NO "LITTLE MISSY" BY YOUR SIDE.
..... .....
WHO THE HELL ARE *YOU?*
HUH?!
OH, RIGHT... I FORGOT.

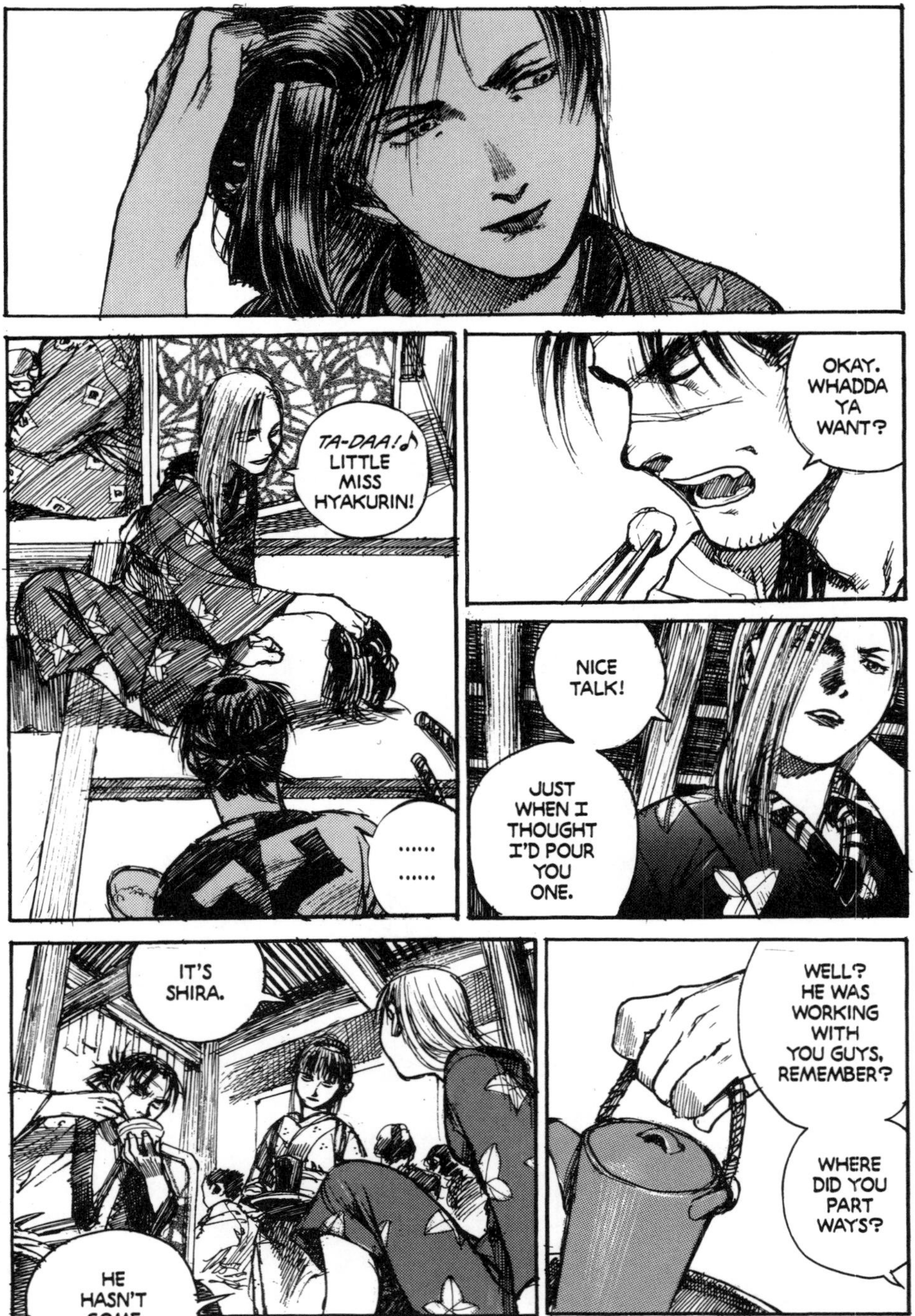
TA-DAA!♪ LITTLE MISS HYAKURIN!
......
......
OKAY. WHADDA YA WANT?
NICE TALK!
JUST WHEN I THOUGHT I'D POUR YOU ONE.
IT'S SHIRA.
HE HASN'T COME BACK.
WELL? HE WAS WORKING WITH YOU GUYS, REMEMBER?
WHERE DID YOU PART WAYS?

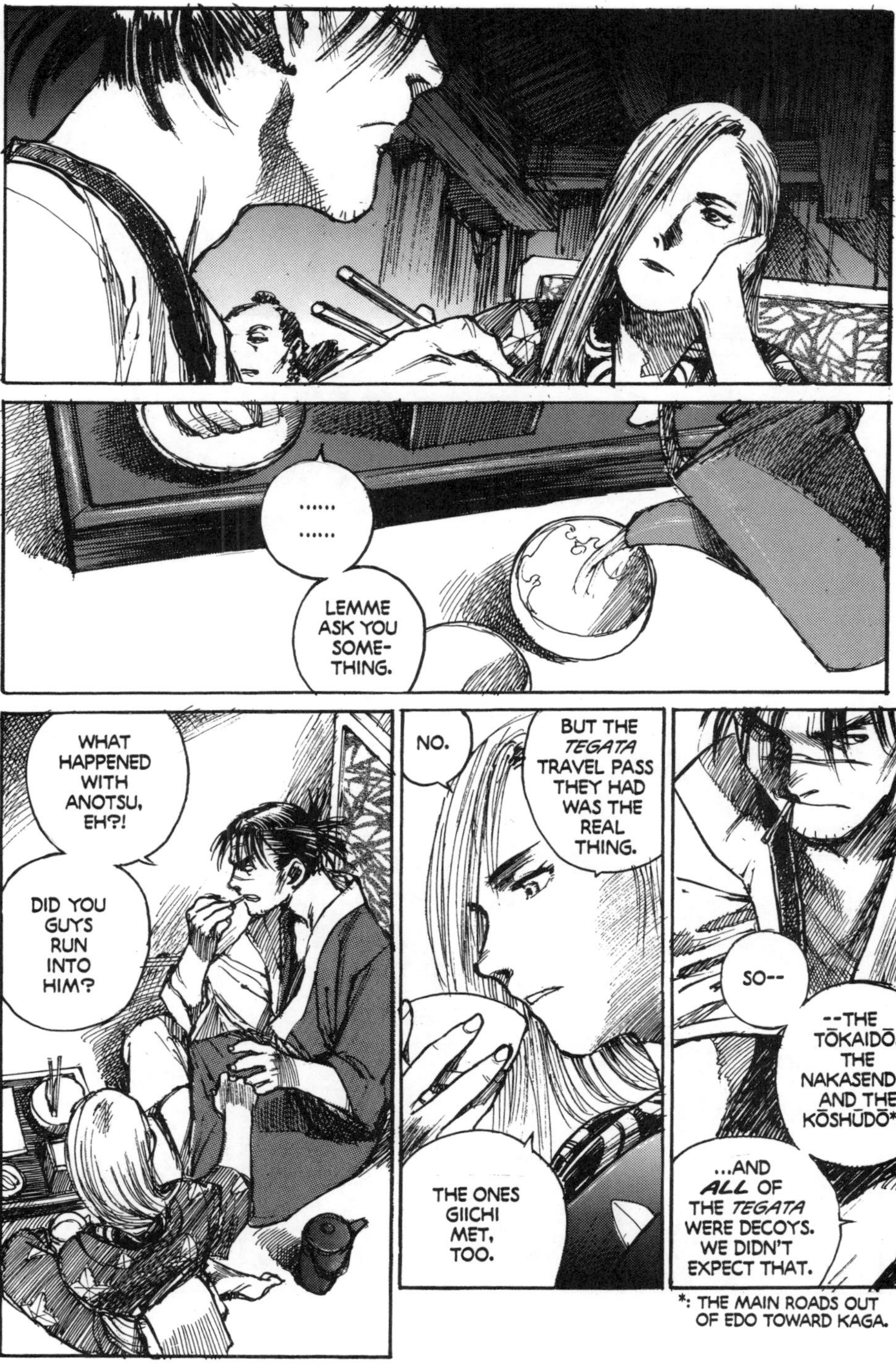
......
......
LEMME ASK YOU SOMETHING.
WHAT HAPPENED WITH ANOTSU, EH?!
DID YOU GUYS RUN INTO HIM?
NO.
BUT THE *TEGATA* TRAVEL PASS THEY HAD WAS THE REAL THING.
THE ONES GIICHI MET, TOO.
SO--
--THE TŌKAIDŌ, THE NAKASENDŌ, AND THE KŌSHŪDŌ*...
...AND ***ALL*** OF THE *TEGATA* WERE DECOYS. WE DIDN'T EXPECT THAT.

*: THE MAIN ROADS OUT OF EDO TOWARD KAGA.

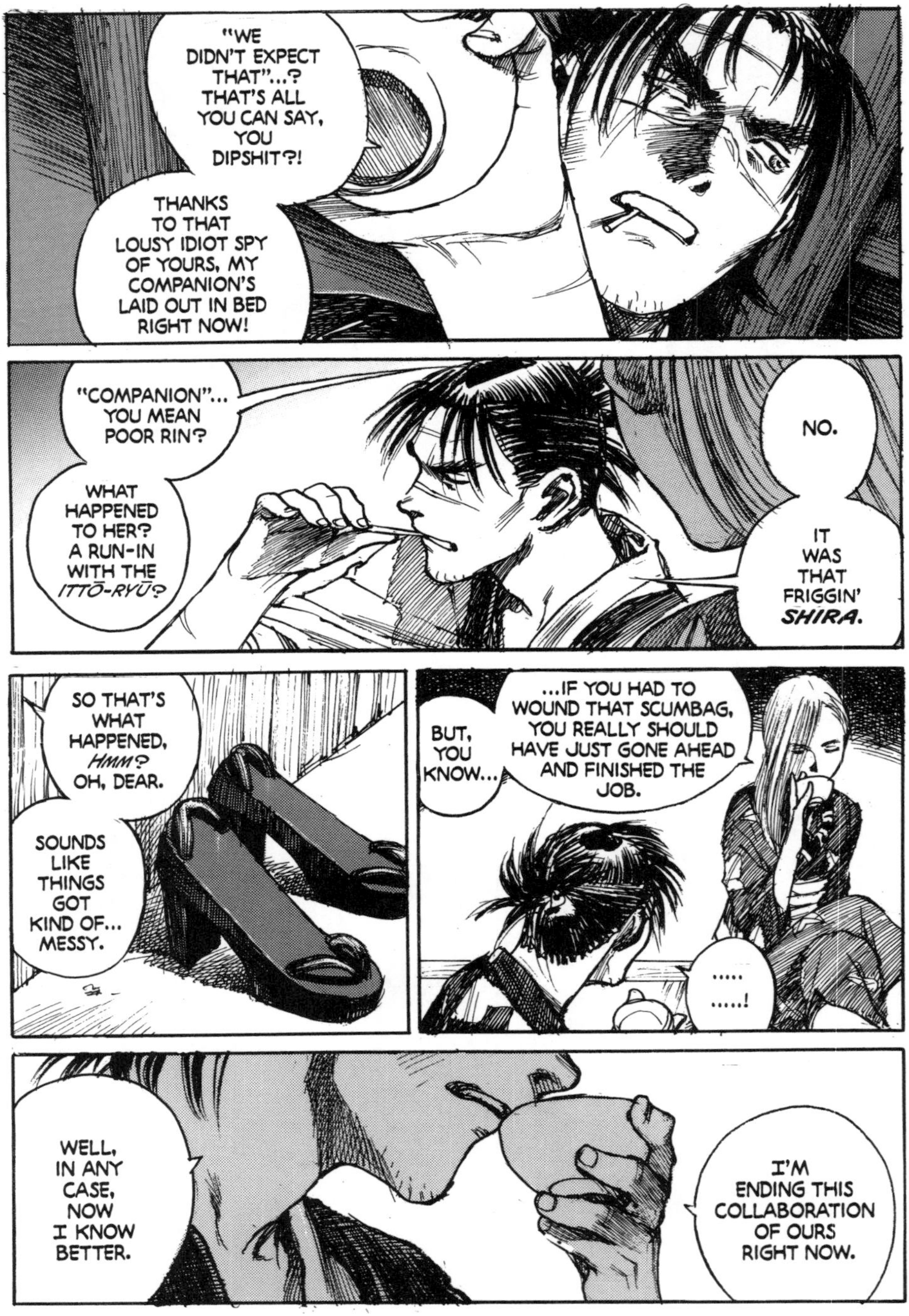
"WE DIDN'T EXPECT THAT"...? THAT'S ALL YOU CAN SAY, YOU DIPSHIT?!
THANKS TO THAT LOUSY IDIOT SPY OF YOURS, MY COMPANION'S LAID OUT IN BED RIGHT NOW!
"COMPANION"... YOU MEAN POOR RIN?
WHAT HAPPENED TO HER? A RUN-IN WITH THE *ITTŌ-RYŪ*?
NO.
IT WAS THAT FRIGGIN' ***SHIRA***.
SO THAT'S WHAT HAPPENED, *HMM*? OH, DEAR.
SOUNDS LIKE THINGS GOT KIND OF... MESSY.
BUT, YOU KNOW...
...IF YOU HAD TO WOUND THAT SCUMBAG, YOU REALLY SHOULD HAVE JUST GONE AHEAD AND FINISHED THE JOB.
..... .....!
WELL, IN ANY CASE, NOW I KNOW BETTER.
I'M ENDING THIS COLLABORATION OF OURS RIGHT NOW.

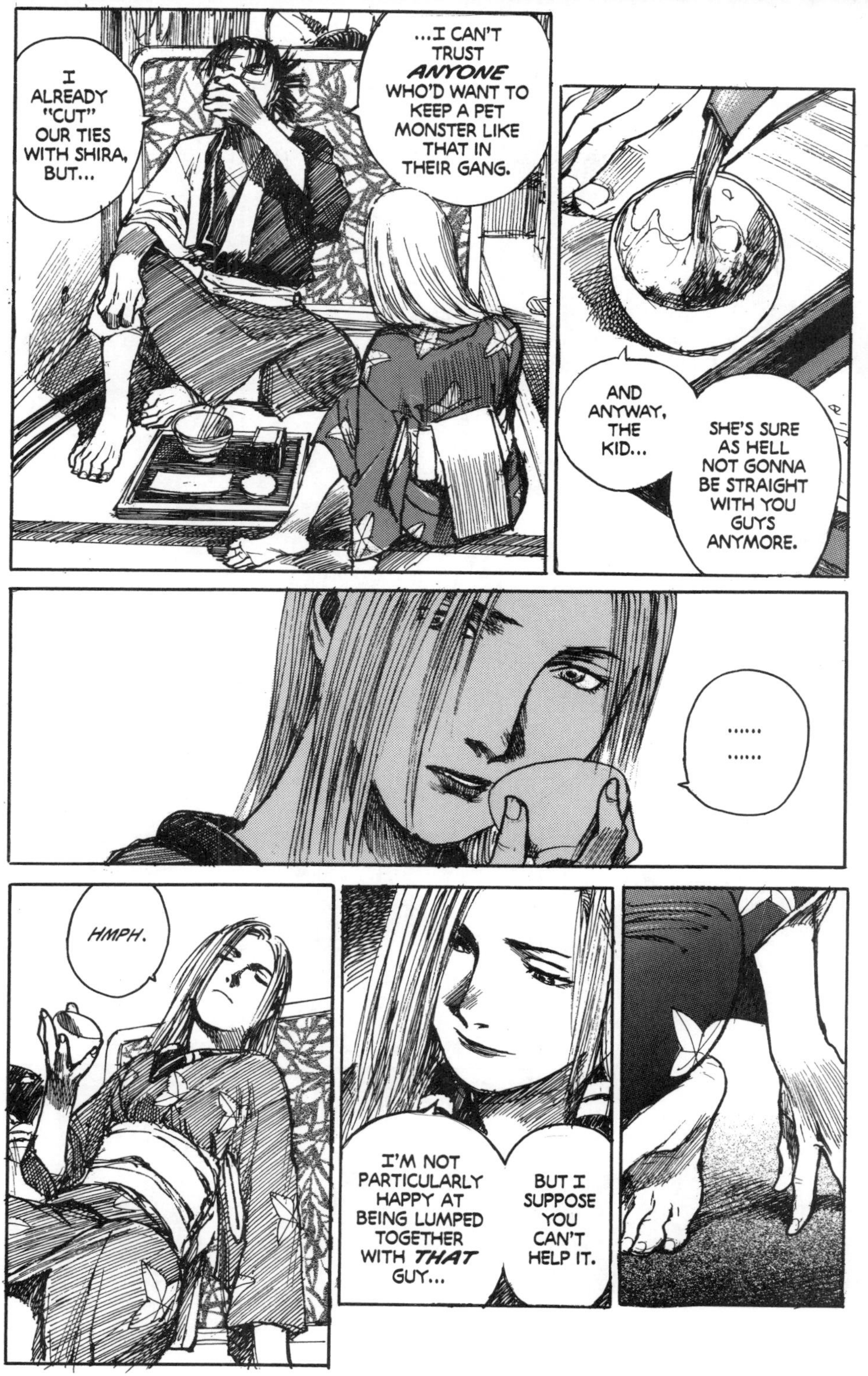

I ALREADY "CUT" OUR TIES WITH SHIRA, BUT...
...I CAN'T TRUST ANYONE WHO'D WANT TO KEEP A PET MONSTER LIKE THAT IN THEIR GANG.
AND ANYWAY, THE KID...
SHE'S SURE AS HELL NOT GONNA BE STRAIGHT WITH YOU GUYS ANYMORE.
......
......
HMPH.
I'M NOT PARTICULARLY HAPPY AT BEING LUMPED TOGETHER WITH THAT GUY...
BUT I SUPPOSE YOU CAN'T HELP IT.

BY THE WAY... ...I WILL TELL YOU *ONE* THING.

GIICHI FOUND OUT SOMETHING--

--WHERE ANOTSU WILL BE STAYING IN KAGA.

*NYA HA HA HA!* BUT, YOU KNOW... TO TELL THE TRUTH...

...EVEN THOUGH WE KNOW THAT NOW, IT'S TOTALLY MEANINGLESS.

WE'RE IN THE SAME BOAT YOU ARE, SEE?

IN THE *MUGAI-RYŪ...*

...IT'S ONE OF OUR OFFICIAL REGULATIONS THAT WE CAN'T CHASE OUR ENEMIES THROUGH THE CHECKPOINTS.

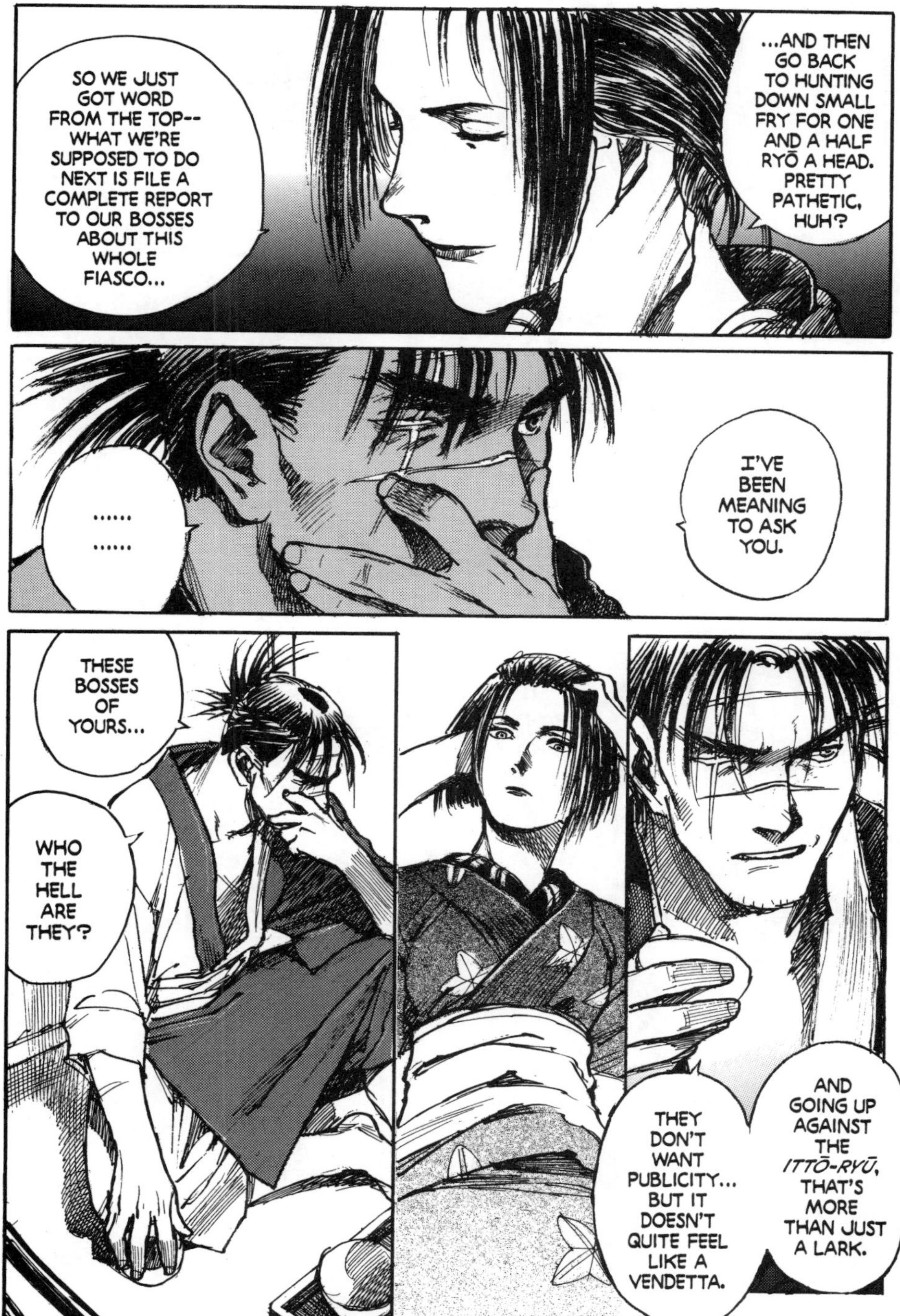
SO WE JUST GOT WORD FROM THE TOP-- WHAT WE'RE SUPPOSED TO DO NEXT IS FILE A COMPLETE REPORT TO OUR BOSSES ABOUT THIS WHOLE FIASCO...
...AND THEN GO BACK TO HUNTING DOWN SMALL FRY FOR ONE AND A HALF RYŌ A HEAD. PRETTY PATHETIC, HUH?
...... ......
I'VE BEEN MEANING TO ASK YOU.
THESE BOSSES OF YOURS...
WHO THE HELL ARE THEY?
THEY DON'T WANT PUBLICITY... BUT IT DOESN'T QUITE FEEL LIKE A VENDETTA.
AND GOING UP AGAINST THE *ITTŌ-RYŪ*, THAT'S MORE THAN JUST A LARK.

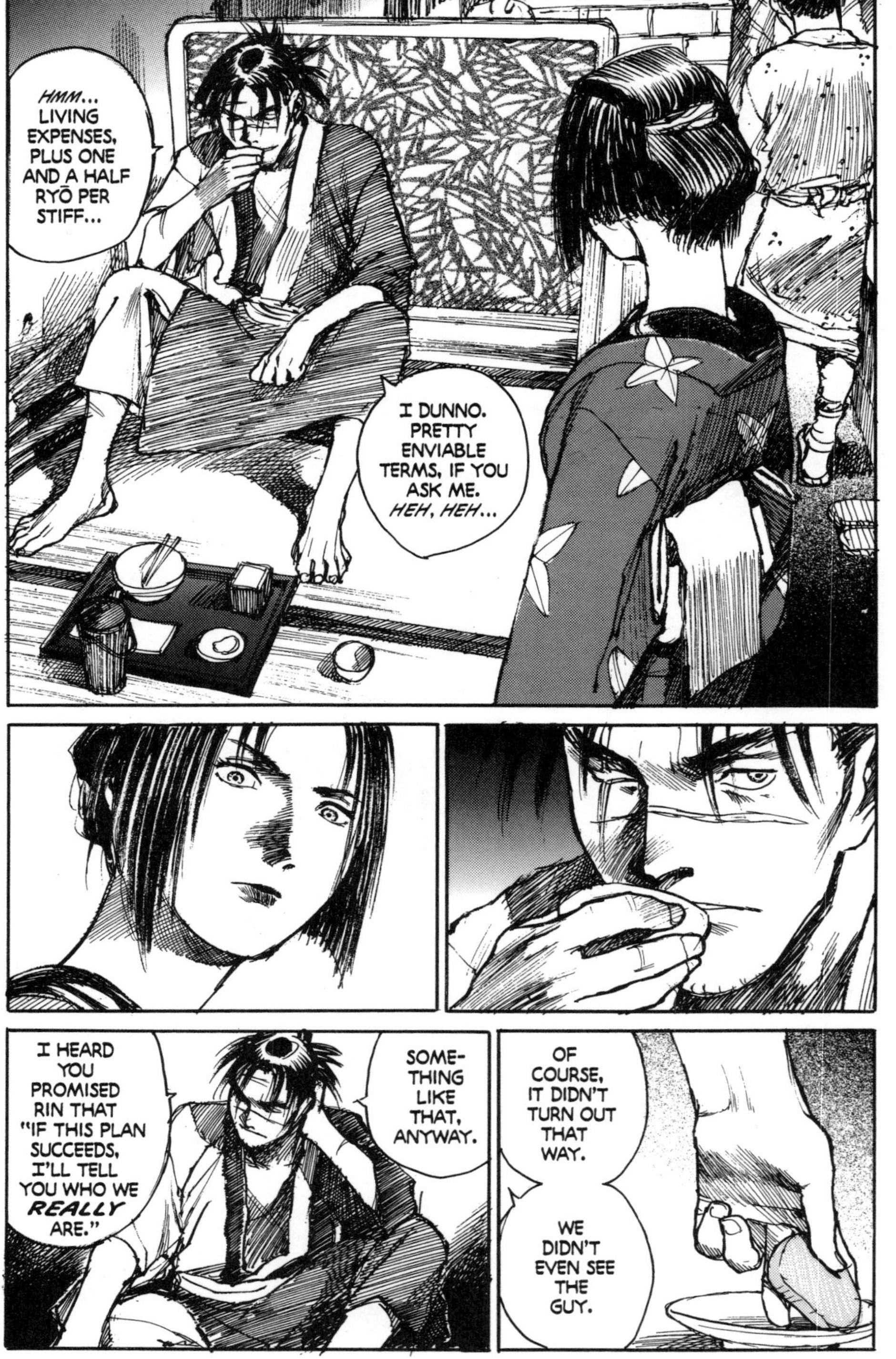

HMM... LIVING EXPENSES, PLUS ONE AND A HALF RYŌ PER STIFF...
I DUNNO. PRETTY ENVIABLE TERMS, IF YOU ASK ME. HEH, HEH...
I HEARD YOU PROMISED RIN THAT "IF THIS PLAN SUCCEEDS, I'LL TELL YOU WHO WE REALLY ARE."
SOME-THING LIKE THAT, ANYWAY.
OF COURSE, IT DIDN'T TURN OUT THAT WAY.
WE DIDN'T EVEN SEE THE GUY.

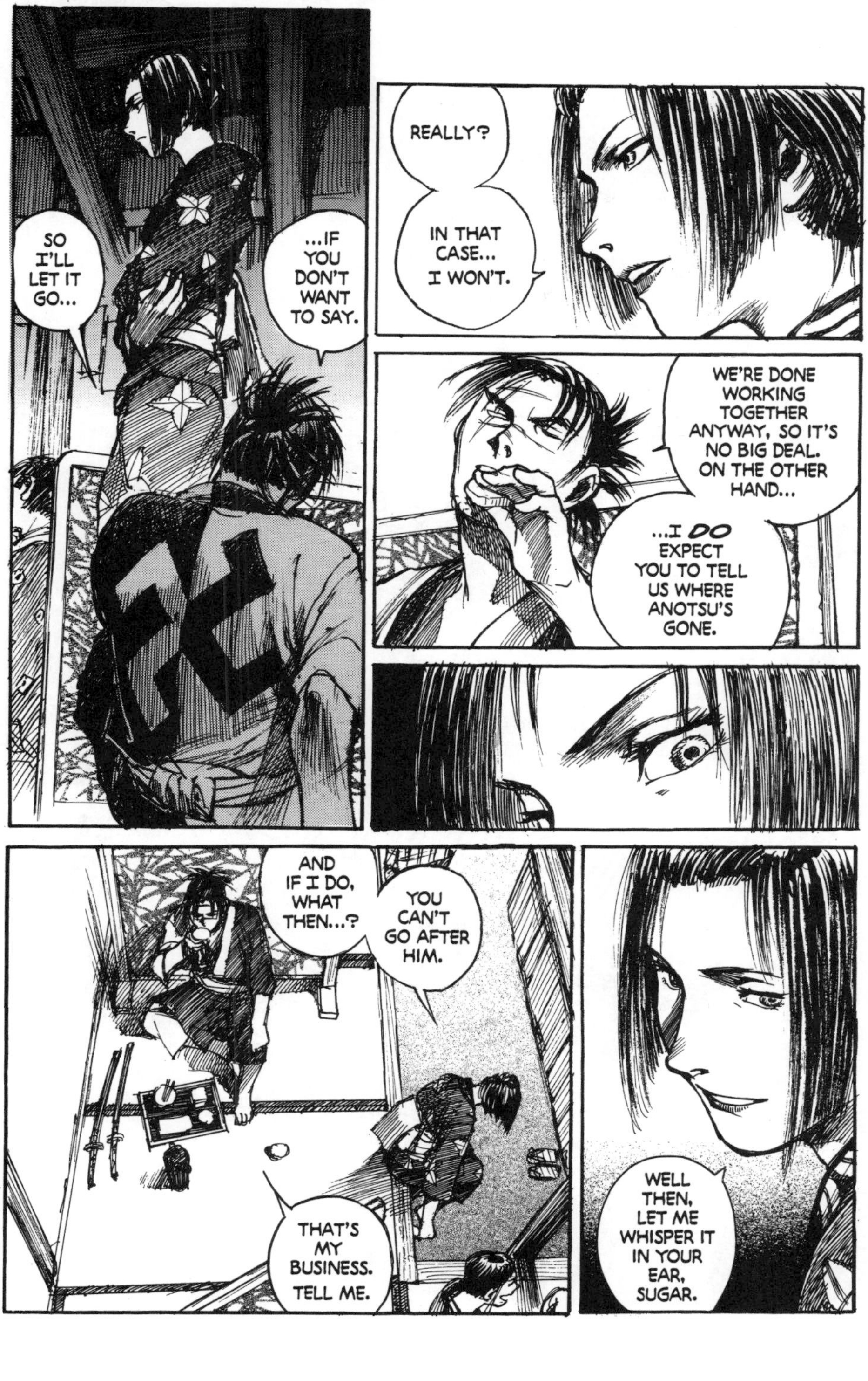
SO I'LL LET IT GO...
...IF YOU DON'T WANT TO SAY.
REALLY?
IN THAT CASE... I WON'T.
WE'RE DONE WORKING TOGETHER ANYWAY, SO IT'S NO BIG DEAL. ON THE OTHER HAND...
...I *DO* EXPECT YOU TO TELL US WHERE ANOTSU'S GONE.
AND IF I DO, WHAT THEN...?
YOU CAN'T GO AFTER HIM.
THAT'S MY BUSINESS. TELL ME.
WELL THEN, LET ME WHISPER IT IN YOUR EAR, SUGAR.

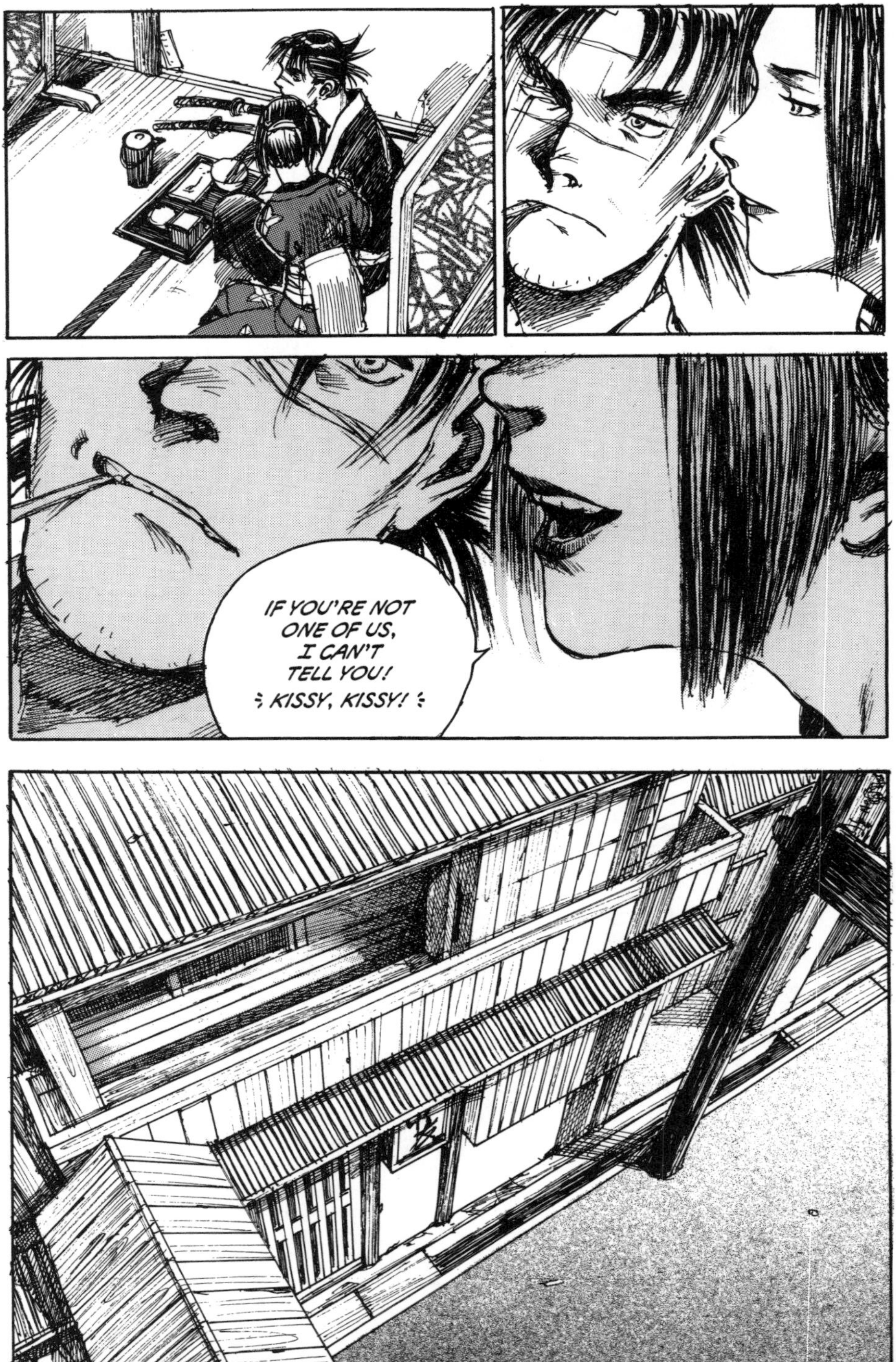
IF YOU'RE NOT ONE OF US, I CAN'T TELL YOU! ⁘ KISSY, KISSY! ⁘

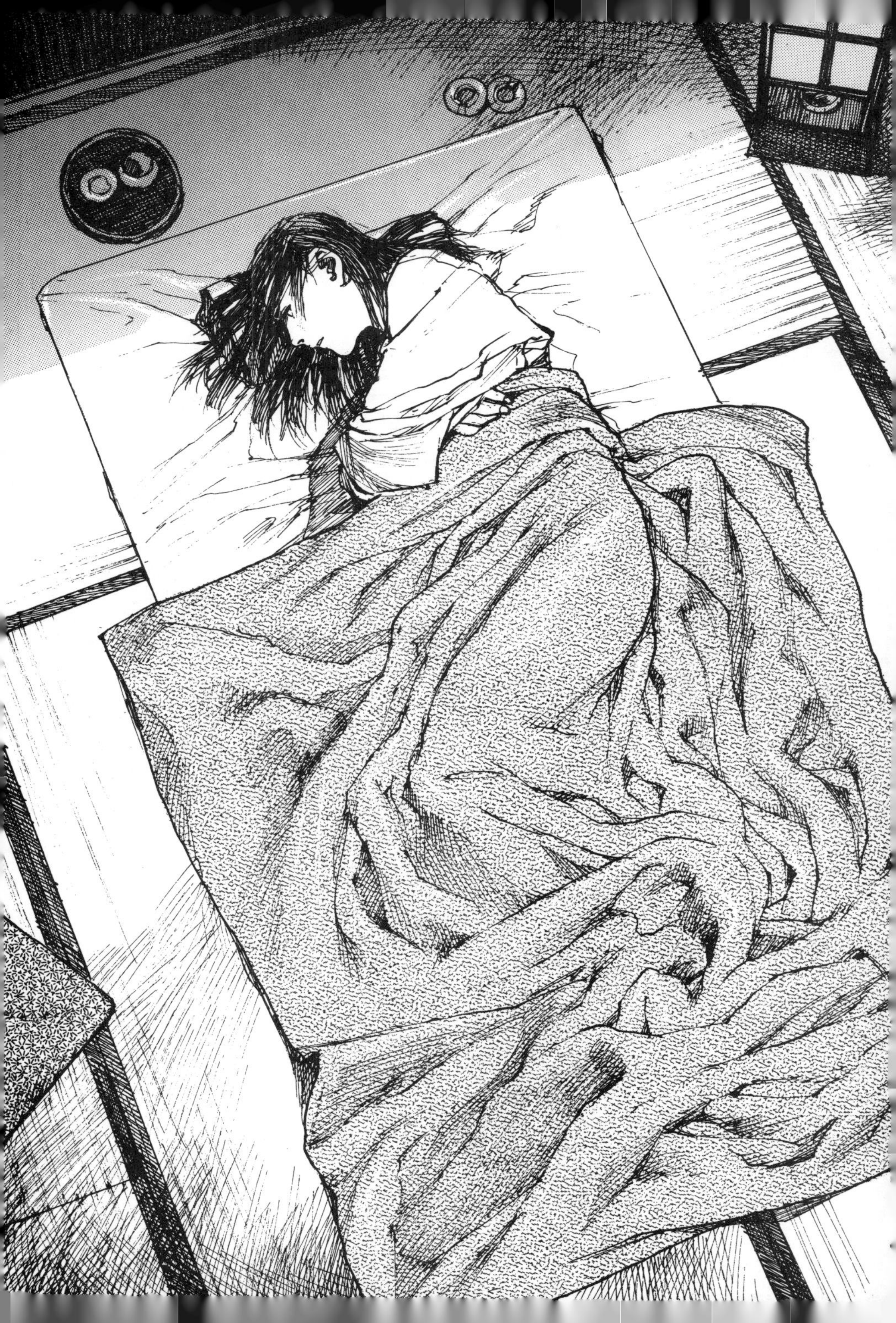

......
......

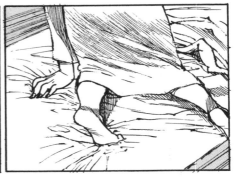

OW OW OW OWW- OOH!

GOD... EVERY BONE IN MY BODY ACHES...

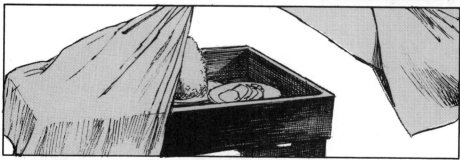

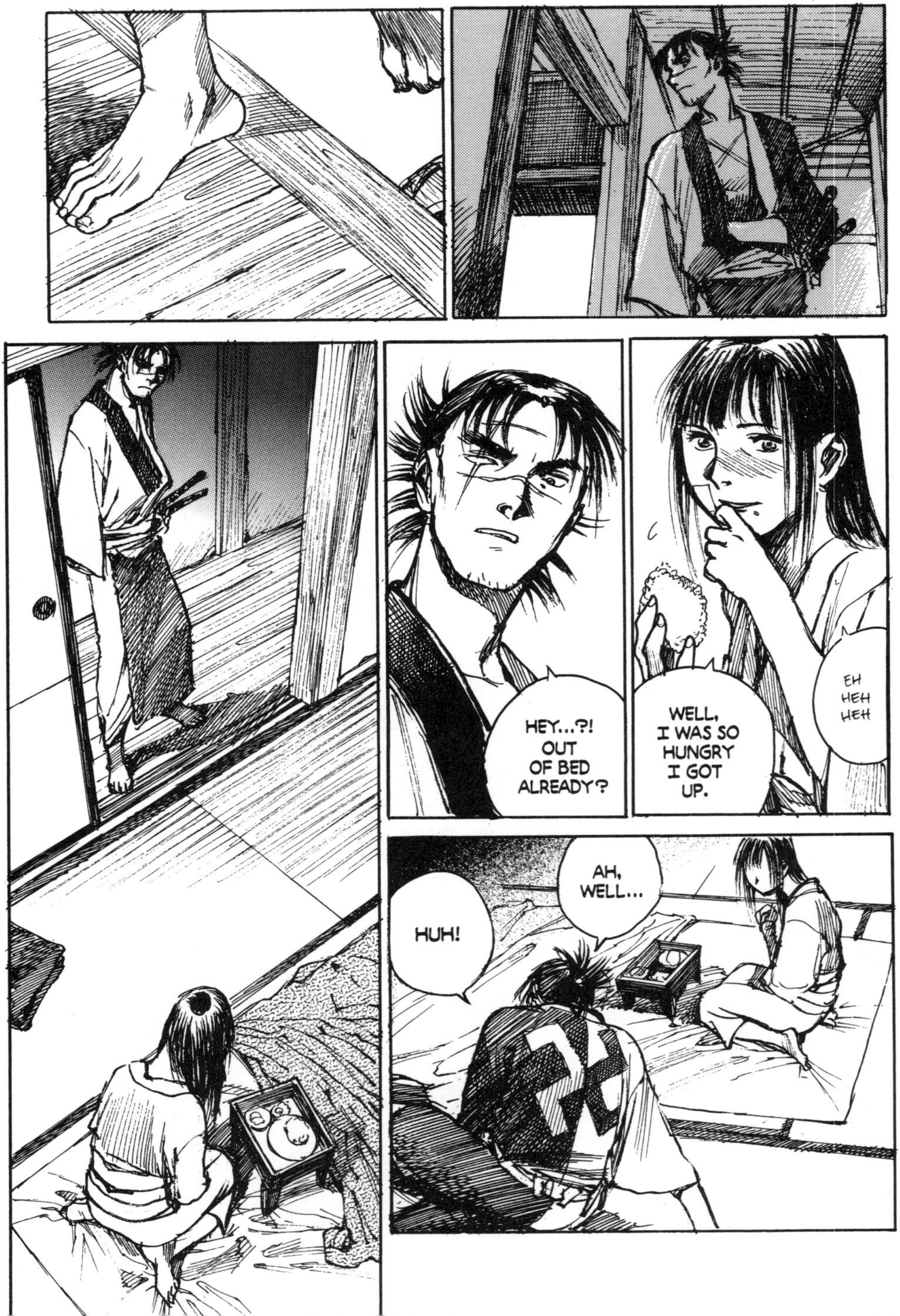
HEY...?! OUT OF BED ALREADY?
WELL, I WAS SO HUNGRY I GOT UP.
EH HEH HEH
HUH!
AH, WELL...

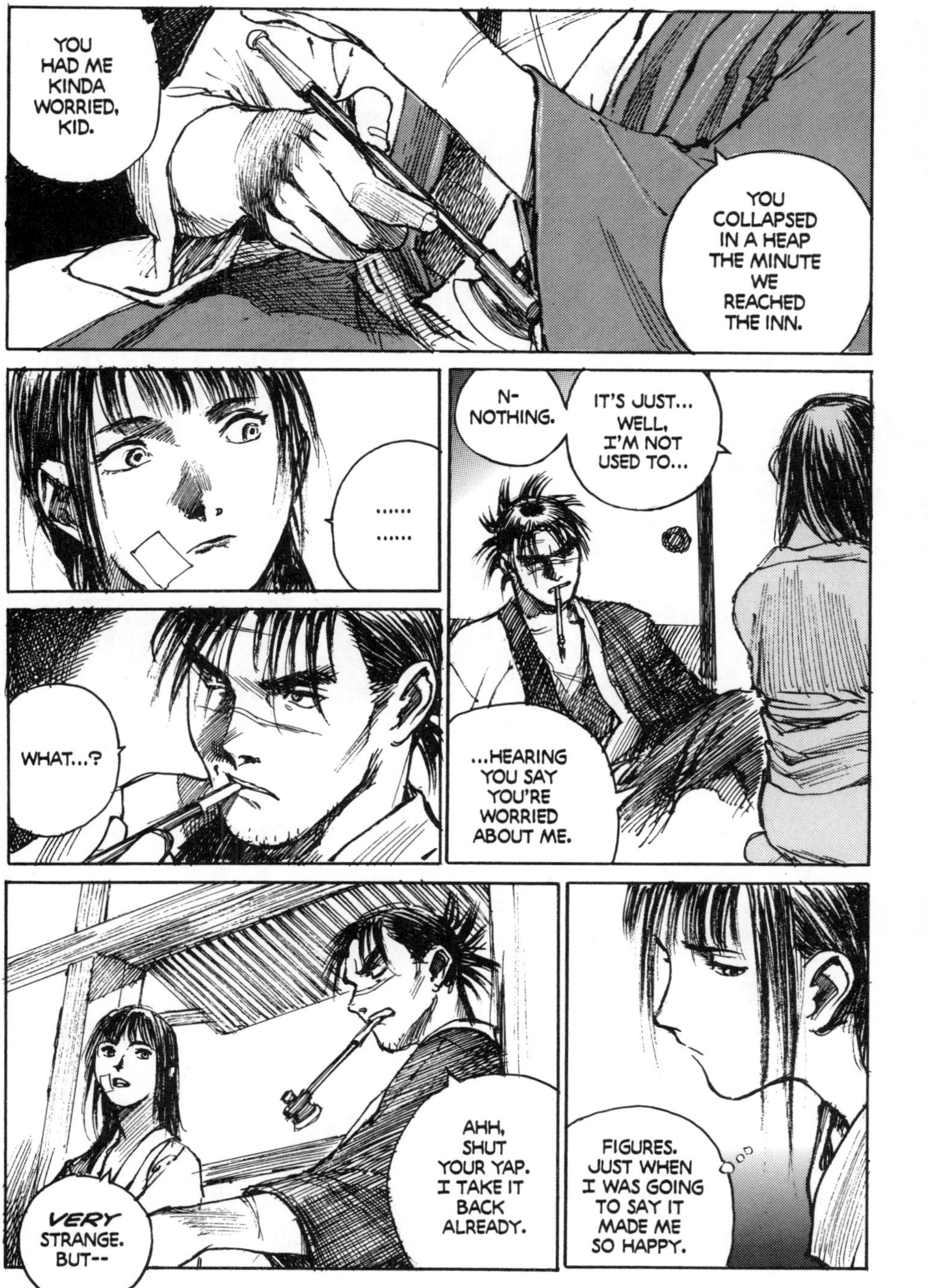
YOU HAD ME KINDA WORRIED, KID.
YOU COLLAPSED IN A HEAP THE MINUTE WE REACHED THE INN.
......
......
N-NOTHING.
IT'S JUST... WELL, I'M NOT USED TO...
WHAT...?
...HEARING YOU SAY YOU'RE WORRIED ABOUT ME.
*VERY* STRANGE. BUT--
AHH, SHUT YOUR YAP. I TAKE IT BACK ALREADY.
FIGURES. JUST WHEN I WAS GOING TO SAY IT MADE ME SO HAPPY.

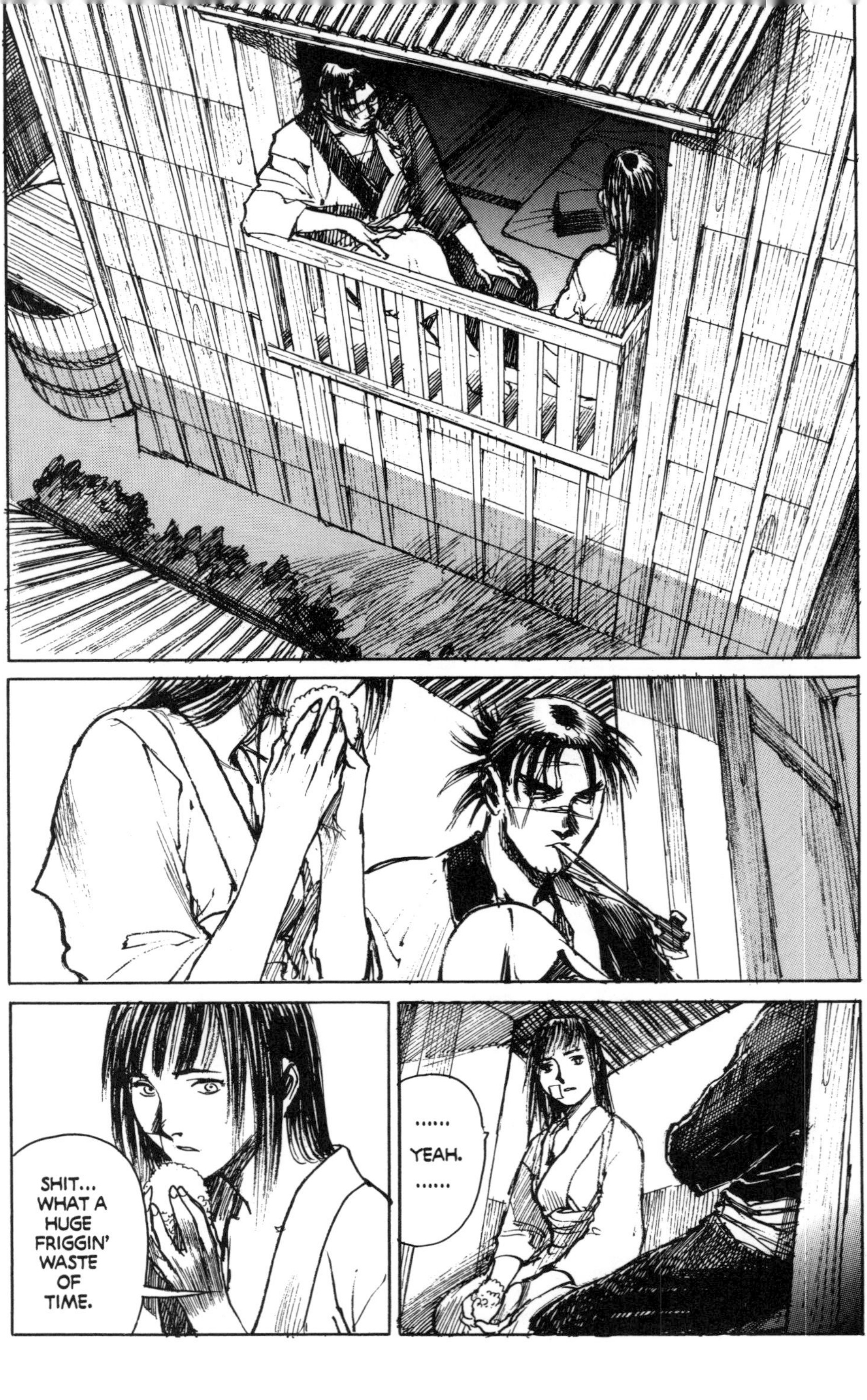
SHIT... WHAT A HUGE FRIGGIN' WASTE OF TIME.
...... YEAH. ......

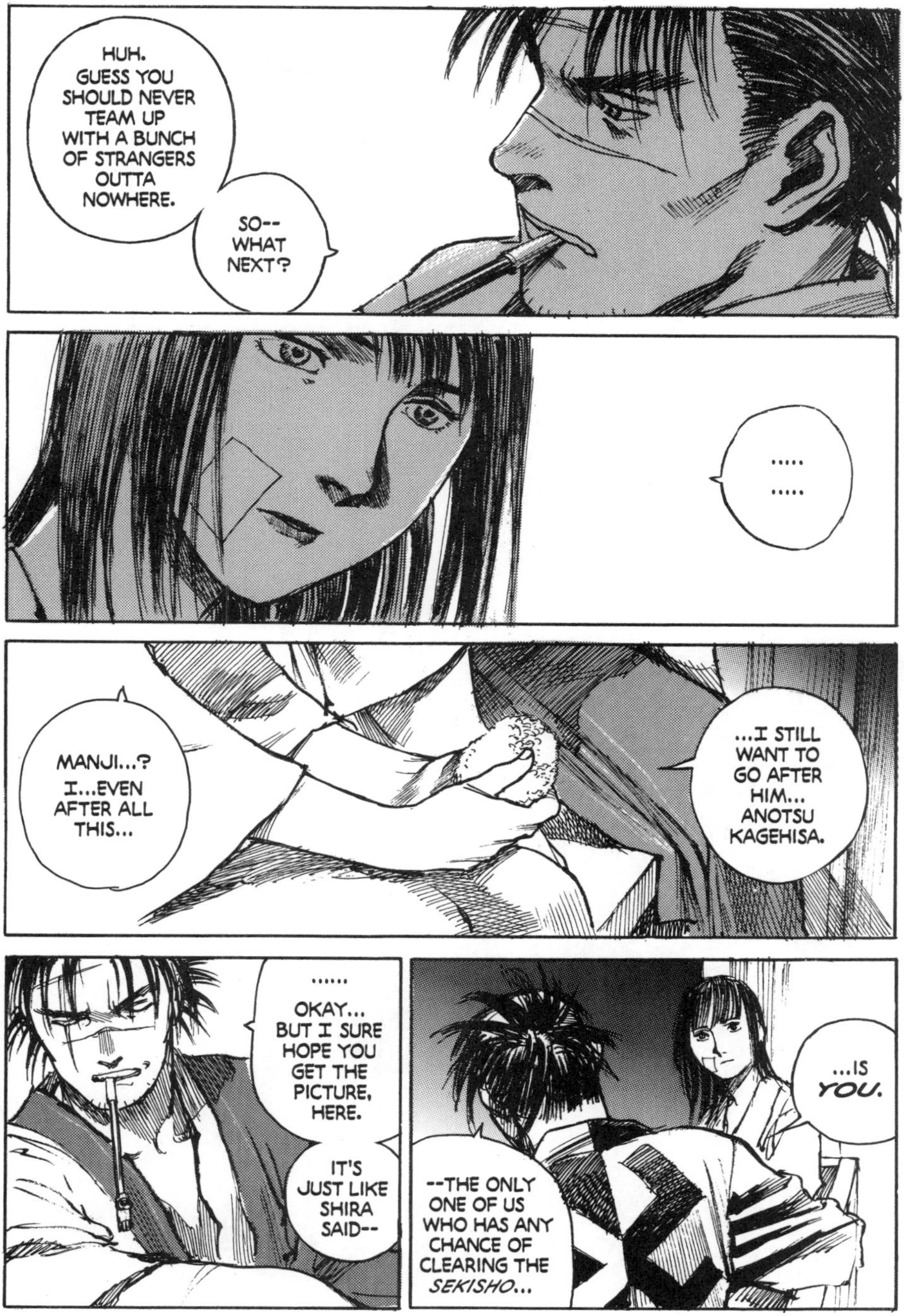
HUH. GUESS YOU SHOULD NEVER TEAM UP WITH A BUNCH OF STRANGERS OUTTA NOWHERE.
SO-- WHAT NEXT?
..... .....
MANJI...? I...EVEN AFTER ALL THIS...
...I STILL WANT TO GO AFTER HIM... ANOTSU KAGEHISA.
...... OKAY... BUT I SURE HOPE YOU GET THE PICTURE, HERE.
IT'S JUST LIKE SHIRA SAID--
--THE ONLY ONE OF US WHO HAS ANY CHANCE OF CLEARING THE *SEKISHO*...
...IS *YOU.*

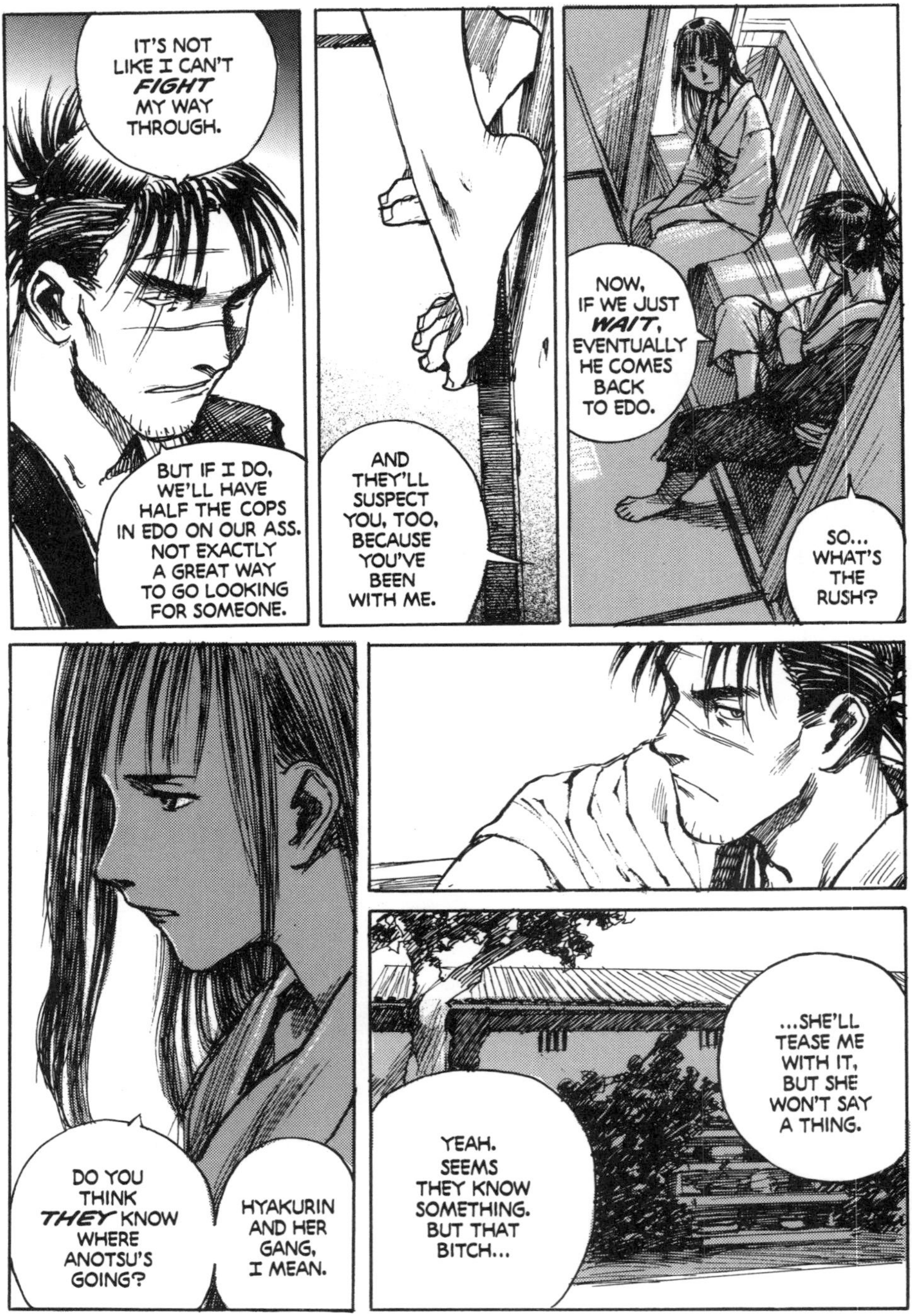
IT'S NOT LIKE I CAN'T *FIGHT* MY WAY THROUGH.
BUT IF I DO, WE'LL HAVE HALF THE COPS IN EDO ON OUR ASS. NOT EXACTLY A GREAT WAY TO GO LOOKING FOR SOMEONE.
AND THEY'LL SUSPECT YOU, TOO, BECAUSE YOU'VE BEEN WITH ME.
NOW, IF WE JUST *WAIT*, EVENTUALLY HE COMES BACK TO EDO.
SO... WHAT'S THE RUSH?
DO YOU THINK *THEY* KNOW WHERE ANOTSU'S GOING?
HYAKURIN AND HER GANG, I MEAN.
YEAH. SEEMS THEY KNOW SOMETHING. BUT THAT BITCH...
...SHE'LL TEASE ME WITH IT, BUT SHE WON'T SAY A THING.

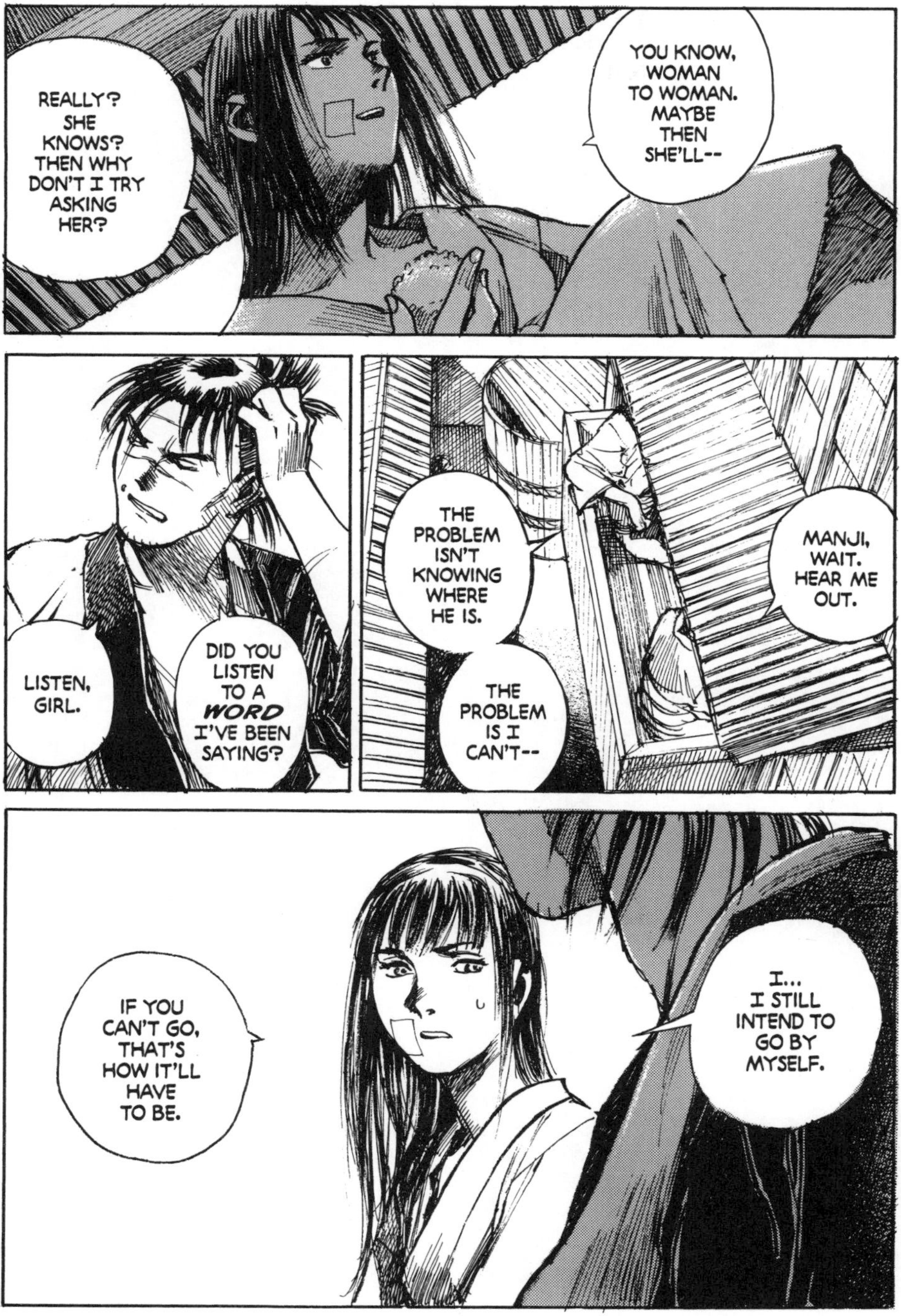
REALLY? SHE KNOWS? THEN WHY DON'T I TRY ASKING HER?
YOU KNOW, WOMAN TO WOMAN. MAYBE THEN SHE'LL--
LISTEN, GIRL.
DID YOU LISTEN TO A *WORD* I'VE BEEN SAYING?
THE PROBLEM ISN'T KNOWING WHERE HE IS.
THE PROBLEM IS I CAN'T--
MANJI, WAIT. HEAR ME OUT.
IF YOU CAN'T GO, THAT'S HOW IT'LL HAVE TO BE.
I... I STILL INTEND TO GO BY MYSELF.

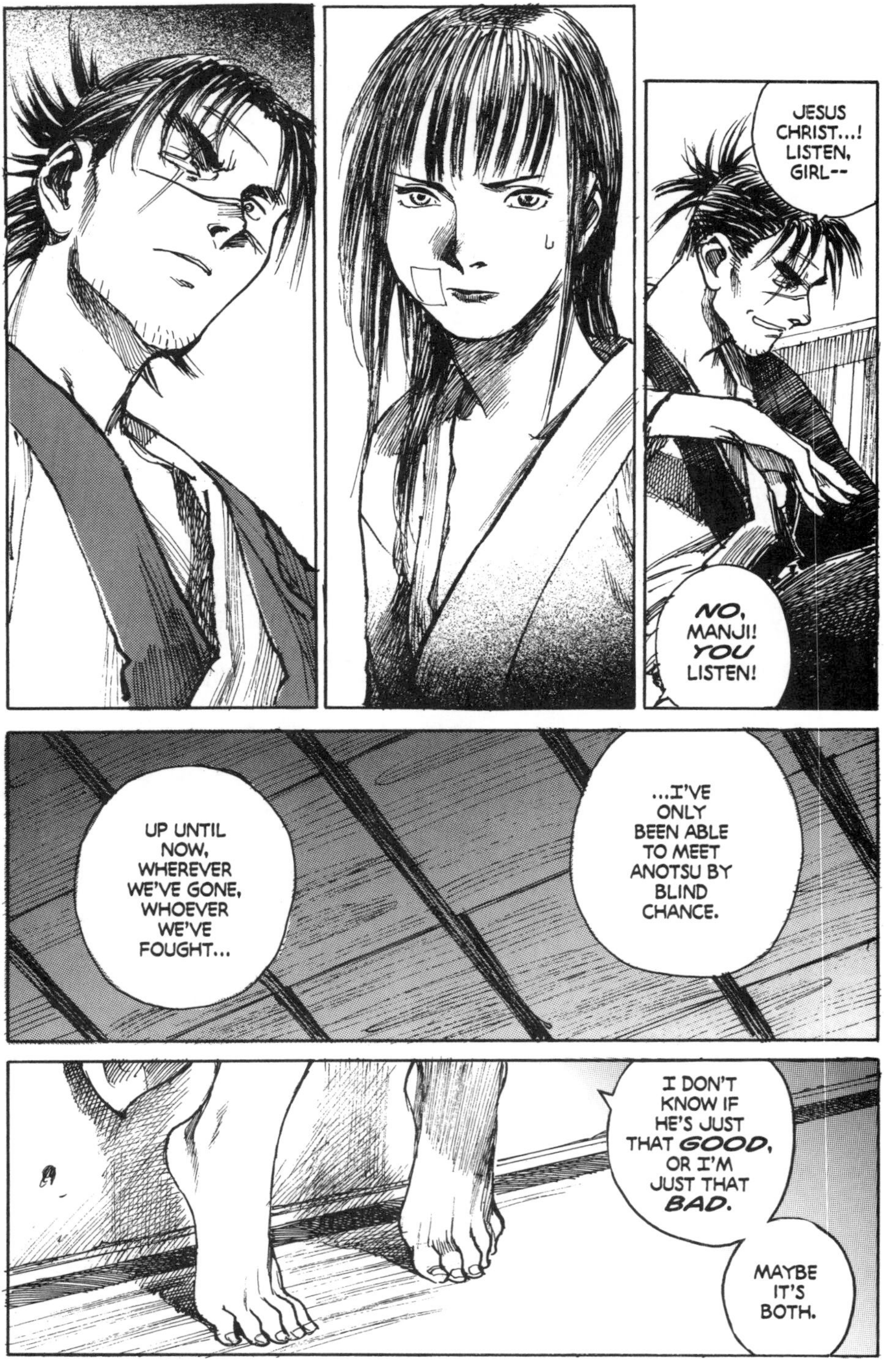
JESUS CHRIST...! LISTEN, GIRL--
NO, MANJI! YOU LISTEN!
UP UNTIL NOW, WHEREVER WE'VE GONE, WHOEVER WE'VE FOUGHT...
...I'VE ONLY BEEN ABLE TO MEET ANOTSU BY BLIND CHANCE.
I DON'T KNOW IF HE'S JUST THAT GOOD, OR I'M JUST THAT BAD.
MAYBE IT'S BOTH.

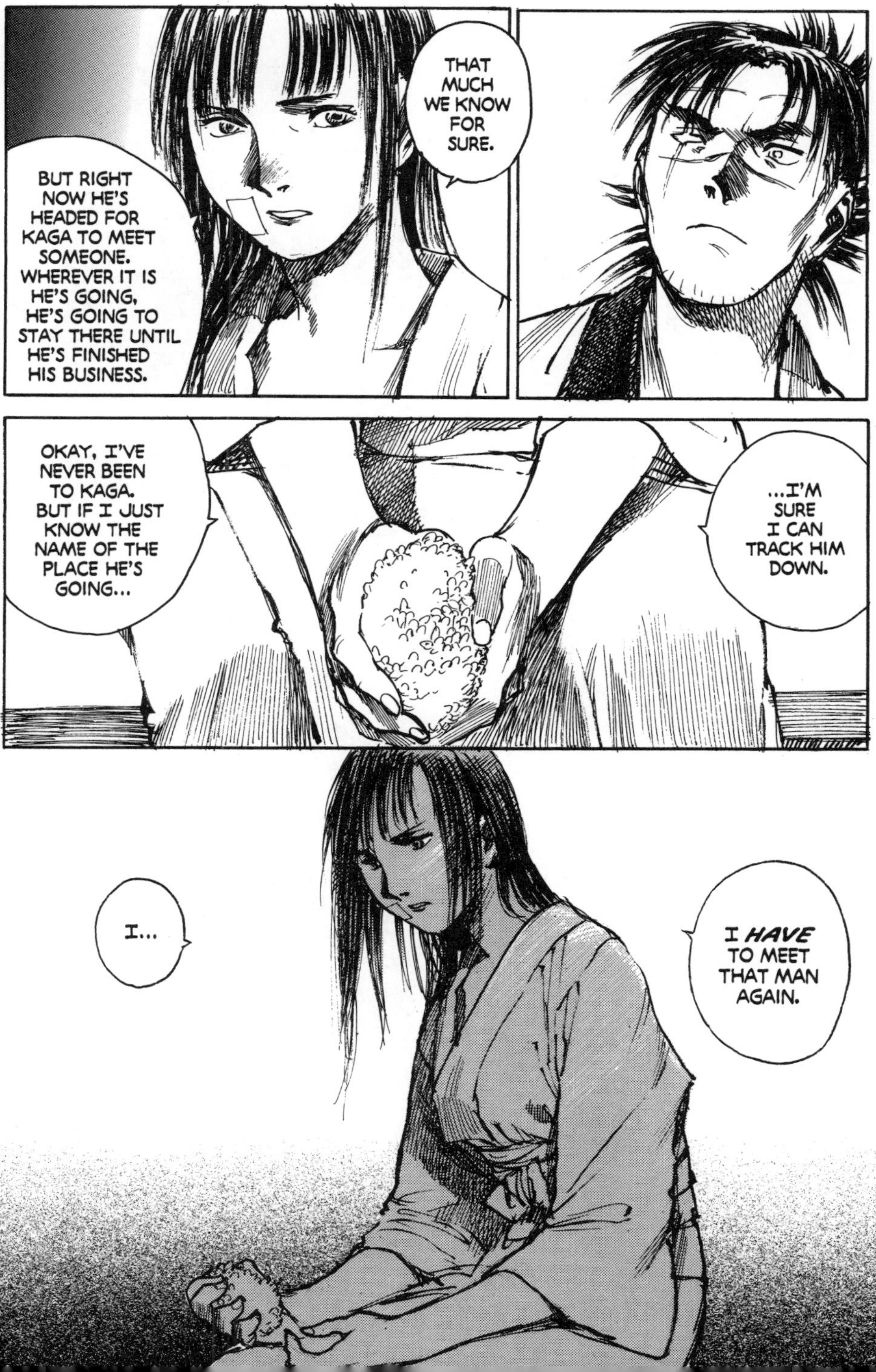
THAT MUCH WE KNOW FOR SURE.
BUT RIGHT NOW HE'S HEADED FOR KAGA TO MEET SOMEONE. WHEREVER IT IS HE'S GOING, HE'S GOING TO STAY THERE UNTIL HE'S FINISHED HIS BUSINESS.
OKAY, I'VE NEVER BEEN TO KAGA. BUT IF I JUST KNOW THE NAME OF THE PLACE HE'S GOING...
...I'M SURE I CAN TRACK HIM DOWN.
I...
I *HAVE* TO MEET THAT MAN AGAIN.

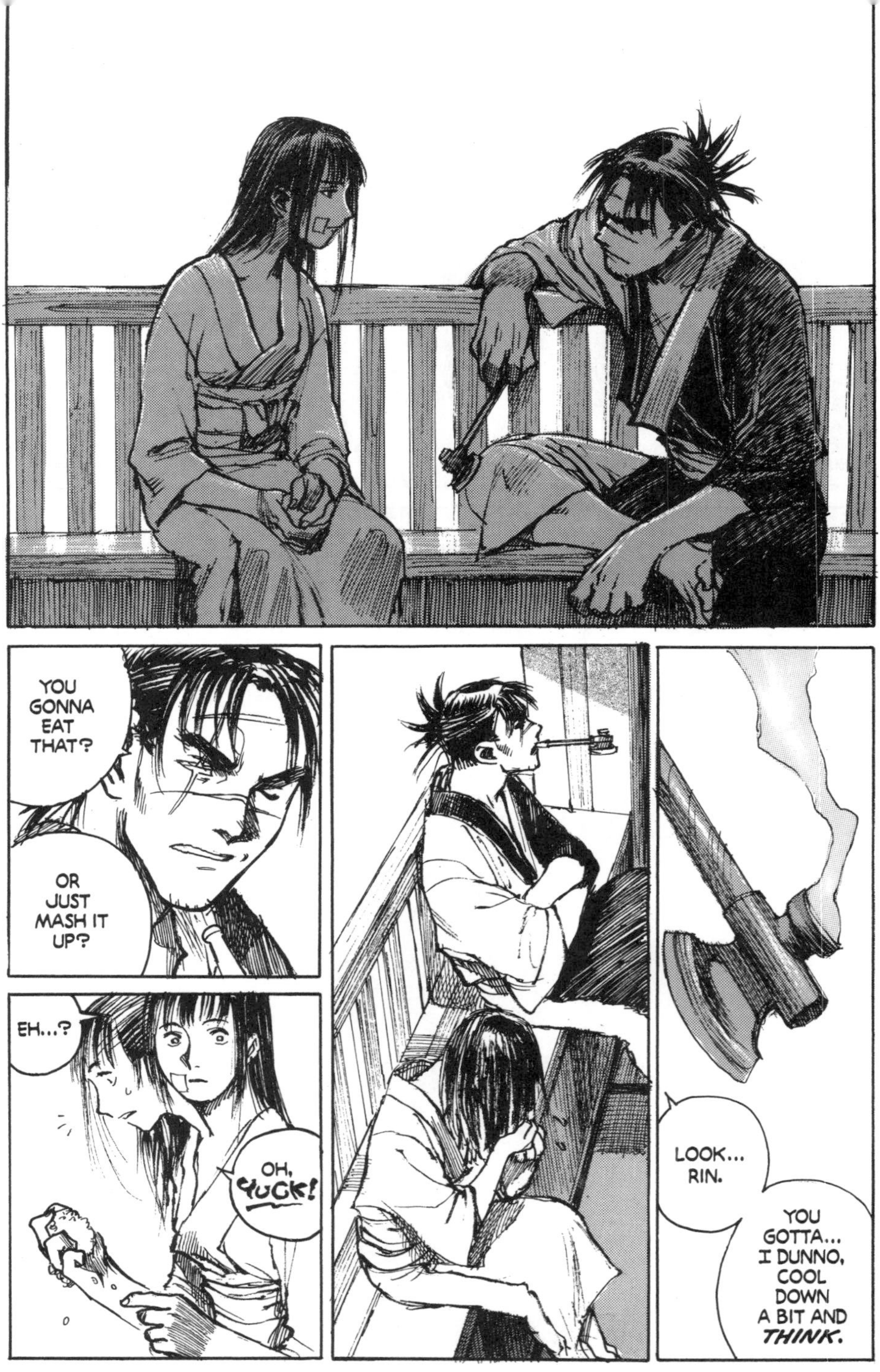
YOU GONNA EAT THAT?
OR JUST MASH IT UP?
EH...?
OH, YUCK!
LOOK... RIN.
YOU GOTTA... I DUNNO, COOL DOWN A BIT AND *THINK*.

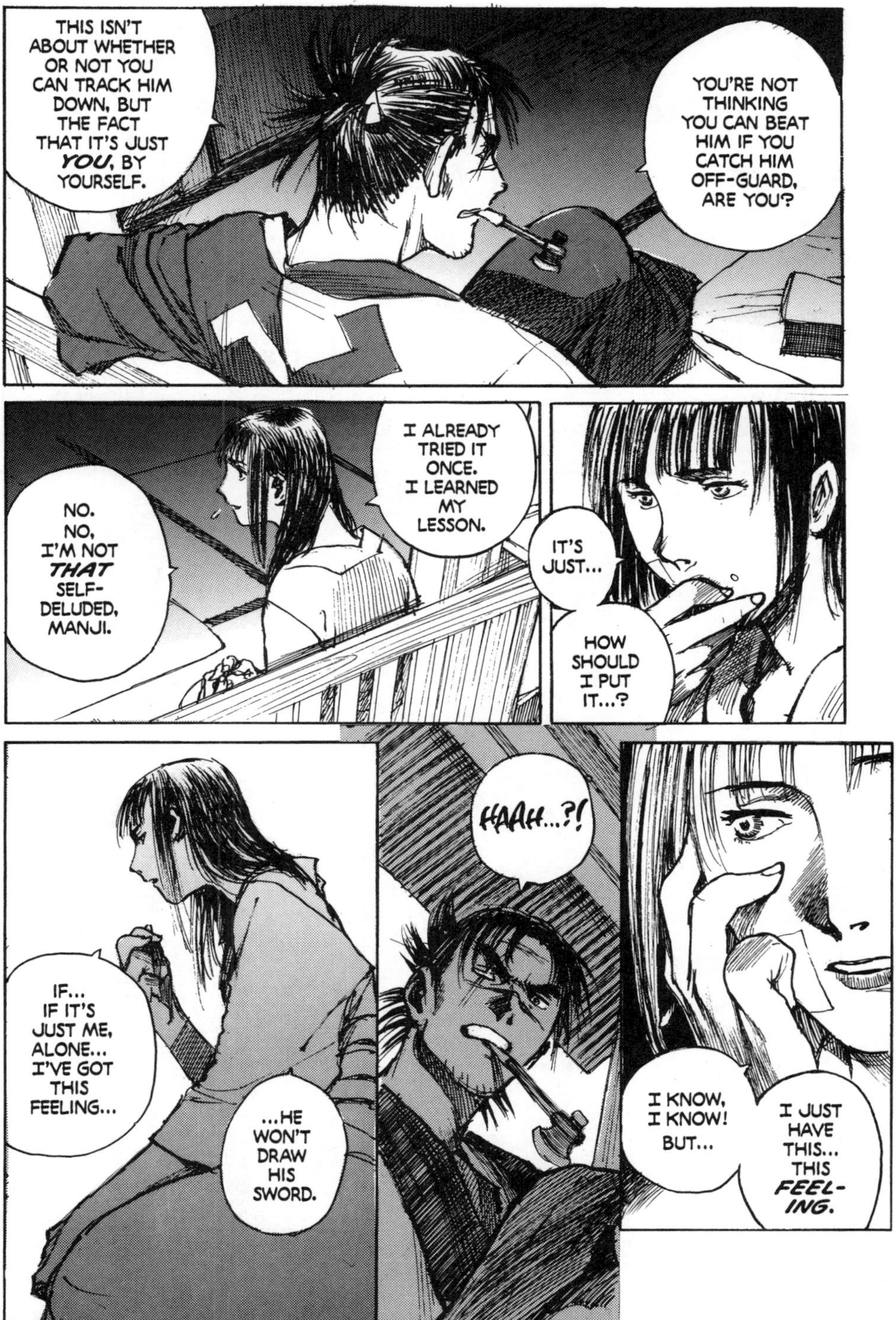
THIS ISN'T ABOUT WHETHER OR NOT YOU CAN TRACK HIM DOWN, BUT THE FACT THAT IT'S JUST *YOU*, BY YOURSELF.
YOU'RE NOT THINKING YOU CAN BEAT HIM IF YOU CATCH HIM OFF-GUARD, ARE YOU?
NO. NO, I'M NOT *THAT* SELF-DELUDED, MANJI.
I ALREADY TRIED IT ONCE. I LEARNED MY LESSON.
IT'S JUST...
HOW SHOULD I PUT IT...?
IF... IF IT'S JUST ME, ALONE... I'VE GOT THIS FEELING...
...HE WON'T DRAW HIS SWORD.
HAAH...?!
I KNOW, I KNOW! BUT...
I JUST HAVE THIS... THIS *FEELING*.

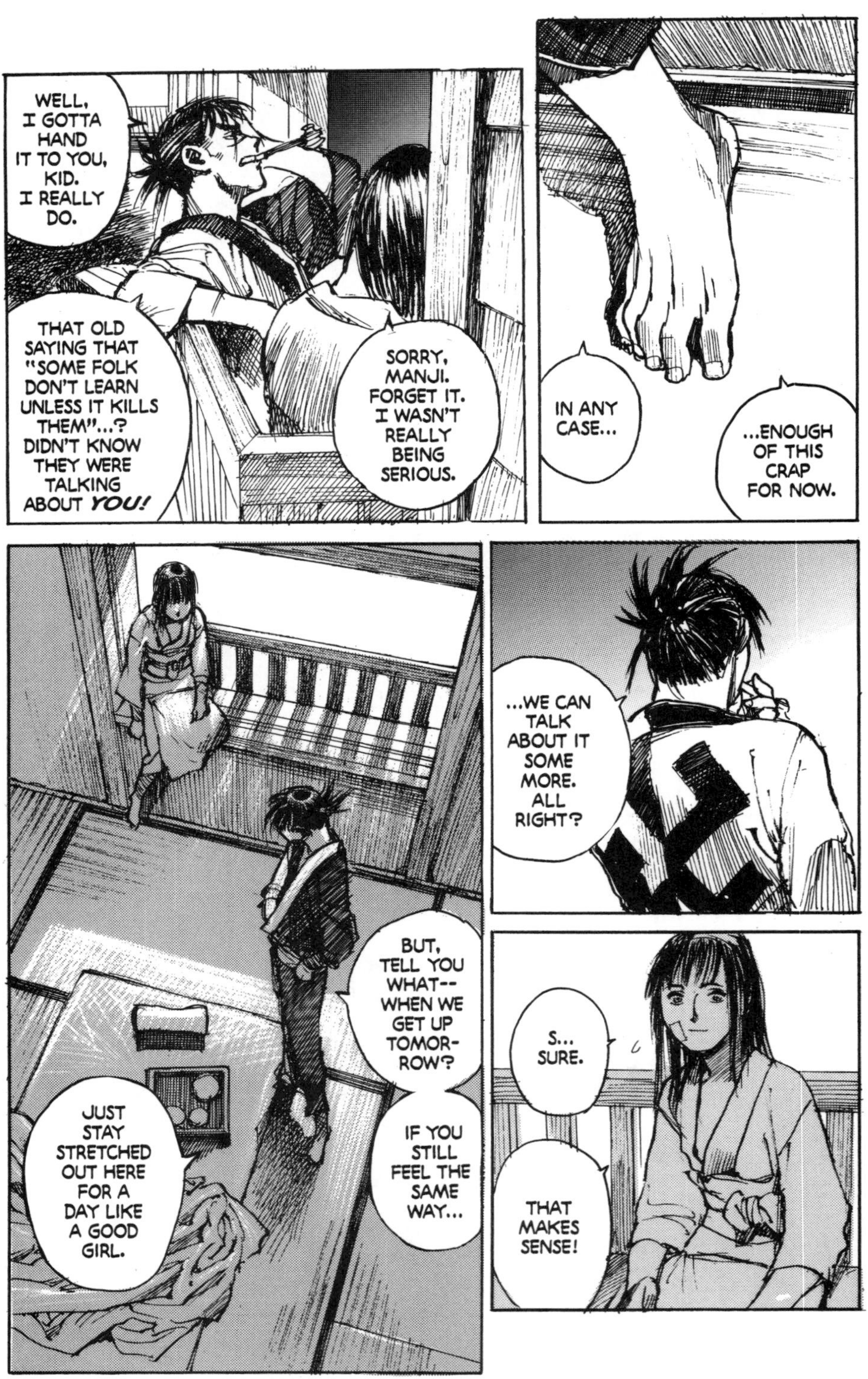
WELL, I GOTTA HAND IT TO YOU, KID. I REALLY DO.
THAT OLD SAYING THAT "SOME FOLK DON'T LEARN UNLESS IT KILLS THEM"...? DIDN'T KNOW THEY WERE TALKING ABOUT *YOU!*
SORRY, MANJI. FORGET IT. I WASN'T REALLY BEING SERIOUS.
IN ANY CASE...
...ENOUGH OF THIS CRAP FOR NOW.
BUT, TELL YOU WHAT-- WHEN WE GET UP TOMOR-ROW?
IF YOU STILL FEEL THE SAME WAY...
JUST STAY STRETCHED OUT HERE FOR A DAY LIKE A GOOD GIRL.
...WE CAN TALK ABOUT IT SOME MORE. ALL RIGHT?
S... SURE.
THAT MAKES SENSE!

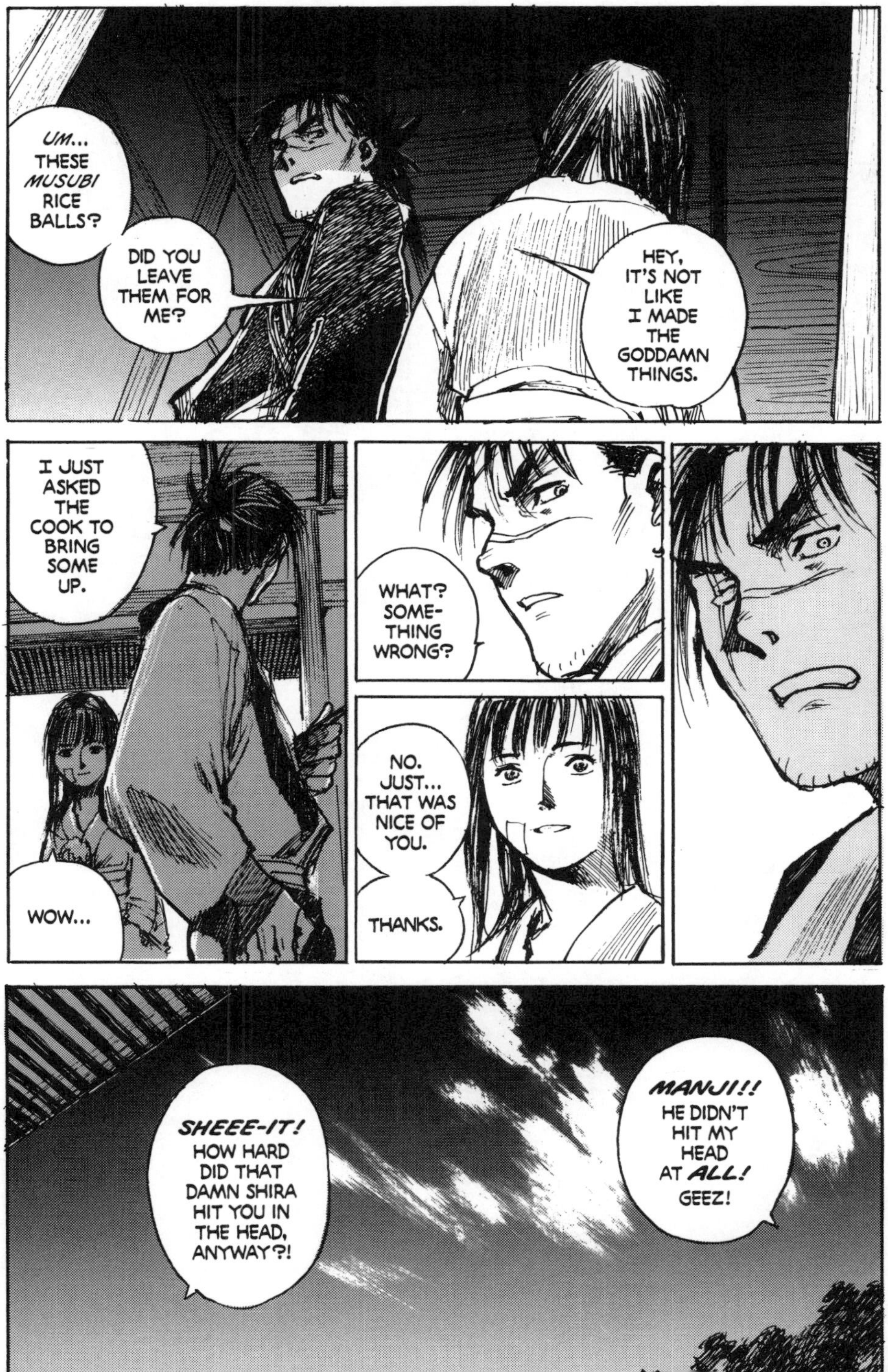
UM... THESE MUSUBI RICE BALLS?
DID YOU LEAVE THEM FOR ME?
HEY, IT'S NOT LIKE I MADE THE GODDAMN THINGS.
I JUST ASKED THE COOK TO BRING SOME UP.
WOW...
WHAT? SOME-THING WRONG?
NO. JUST... THAT WAS NICE OF YOU.
THANKS.
SHEEE-IT! HOW HARD DID THAT DAMN SHIRA HIT YOU IN THE HEAD, ANYWAY?!
MANJI!! HE DIDN'T HIT MY HEAD AT ALL! GEEZ!

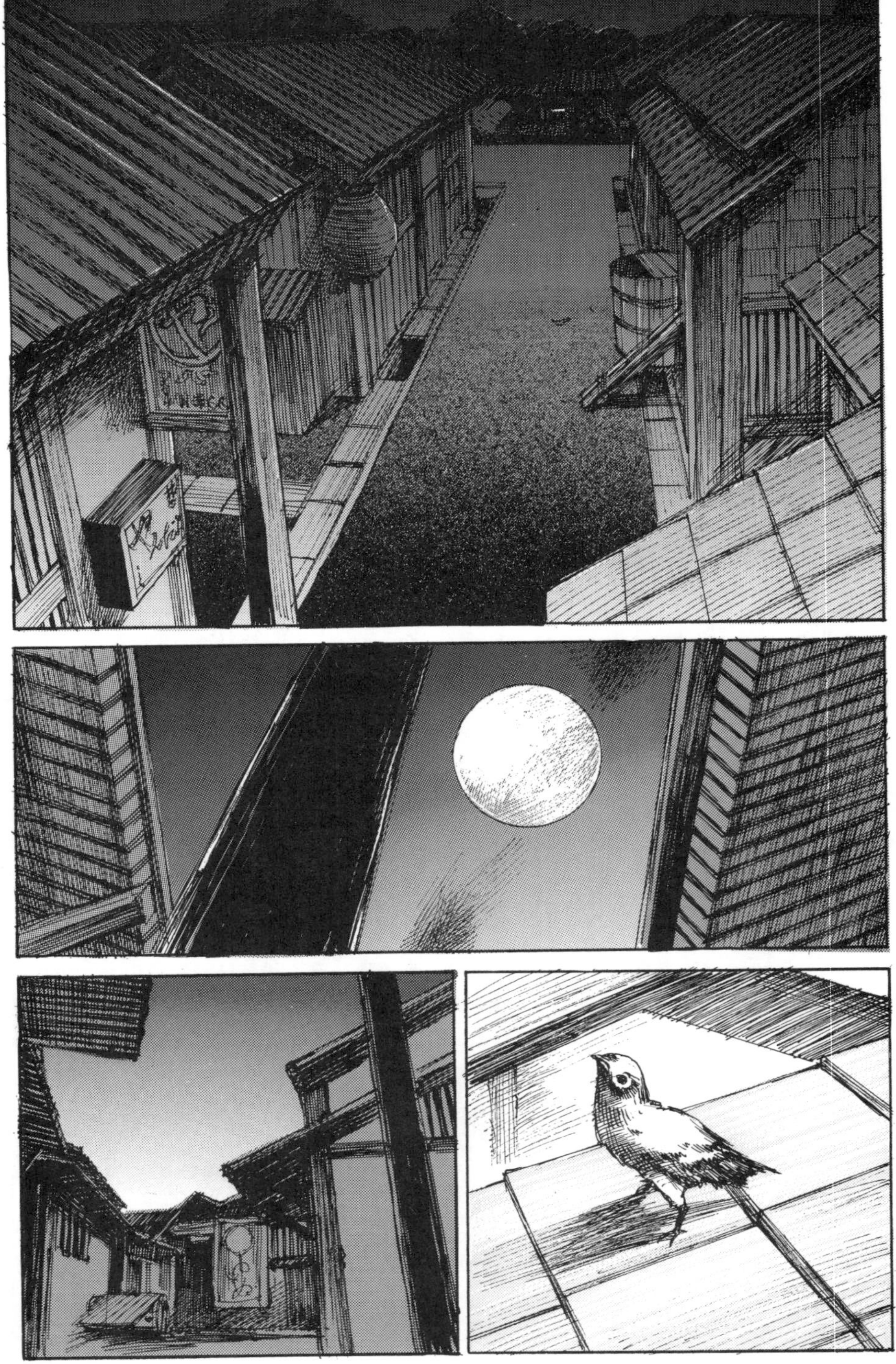

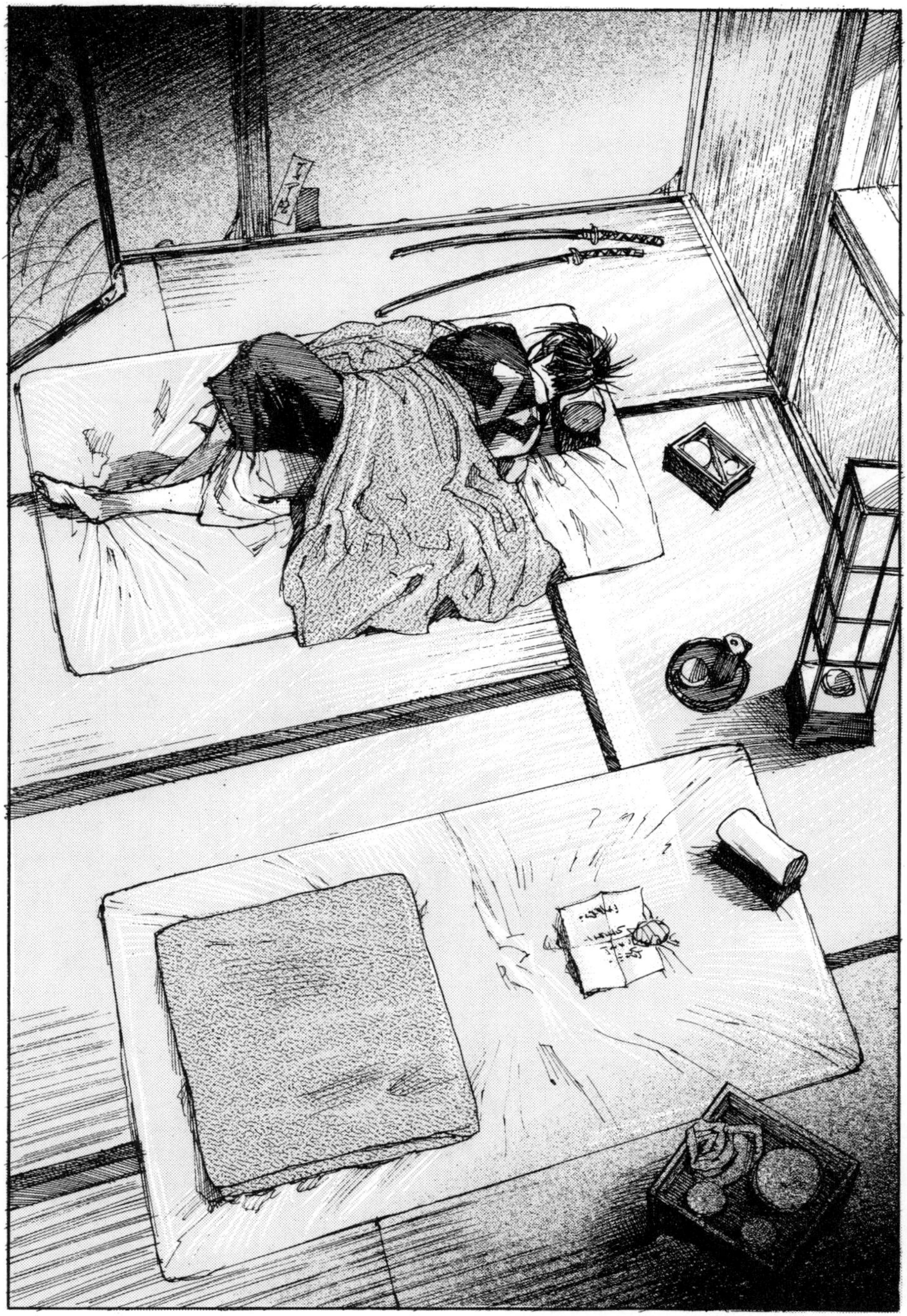

"I'M LEAVING SOME MONEY FOR THE ROOM. FORGIVE ME."

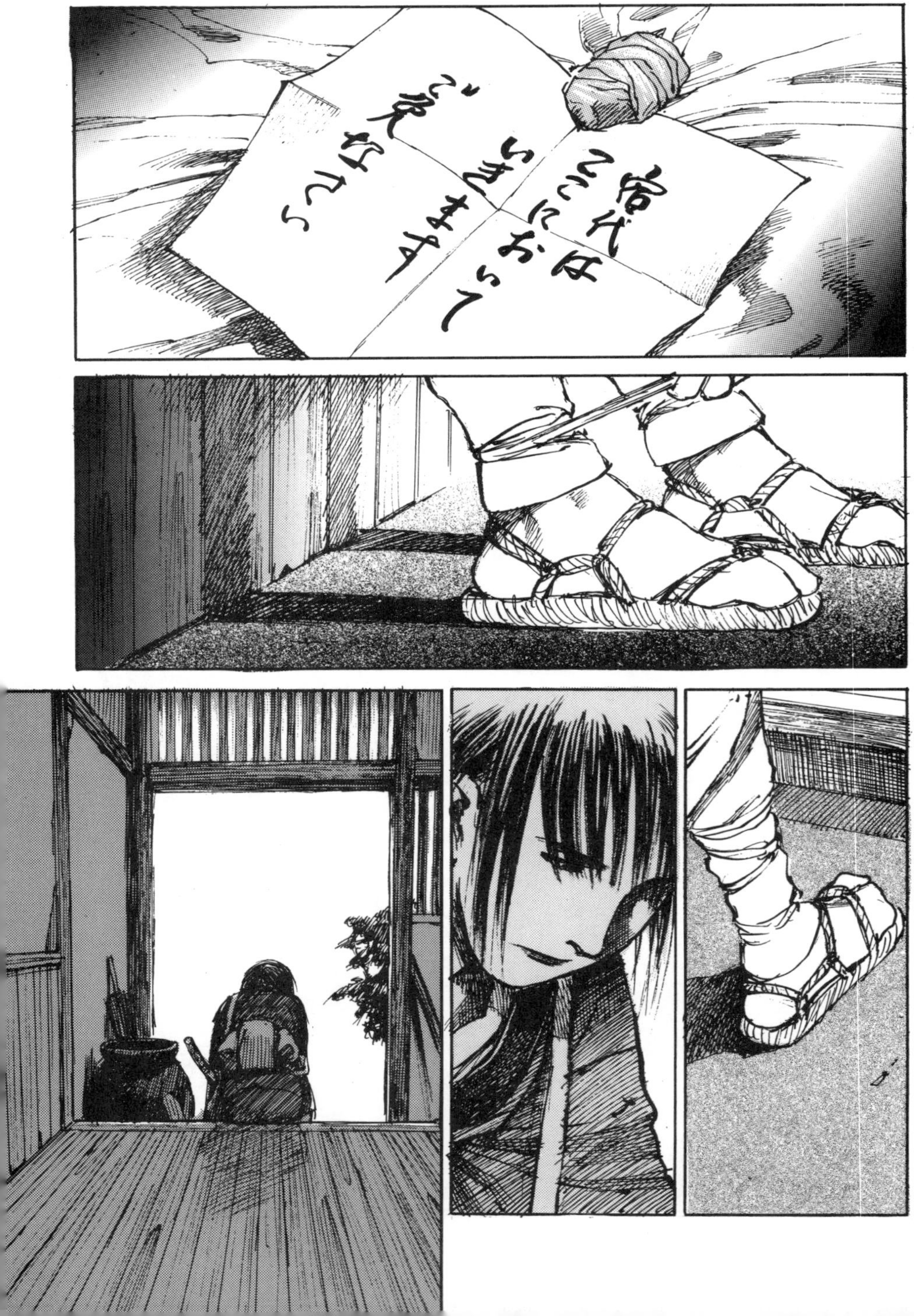
宿代は
ここにおいて
いきます
ご免なさい

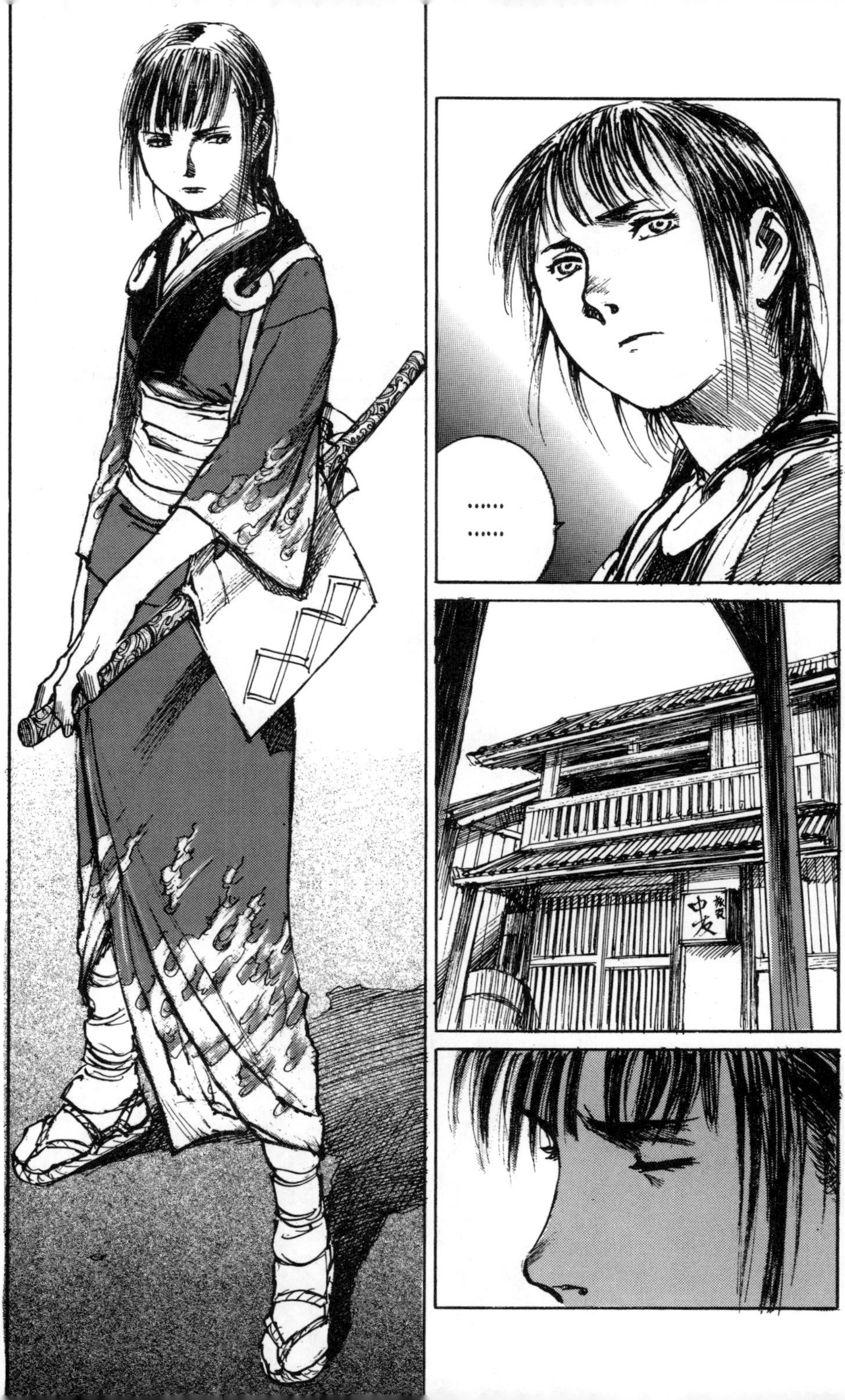
……
……

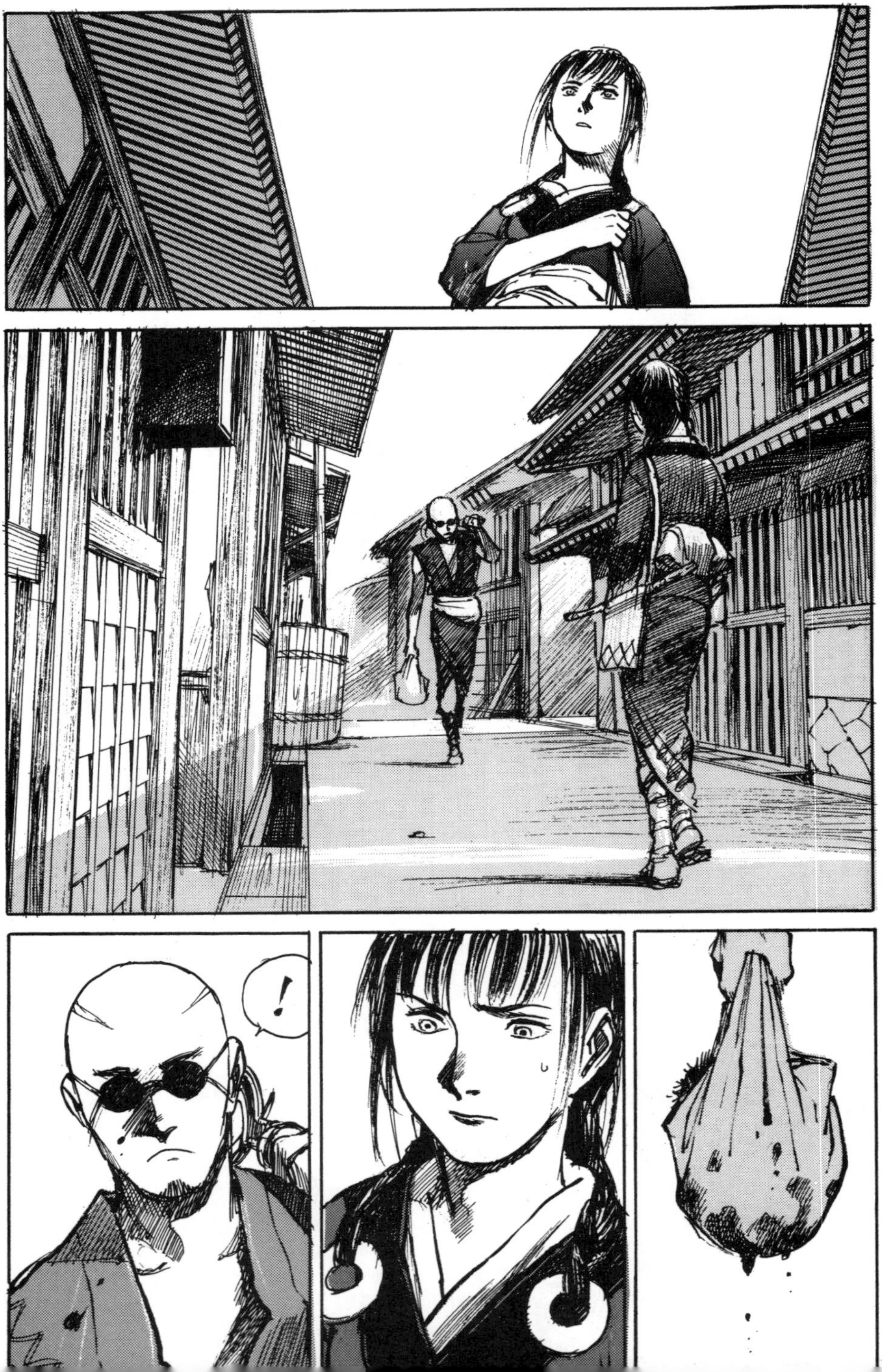
!

Uh... EXCUSE ME... BUT...

.....
.....

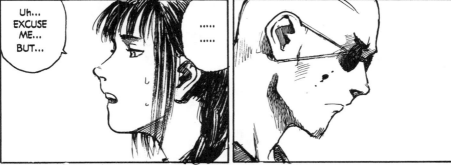

.....
.....

THE *SHINGYŌTŌ-RYŪ* SWORD SCHOOL, *IBANE SHINANJO.* I DON'T KNOW THE EXACT LOCATION.

YOU CAN ASK WHEN YOU GET TO KAGA.

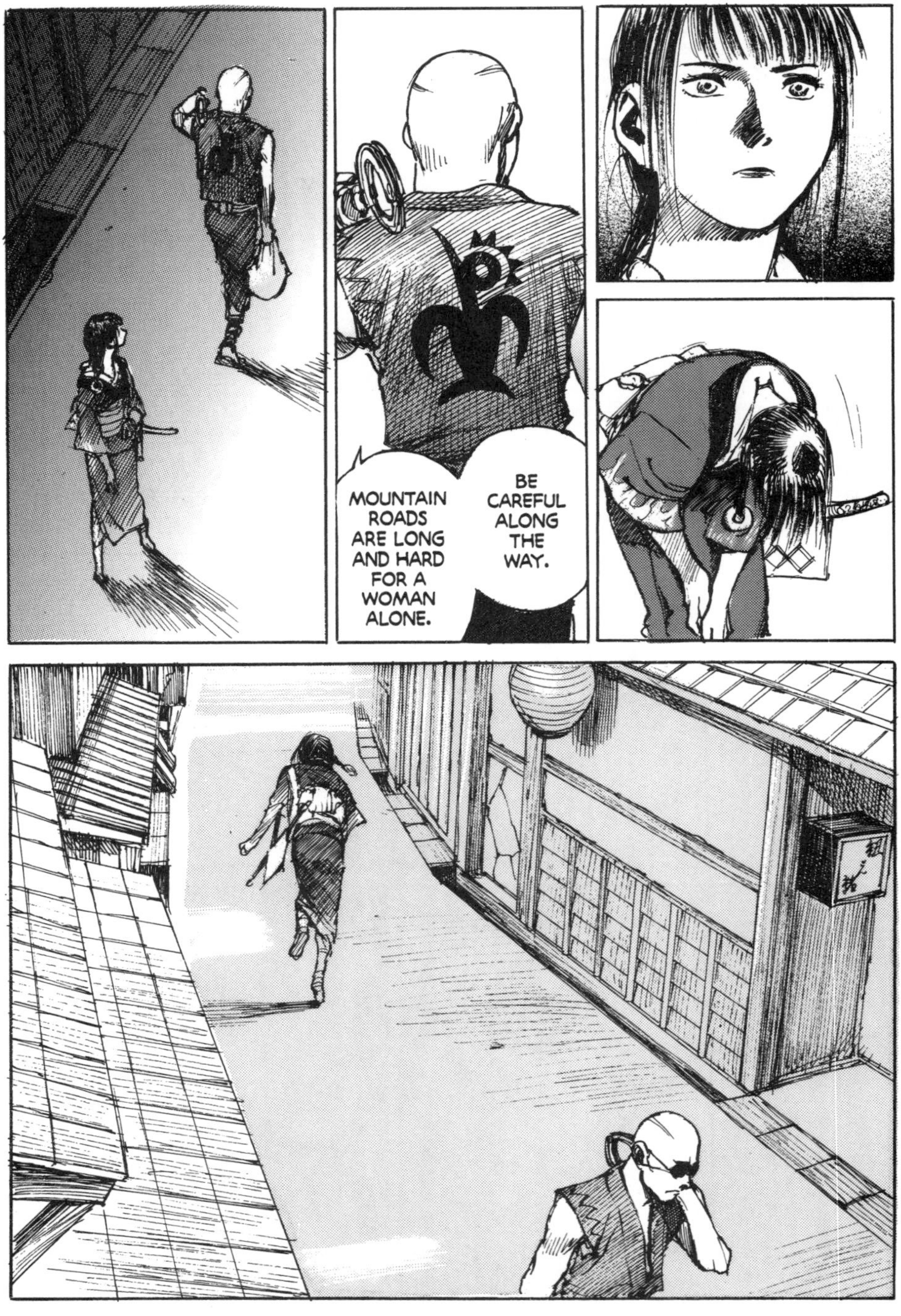
MOUNTAIN ROADS ARE LONG AND HARD FOR A WOMAN ALONE.
BE CAREFUL ALONG THE WAY.

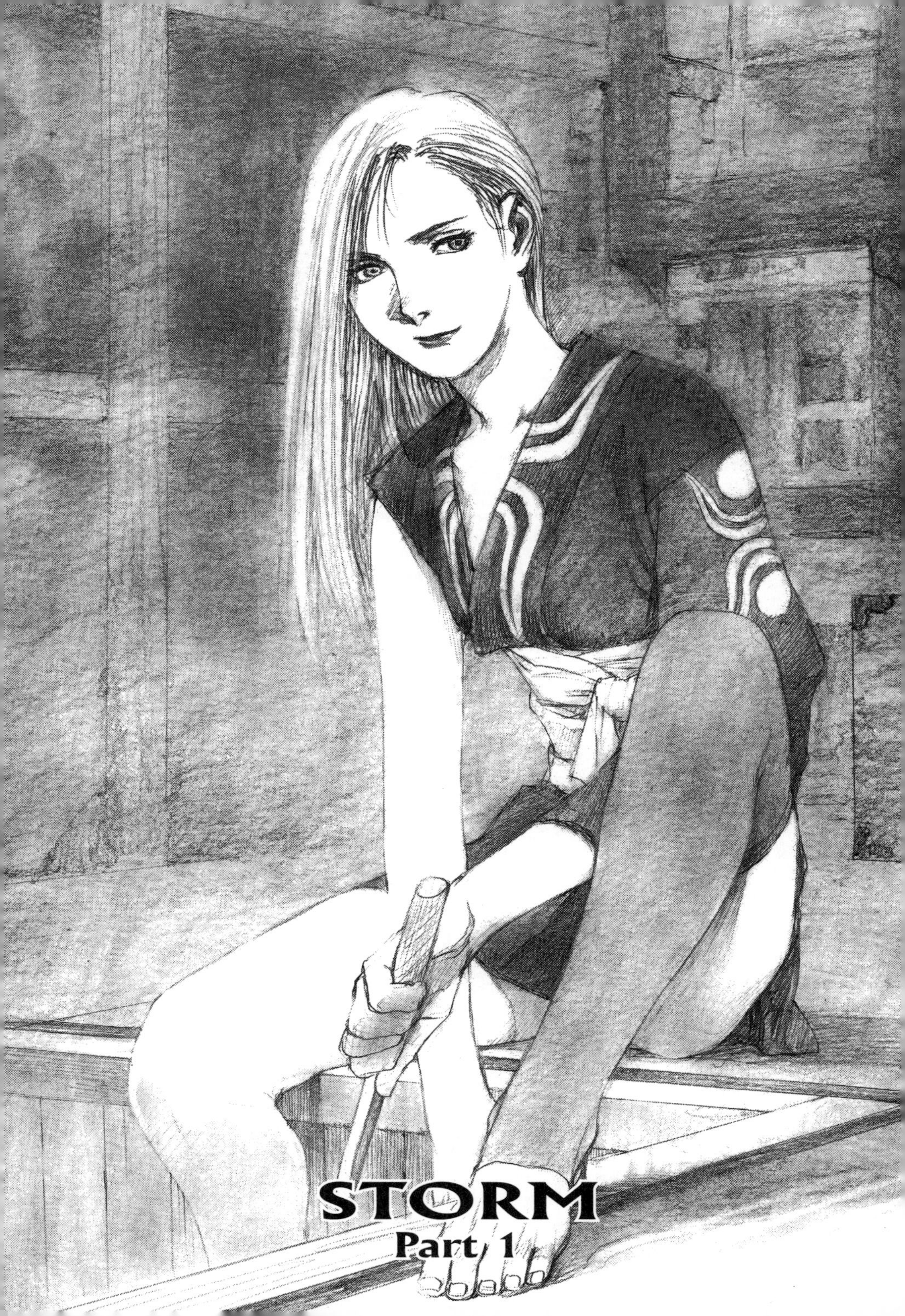
STORM
Part 1

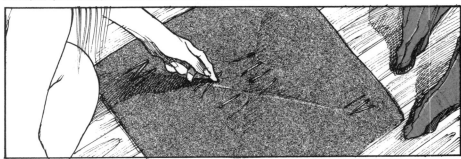

……

……

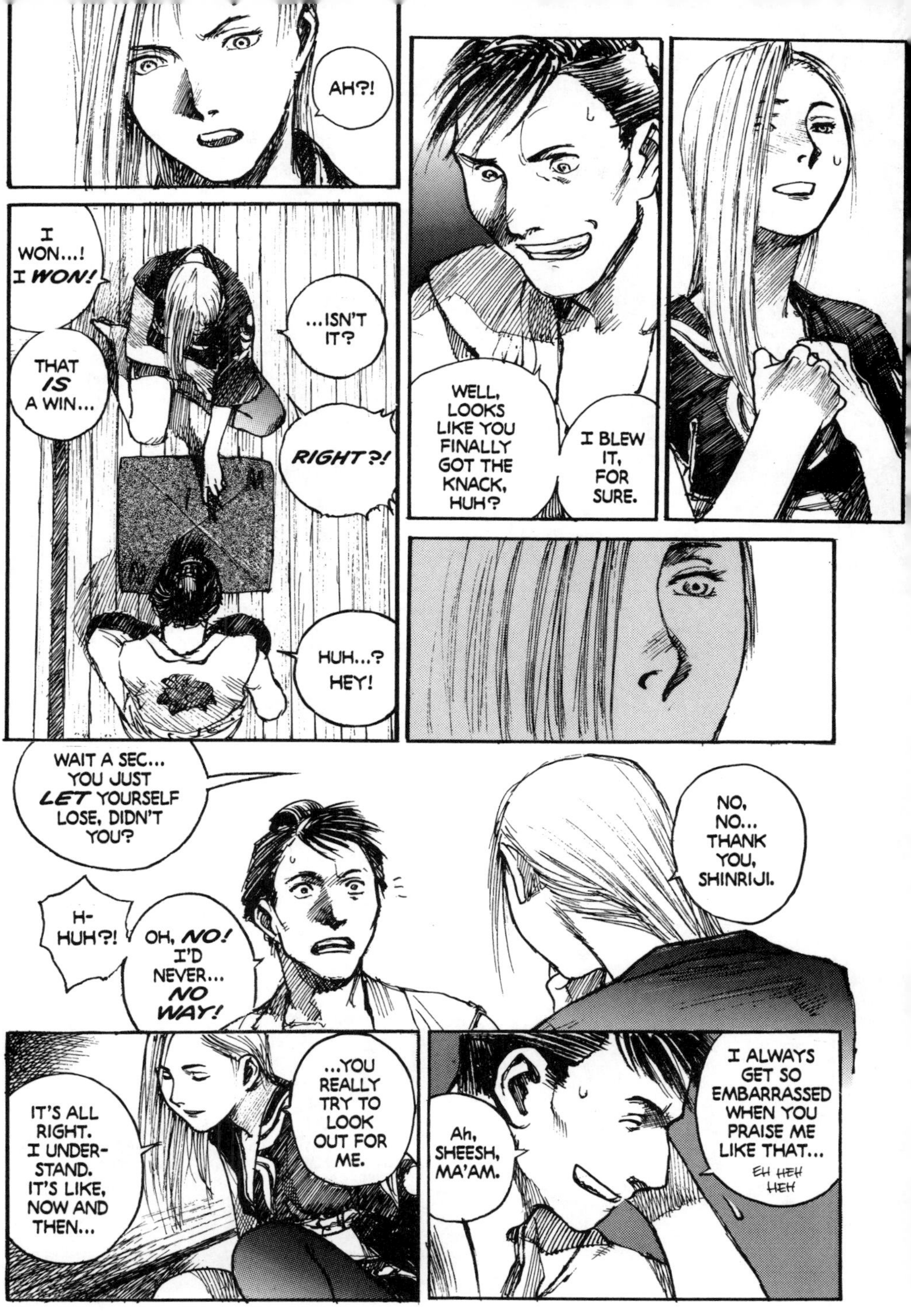

AH?!
WELL, LOOKS LIKE YOU FINALLY GOT THE KNACK, HUH?
I BLEW IT, FOR SURE.
I WON...! I *WON!*
THAT *IS* A WIN...
...ISN'T IT?
*RIGHT?!*
HUH...? HEY!
WAIT A SEC... YOU JUST *LET* YOURSELF LOSE, DIDN'T YOU?
H-HUH?!
OH, *NO!* I'D NEVER... *NO WAY!*
NO, NO... THANK YOU, SHINRIJI.
IT'S ALL RIGHT. I UNDER-STAND. IT'S LIKE, NOW AND THEN...
...YOU REALLY TRY TO LOOK OUT FOR ME.
Ah, SHEESH, MA'AM.
I ALWAYS GET SO EMBARRASSED WHEN YOU PRAISE ME LIKE THAT...
EH HEH HEH

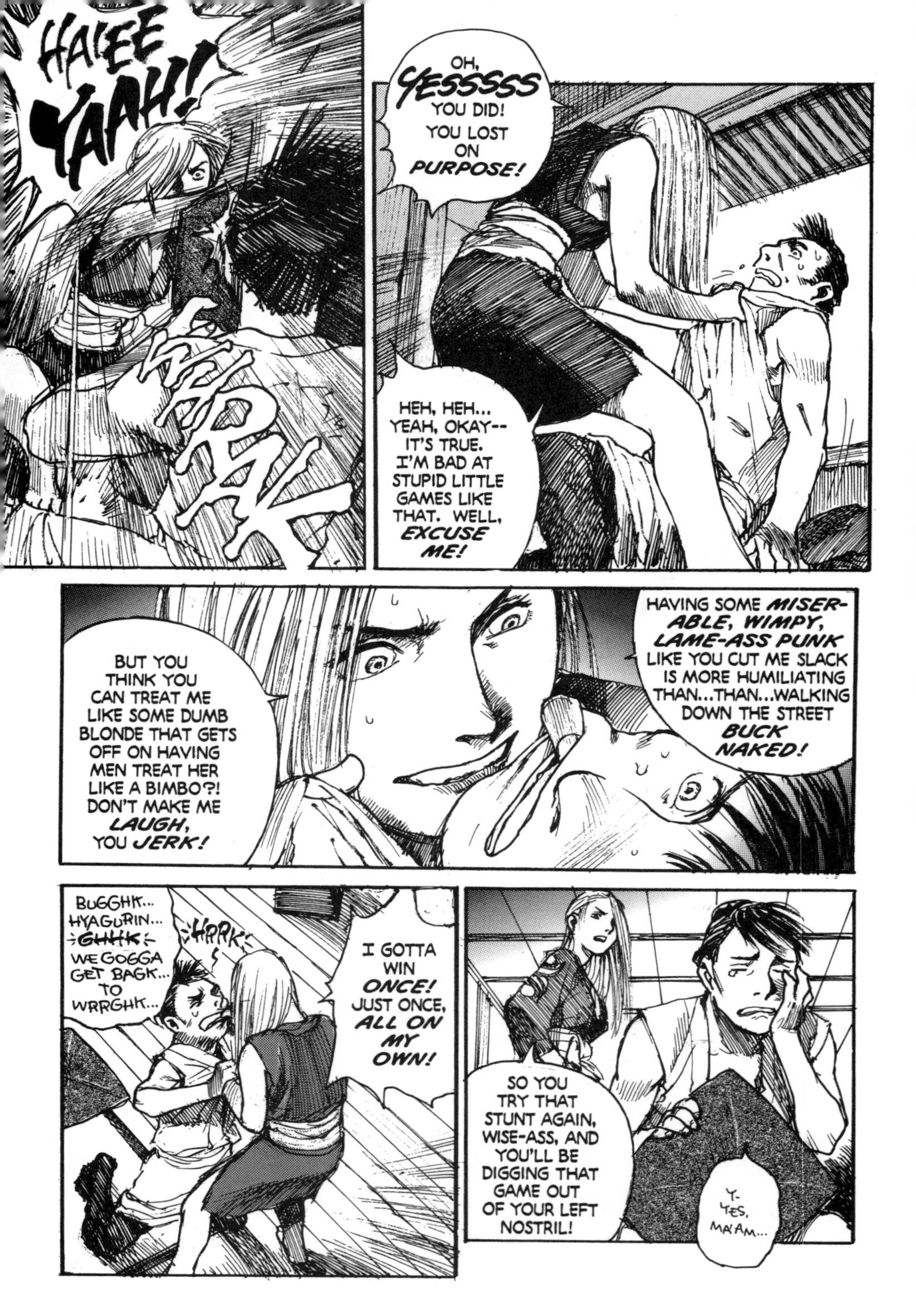
HAIEE YAAH!
WHAK
OH, YESSSSS YOU DID! YOU LOST ON PURPOSE!
HEH, HEH... YEAH, OKAY-- IT'S TRUE. I'M BAD AT STUPID LITTLE GAMES LIKE THAT. WELL, EXCUSE ME!
BUT YOU THINK YOU CAN TREAT ME LIKE SOME DUMB BLONDE THAT GETS OFF ON HAVING MEN TREAT HER LIKE A BIMBO?! DON'T MAKE ME LAUGH, YOU JERK!
HAVING SOME MISER-ABLE, WIMPY, LAME-ASS PUNK LIKE YOU CUT ME SLACK IS MORE HUMILIATING THAN...THAN...WALKING DOWN THE STREET BUCK NAKED!
BUGGHK... HYAGURIN... GHHK WE GOGGA GET BAGK... TO WRRGHK...
HRRK!
I GOTTA WIN ONCE! JUST ONCE, ALL ON MY OWN!
SO YOU TRY THAT STUNT AGAIN, WISE-ASS, AND YOU'LL BE DIGGING THAT GAME OUT OF YOUR LEFT NOSTRIL!
Y-YES, MA'AM...

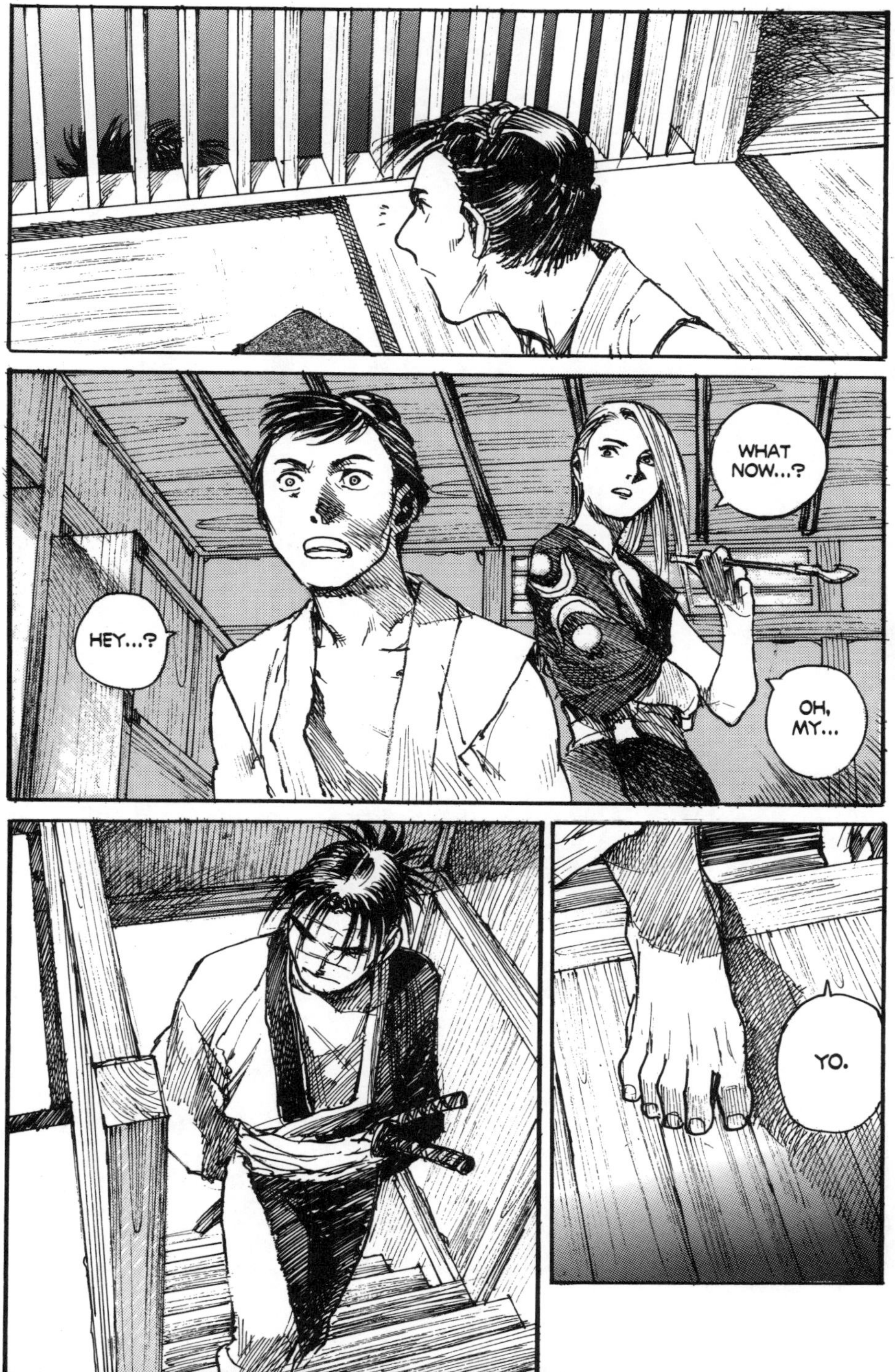
WHAT NOW...?
HEY...?
OH, MY...
YO.

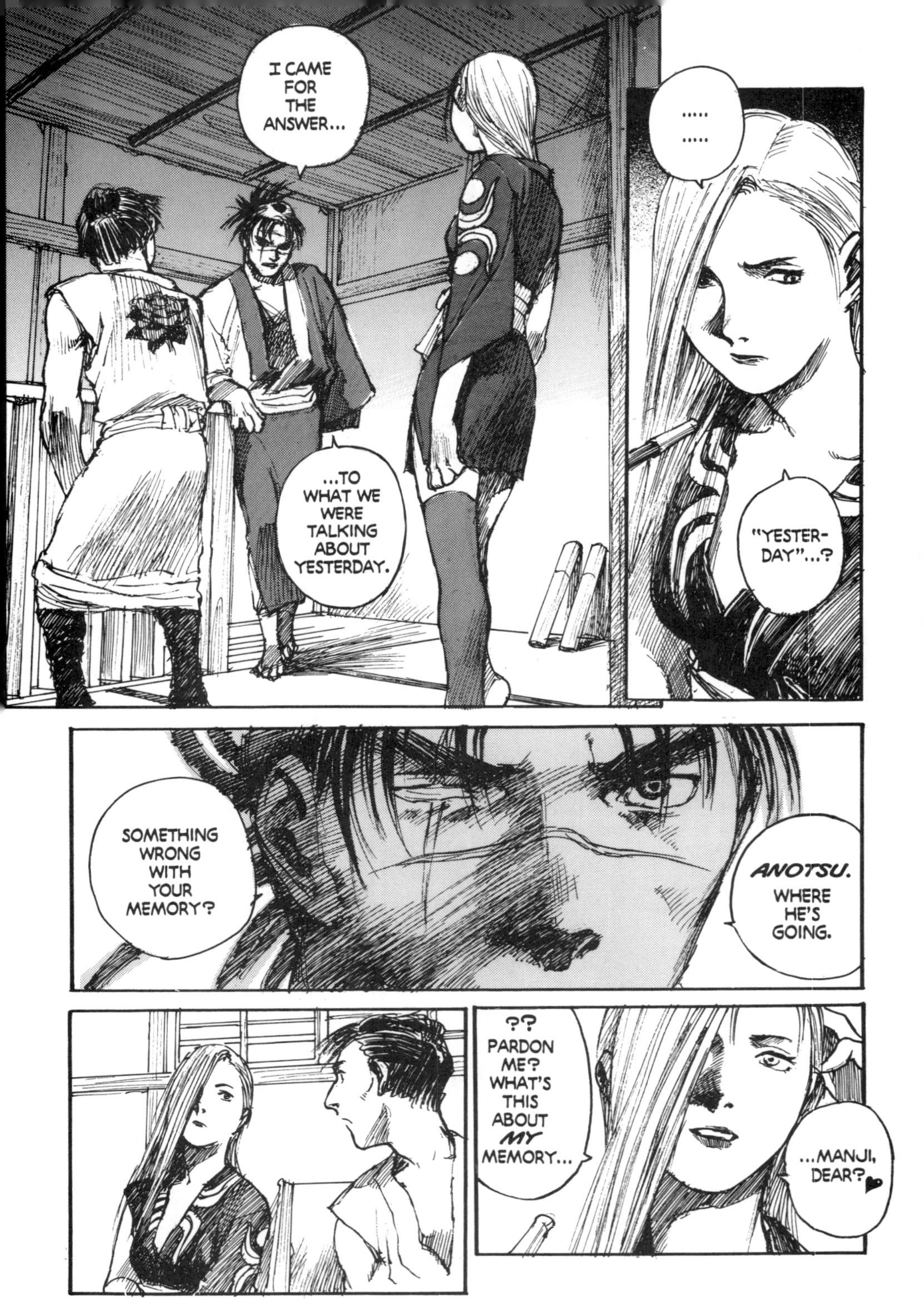
I CAME FOR THE ANSWER...
...TO WHAT WE WERE TALKING ABOUT YESTERDAY.
.....
.....
"YESTER-DAY"...?
SOMETHING WRONG WITH YOUR MEMORY?
ANOTSU. WHERE HE'S GOING.
?? PARDON ME? WHAT'S THIS ABOUT MY MEMORY...
...MANJI, DEAR?

YOU'RE THE ONE WITH MEMORY PROBLEMS, NOT ME.

"IF YOU'RE NOT ONE OF US, I CAN'T TELL YOU!"

THE SITUATION HAS CHANGED. I'M NOT LEAVING WITHOUT AN ANSWER.

OH, REALLY? THEN YOU'VE DECIDED TO SIGN ON AGAIN...?

NO.

NOW, *TALK.* WHERE'S HE GOING?

WELL, GOSH-A-ROOTIE! UNFORTUNATELY, ME AND OL' SHINRIJI HERE WERE JUST HEADING OUT FOR SOME GRUB.

COULDN'T YOU COME BACK SOME OTHER TIME? WE CAN TALK THEN...OR MAYBE MEAN MISTER MANJI WOULD LIKE TO *JOIN* US...?

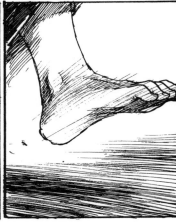

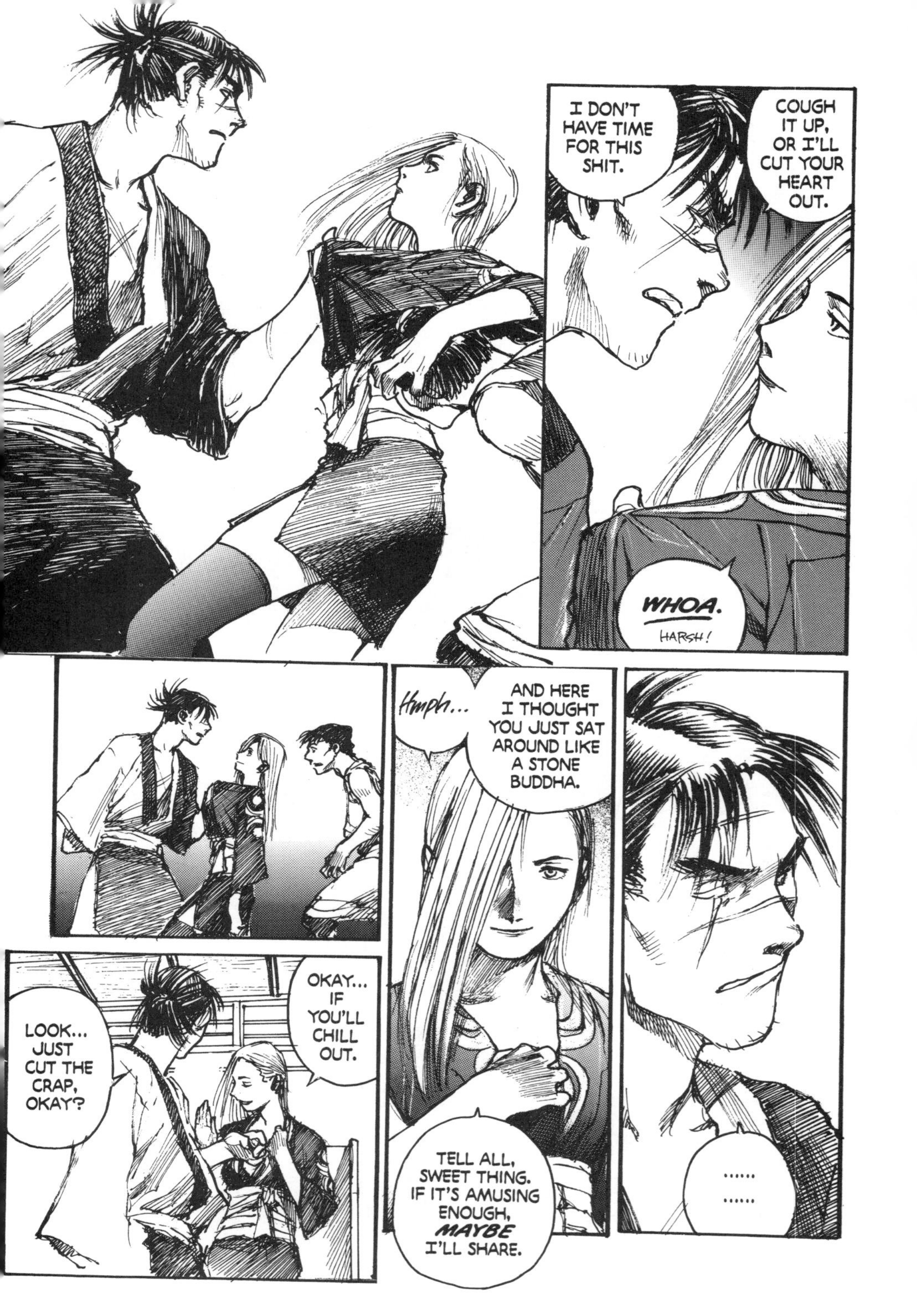
I DON'T HAVE TIME FOR THIS SHIT.
COUGH IT UP, OR I'LL CUT YOUR HEART OUT.
WHOA.
HARSH!
LOOK... JUST CUT THE CRAP, OKAY?
OKAY... IF YOU'LL CHILL OUT.
Hmph...
AND HERE I THOUGHT YOU JUST SAT AROUND LIKE A STONE BUDDHA.
TELL ALL, SWEET THING. IF IT'S AMUSING ENOUGH, MAYBE I'LL SHARE.
......
......

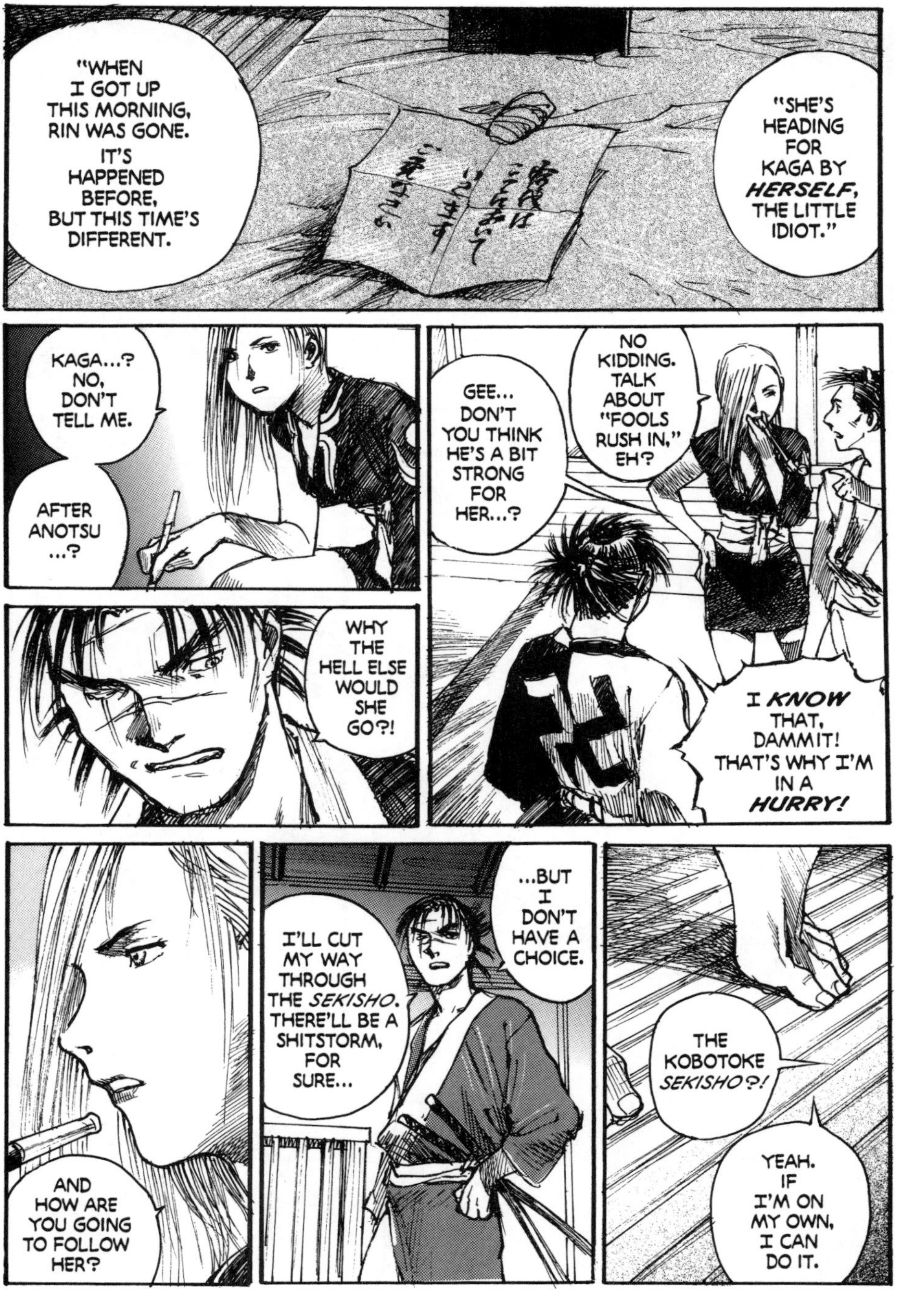
"WHEN I GOT UP THIS MORNING, RIN WAS GONE. IT'S HAPPENED BEFORE, BUT THIS TIME'S DIFFERENT.
"SHE'S HEADING FOR KAGA BY *HERSELF*, THE LITTLE IDIOT."
KAGA...? NO, DON'T TELL ME.
AFTER ANOTSU ...?
WHY THE HELL ELSE WOULD SHE GO?!
NO KIDDING. TALK ABOUT "FOOLS RUSH IN," EH?
GEE... DON'T YOU THINK HE'S A BIT STRONG FOR HER...?
I *KNOW* THAT, DAMMIT! THAT'S WHY I'M IN A *HURRY!*
AND HOW ARE YOU GOING TO FOLLOW HER?
I'LL CUT MY WAY THROUGH THE *SEKISHO*. THERE'LL BE A SHITSTORM, FOR SURE...
...BUT I DON'T HAVE A CHOICE.
THE KOBOTOKE *SEKISHO*?!
YEAH. IF I'M ON MY OWN, I CAN DO IT.

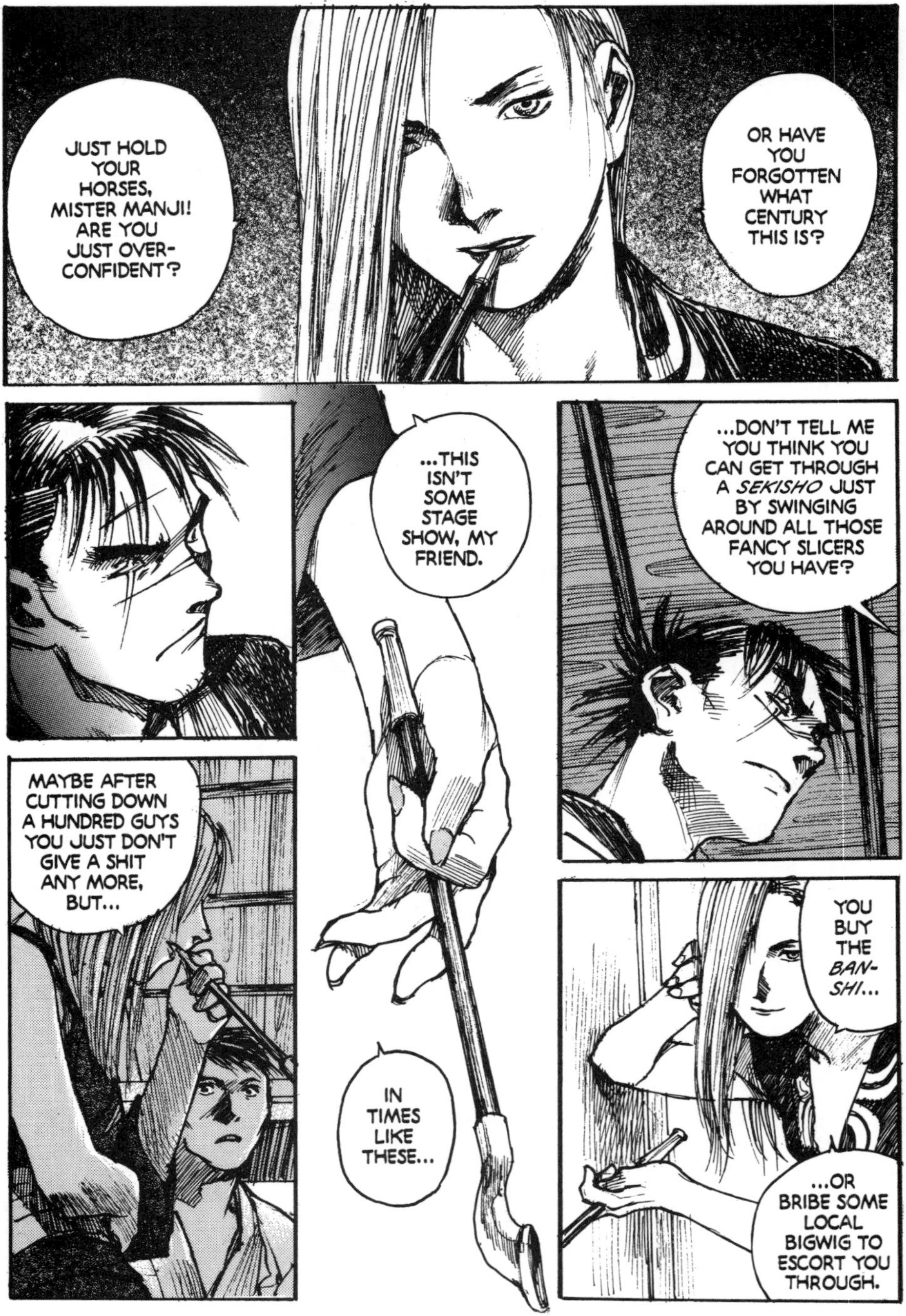
JUST HOLD YOUR HORSES, MISTER MANJI! ARE YOU JUST OVER-CONFIDENT?
OR HAVE YOU FORGOTTEN WHAT CENTURY THIS IS?
...THIS ISN'T SOME STAGE SHOW, MY FRIEND.
...DON'T TELL ME YOU THINK YOU CAN GET THROUGH A *SEKISHO* JUST BY SWINGING AROUND ALL THOSE FANCY SLICERS YOU HAVE?
MAYBE AFTER CUTTING DOWN A HUNDRED GUYS YOU JUST DON'T GIVE A SHIT ANY MORE, BUT...
IN TIMES LIKE THESE...
YOU BUY THE *BAN-SHI*...
...OR BRIBE SOME LOCAL BIGWIG TO ESCORT YOU THROUGH.

WHAT IT REALLY COMES DOWN TO, WHAT *REALLY* MATTERS, IS...

...*CASH-OLA!*

BUT EVEN *THAT'S* NO GUARANTEE.

TRUTH IS, IT'S RARER FOR THINGS TO GO *RIGHT*.

AND IF IT GOES WRONG, AND YOU END UP HAVING TO ESCAPE FROM ALL THOSE *BANSHI*...

...HOW ARE YOU GONNA TRACK HER DOWN?

WOMEN GET STOPPED AT THE *SEKISHO*, EVEN *WITH* A *TEGATA*. AND BESIDES, THE GIRL DOESN'T KNOW KAGA ANY BETTER THAN YOU DO.

SO DON'T GET YOUR SHORTS IN A KNOT.

SHE'S NOT GOING TO CATCH ANOTSU *THAT* EASY.

SO WHY DON'T YOU TRY SOMETHING MORE SENSI-BLE...?

LIKE *WHAT*, DAMN IT?! THE BOTTOM LINE IS...

...*NO MONEY, NO CHOICE!* RIGHT?

NO, NO, NO!

WHAT I'M SAYING IS...

...DON'T THINK OF HOW TO CLEAR THE *SEKISHO.*

THINK A STEP AHEAD.

?

LET'S CUT TO THE CHASE.

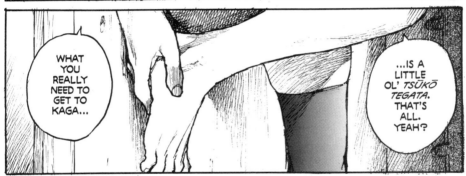

WHAT YOU REALLY NEED TO GET TO KAGA...

...IS A LITTLE OL' *TSŪKŌ TEGATA.* THAT'S ALL. YEAH?

"CUT TO THE CHASE," SHE SAYS. "GET A *TEGATA,*" SHE SAYS. LOOK, BLONDIE...

...FOR *ME,* THAT'S HARDER THAN CUTTING MY WAY THROUGH THE DAMN *SEKISHO!*

DON'T YOU HAVE A FRIGGIN' *CLUE?* EH?!

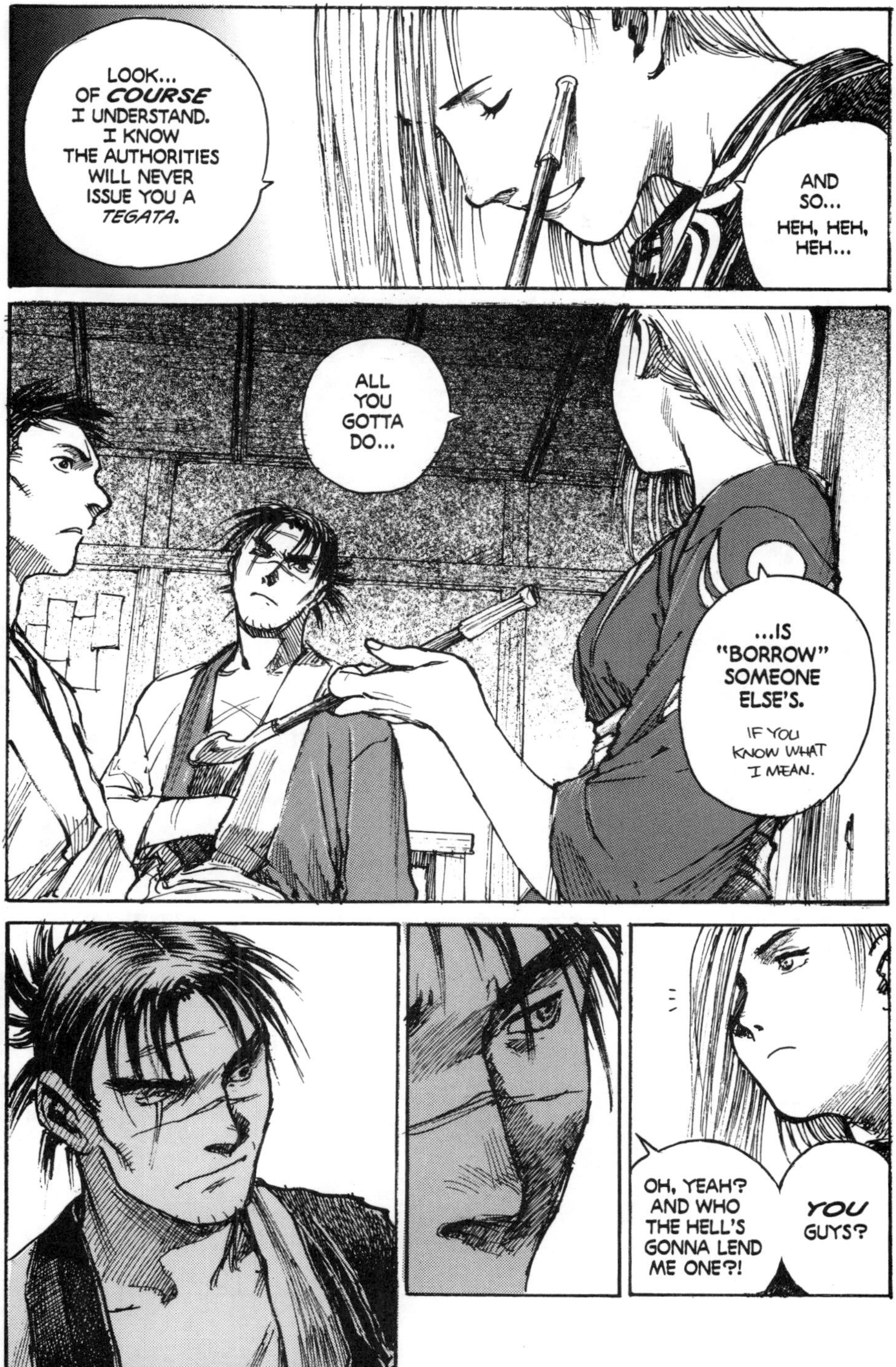
LOOK... OF *COURSE* I UNDERSTAND. I KNOW THE AUTHORITIES WILL NEVER ISSUE YOU A *TEGATA*.
AND SO... HEH, HEH, HEH...
ALL YOU GOTTA DO...
...IS "BORROW" SOMEONE ELSE'S.
IF YOU KNOW WHAT I MEAN.
OH, YEAH? AND WHO THE HELL'S GONNA LEND ME ONE?!
*YOU* GUYS?

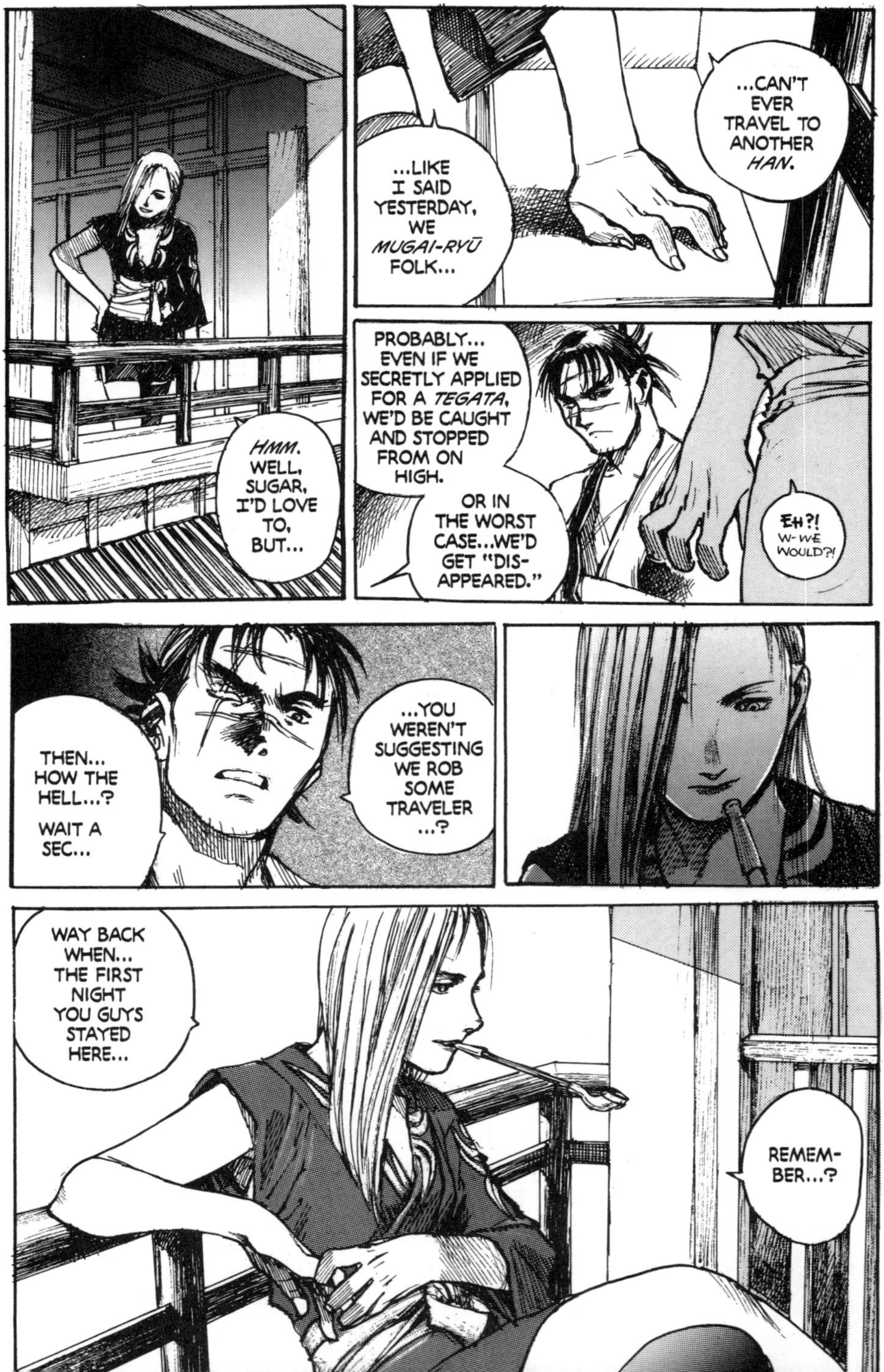
HMM. WELL, SUGAR, I'D LOVE TO, BUT...
...LIKE I SAID YESTERDAY, WE MUGAI-RYŪ FOLK...
...CAN'T EVER TRAVEL TO ANOTHER HAN.
PROBABLY... EVEN IF WE SECRETLY APPLIED FOR A TEGATA, WE'D BE CAUGHT AND STOPPED FROM ON HIGH.
OR IN THE WORST CASE...WE'D GET "DIS-APPEARED."
EH?! W-WE WOULD?!
THEN... HOW THE HELL...?
WAIT A SEC...
...YOU WEREN'T SUGGESTING WE ROB SOME TRAVELER ...?
WAY BACK WHEN... THE FIRST NIGHT YOU GUYS STAYED HERE...
REMEM-BER...?

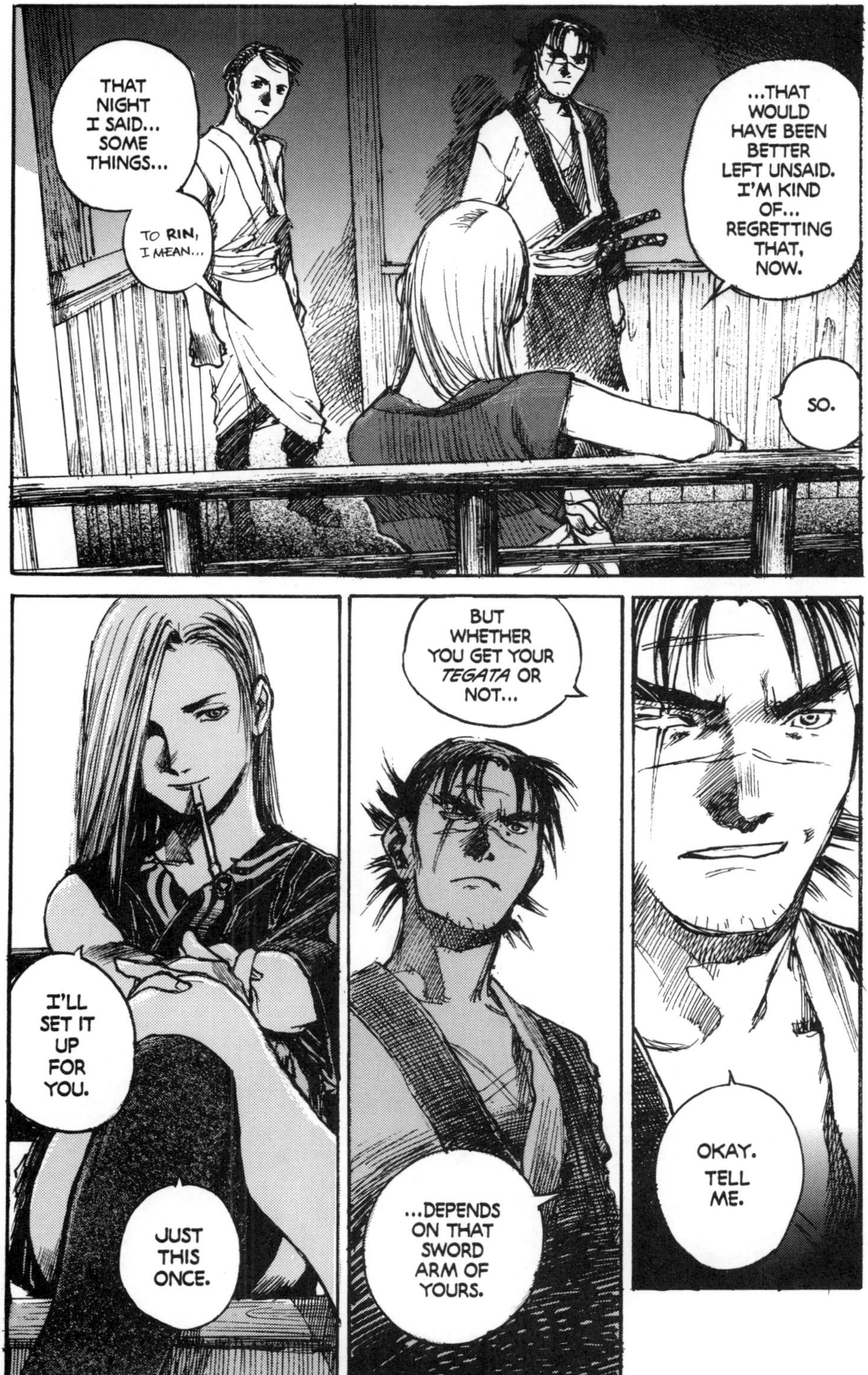
THAT NIGHT I SAID... SOME THINGS...
TO RIN, I MEAN...
...THAT WOULD HAVE BEEN BETTER LEFT UNSAID. I'M KIND OF... REGRETTING THAT, NOW.
SO.
I'LL SET IT UP FOR YOU.
JUST THIS ONCE.
BUT WHETHER YOU GET YOUR *TEGATA* OR NOT...
...DEPENDS ON THAT SWORD ARM OF YOURS.
OKAY. TELL ME.

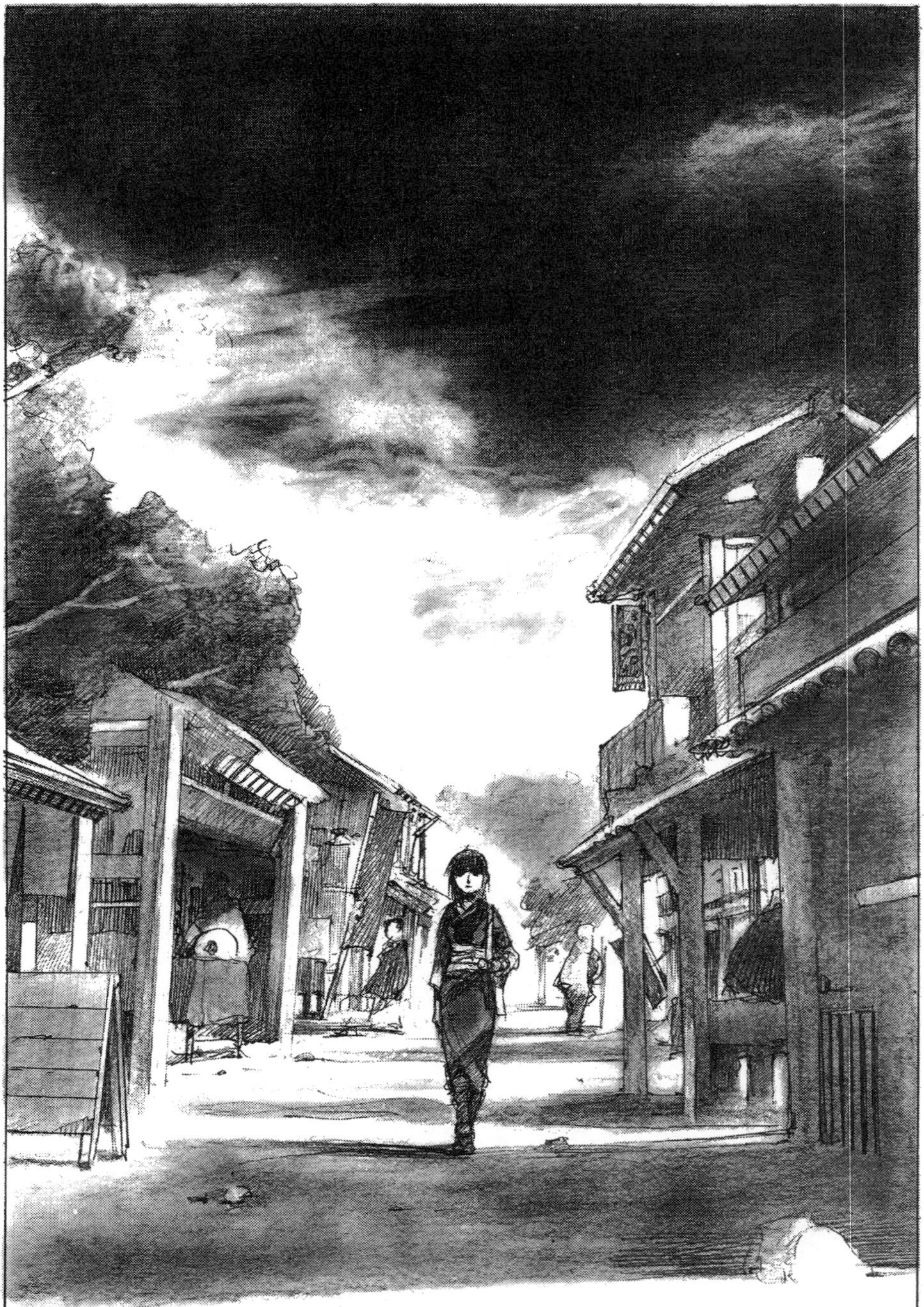

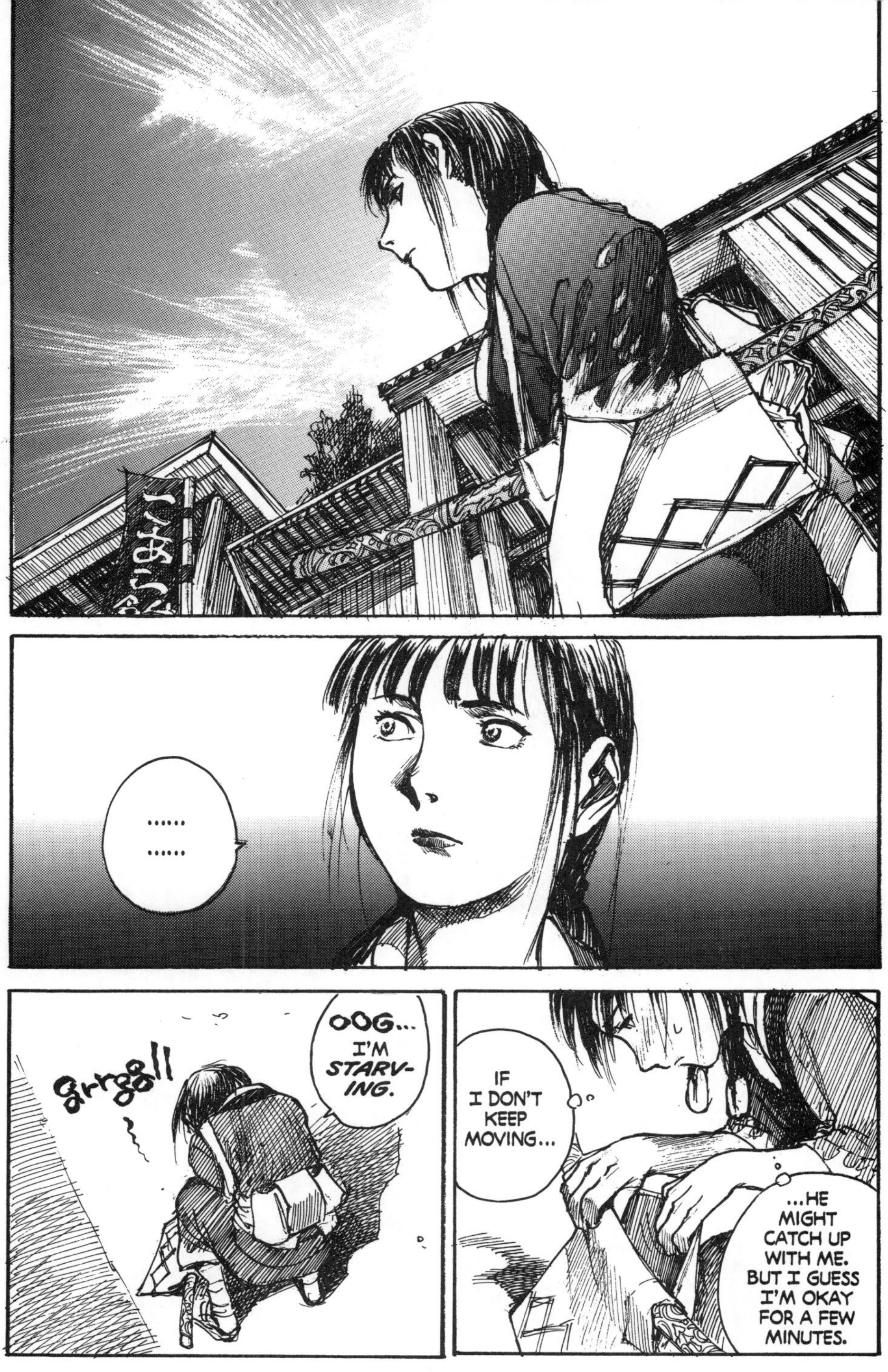
……
……
OOG... I'M STARVING.
IF I DON'T KEEP MOVING...
...HE MIGHT CATCH UP WITH ME. BUT I GUESS I'M OKAY FOR A FEW MINUTES.

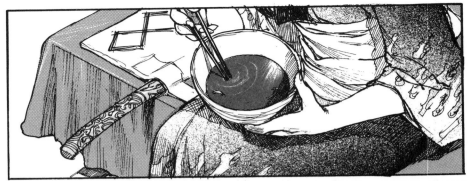

SLRRRP

hahh

IT'S BEEN AGES.

WALKING ALONE.

EATING ALONE...

......

THE LAST TIME MUST HAVE BEEN... WHEN?

WHEN I WAS STILL LOOKING FOR MANJI, I GUESS.

"THAT OLD LADY YAOBIKUNI HAD TOLD ME ABOUT HIM...
GOSH, SUDDENLY I'M ALL NOSTALGIC...
"AND WHEN I FINALLY FOUND HIM, AND WAS SO HAPPY...
"HE SMACKED ME! HARD!"
......
......
IF YOU'RE ALWAYS BEING PROTECTED BY SOME TOUGH GUY...
...YOU'RE NEVER GOING TO BE STRONG YOURSELF. RIGHT?

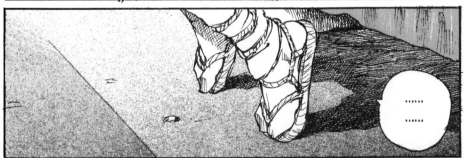

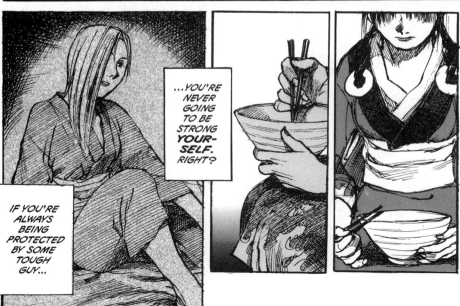

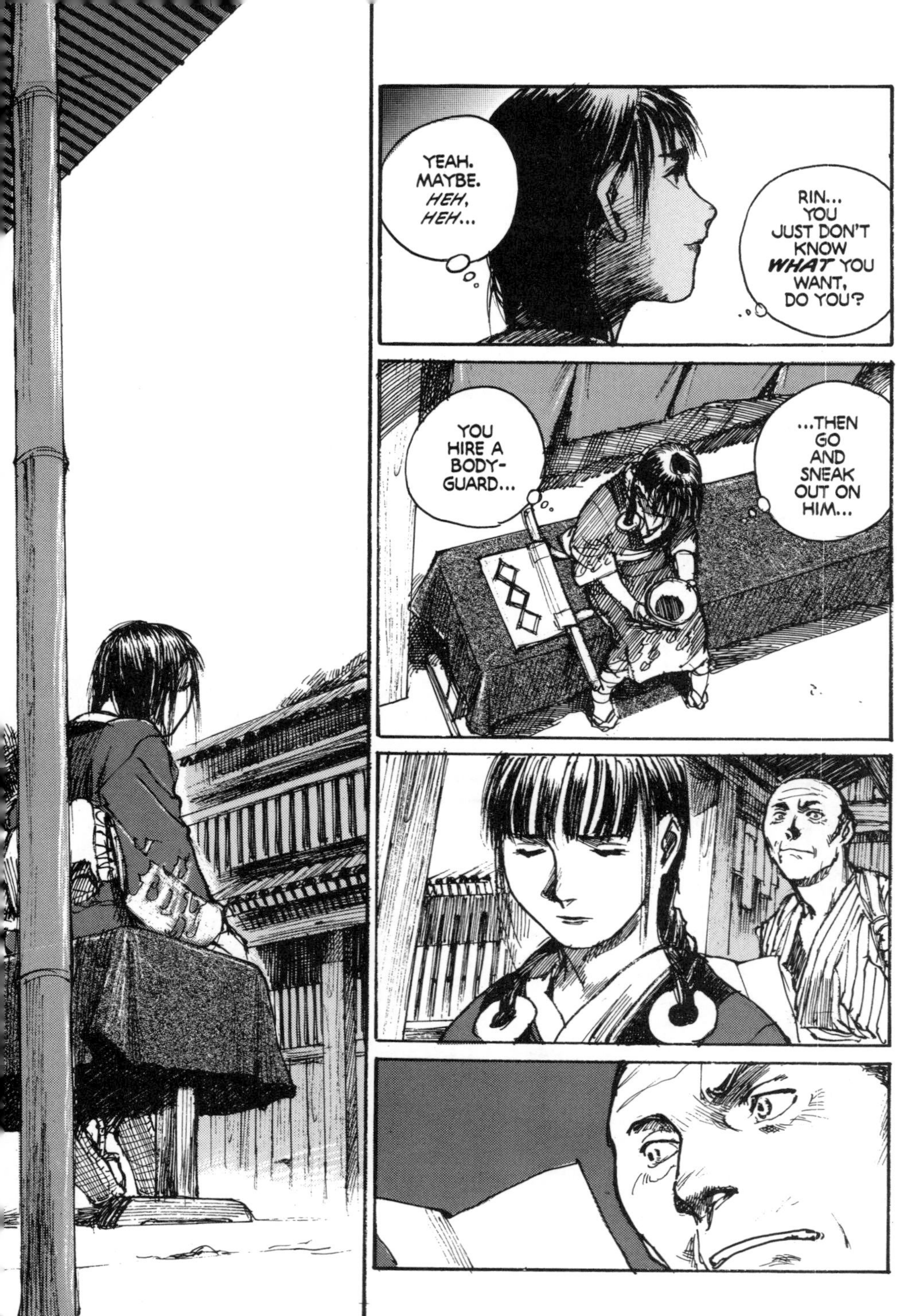
YEAH. MAYBE. *HEH, HEH*...
RIN... YOU JUST DON'T KNOW ***WHAT*** YOU WANT, DO YOU?
YOU HIRE A BODY-GUARD...
...THEN GO AND SNEAK OUT ON HIM...

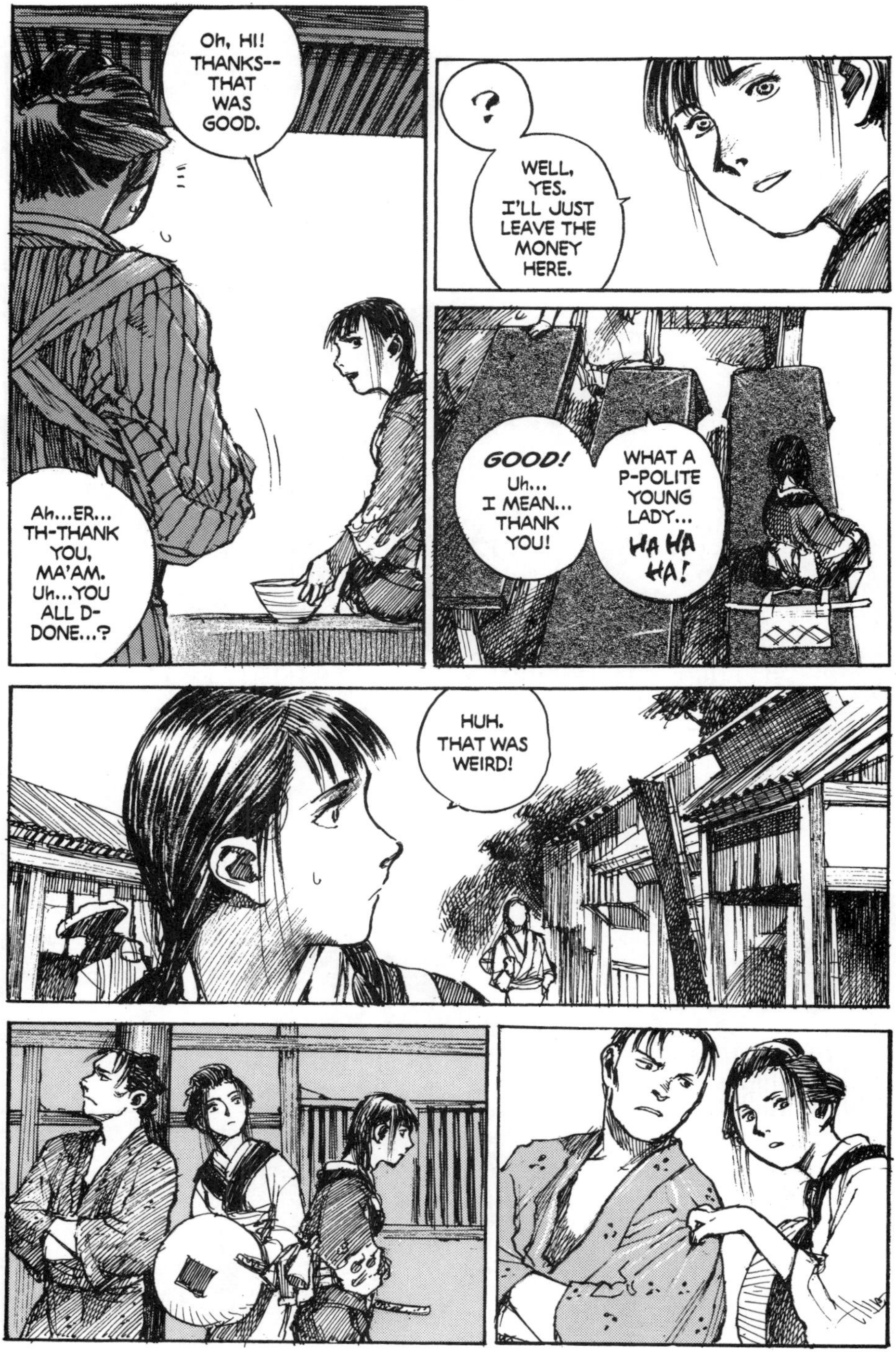
Oh, HI! THANKS-- THAT WAS GOOD.
Ah...ER... TH-THANK YOU, MA'AM. Uh...YOU ALL D-DONE...?
?
WELL, YES. I'LL JUST LEAVE THE MONEY HERE.
GOOD! Uh... I MEAN... THANK YOU!
WHAT A P-POLITE YOUNG LADY... HA HA HA!
HUH. THAT WAS WEIRD!

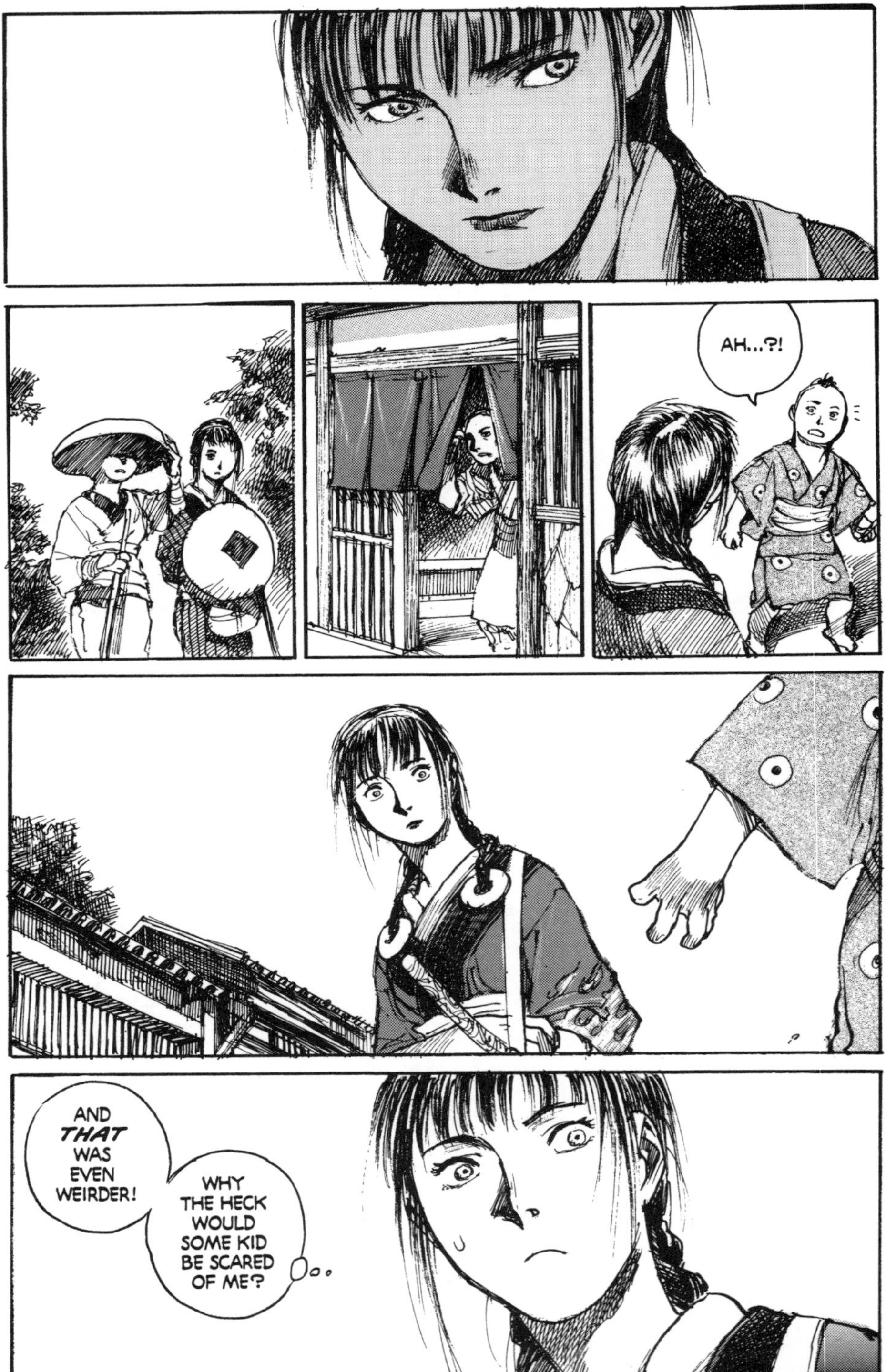
AH...?!
AND *THAT* WAS EVEN WEIRDER!
WHY THE HECK WOULD SOME KID BE SCARED OF ME?

IT'S NOT *THAT* STRANGE TO SEE A WOMAN WITH A SWORD.

I HAD IT ON THE ROAD TO NAITŌ SHINJUKU, TOO, AND NO ONE SAID A THING.

AHH... MAYBE I'M JUST PARANOID OR SOMETHING.

MMM...♥ ONCE YOU GET THIS FAR OUT OF TOWN...

...IT'S SO NICE AND--

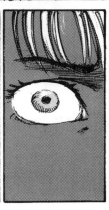

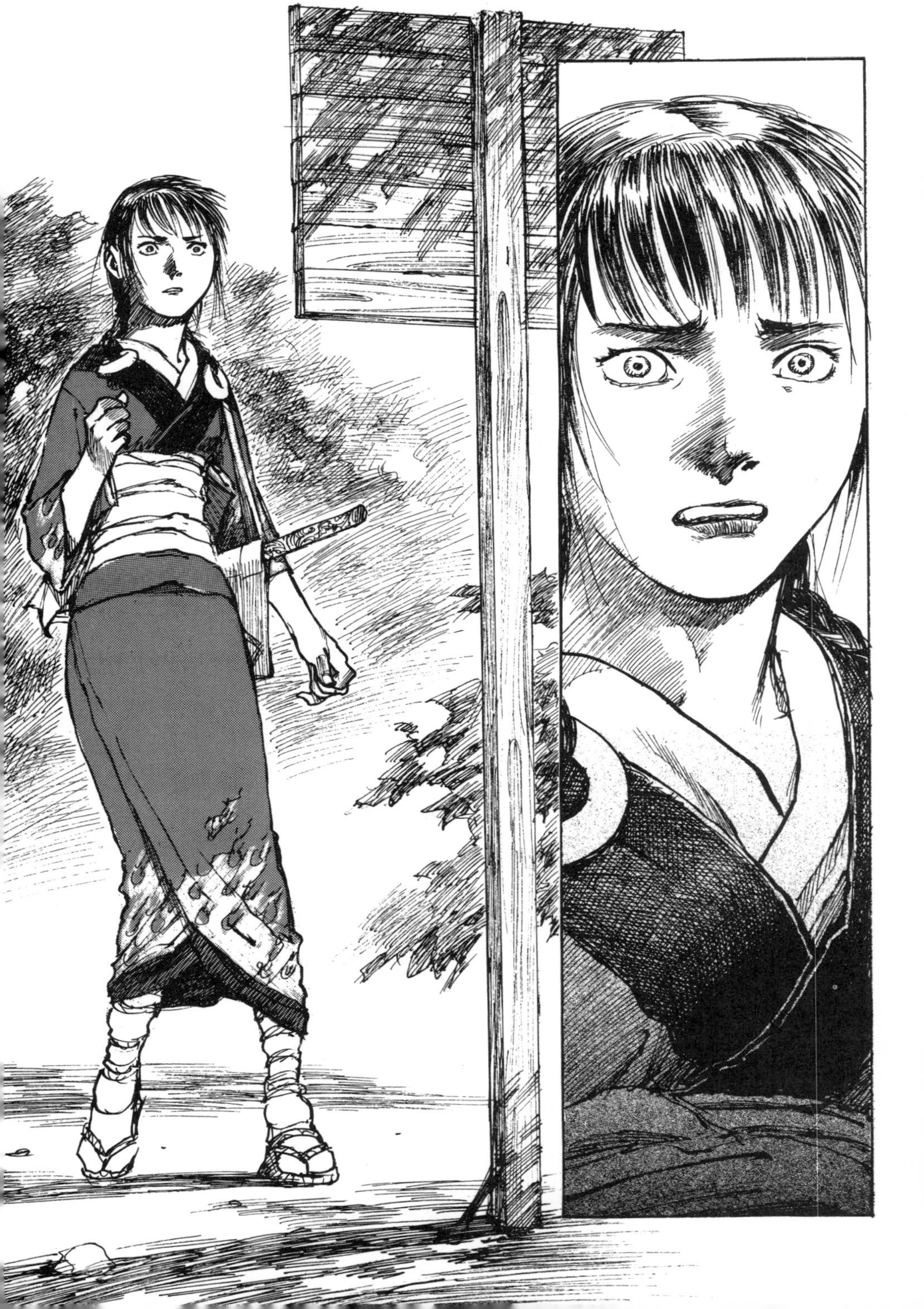

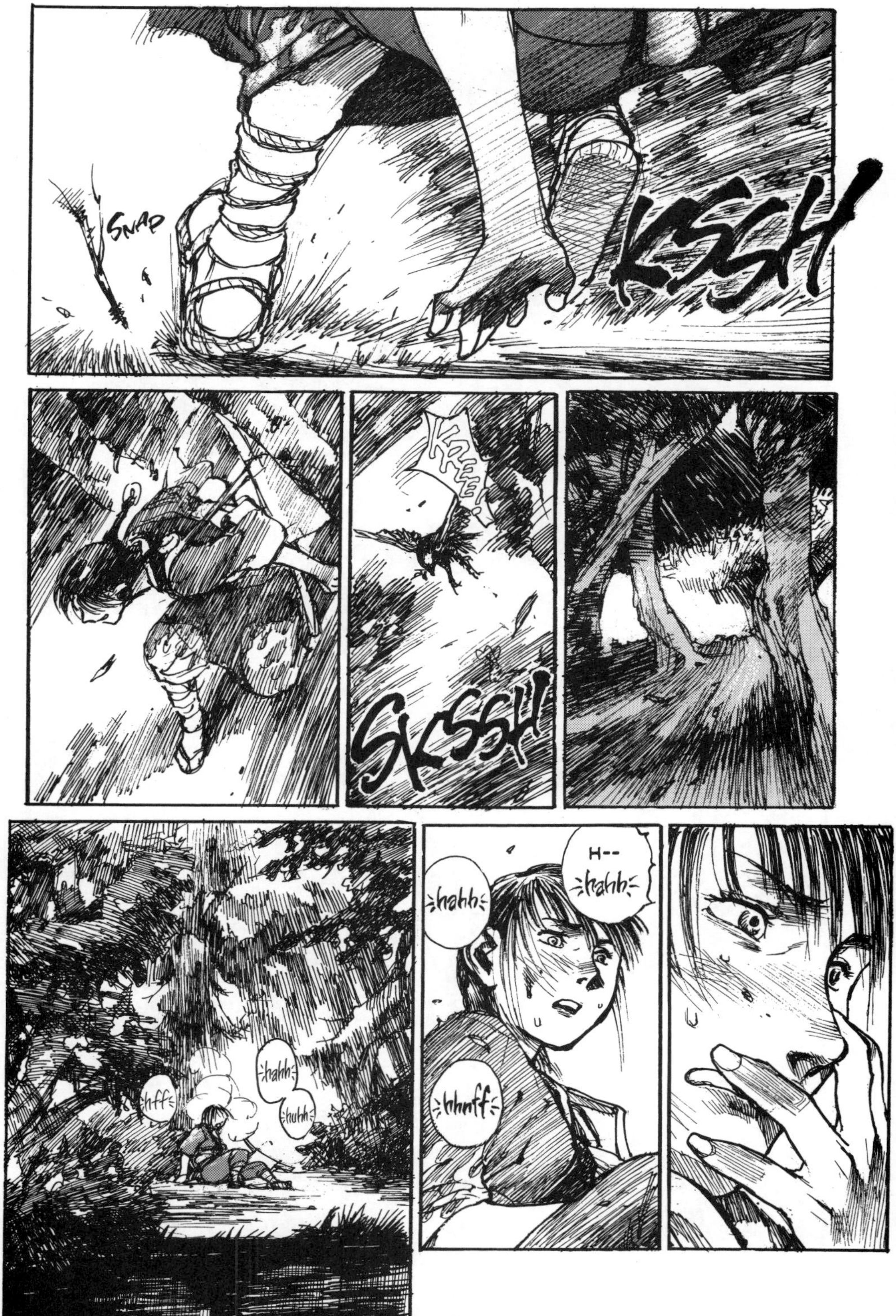
SNAP
KSSH
KREE!
SKSSH
hff
hahh
huhh
H--
hahh
hahh
hhnff

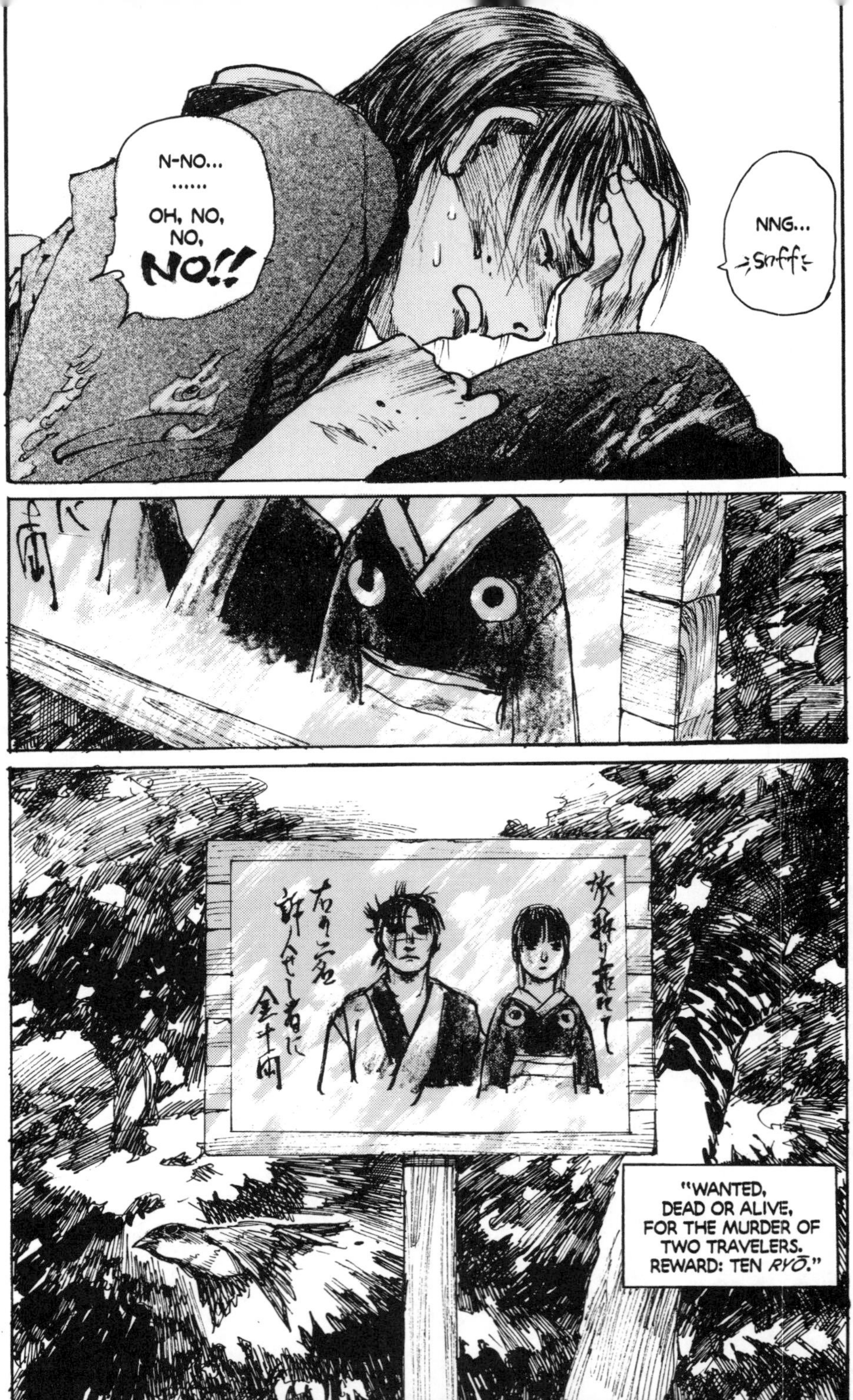
N-NO... ...... OH, NO, NO, NO!!
NNG...
SNFF
"WANTED, DEAD OR ALIVE, FOR THE MURDER OF TWO TRAVELERS. REWARD: TEN *RYŌ*."

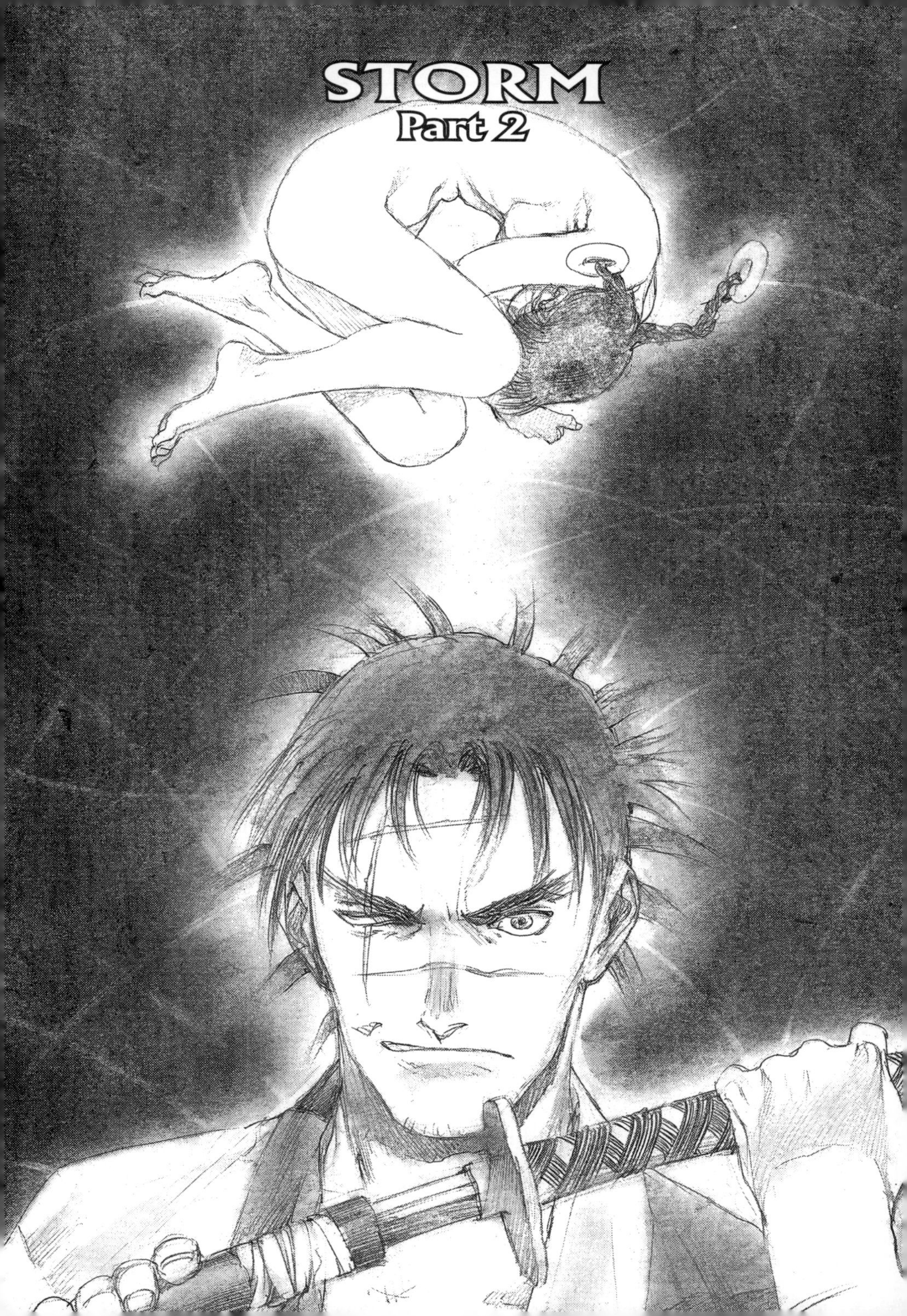
STORM
Part 2

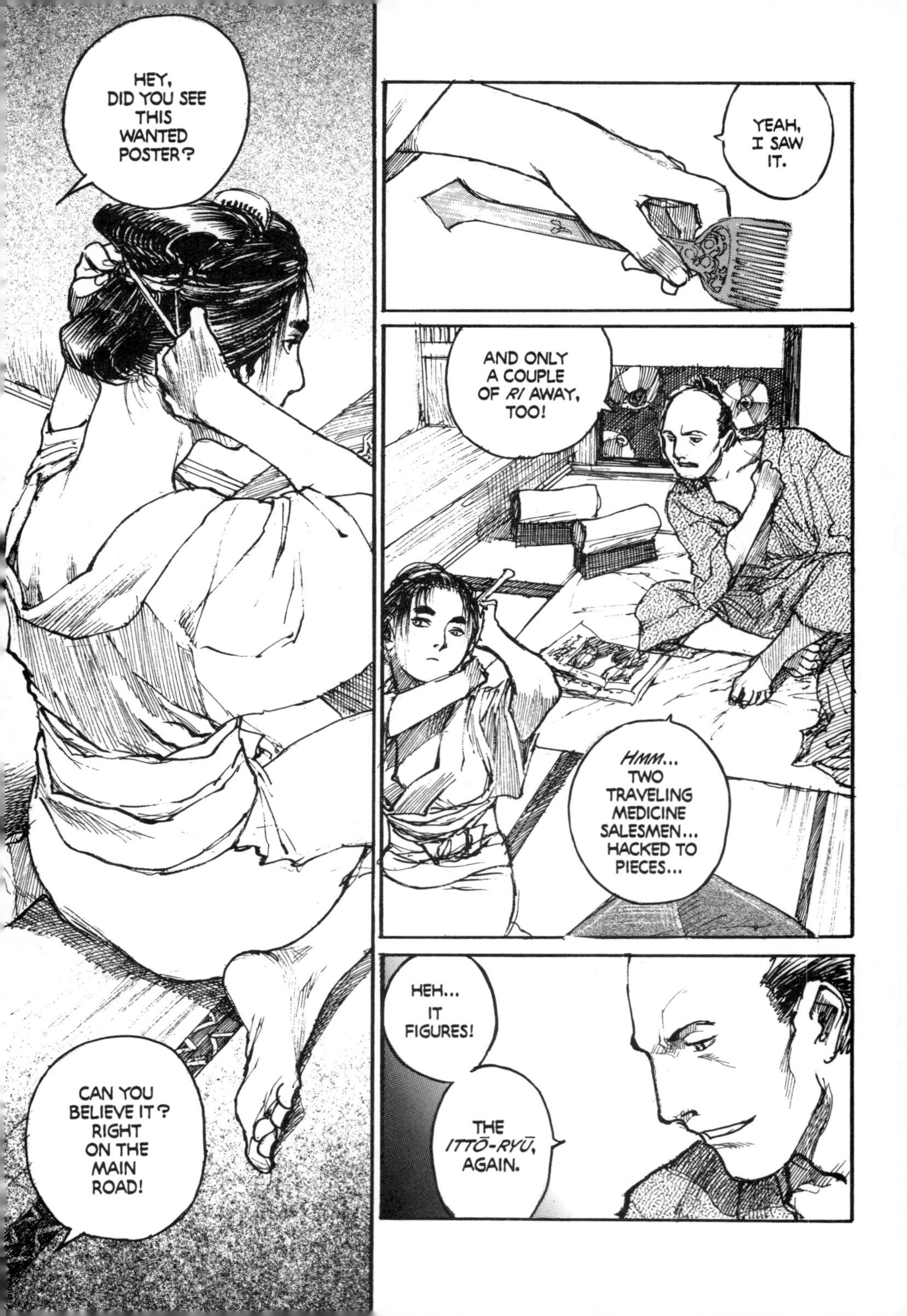
HEY, DID YOU SEE THIS WANTED POSTER?
CAN YOU BELIEVE IT? RIGHT ON THE MAIN ROAD!
YEAH, I SAW IT.
AND ONLY A COUPLE OF *RI* AWAY, TOO!
*HMM*... TWO TRAVELING MEDICINE SALESMEN... HACKED TO PIECES...
HEH... IT FIGURES!
THE *ITTŌ-RYŪ*, AGAIN.

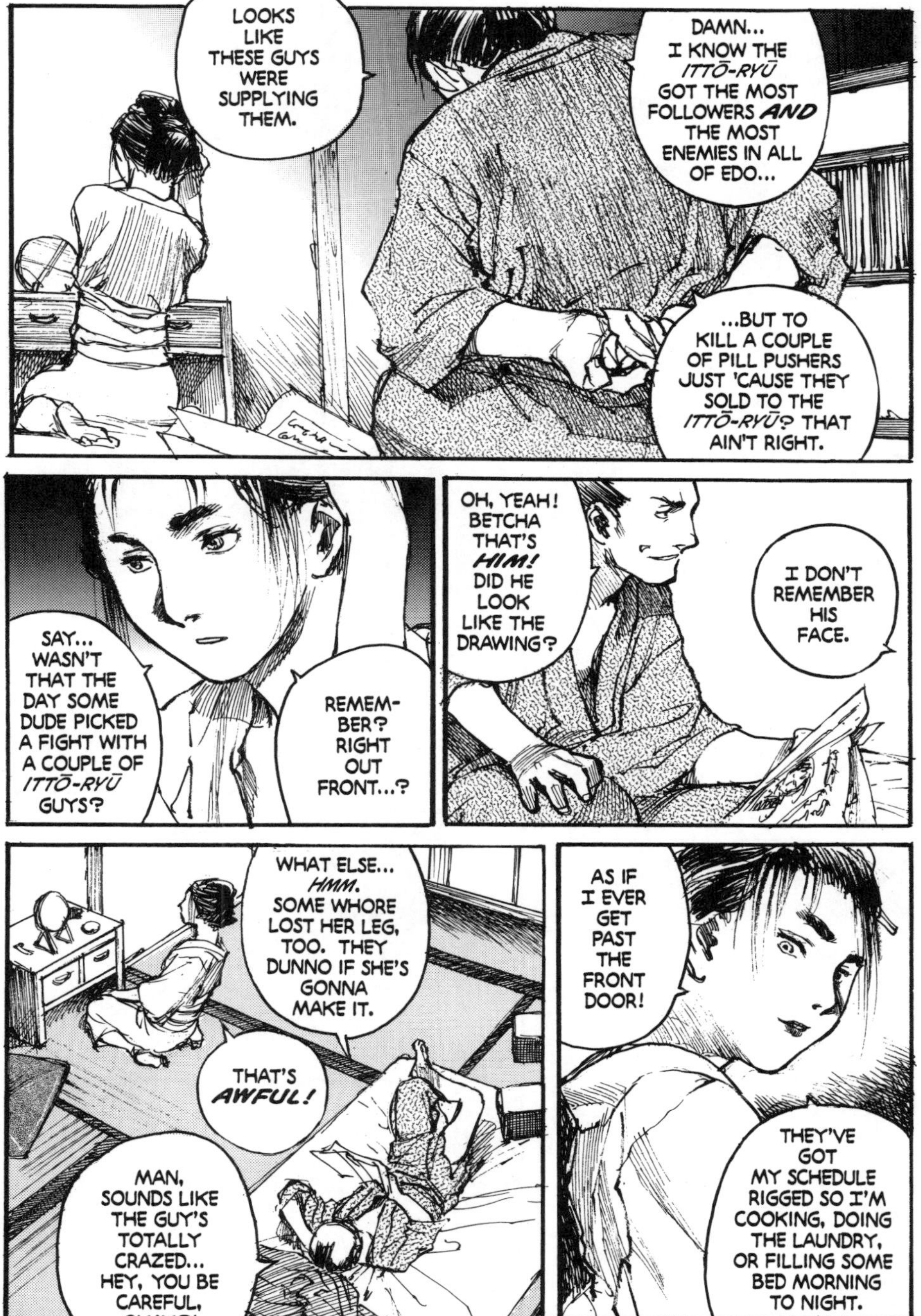
LOOKS LIKE THESE GUYS WERE SUPPLYING THEM.
DAMN... I KNOW THE *ITTŌ-RYŪ* GOT THE MOST FOLLOWERS ***AND*** THE MOST ENEMIES IN ALL OF EDO...
...BUT TO KILL A COUPLE OF PILL PUSHERS JUST 'CAUSE THEY SOLD TO THE *ITTŌ-RYŪ*? THAT AIN'T RIGHT.
SAY... WASN'T THAT THE DAY SOME DUDE PICKED A FIGHT WITH A COUPLE OF *ITTŌ-RYŪ* GUYS?
REMEM-BER? RIGHT OUT FRONT...?
OH, YEAH! BETCHA THAT'S ***HIM!*** DID HE LOOK LIKE THE DRAWING?
I DON'T REMEMBER HIS FACE.
WHAT ELSE... *HMM.* SOME WHORE LOST HER LEG, TOO. THEY DUNNO IF SHE'S GONNA MAKE IT.
THAT'S ***AWFUL!***
MAN, SOUNDS LIKE THE GUY'S TOTALLY CRAZED... HEY, YOU BE CAREFUL, OKAY?!
AS IF I EVER GET PAST THE FRONT DOOR!
THEY'VE GOT MY SCHEDULE RIGGED SO I'M COOKING, DOING THE LAUNDRY, OR FILLING SOME BED MORNING TO NIGHT.

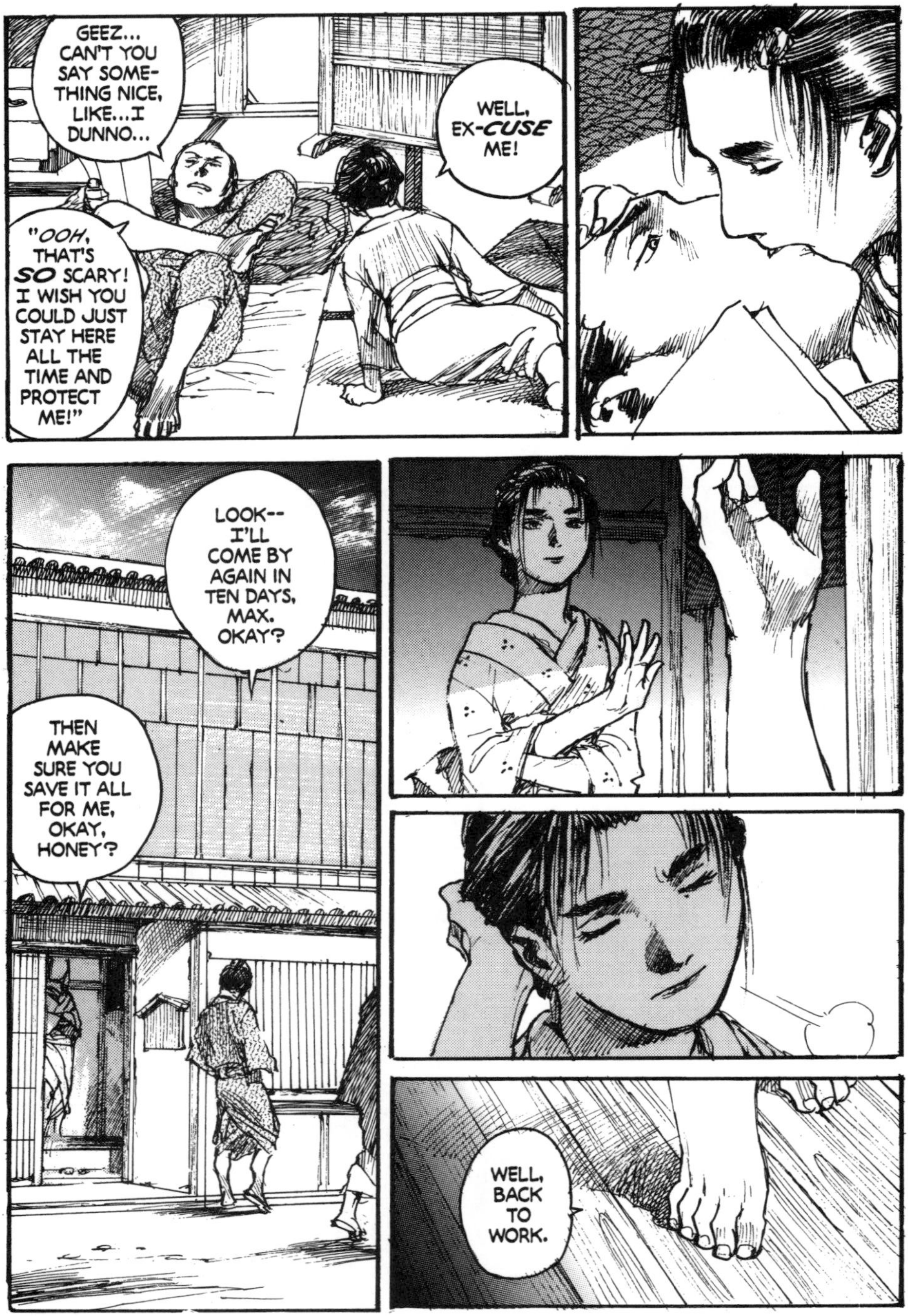
GEEZ... CAN'T YOU SAY SOMETHING NICE, LIKE...I DUNNO...
"OOH, THAT'S SO SCARY! I WISH YOU COULD JUST STAY HERE ALL THE TIME AND PROTECT ME!"
WELL, EX-CUSE ME!
LOOK-- I'LL COME BY AGAIN IN TEN DAYS, MAX. OKAY?
THEN MAKE SURE YOU SAVE IT ALL FOR ME, OKAY, HONEY?
WELL, BACK TO WORK.

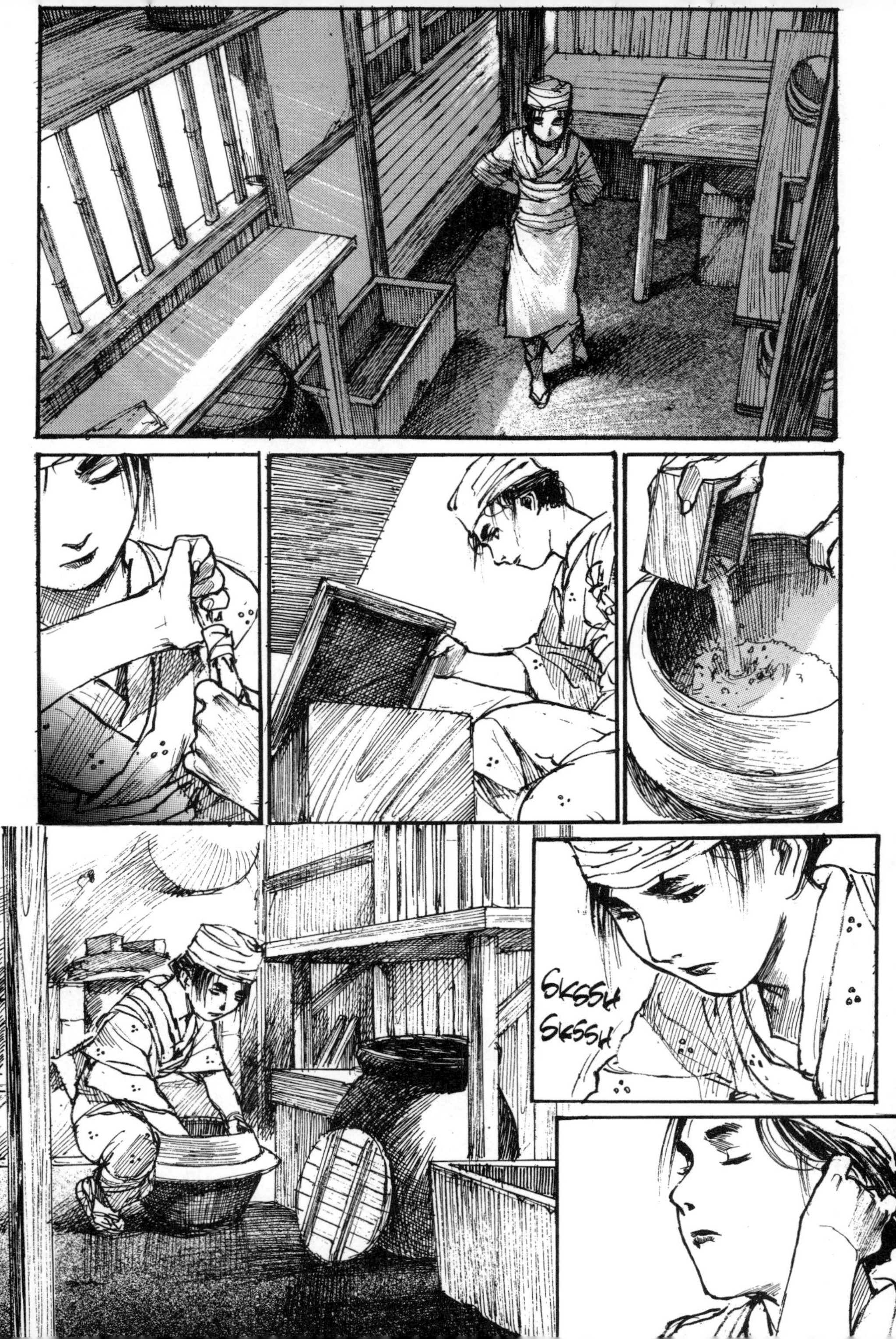
SKSSH
SKSSH

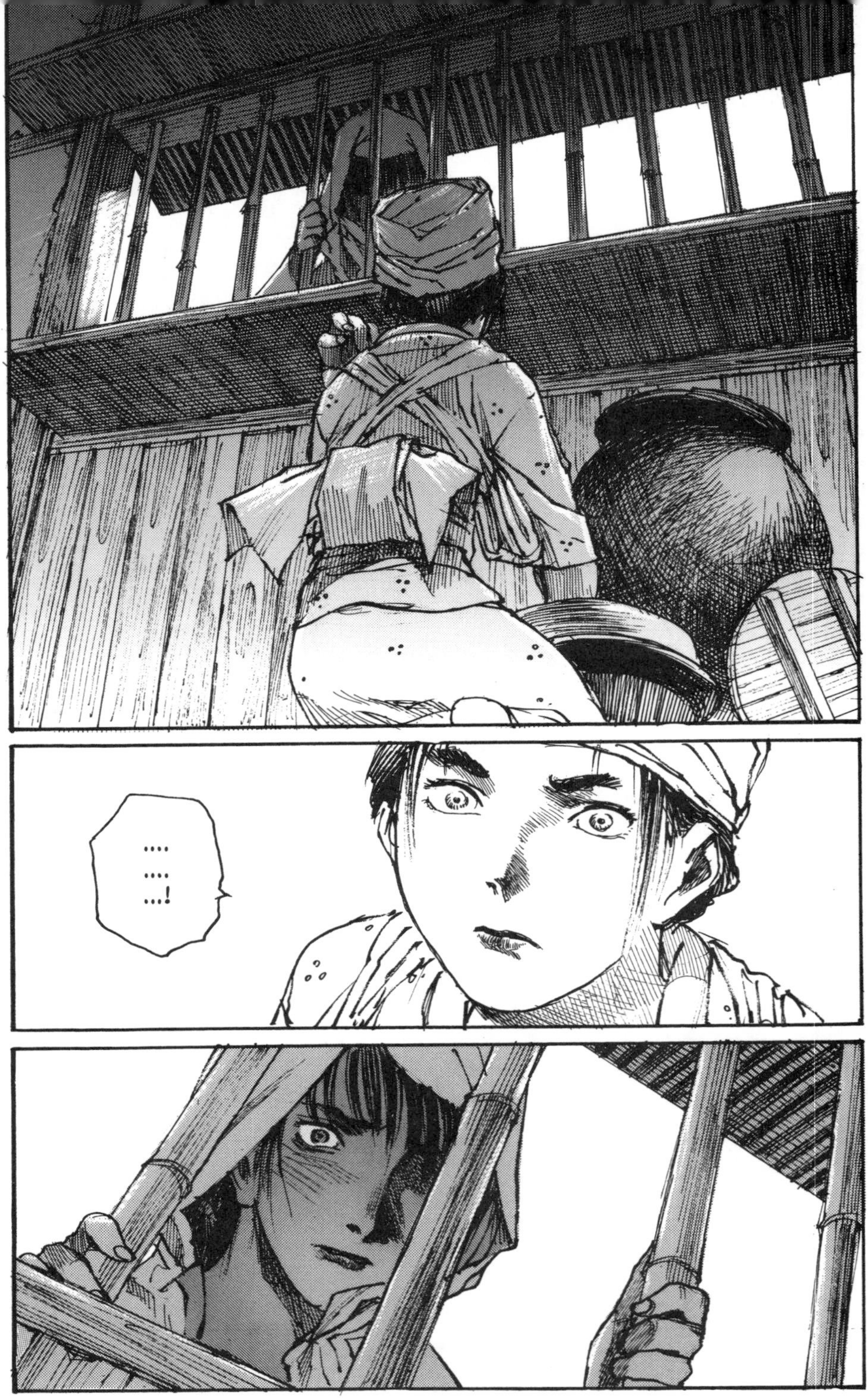
....
....
...!

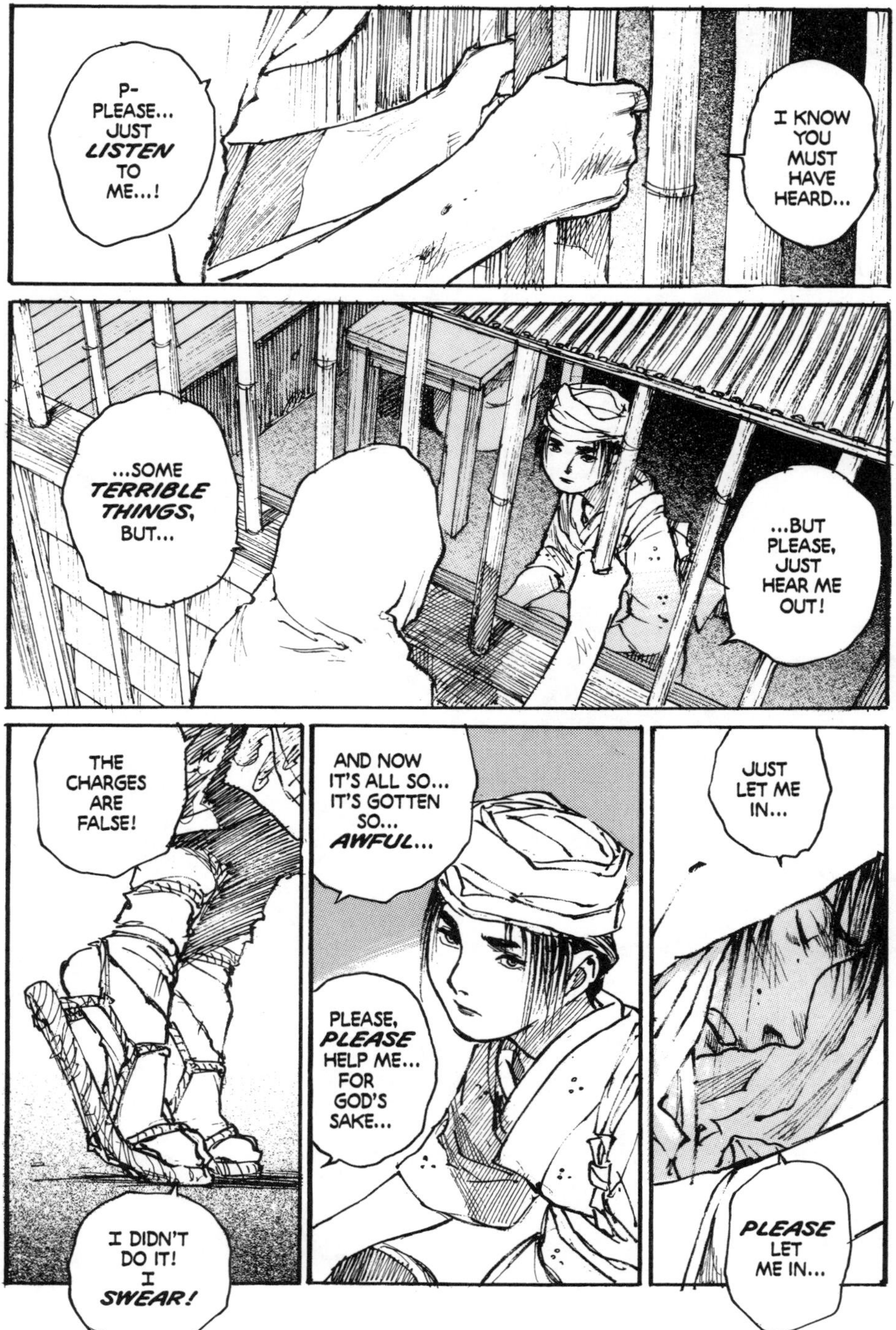
P-PLEASE... JUST *LISTEN* TO ME...!
I KNOW YOU MUST HAVE HEARD...
...SOME *TERRIBLE THINGS*, BUT...
...BUT PLEASE, JUST HEAR ME OUT!
THE CHARGES ARE FALSE!
I DIDN'T DO IT! I *SWEAR!*
AND NOW IT'S ALL SO... IT'S GOTTEN SO... *AWFUL*...
PLEASE, *PLEASE* HELP ME... FOR GOD'S SAKE...
JUST LET ME IN...
*PLEASE* LET ME IN...

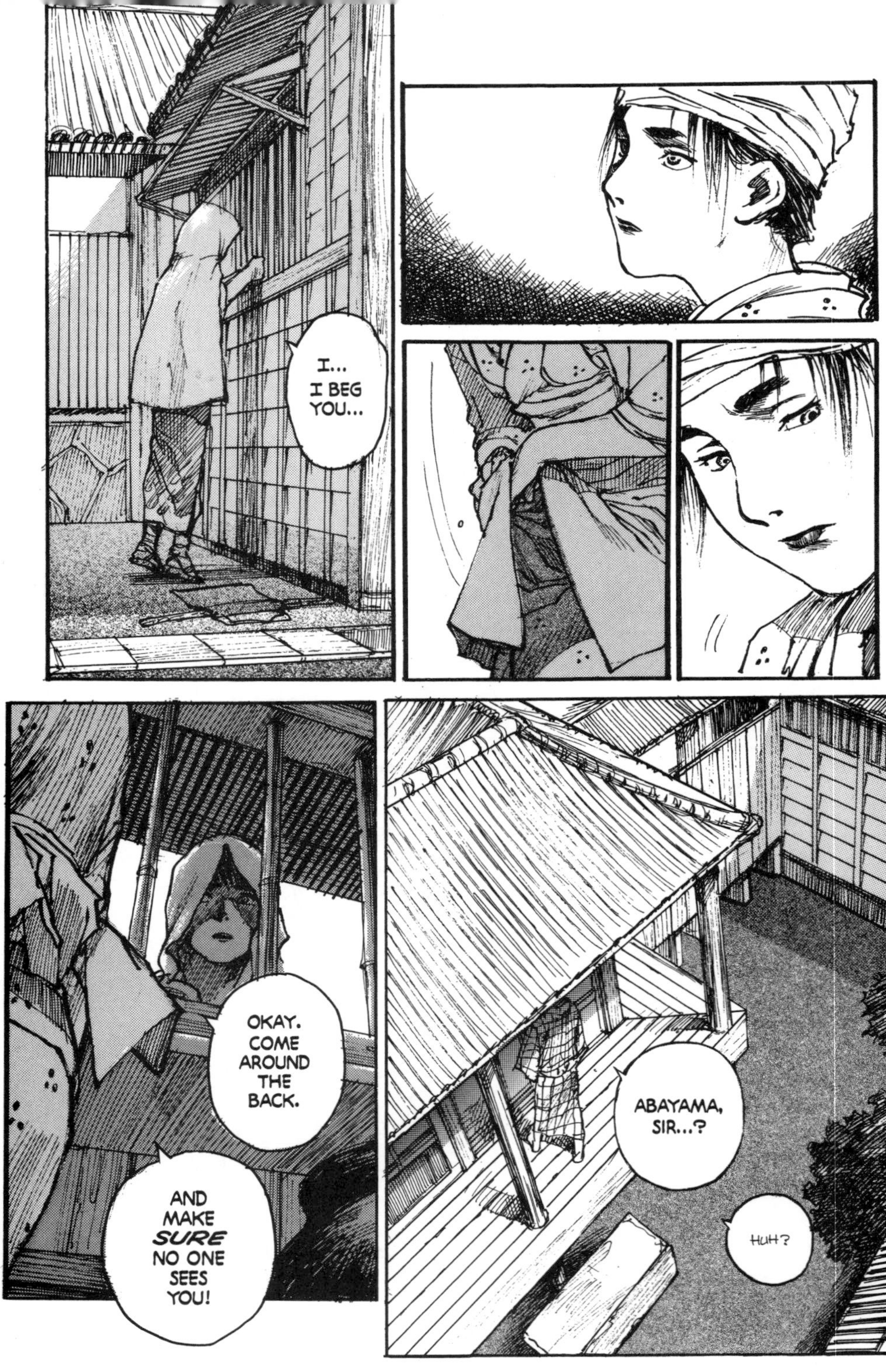

I... I BEG YOU...
OKAY. COME AROUND THE BACK.
AND MAKE *SURE* NO ONE SEES YOU!
ABAYAMA, SIR...?
HUH?

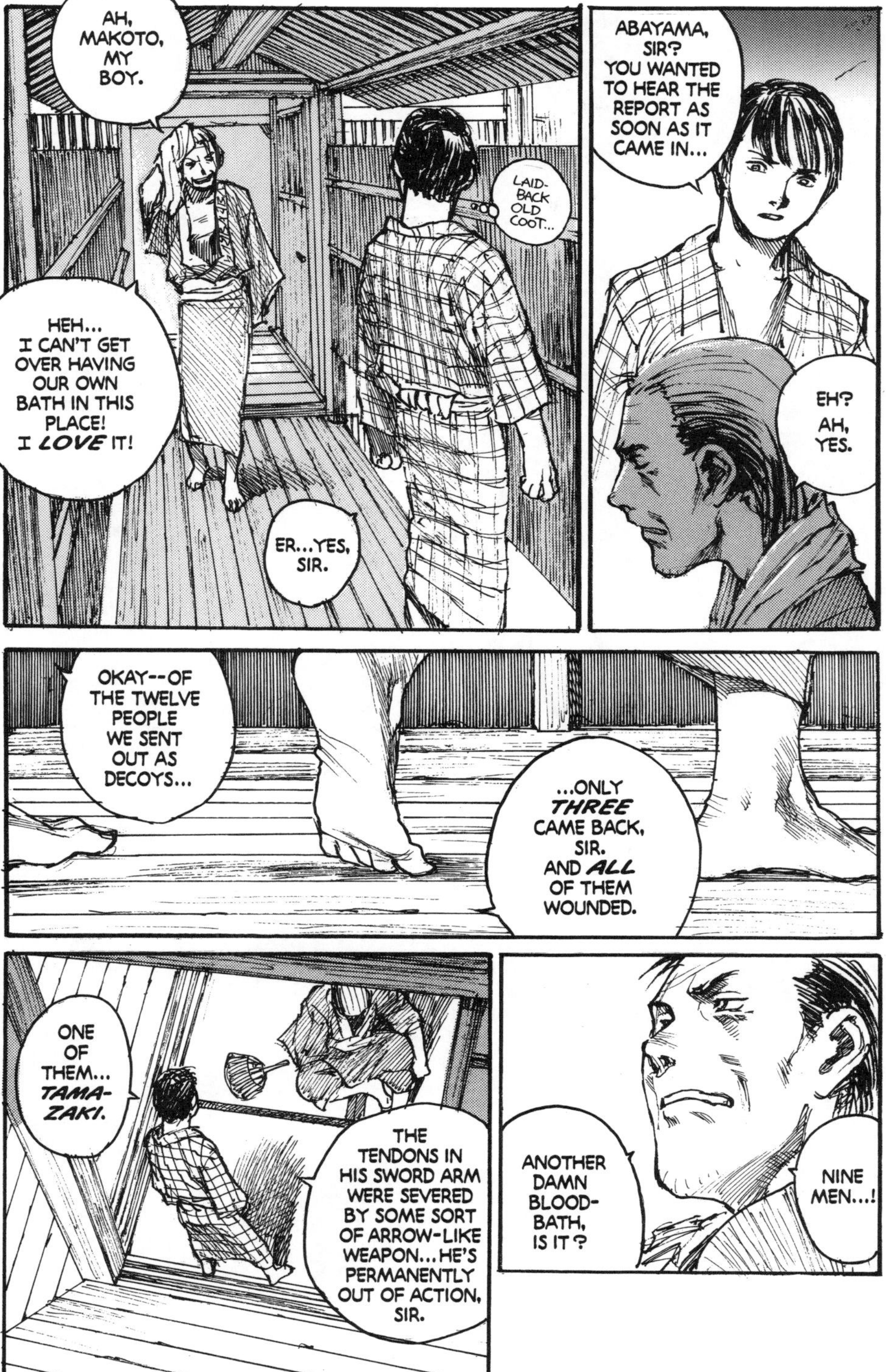
AH, MAKOTO, MY BOY.
LAID-BACK OLD COOT...
HEH... I CAN'T GET OVER HAVING OUR OWN BATH IN THIS PLACE! I *LOVE* IT!
ER...YES, SIR.
ABAYAMA, SIR? YOU WANTED TO HEAR THE REPORT AS SOON AS IT CAME IN...
EH? AH, YES.
OKAY--OF THE TWELVE PEOPLE WE SENT OUT AS DECOYS...
...ONLY *THREE* CAME BACK, SIR. AND *ALL* OF THEM WOUNDED.
ONE OF THEM... *TAMAZAKI.*
THE TENDONS IN HIS SWORD ARM WERE SEVERED BY SOME SORT OF ARROW-LIKE WEAPON... HE'S PERMANENTLY OUT OF ACTION, SIR.
ANOTHER DAMN BLOOD-BATH, IS IT?
NINE MEN...!

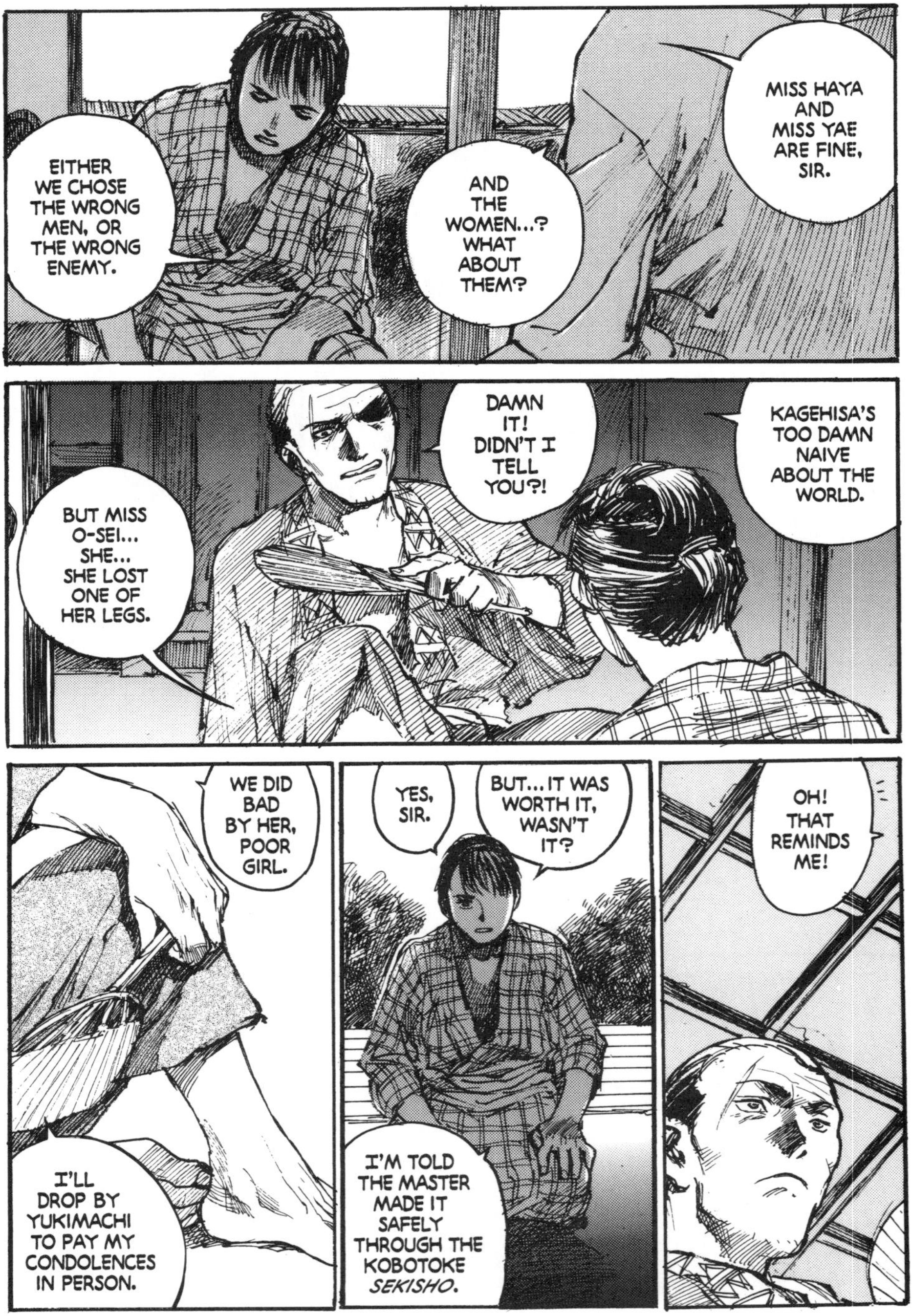
EITHER WE CHOSE THE WRONG MEN, OR THE WRONG ENEMY.
AND THE WOMEN...? WHAT ABOUT THEM?
MISS HAYA AND MISS YAE ARE FINE, SIR.
BUT MISS O-SEI... SHE... SHE LOST ONE OF HER LEGS.
DAMN IT! DIDN'T I TELL YOU?!
KAGEHISA'S TOO DAMN NAIVE ABOUT THE WORLD.
WE DID BAD BY HER, POOR GIRL.
I'LL DROP BY YUKIMACHI TO PAY MY CONDOLENCES IN PERSON.
YES, SIR.
BUT... IT WAS WORTH IT, WASN'T IT?
I'M TOLD THE MASTER MADE IT SAFELY THROUGH THE KOBOTOKE *SEKISHO*.
OH! THAT REMINDS ME!

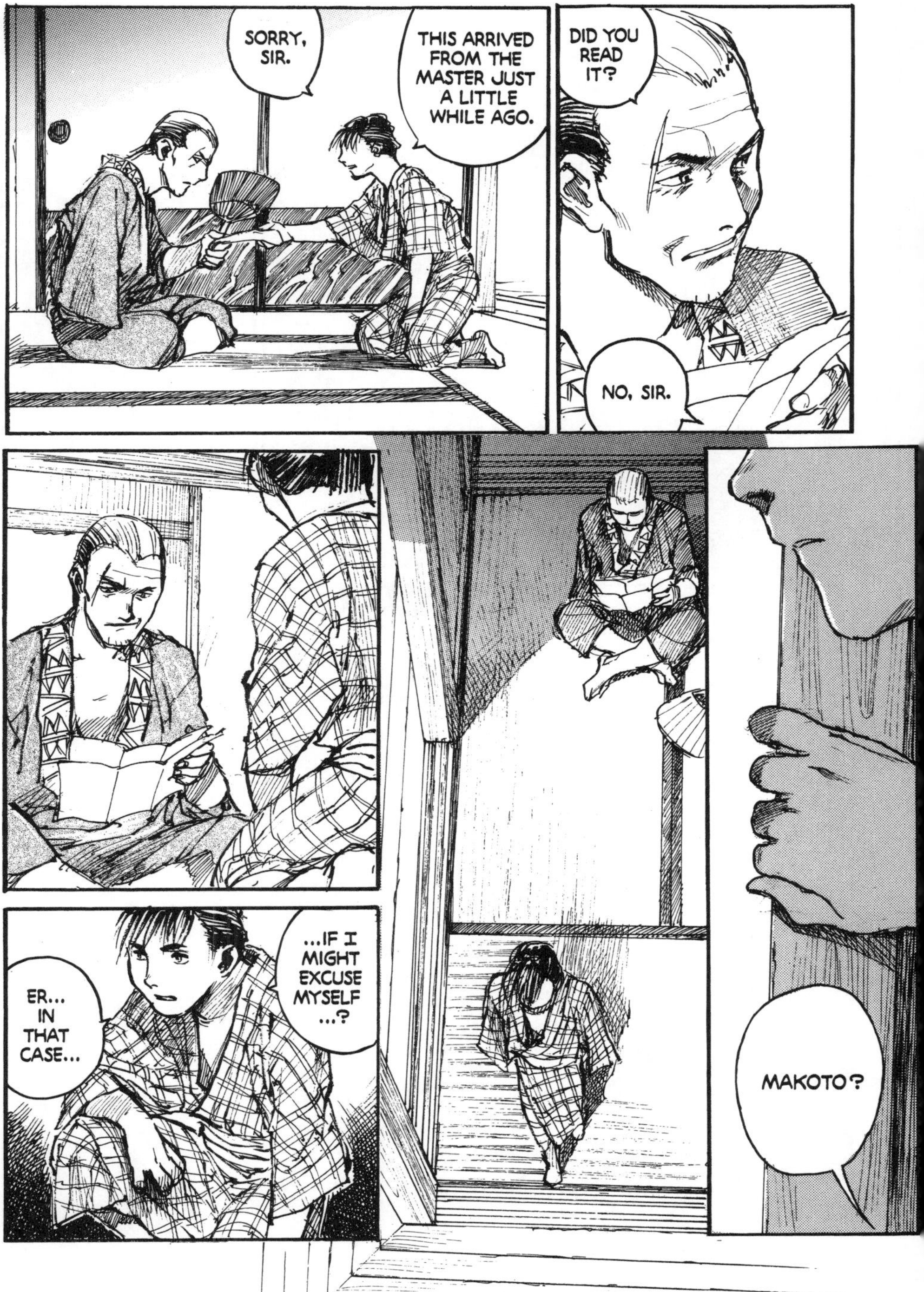
SORRY, SIR.
THIS ARRIVED FROM THE MASTER JUST A LITTLE WHILE AGO.
DID YOU READ IT?
NO, SIR.
ER... IN THAT CASE...
...IF I MIGHT EXCUSE MYSELF ...?
MAKOTO?

NOT TELLING YOU ABOUT THE DECOYS...

I DIDN'T PLAY STRAIGHT WITH YOU, EITHER.

YES...?

Uh...

THAT'S OKAY, SIR.

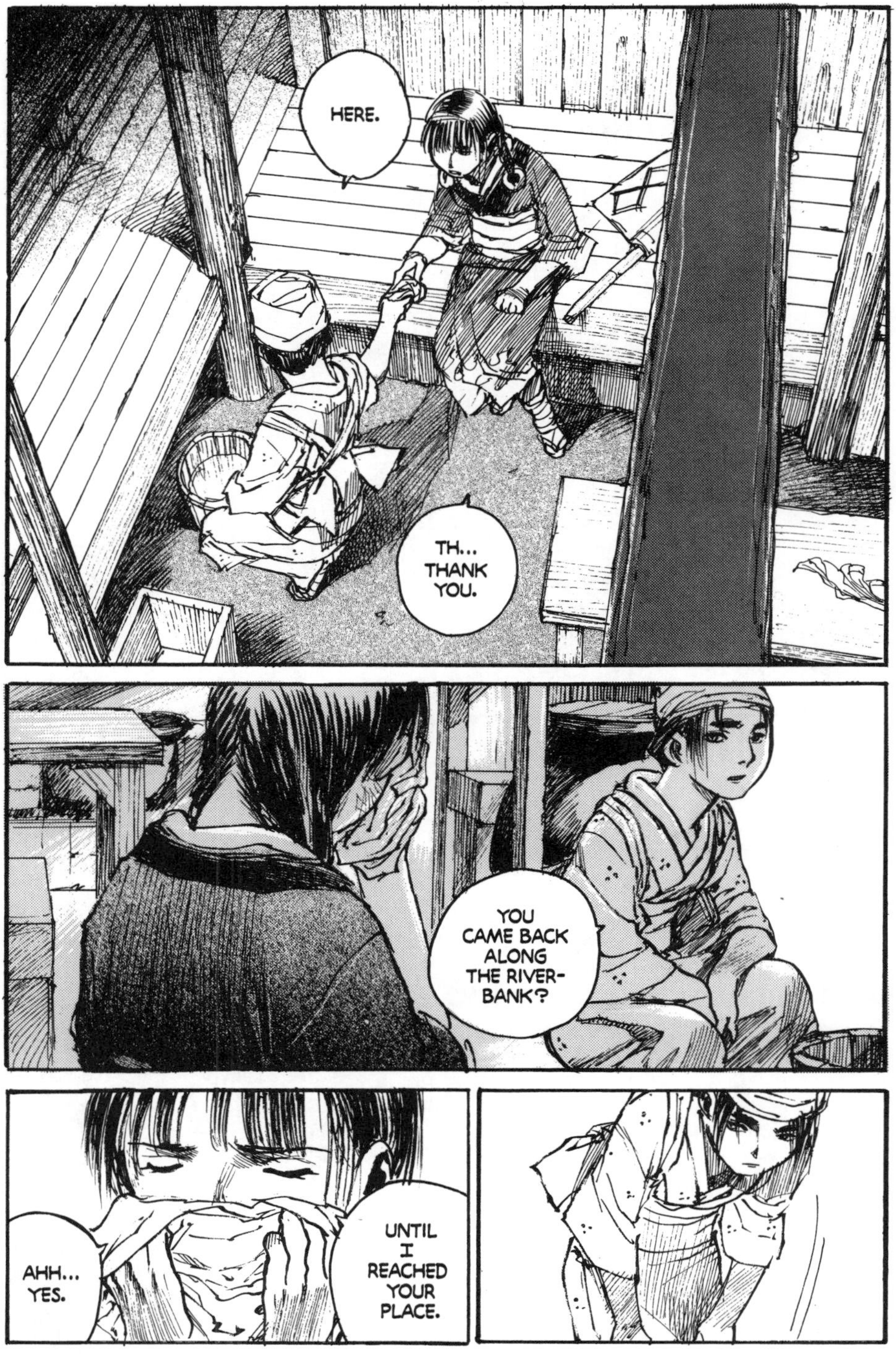
HERE.
TH... THANK YOU.
YOU CAME BACK ALONG THE RIVER-BANK?
AHH... YES.
UNTIL I REACHED YOUR PLACE.

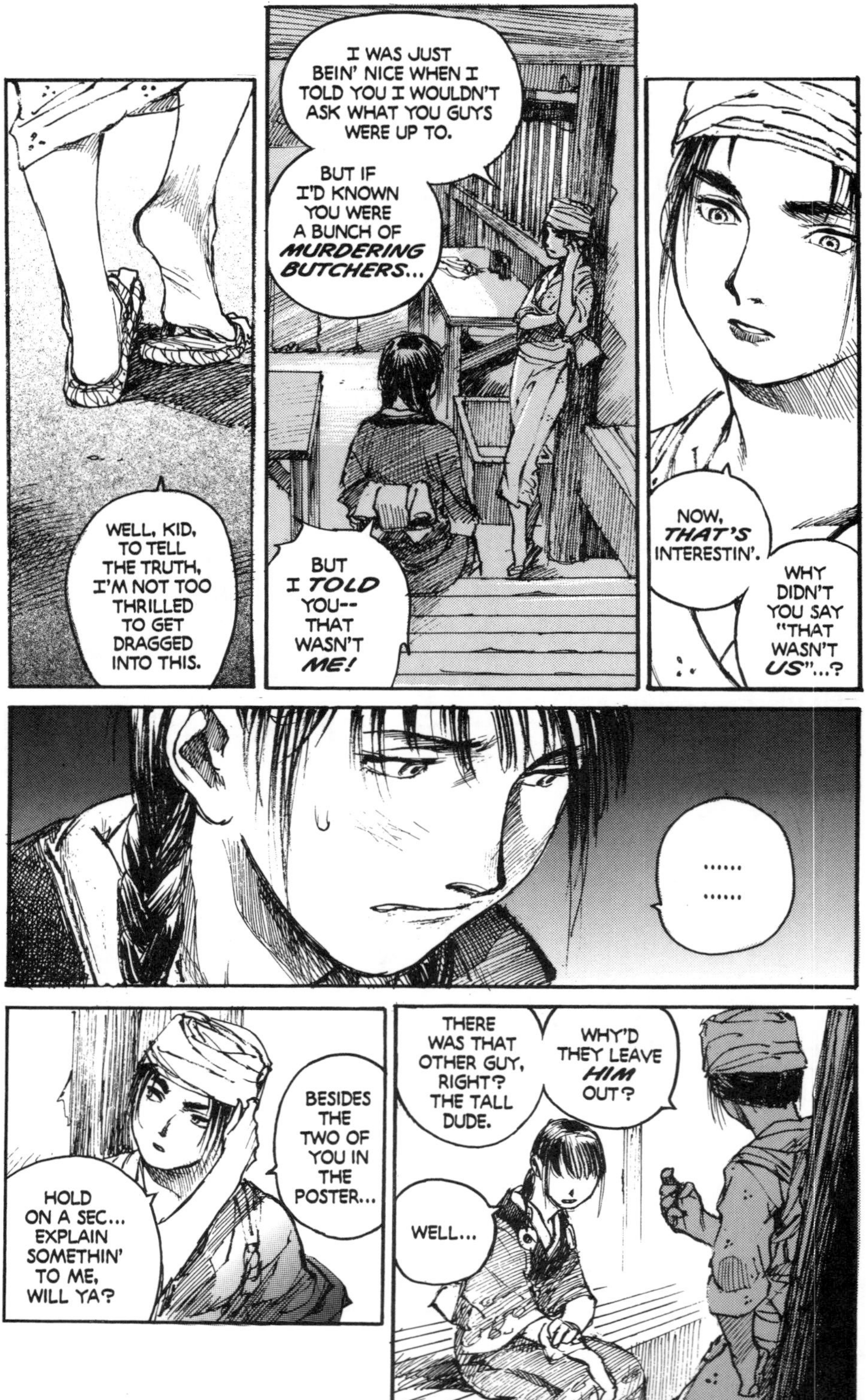
WELL, KID, TO TELL THE TRUTH, I'M NOT TOO THRILLED TO GET DRAGGED INTO THIS.
I WAS JUST BEIN' NICE WHEN I TOLD YOU I WOULDN'T ASK WHAT YOU GUYS WERE UP TO.
BUT IF I'D KNOWN YOU WERE A BUNCH OF *MURDERING BUTCHERS*...
BUT I *TOLD* YOU-- THAT WASN'T *ME!*
NOW, *THAT'S* INTERESTIN'.
WHY DIDN'T YOU SAY "THAT WASN'T *US*"...?
...... ......
HOLD ON A SEC... EXPLAIN SOMETHIN' TO ME, WILL YA?
BESIDES THE TWO OF YOU IN THE POSTER...
THERE WAS THAT OTHER GUY, RIGHT? THE TALL DUDE.
WHY'D THEY LEAVE *HIM* OUT?
WELL...

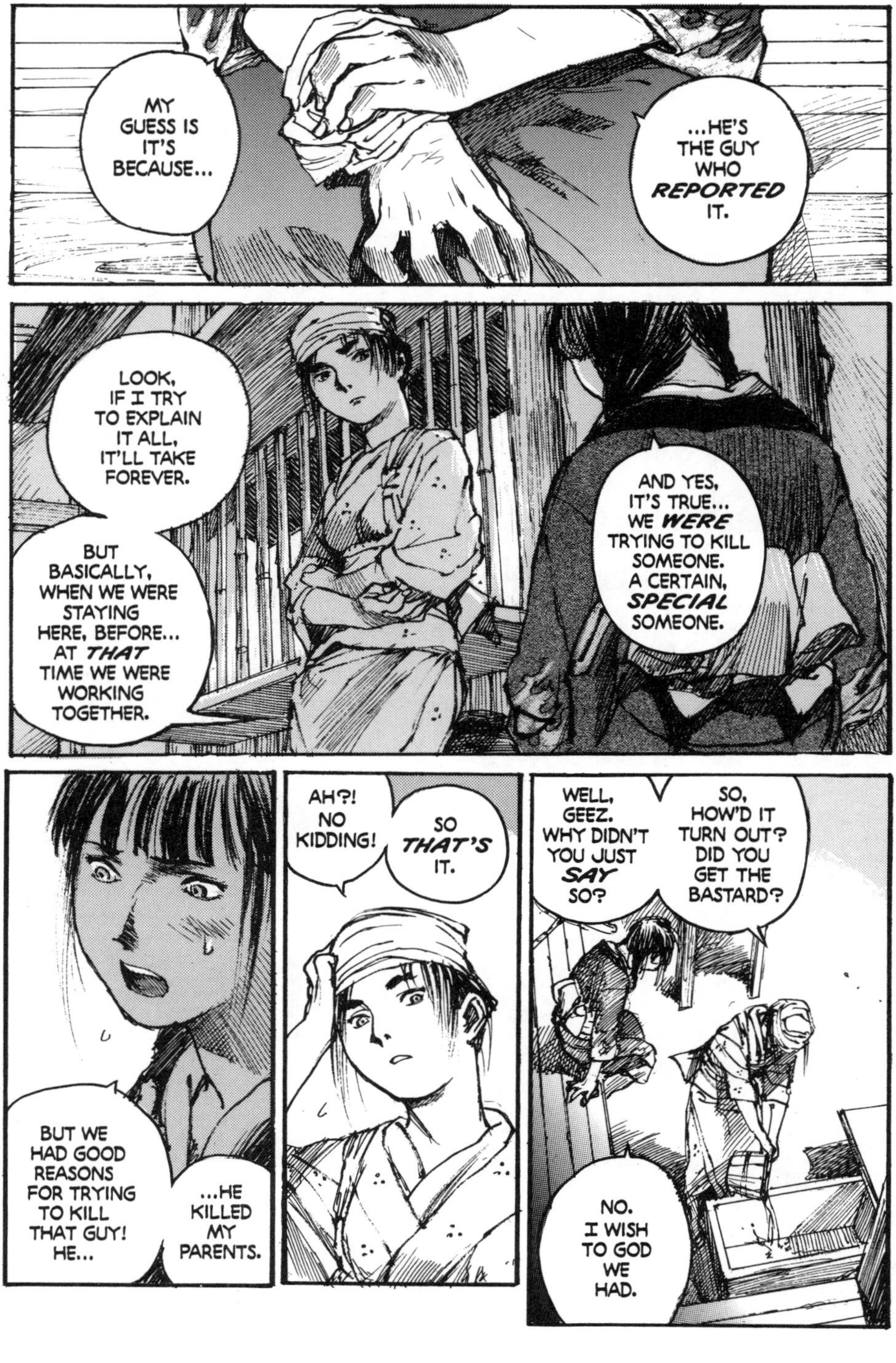
MY GUESS IS IT'S BECAUSE...
...HE'S THE GUY WHO *REPORTED* IT.
LOOK, IF I TRY TO EXPLAIN IT ALL, IT'LL TAKE FOREVER.
BUT BASICALLY, WHEN WE WERE STAYING HERE, BEFORE... AT *THAT* TIME WE WERE WORKING TOGETHER.
AND YES, IT'S TRUE... WE *WERE* TRYING TO KILL SOMEONE. A CERTAIN, *SPECIAL* SOMEONE.
BUT WE HAD GOOD REASONS FOR TRYING TO KILL THAT GUY! HE...
...HE KILLED MY PARENTS.
AH?! NO KIDDING!
SO *THAT'S* IT.
WELL, GEEZ. WHY DIDN'T YOU JUST *SAY* SO?
SO, HOW'D IT TURN OUT? DID YOU GET THE BASTARD?
NO. I WISH TO GOD WE HAD.

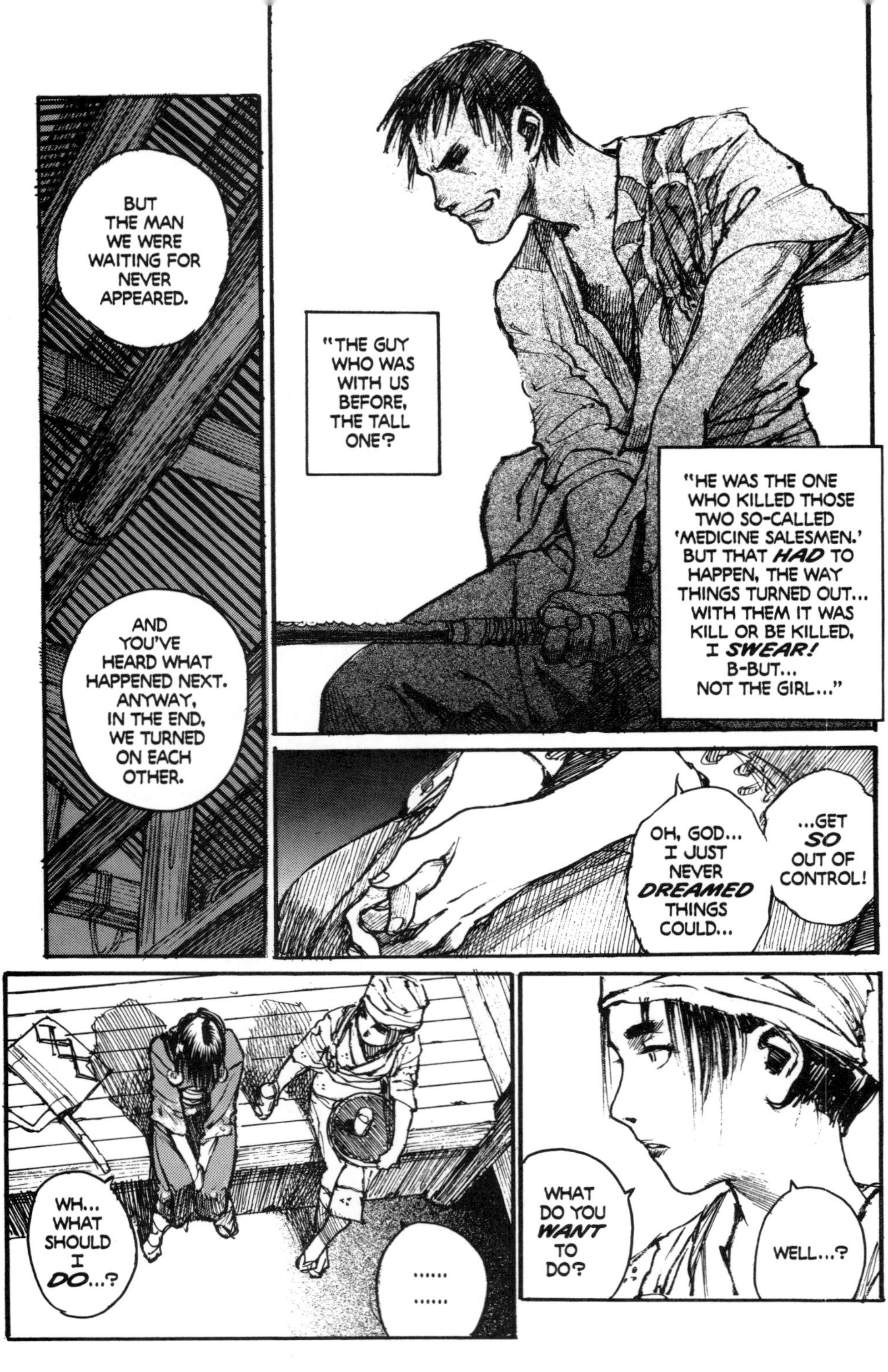
BUT THE MAN WE WERE WAITING FOR NEVER APPEARED.
AND YOU'VE HEARD WHAT HAPPENED NEXT. ANYWAY, IN THE END, WE TURNED ON EACH OTHER.
"THE GUY WHO WAS WITH US BEFORE, THE TALL ONE?
"HE WAS THE ONE WHO KILLED THOSE TWO SO-CALLED 'MEDICINE SALESMEN.' BUT THAT HAD TO HAPPEN, THE WAY THINGS TURNED OUT... WITH THEM IT WAS KILL OR BE KILLED, I SWEAR! B-BUT... NOT THE GIRL..."
OH, GOD... I JUST NEVER DREAMED THINGS COULD...
...GET SO OUT OF CONTROL!
WH... WHAT SHOULD I DO...?
...... ......
WHAT DO YOU WANT TO DO?
WELL...?

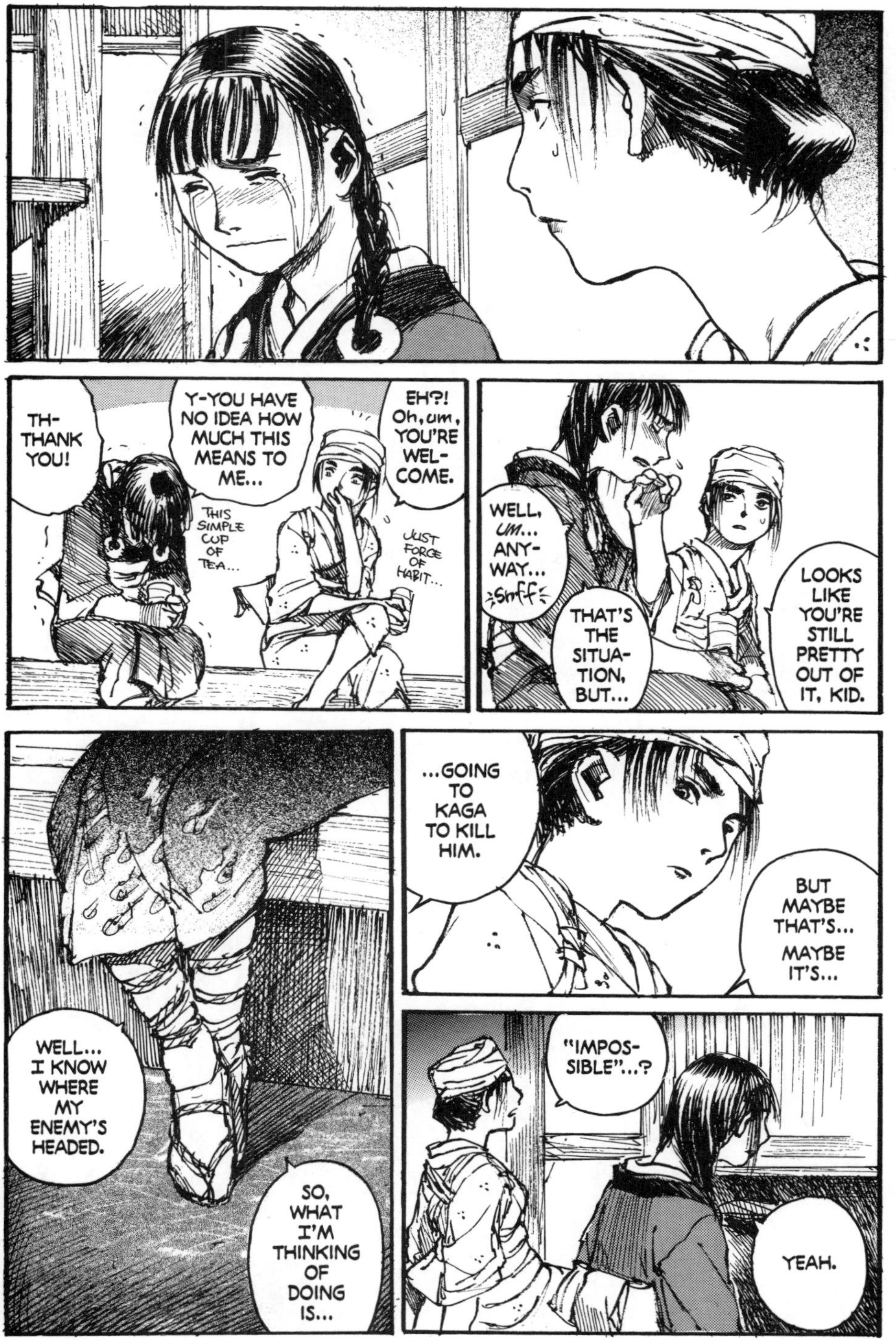
TH-THANK YOU!
Y-YOU HAVE NO IDEA HOW MUCH THIS MEANS TO ME...
THIS SIMPLE CUP OF TEA...
EH?! Oh, um, YOU'RE WELCOME.
JUST FORCE OF HABIT...
WELL, um... ANYWAY...
Sniff
THAT'S THE SITUATION, BUT...
LOOKS LIKE YOU'RE STILL PRETTY OUT OF IT, KID.
WELL... I KNOW WHERE MY ENEMY'S HEADED.
SO, WHAT I'M THINKING OF DOING IS...
...GOING TO KAGA TO KILL HIM.
BUT MAYBE THAT'S... MAYBE IT'S...
"IMPOSSIBLE"...?
YEAH.

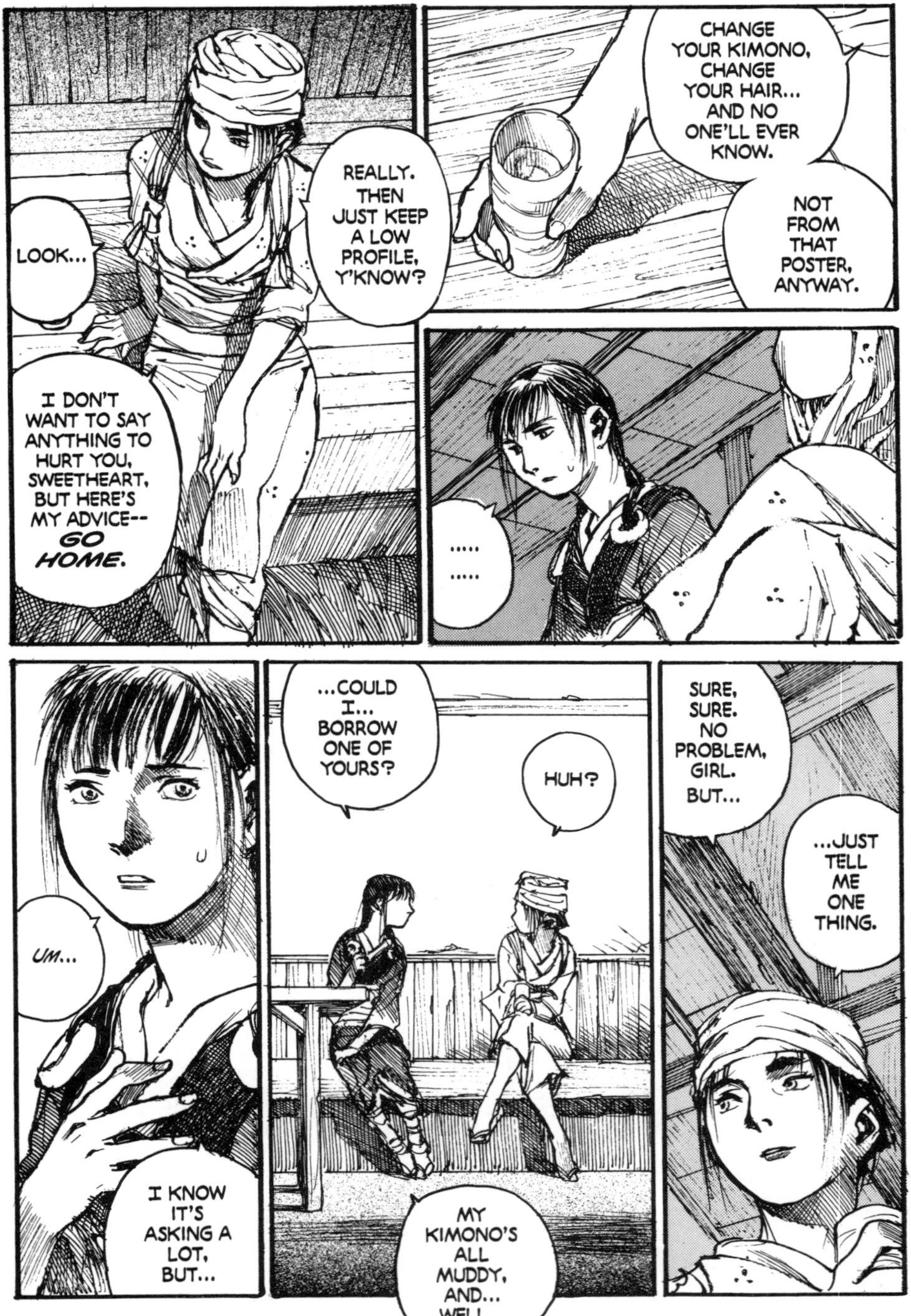
LOOK...
REALLY. THEN JUST KEEP A LOW PROFILE, Y'KNOW?
I DON'T WANT TO SAY ANYTHING TO HURT YOU, SWEETHEART, BUT HERE'S MY ADVICE-- GO HOME.
CHANGE YOUR KIMONO, CHANGE YOUR HAIR... AND NO ONE'LL EVER KNOW.
NOT FROM THAT POSTER, ANYWAY.
..... .....
UM...
I KNOW IT'S ASKING A LOT, BUT...
...COULD I... BORROW ONE OF YOURS?
HUH?
MY KIMONO'S ALL MUDDY, AND... WELL...
SURE, SURE. NO PROBLEM, GIRL. BUT...
...JUST TELL ME ONE THING.

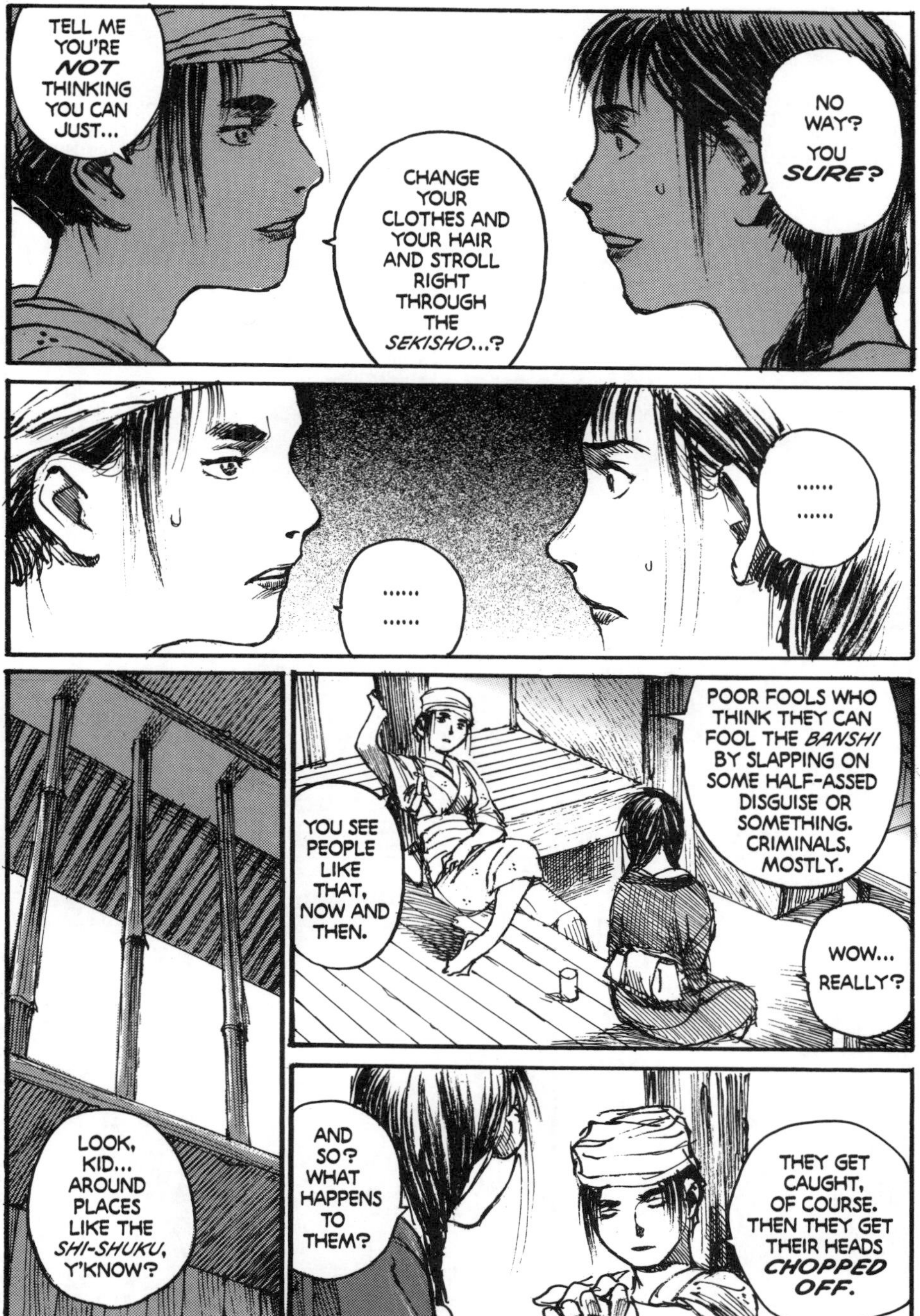
TELL ME YOU'RE *NOT* THINKING YOU CAN JUST...
CHANGE YOUR CLOTHES AND YOUR HAIR AND STROLL RIGHT THROUGH THE *SEKISHO*...?
NO WAY? YOU *SURE?*
...... ......
...... ......
LOOK, KID... AROUND PLACES LIKE THE *SHI-SHUKU*, Y'KNOW?
YOU SEE PEOPLE LIKE THAT, NOW AND THEN.
POOR FOOLS WHO THINK THEY CAN FOOL THE *BANSHI* BY SLAPPING ON SOME HALF-ASSED DISGUISE OR SOMETHING. CRIMINALS, MOSTLY.
WOW... REALLY?
AND SO? WHAT HAPPENS TO THEM?
THEY GET CAUGHT, OF COURSE. THEN THEY GET THEIR HEADS *CHOPPED OFF.*

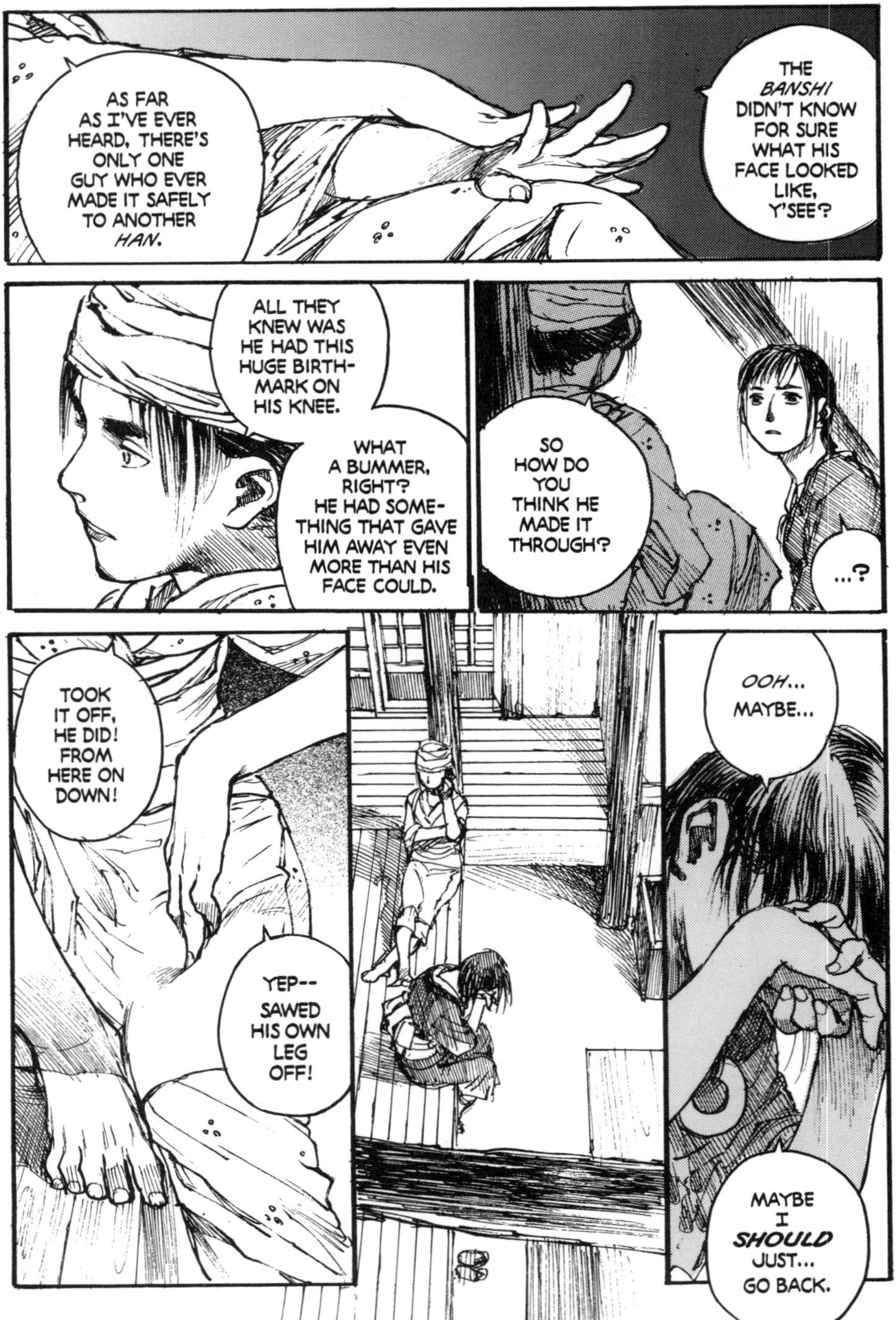
AS FAR AS I'VE EVER HEARD, THERE'S ONLY ONE GUY WHO EVER MADE IT SAFELY TO ANOTHER *HAN*.
THE *BANSHI* DIDN'T KNOW FOR SURE WHAT HIS FACE LOOKED LIKE, Y'SEE?
ALL THEY KNEW WAS HE HAD THIS HUGE BIRTH-MARK ON HIS KNEE.
WHAT A BUMMER, RIGHT? HE HAD SOME-THING THAT GAVE HIM AWAY EVEN MORE THAN HIS FACE COULD.
SO HOW DO YOU THINK HE MADE IT THROUGH?
...?
TOOK IT OFF, HE DID! FROM HERE ON DOWN!
YEP-- SAWED HIS OWN LEG OFF!
*OOH*... MAYBE...
MAYBE I ***SHOULD*** JUST... GO BACK.

D-DAMN IT!
THIS TIME...
*THIS* TIME I
THOUGHT
I HAD HIM
TRAPPED.

*YOU'RE*
THE ONE
WHO'S
TRAPPED,
HON.

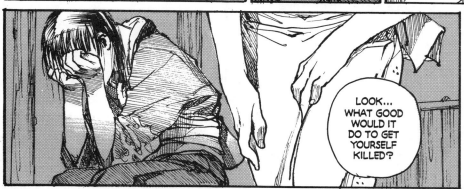

LOOK...
WHAT GOOD
WOULD IT
DO TO GET
YOURSELF
KILLED?

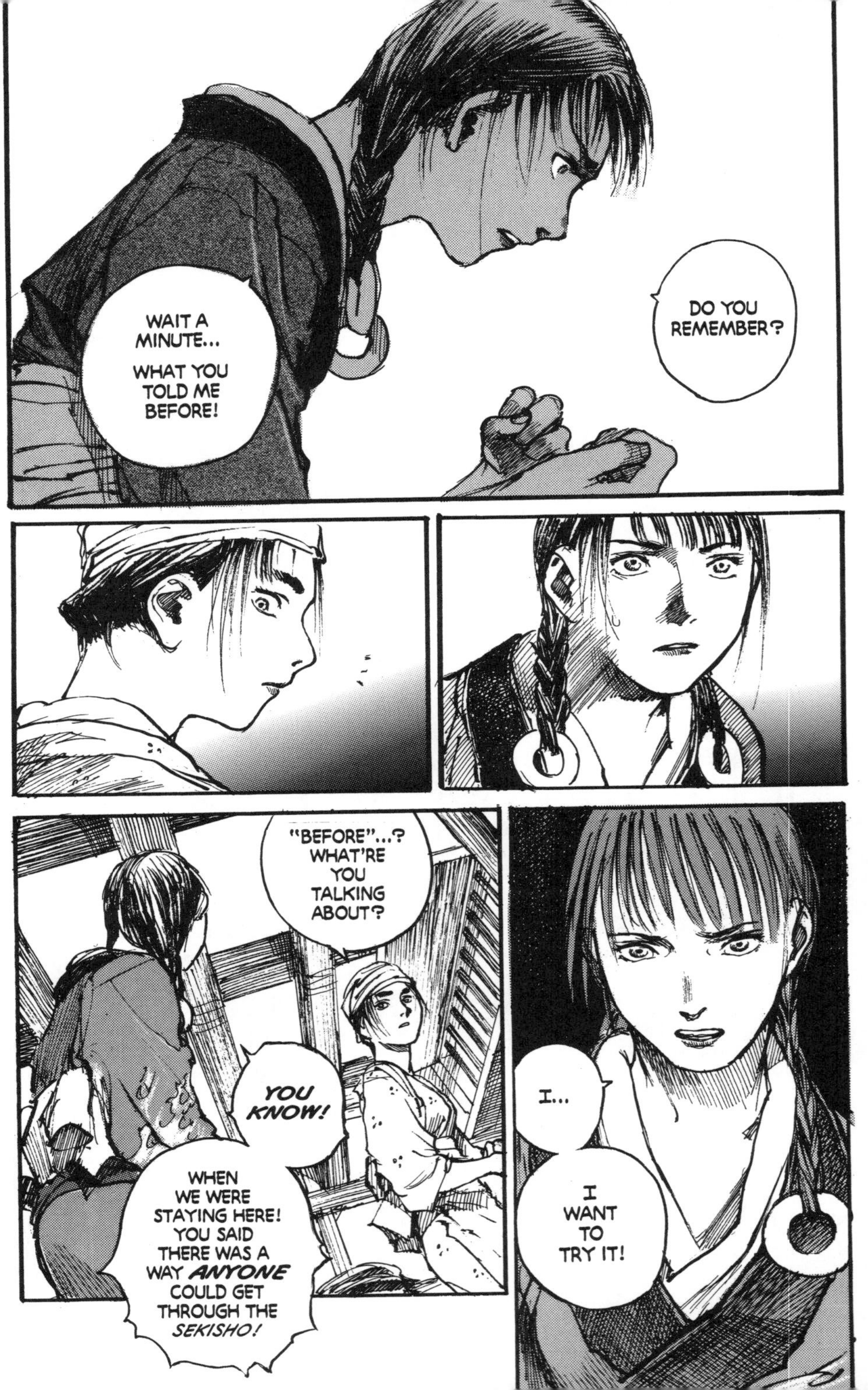
WAIT A MINUTE...
WHAT YOU TOLD ME BEFORE!
DO YOU REMEMBER?
"BEFORE"...? WHAT'RE YOU TALKING ABOUT?
*YOU KNOW!*
WHEN WE WERE STAYING HERE! YOU SAID THERE WAS A WAY *ANYONE* COULD GET THROUGH THE *SEKISHO!*
I...
I WANT TO TRY IT!

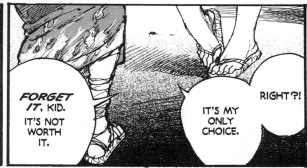

*FORGET IT*, KID. IT'S NOT WORTH IT.

IT'S MY ONLY CHOICE.

RIGHT?!

IN THE EYES OF THE WORLD, I'M A *CRIMINAL*, WANTED DEAD OR ALIVE!

I DON'T KNOW IF I CAN EVEN GET BACK TO EDO IN ONE PIECE!

BUT...

...IF I CAN MAKE IT TO ANOTHER *HAN*, I'M *FREE!* THEN *EVERYTHING* WORKS!

THERE'S NOWHERE LEFT EXCEPT STRAIGHT AHEAD, TO FIND THE MAN WHO MURDERED MY PARENTS!

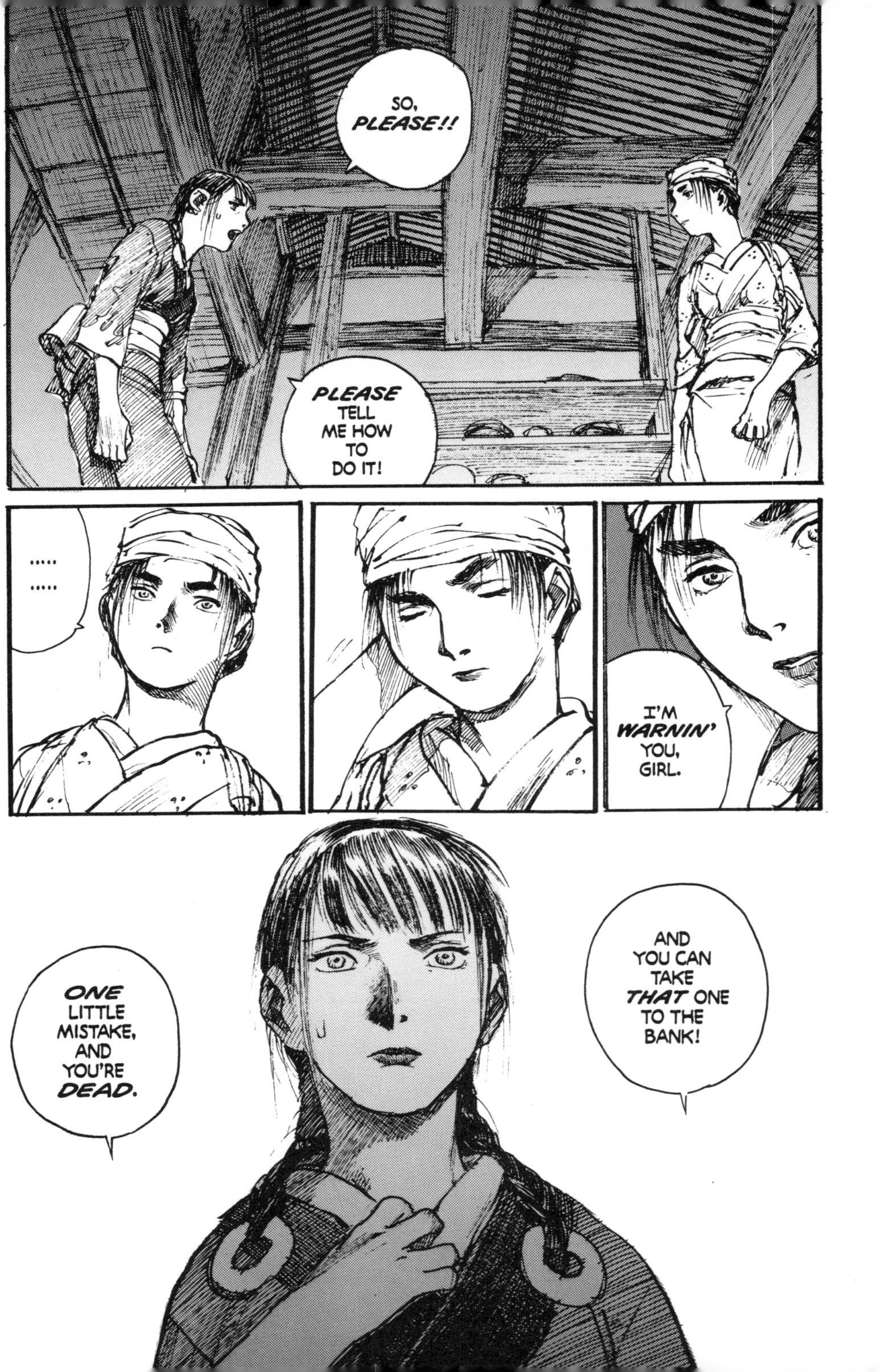

SO, *PLEASE!!*
*PLEASE* TELL ME HOW TO DO IT!
…… ……
I'M *WARNIN'* YOU, GIRL.
*ONE* LITTLE MISTAKE, AND YOU'RE *DEAD*.
AND YOU CAN TAKE *THAT* ONE TO THE BANK!

# STIGMA
## Part 1

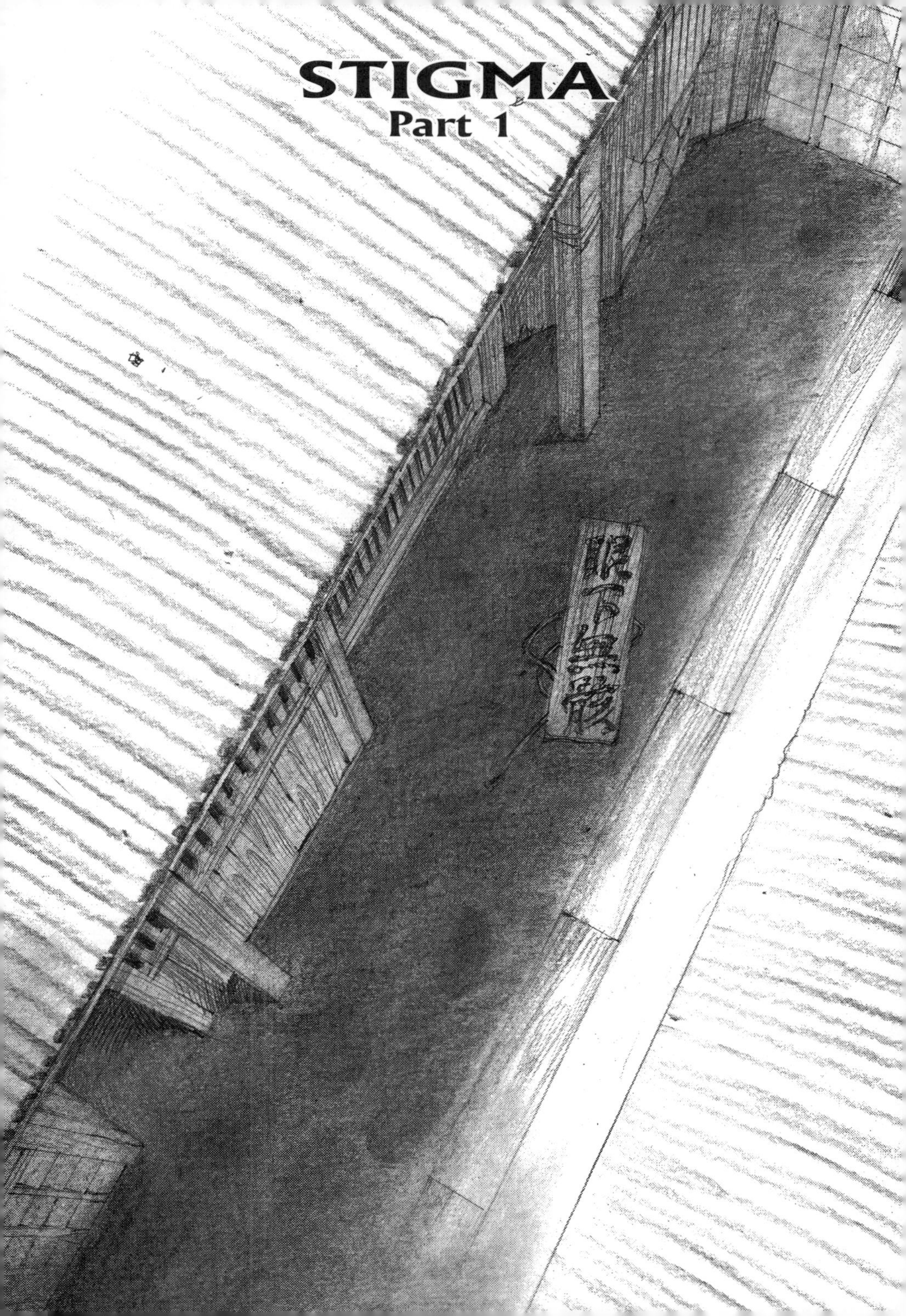

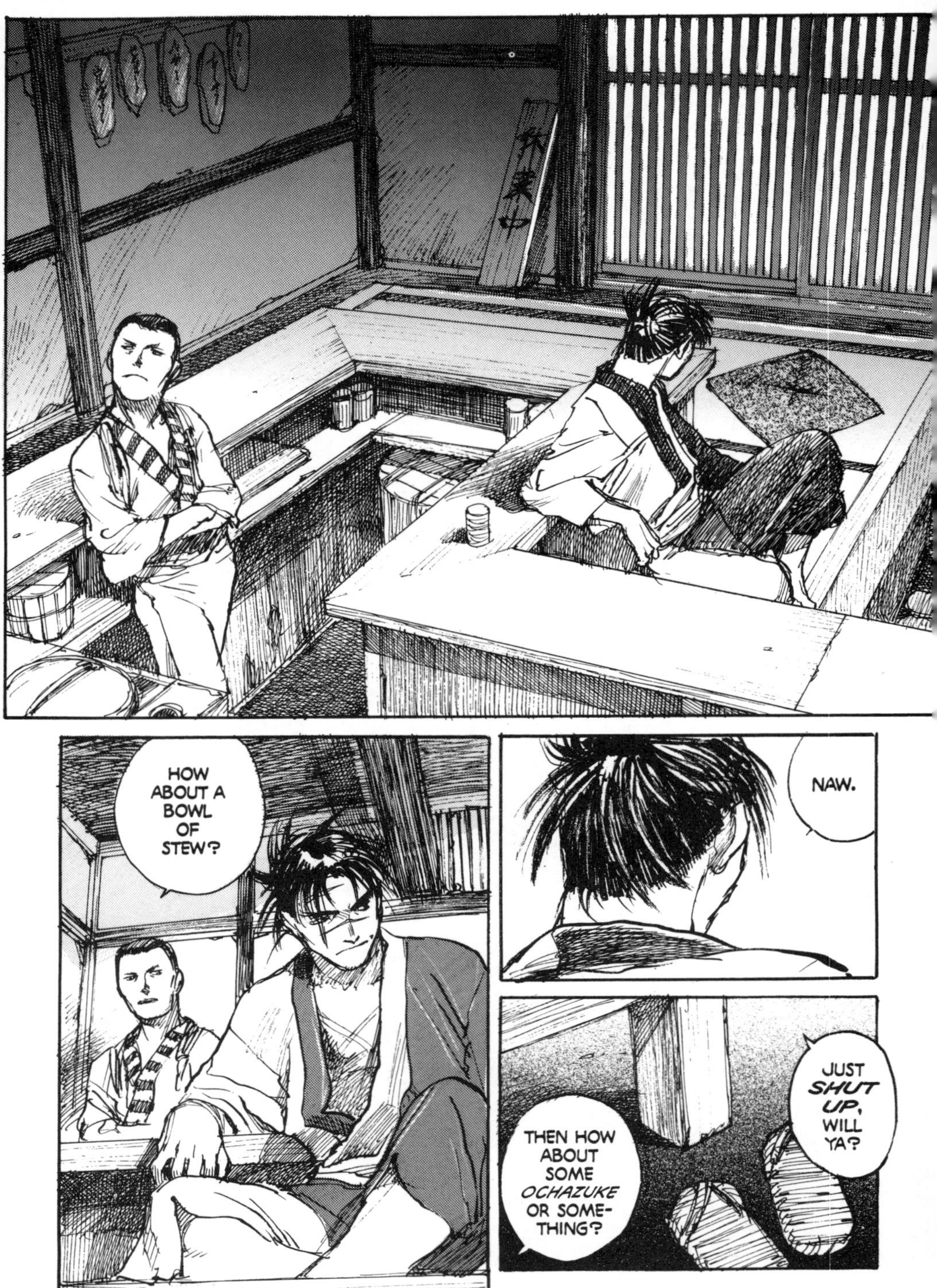
HOW ABOUT A BOWL OF STEW?
NAW.
THEN HOW ABOUT SOME *OCHAZUKE* OR SOME-THING?
JUST ***SHUT UP***, WILL YA?

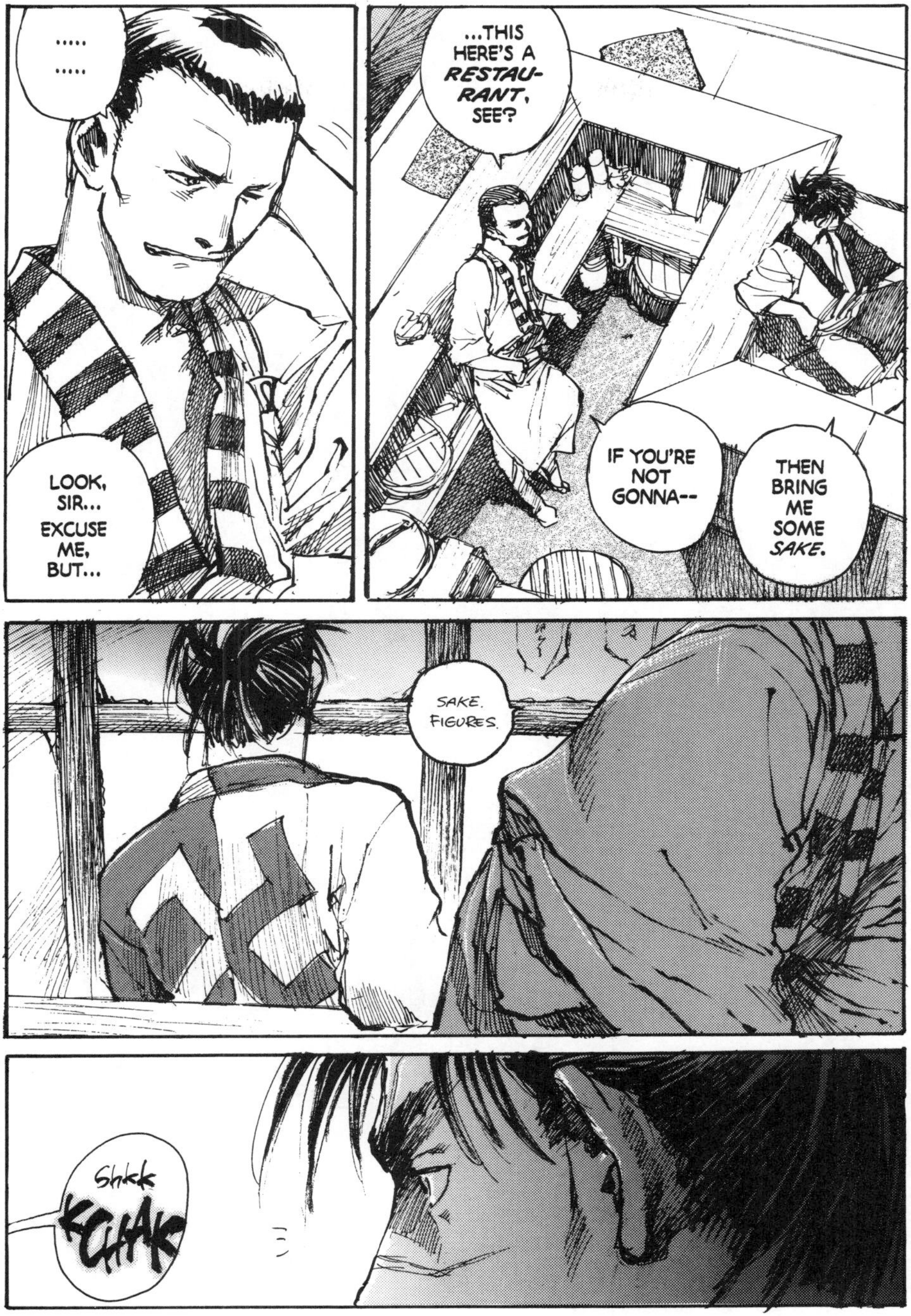
.....
.....
LOOK, SIR... EXCUSE ME, BUT...
...THIS HERE'S A *RESTAURANT*, SEE?
IF YOU'RE NOT GONNA--
THEN BRING ME SOME *SAKE*.
SAKE. FIGURES.
Shkk
KCHAK

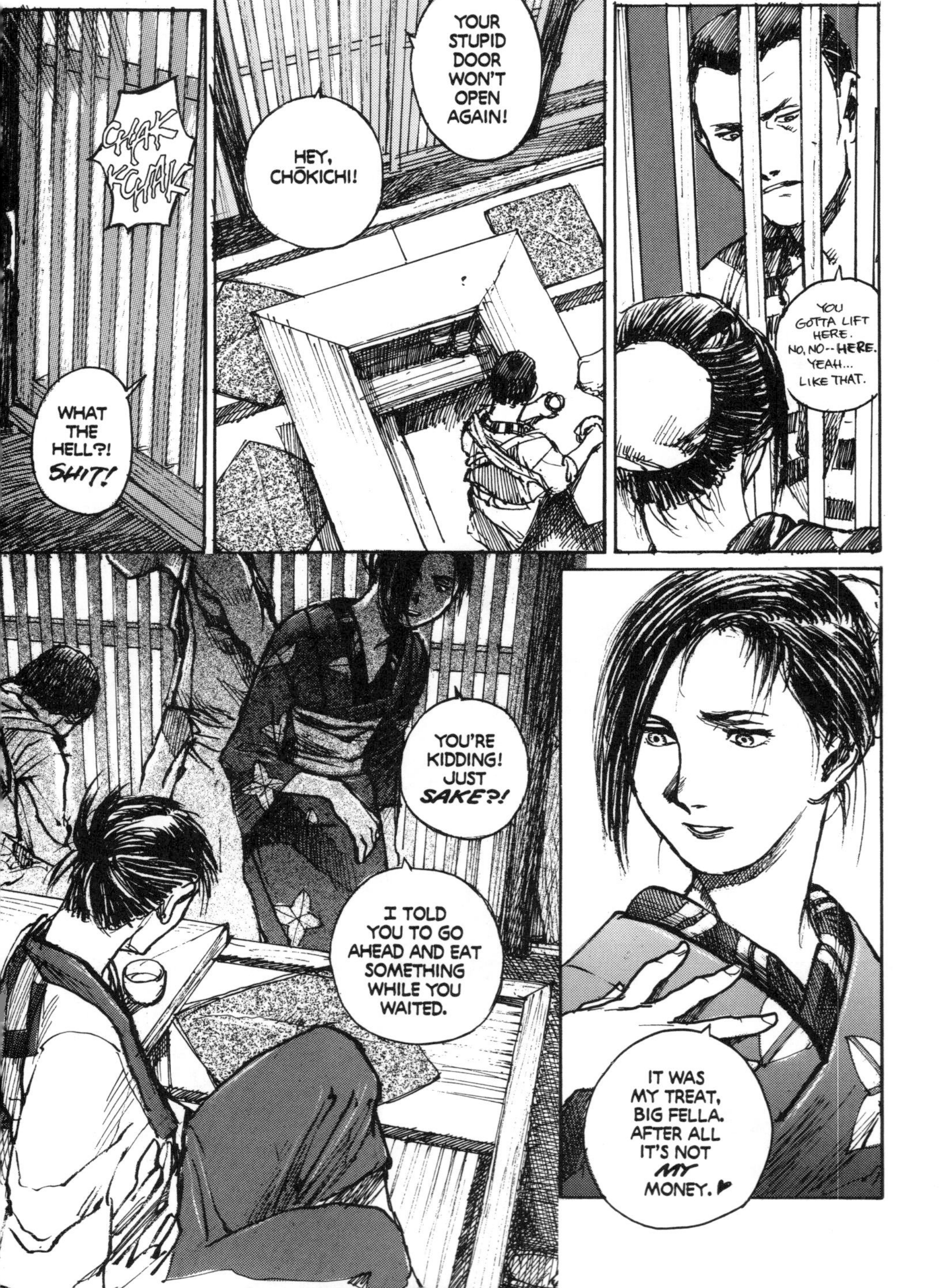
CHAK KCHAK
WHAT THE HELL?! SHIT!
HEY, CHŌKICHI!
YOUR STUPID DOOR WON'T OPEN AGAIN!
YOU GOTTA LIFT HERE. NO, NO--HERE. YEAH... LIKE THAT.
YOU'RE KIDDING! JUST SAKE?!
I TOLD YOU TO GO AHEAD AND EAT SOMETHING WHILE YOU WAITED.
IT WAS MY TREAT, BIG FELLA. AFTER ALL IT'S NOT MY MONEY. ♥

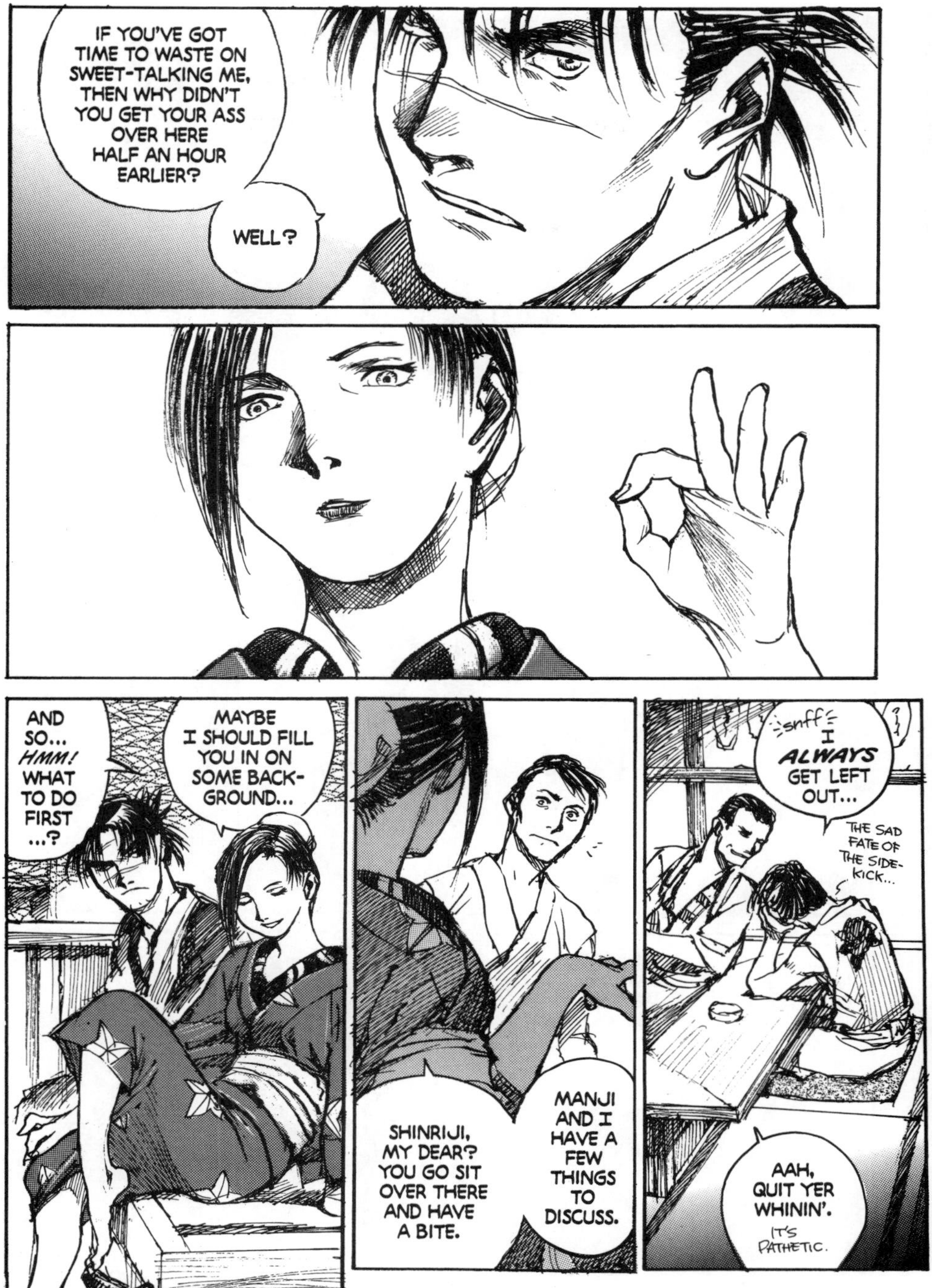
IF YOU'VE GOT TIME TO WASTE ON SWEET-TALKING ME, THEN WHY DIDN'T YOU GET YOUR ASS OVER HERE HALF AN HOUR EARLIER?
WELL?
AND SO... *HMM!* WHAT TO DO FIRST ...?
MAYBE I SHOULD FILL YOU IN ON SOME BACK-GROUND...
SHINRIJI, MY DEAR? YOU GO SIT OVER THERE AND HAVE A BITE.
MANJI AND I HAVE A FEW THINGS TO DISCUSS.
snff
I **ALWAYS** GET LEFT OUT...
THE SAD FATE OF THE SIDE-KICK...
AAH, QUIT YER WHININ'.
IT'S PATHETIC.

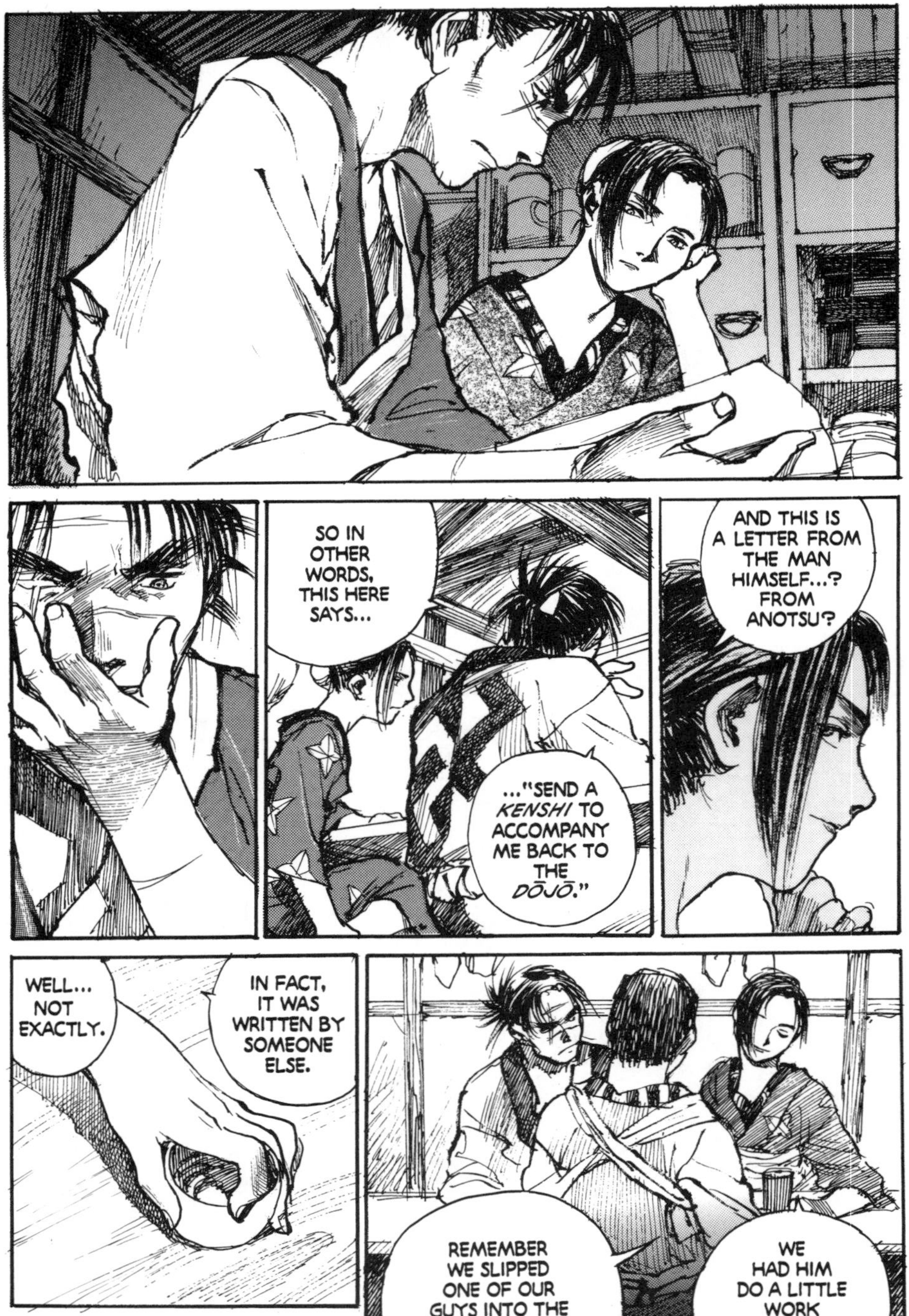
SO IN OTHER WORDS, THIS HERE SAYS...
..."SEND A *KENSHI* TO ACCOMPANY ME BACK TO THE *DŌJŌ*."
AND THIS IS A LETTER FROM THE MAN HIMSELF...? FROM ANOTSU?
WELL... NOT EXACTLY.
IN FACT, IT WAS WRITTEN BY SOMEONE ELSE.
REMEMBER WE SLIPPED ONE OF OUR GUYS INTO THE ITTŌ-RYŪ...?
WE HAD HIM DO A LITTLE WORK FOR US.

THE ITTŌ-RYŪ RUNS THIS *DŌJŌ* OVER IN MUKŌ-JIMA, SEE? THERE'S THIS OLD GEEZER THERE NOW, NAME OF *ABAYAMA*.

HE'S THE ITTŌ-RYŪ'S "ACTING LEADER" WHILE ANOTSU'S GONE.

ANYWAY, ABAYAMA'S GOT THIS KID HE'S USING FOR ALL HIS ERRANDS AND JUNK.

THAT'S OUR "SPECIAL FRIEND."

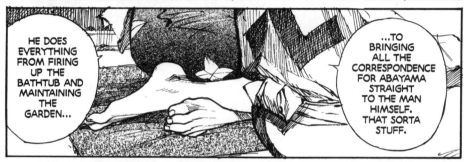

HE DOES EVERYTHING FROM FIRING UP THE BATHTUB AND MAINTAINING THE GARDEN...

...TO BRINGING ALL THE CORRESPONDENCE FOR ABAYAMA STRAIGHT TO THE MAN HIMSELF. THAT SORTA STUFF.

HOLD ON.

DON'T TELL ME THE PERSON WHO WROTE THIS--

IN ANY CASE, *IF* THEY DO WHAT THIS LETTER SAYS...

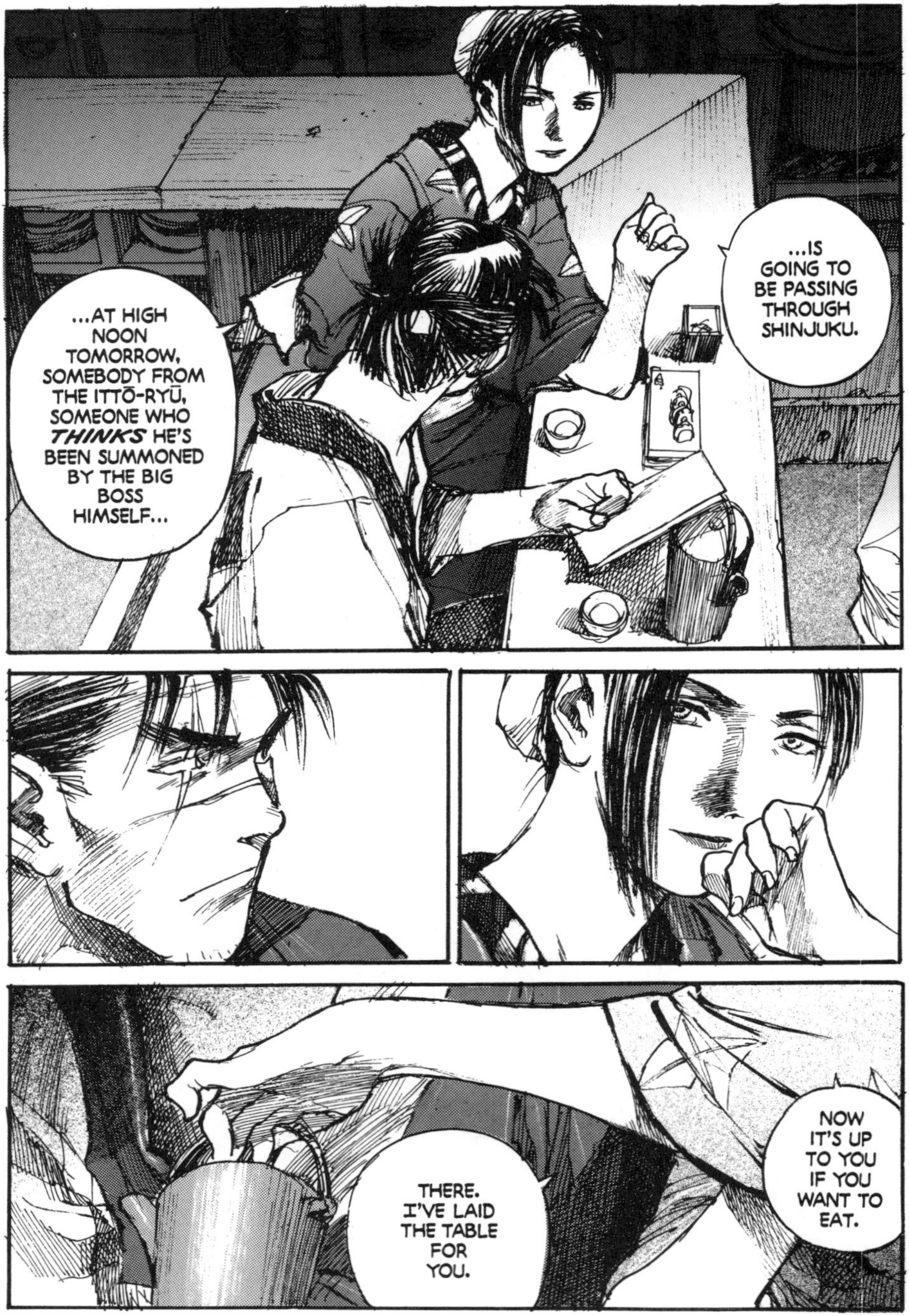
...AT HIGH NOON TOMORROW, SOMEBODY FROM THE ITTŌ-RYŪ, SOMEONE WHO *THINKS* HE'S BEEN SUMMONED BY THE BIG BOSS HIMSELF...
...IS GOING TO BE PASSING THROUGH SHINJUKU.
THERE. I'VE LAID THE TABLE FOR YOU.
NOW IT'S UP TO YOU IF YOU WANT TO EAT.

CHŌ, HON! TWO *OCHAZUKE!*

HEY! LEAVING SO SOON?

I HEARD EVERYTHING I NEED.

AND EVERY MINUTE COUNTS. SO...YEAH.

WAIT A MINUTE, DAMN IT! *LISTEN!* I'M NOT DONE YET, MANJI!

HAVEN'T YOU HEARD?

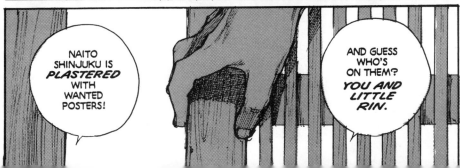

NAITO SHINJUKU IS *PLASTERED* WITH WANTED POSTERS!

AND GUESS WHO'S ON THEM? *YOU AND LITTLE RIN.*

HUH...I CAN SEE *YOU* BEING ON THEM, BUT POOR LITTLE RIN... SO, WHAT DID IT?

THAT BUSINESS THE OTHER DAY?

WHAT THE F--?!

SEE? DIDN'T KNOW THAT, DID YOU?

NOT THAT I KNEW MYSELF UNTIL JUST A WHILE AGO.

*SHIRA...!* THAT PIECE OF *SHIT!*

STOP BY OUR HIDEOUT ON YOUR WAY OUT OF TOWN, 'KAY?

YOU CAN TAKE A *KASA*\*... AND MAYBE ONE OF SHINRIJI'S *KIMONO* WHILE YOU'RE AT IT.

AFTER ALL, IT WAS ME WHO TEAMED YOU WITH SHIRA.

IF HE REALLY *IS* THE ONE BEHIND THOSE POSTERS, WELL...IT'S THE LEAST I CAN DO.

\* : A BASKETWORK HAT THAT CAN CONCEAL THE FACE.

NOW, YOU TAKE CARE OF HER, YOU HEAR?

OUR LITTLE RIN.

LOOK... HYAKURIN.

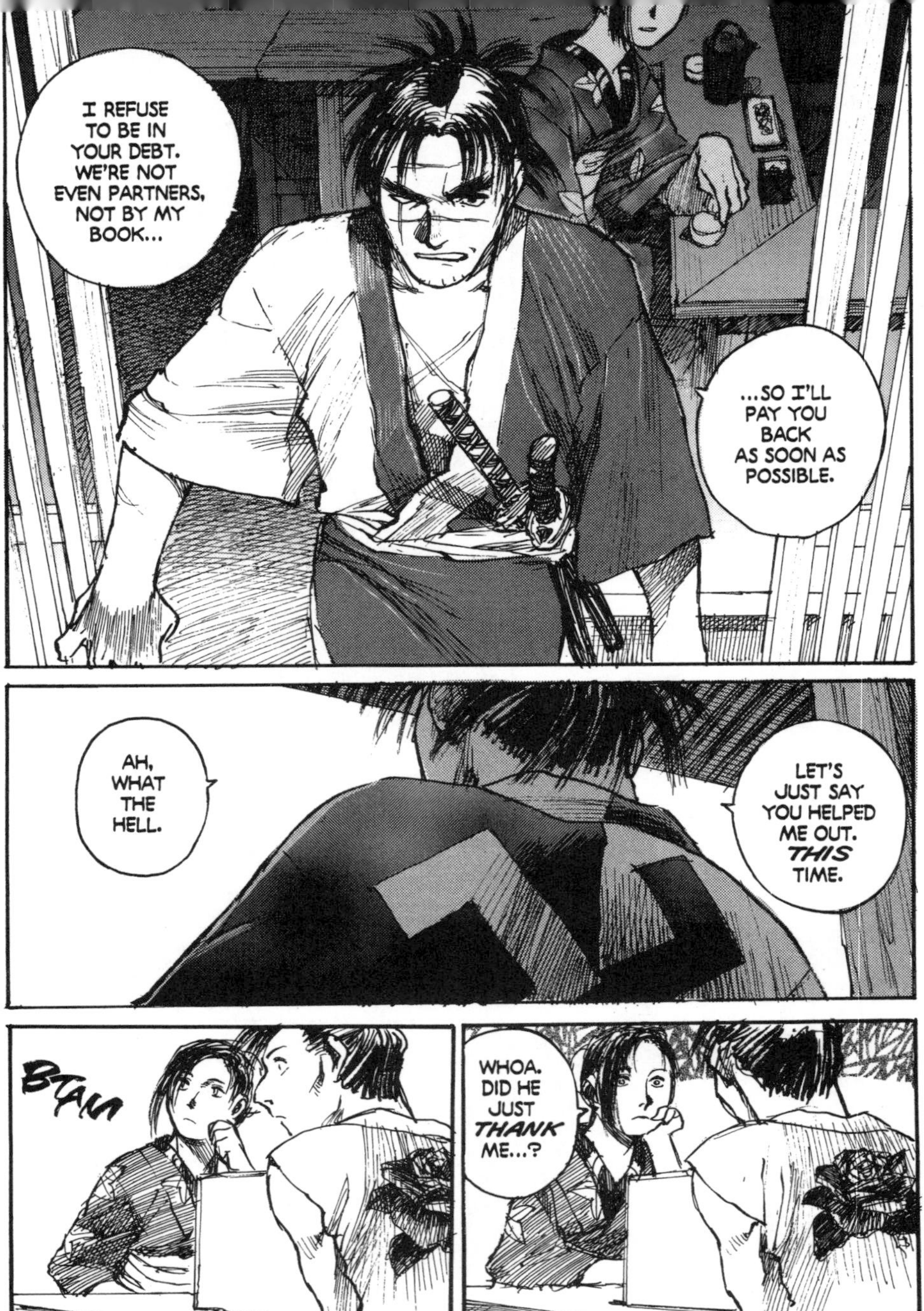
I REFUSE TO BE IN YOUR DEBT. WE'RE NOT EVEN PARTNERS, NOT BY MY BOOK...
...SO I'LL PAY YOU BACK AS SOON AS POSSIBLE.
AH, WHAT THE HELL.
LET'S JUST SAY YOU HELPED ME OUT. THIS TIME.
BTAM
WHOA. DID HE JUST THANK ME...?

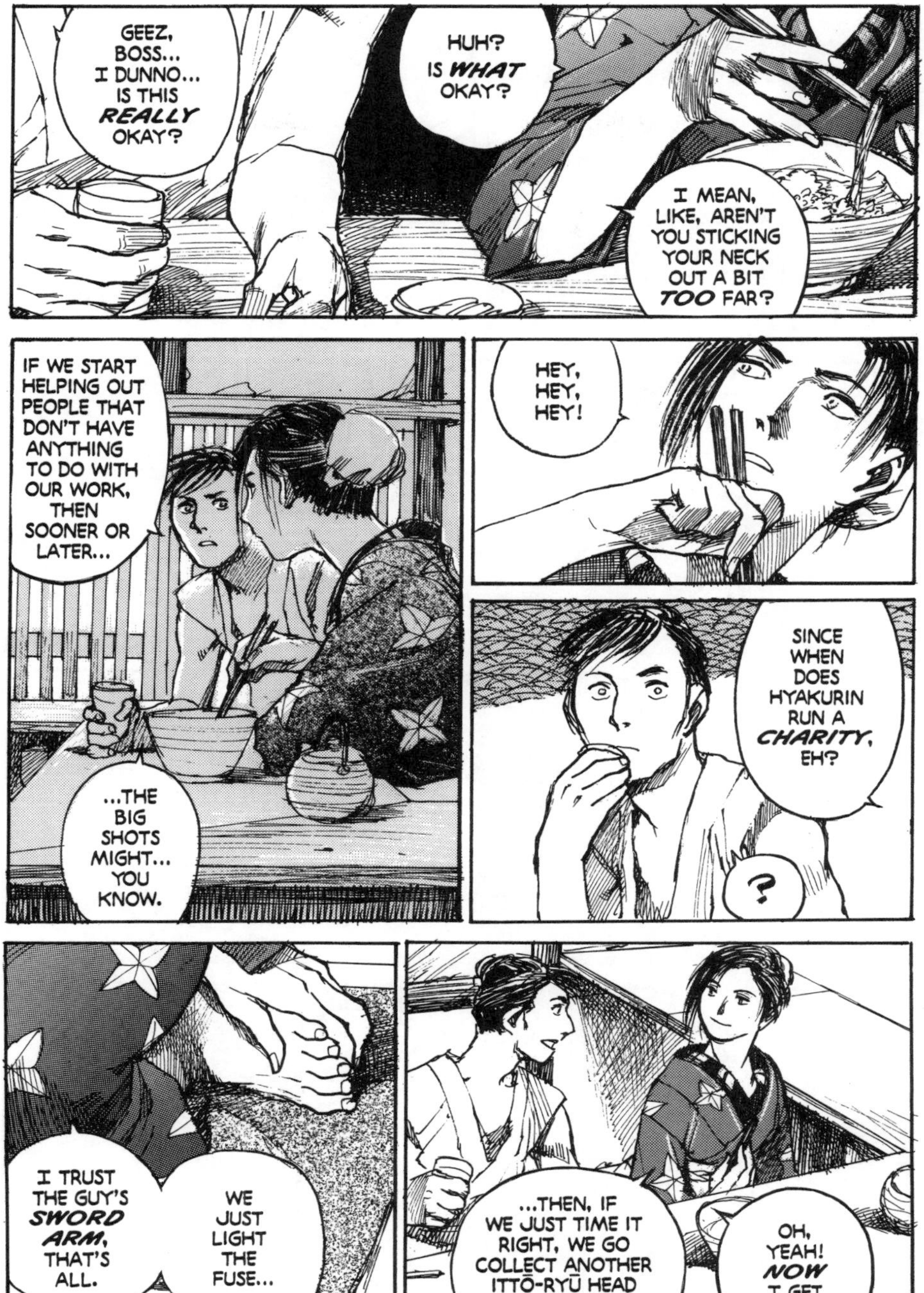
GEEZ, BOSS... I DUNNO... IS THIS REALLY OKAY?
HUH? IS WHAT OKAY?
I MEAN, LIKE, AREN'T YOU STICKING YOUR NECK OUT A BIT TOO FAR?
IF WE START HELPING OUT PEOPLE THAT DON'T HAVE ANYTHING TO DO WITH OUR WORK, THEN SOONER OR LATER...
...THE BIG SHOTS MIGHT... YOU KNOW.
HEY, HEY, HEY!
SINCE WHEN DOES HYAKURIN RUN A CHARITY, EH?
?
I TRUST THE GUY'S SWORD ARM, THAT'S ALL.
WE JUST LIGHT THE FUSE...
...THEN, IF WE JUST TIME IT RIGHT, WE GO COLLECT ANOTHER ITTŌ-RYŪ HEAD WITHOUT LIFTING A FINGER.
OH, YEAH! NOW I GET IT!

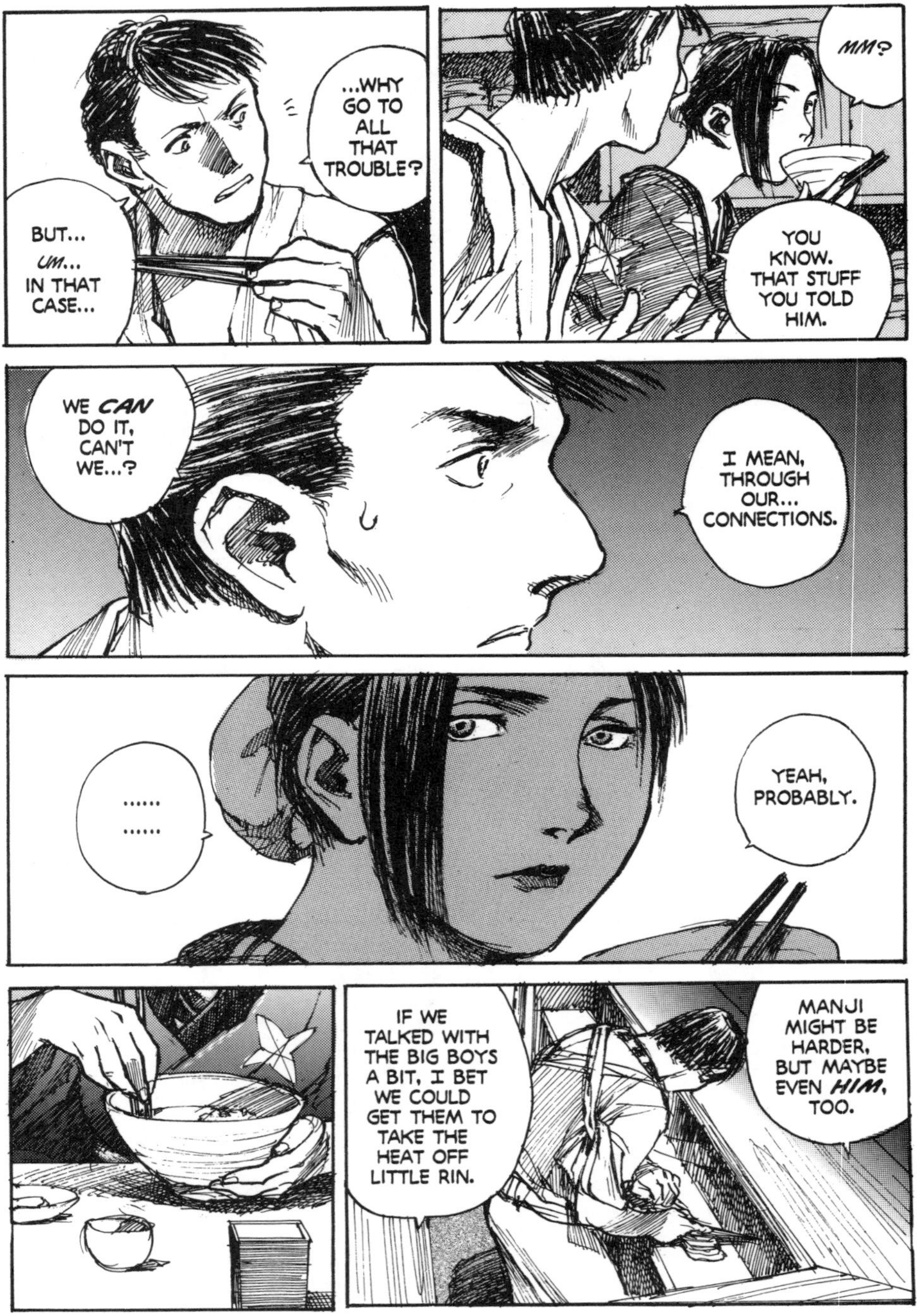
...WHY GO TO ALL THAT TROUBLE?
BUT... UM... IN THAT CASE...
MM?
YOU KNOW. THAT STUFF YOU TOLD HIM.
WE CAN DO IT, CAN'T WE...?
I MEAN, THROUGH OUR... CONNECTIONS.
......
......
YEAH, PROBABLY.
IF WE TALKED WITH THE BIG BOYS A BIT, I BET WE COULD GET THEM TO TAKE THE HEAT OFF LITTLE RIN.
MANJI MIGHT BE HARDER, BUT MAYBE EVEN HIM, TOO.

IN FACT, NOW THAT I THINK ABOUT IT... IT SHOULDN'T BE THAT HARD AT ALL.

BUT IF WE DID THAT, THEN... WELL, HE'S NO FOOL.

HE MAY CATCH ON TO WHO WE *REALLY* ARE.

BUT... EVEN *AFTER* HE FINDS OUT...

...DON'T YA THINK HE'D *STILL* WANT TO WORK WITH US?

*MMM...* MAYBE SO.

BUT IN REALITY...

...WHAT'S THE DIFFERENCE, RIGHT?

ME?

I'D LIKE TO LEAVE THINGS *AMBIGU-OUS*... JUST A WEE BIT LONGER.

IF WE BLOW OUR COVER TO HIM...

...AND HE DECIDES NOT TO WORK WITH US, THEN... WELL...

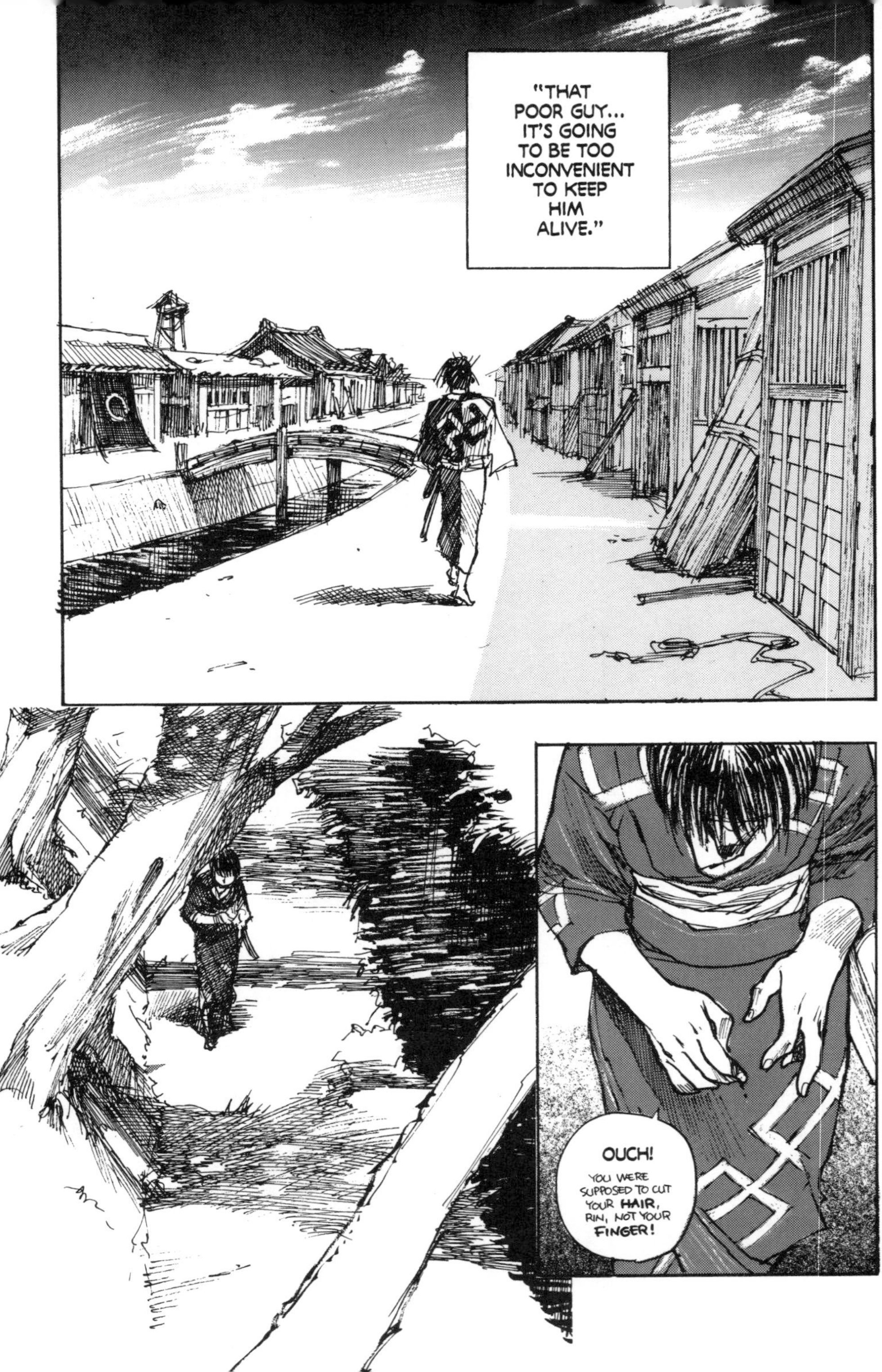
"THAT POOR GUY... IT'S GOING TO BE TOO INCONVENIENT TO KEEP HIM ALIVE."
OUCH! YOU WERE SUPPOSED TO CUT YOUR HAIR, RIN, NOT YOUR FINGER!

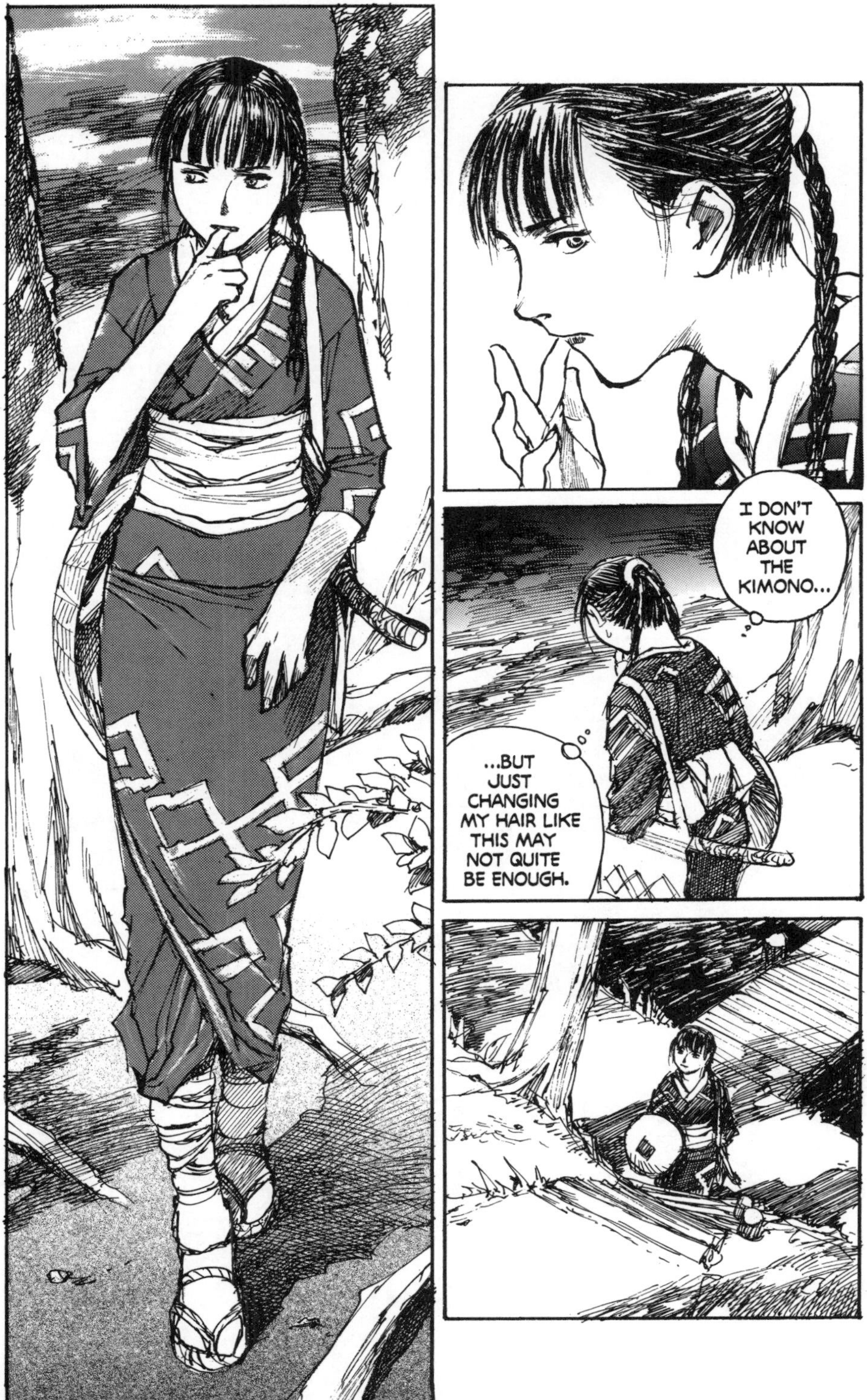
I DON'T KNOW ABOUT THE KIMONO...
...BUT JUST CHANGING MY HAIR LIKE THIS MAY NOT QUITE BE ENOUGH.

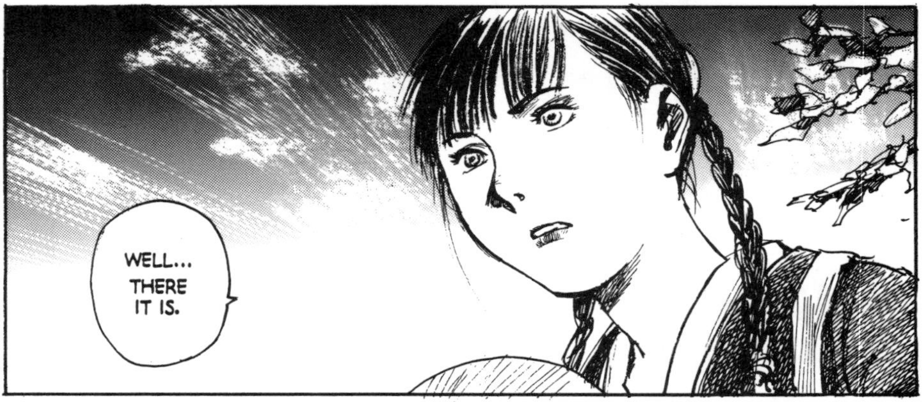
WELL... THERE IT IS.

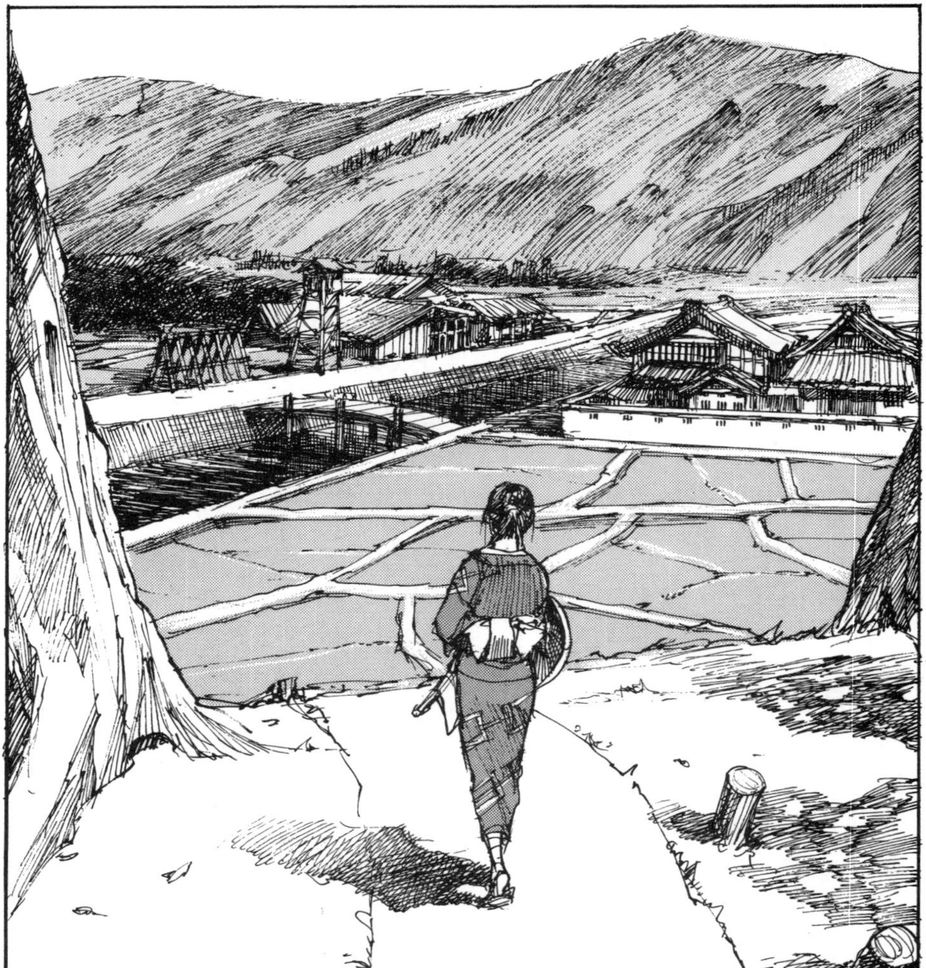

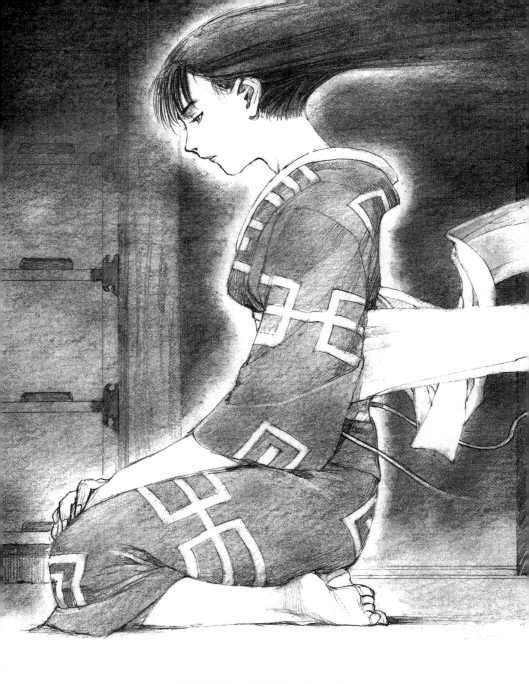

# STIGMA
## Part 2

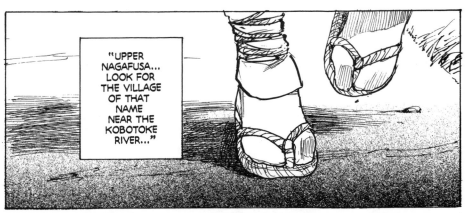

"UPPER NAGAFUSA... LOOK FOR THE VILLAGE OF THAT NAME NEAR THE KOBOTOKE RIVER..."

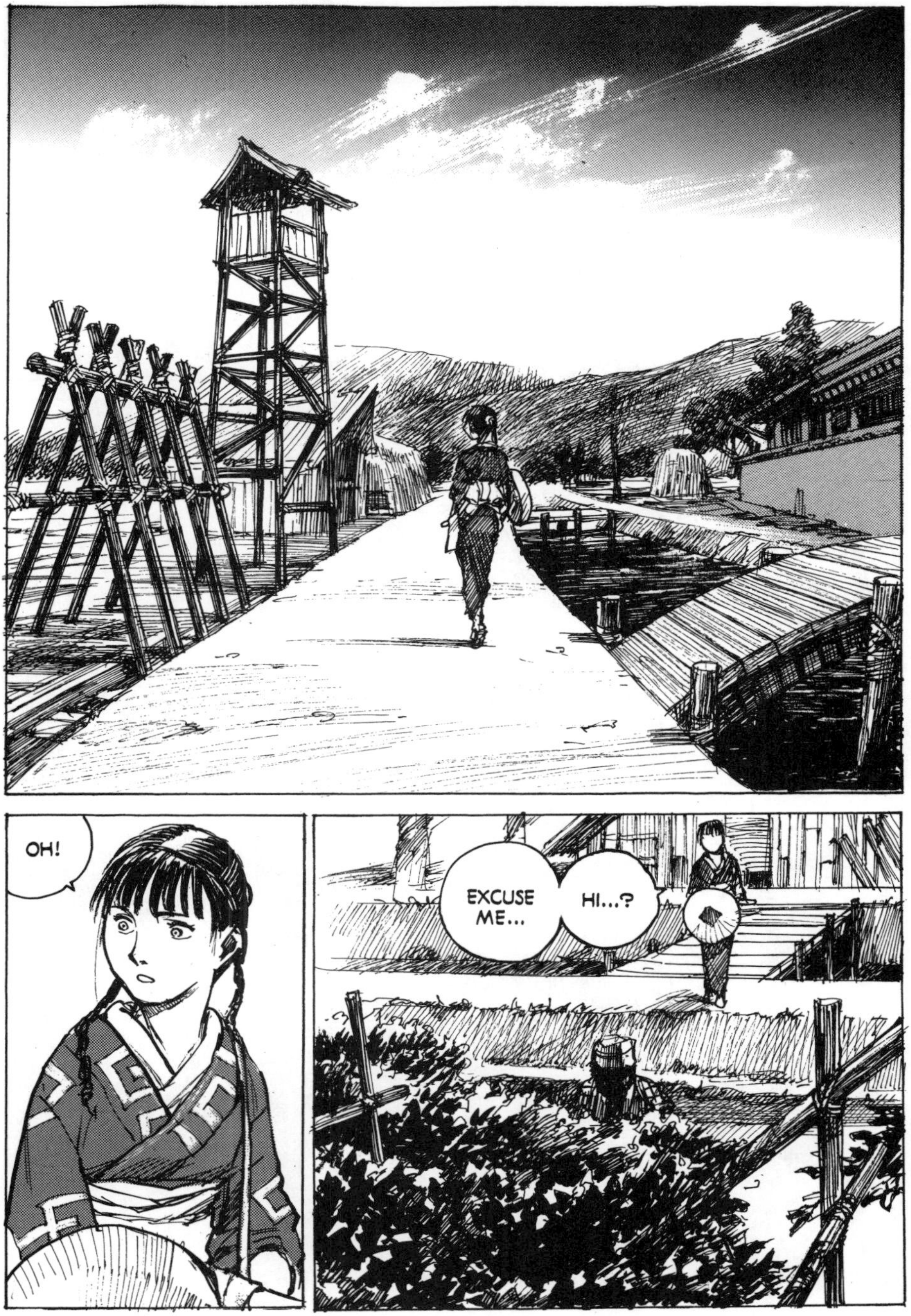
OH!
EXCUSE ME...
HI...?

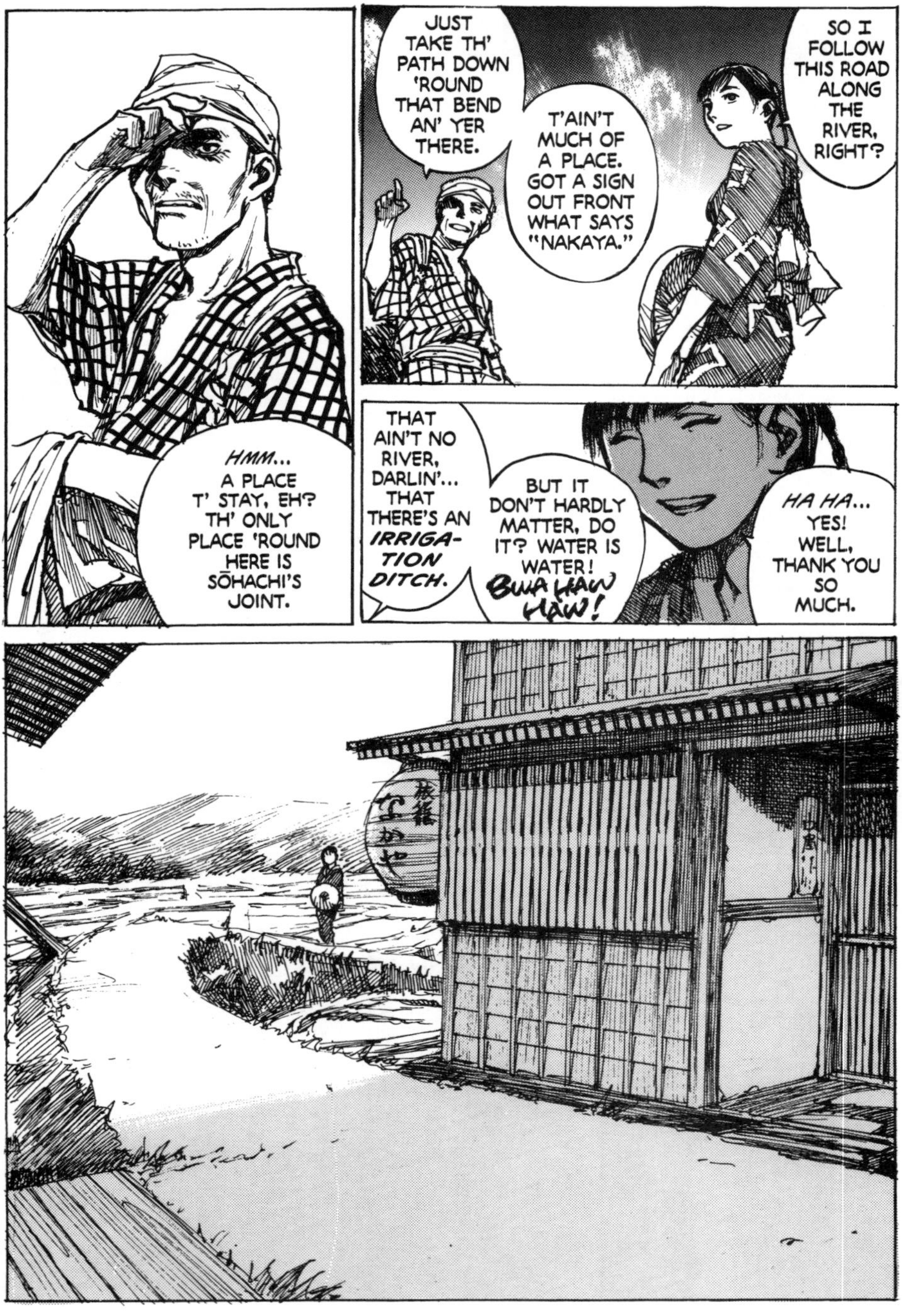
HMM... A PLACE T' STAY, EH? TH' ONLY PLACE 'ROUND HERE IS SŌHACHI'S JOINT.
JUST TAKE TH' PATH DOWN 'ROUND THAT BEND AN' YER THERE.
T'AIN'T MUCH OF A PLACE. GOT A SIGN OUT FRONT WHAT SAYS "NAKAYA."
SO I FOLLOW THIS ROAD ALONG THE RIVER, RIGHT?
THAT AIN'T NO RIVER, DARLIN'... THAT THERE'S AN IRRIGATION DITCH.
BUT IT DON'T HARDLY MATTER, DO IT? WATER IS WATER!
BUWA HAW HAW!
HA HA... YES! WELL, THANK YOU SO MUCH.

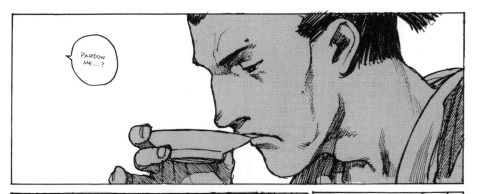

PARDON ME...?

ER...
EXCUSE ME...?

SŌ-HACHI!

......
......?

HUH?!

WE GOT A GUEST?!

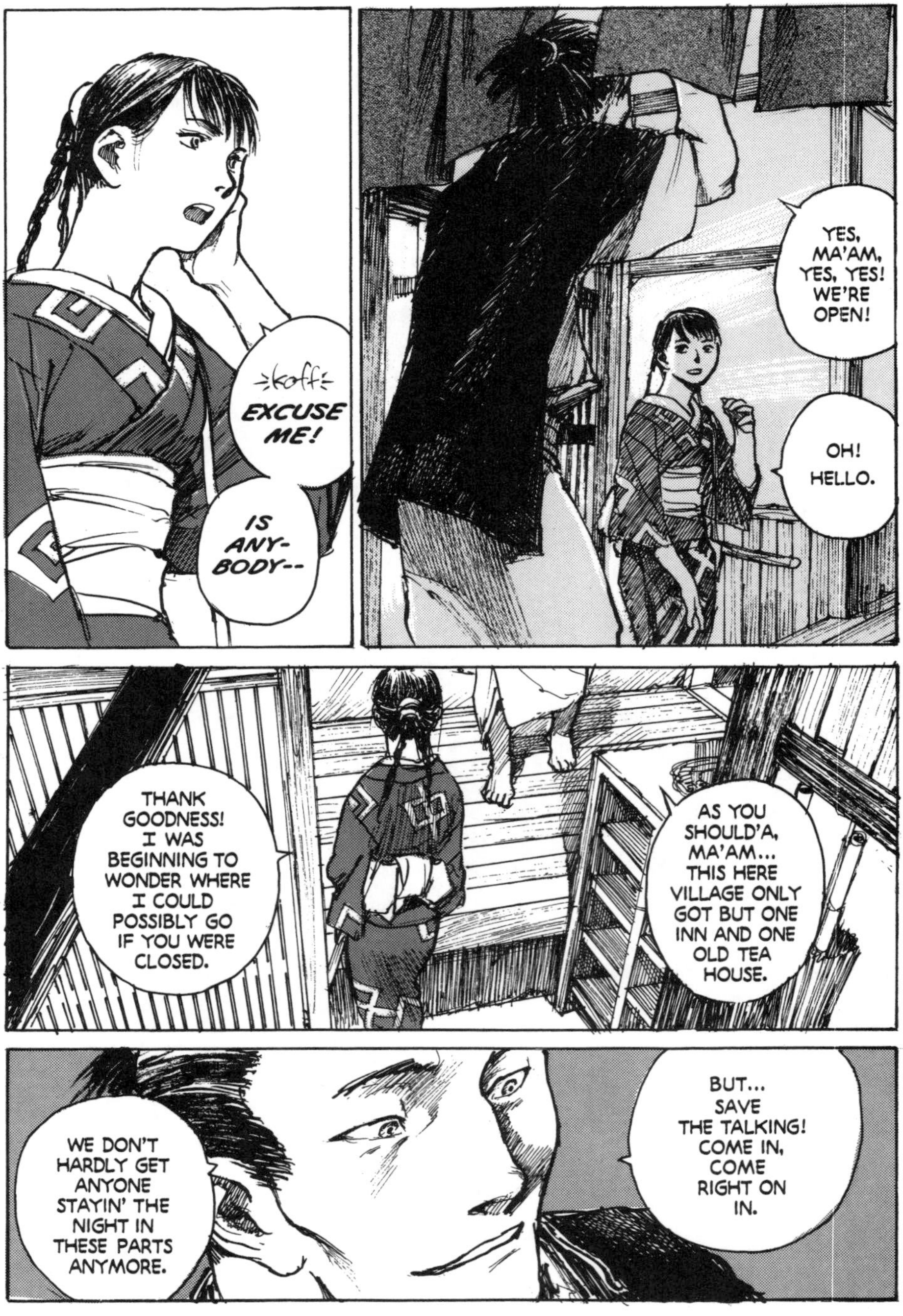
koff
EXCUSE ME!
IS ANYBODY--
YES, MA'AM, YES, YES! WE'RE OPEN!
OH! HELLO.
THANK GOODNESS! I WAS BEGINNING TO WONDER WHERE I COULD POSSIBLY GO IF YOU WERE CLOSED.
AS YOU SHOULD'A, MA'AM... THIS HERE VILLAGE ONLY GOT BUT ONE INN AND ONE OLD TEA HOUSE.
WE DON'T HARDLY GET ANYONE STAYIN' THE NIGHT IN THESE PARTS ANYMORE.
BUT... SAVE THE TALKING! COME IN, COME RIGHT ON IN.

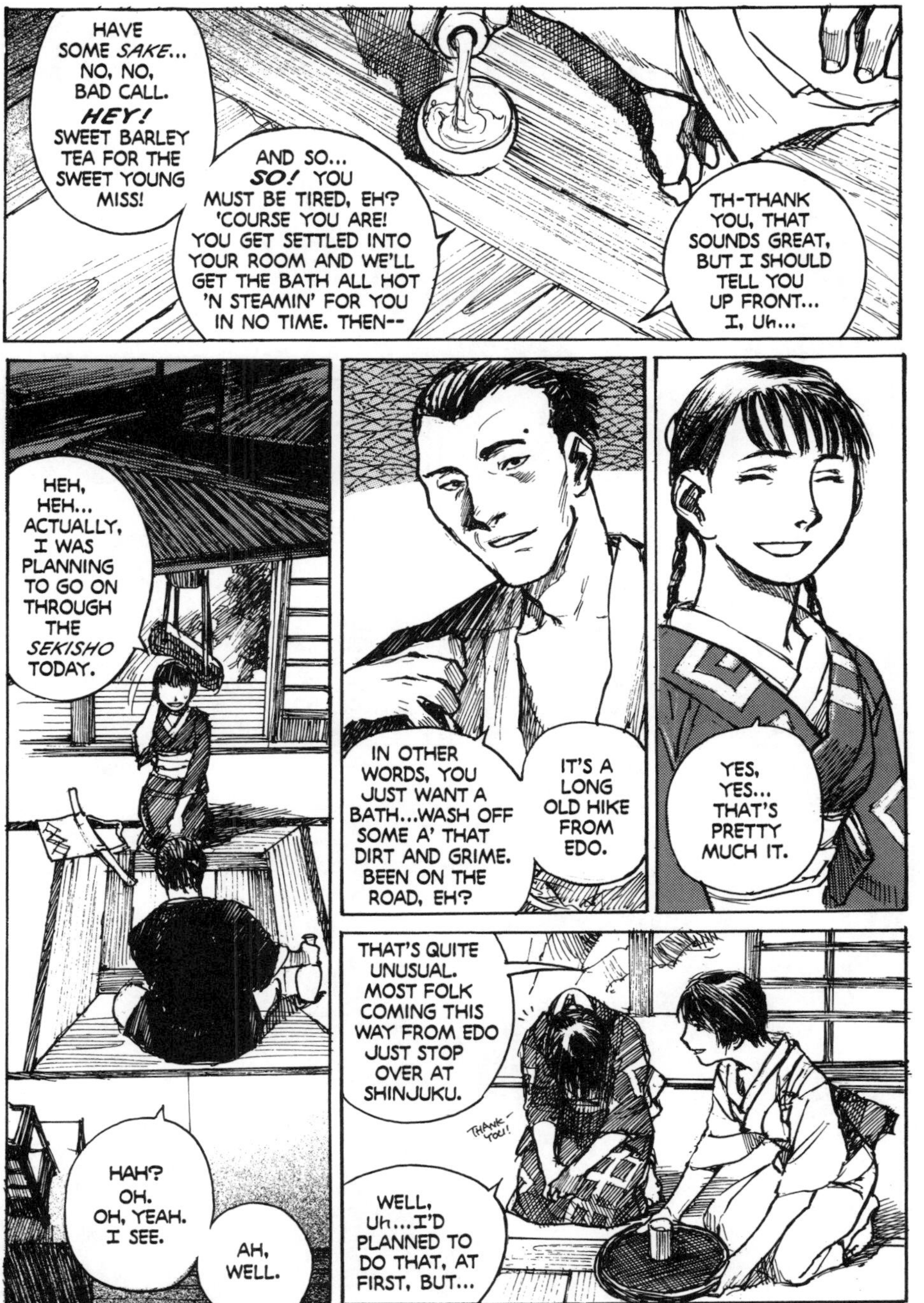
HAVE SOME SAKE... NO, NO, BAD CALL. HEY! SWEET BARLEY TEA FOR THE SWEET YOUNG MISS!
AND SO... SO! YOU MUST BE TIRED, EH? 'COURSE YOU ARE! YOU GET SETTLED INTO YOUR ROOM AND WE'LL GET THE BATH ALL HOT 'N STEAMIN' FOR YOU IN NO TIME. THEN--
TH-THANK YOU, THAT SOUNDS GREAT, BUT I SHOULD TELL YOU UP FRONT... I, Uh...
HEH, HEH... ACTUALLY, I WAS PLANNING TO GO ON THROUGH THE SEKISHO TODAY.
IN OTHER WORDS, YOU JUST WANT A BATH...WASH OFF SOME A' THAT DIRT AND GRIME. BEEN ON THE ROAD, EH?
IT'S A LONG OLD HIKE FROM EDO.
YES, YES... THAT'S PRETTY MUCH IT.
HAH? OH. OH, YEAH. I SEE.
AH, WELL.
THAT'S QUITE UNUSUAL. MOST FOLK COMING THIS WAY FROM EDO JUST STOP OVER AT SHINJUKU.
THANK YOU!
WELL, Uh...I'D PLANNED TO DO THAT, AT FIRST, BUT...

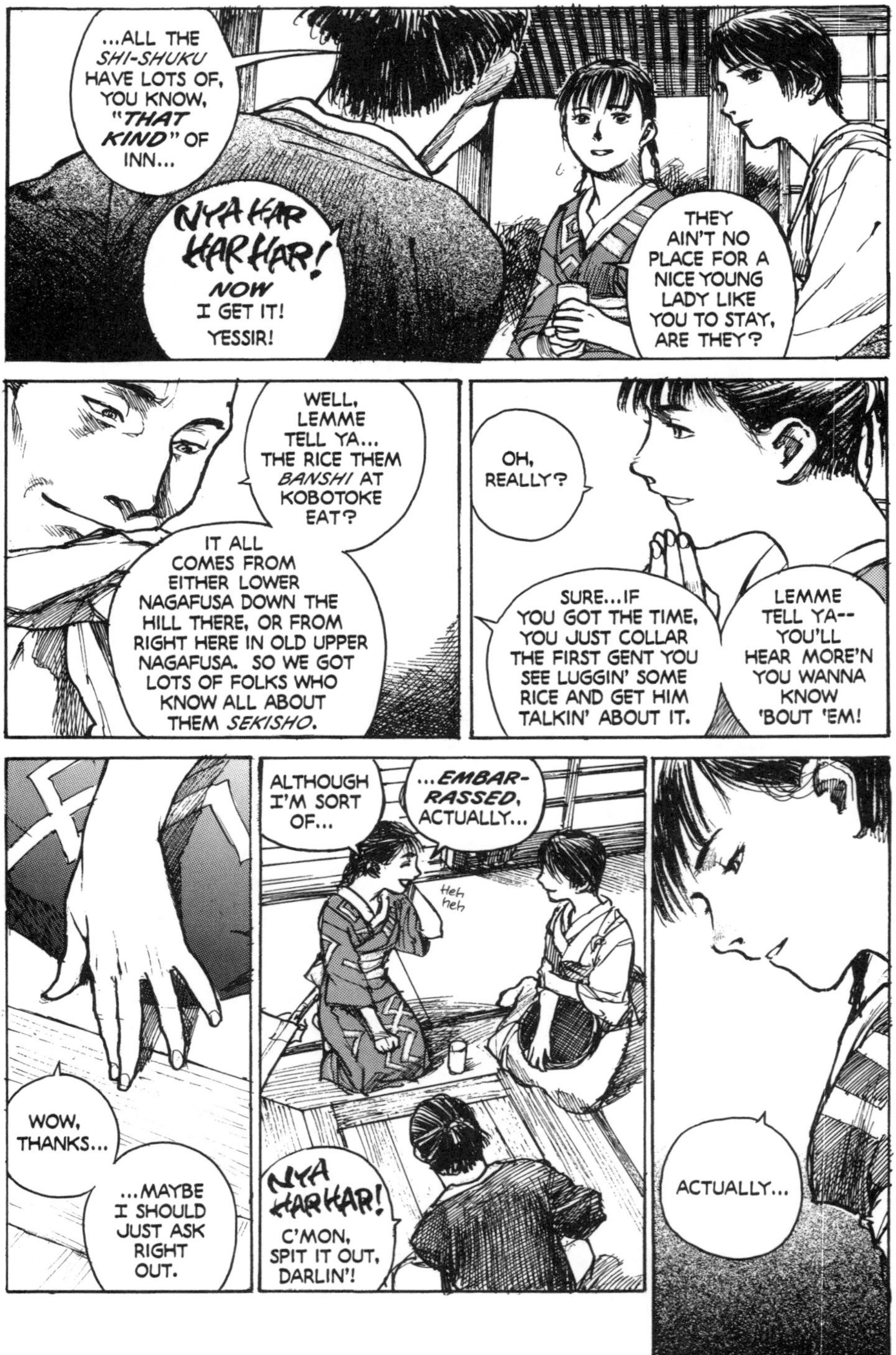
...ALL THE SHI-SHUKU HAVE LOTS OF, YOU KNOW, "THAT KIND" OF INN...
NYA HAR HAR HAR!
NOW I GET IT! YESSIR!
THEY AIN'T NO PLACE FOR A NICE YOUNG LADY LIKE YOU TO STAY, ARE THEY?
WELL, LEMME TELL YA... THE RICE THEM BANSHI AT KOBOTOKE EAT?
IT ALL COMES FROM EITHER LOWER NAGAFUSA DOWN THE HILL THERE, OR FROM RIGHT HERE IN OLD UPPER NAGAFUSA. SO WE GOT LOTS OF FOLKS WHO KNOW ALL ABOUT THEM SEKISHO.
OH, REALLY?
SURE...IF YOU GOT THE TIME, YOU JUST COLLAR THE FIRST GENT YOU SEE LUGGIN' SOME RICE AND GET HIM TALKIN' ABOUT IT.
LEMME TELL YA-- YOU'LL HEAR MORE'N YOU WANNA KNOW 'BOUT 'EM!
WOW, THANKS...
...MAYBE I SHOULD JUST ASK RIGHT OUT.
ALTHOUGH I'M SORT OF...
...EMBARRASSED, ACTUALLY...
Heh heh
NYA HAR HAR!
C'MON, SPIT IT OUT, DARLIN'!
ACTUALLY...

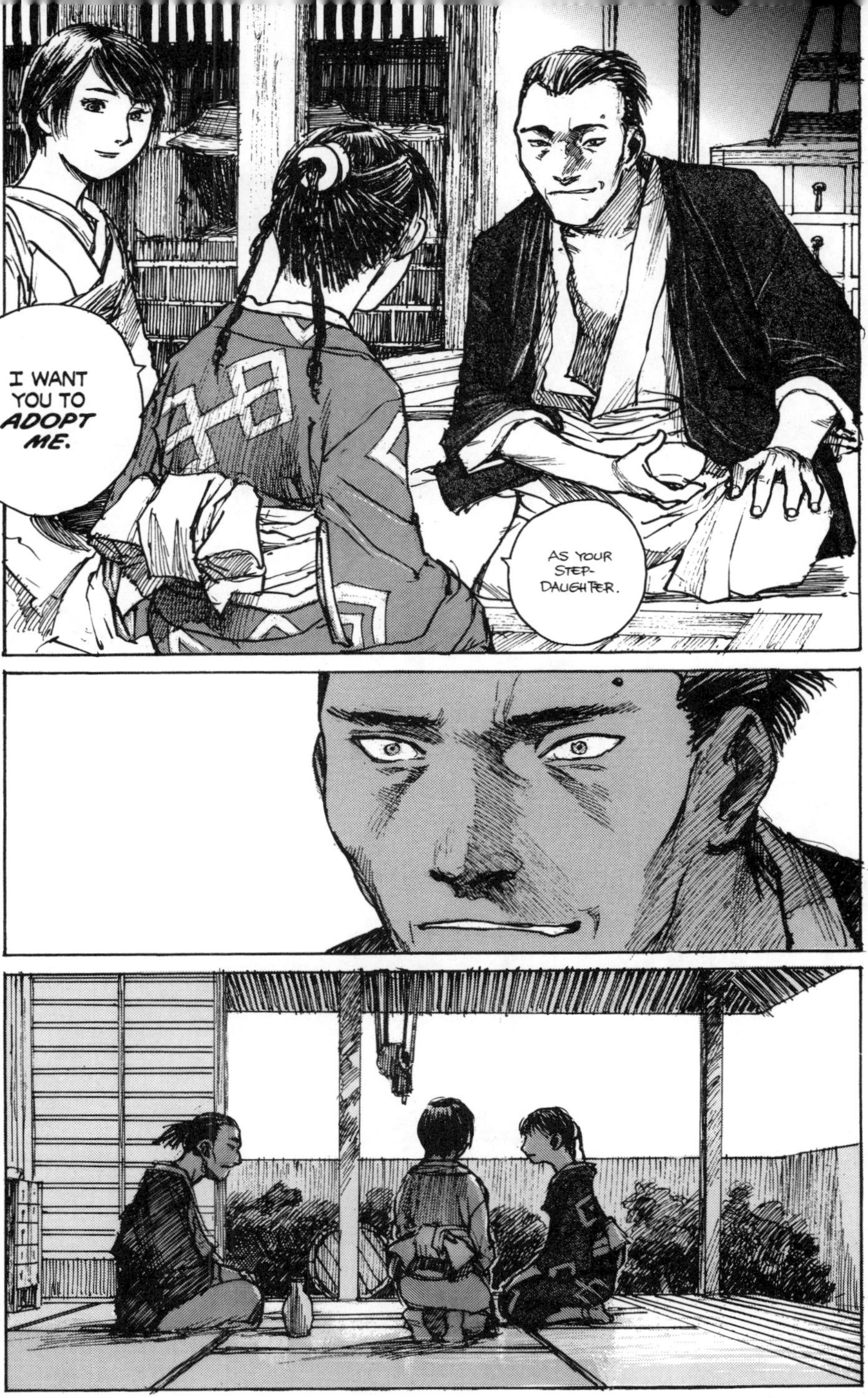
I WANT YOU TO ADOPT ME.
AS YOUR STEP-DAUGHTER.

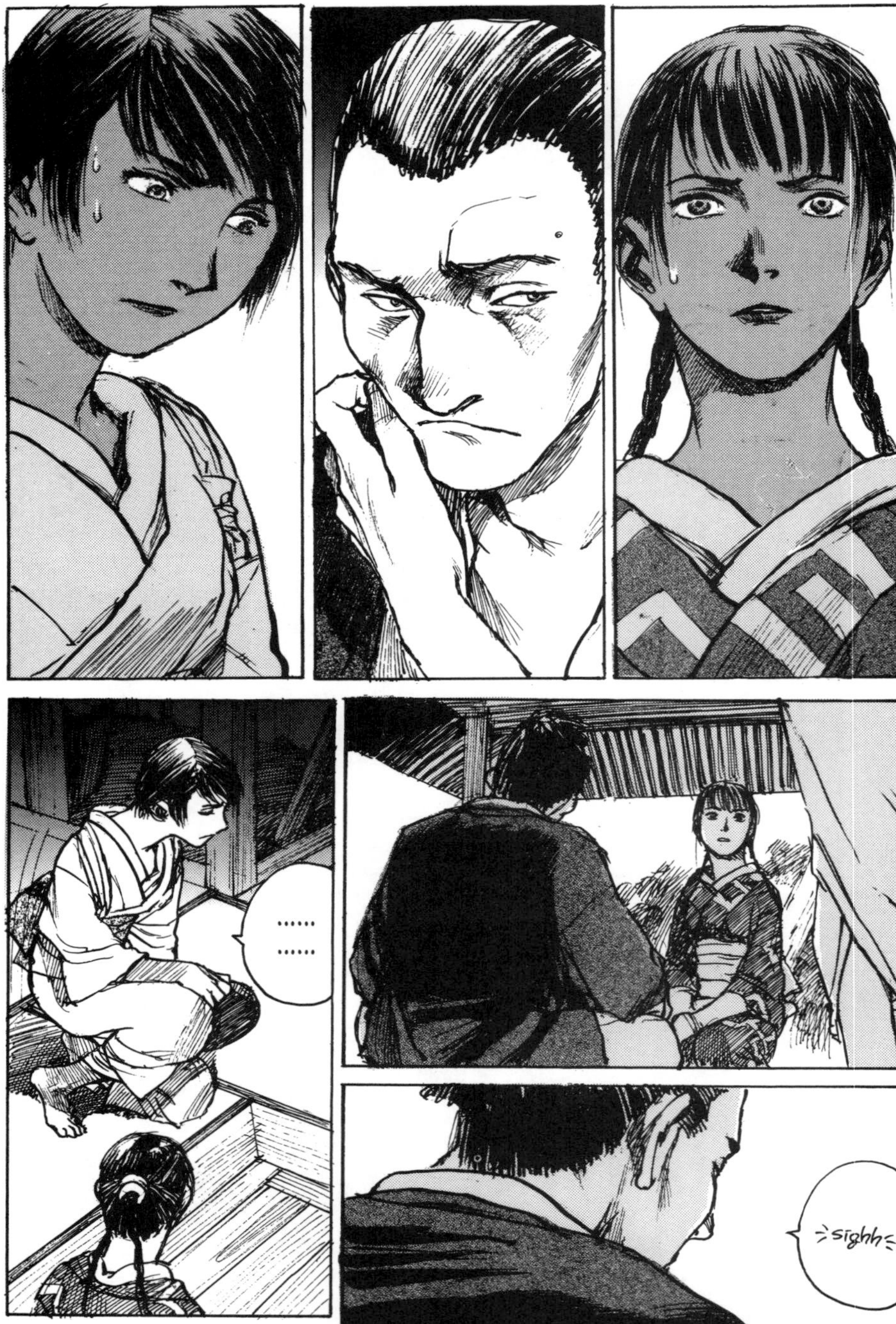
……
……
sighh

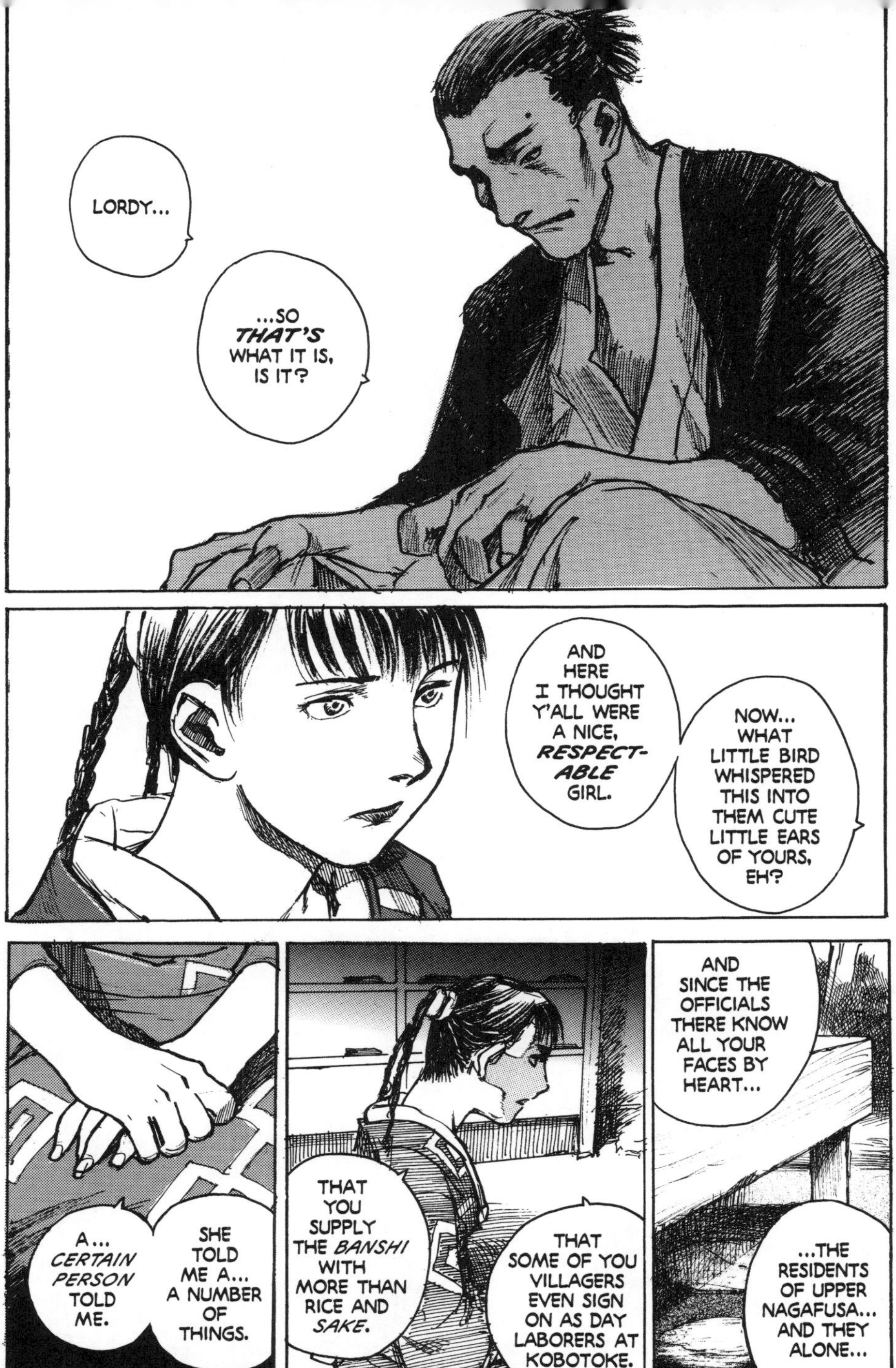
LORDY...
...SO *THAT'S* WHAT IT IS, IS IT?
AND HERE I THOUGHT Y'ALL WERE A NICE, *RESPECTABLE* GIRL.
NOW... WHAT LITTLE BIRD WHISPERED THIS INTO THEM CUTE LITTLE EARS OF YOURS, EH?
A... *CERTAIN PERSON* TOLD ME.
SHE TOLD ME A... A NUMBER OF THINGS.
THAT YOU SUPPLY THE *BANSHI* WITH MORE THAN RICE AND *SAKE*.
THAT SOME OF YOU VILLAGERS EVEN SIGN ON AS DAY LABORERS AT KOBOTOKE.
AND SINCE THE OFFICIALS THERE KNOW ALL YOUR FACES BY HEART...
...THE RESIDENTS OF UPPER NAGAFUSA... AND THEY ALONE...

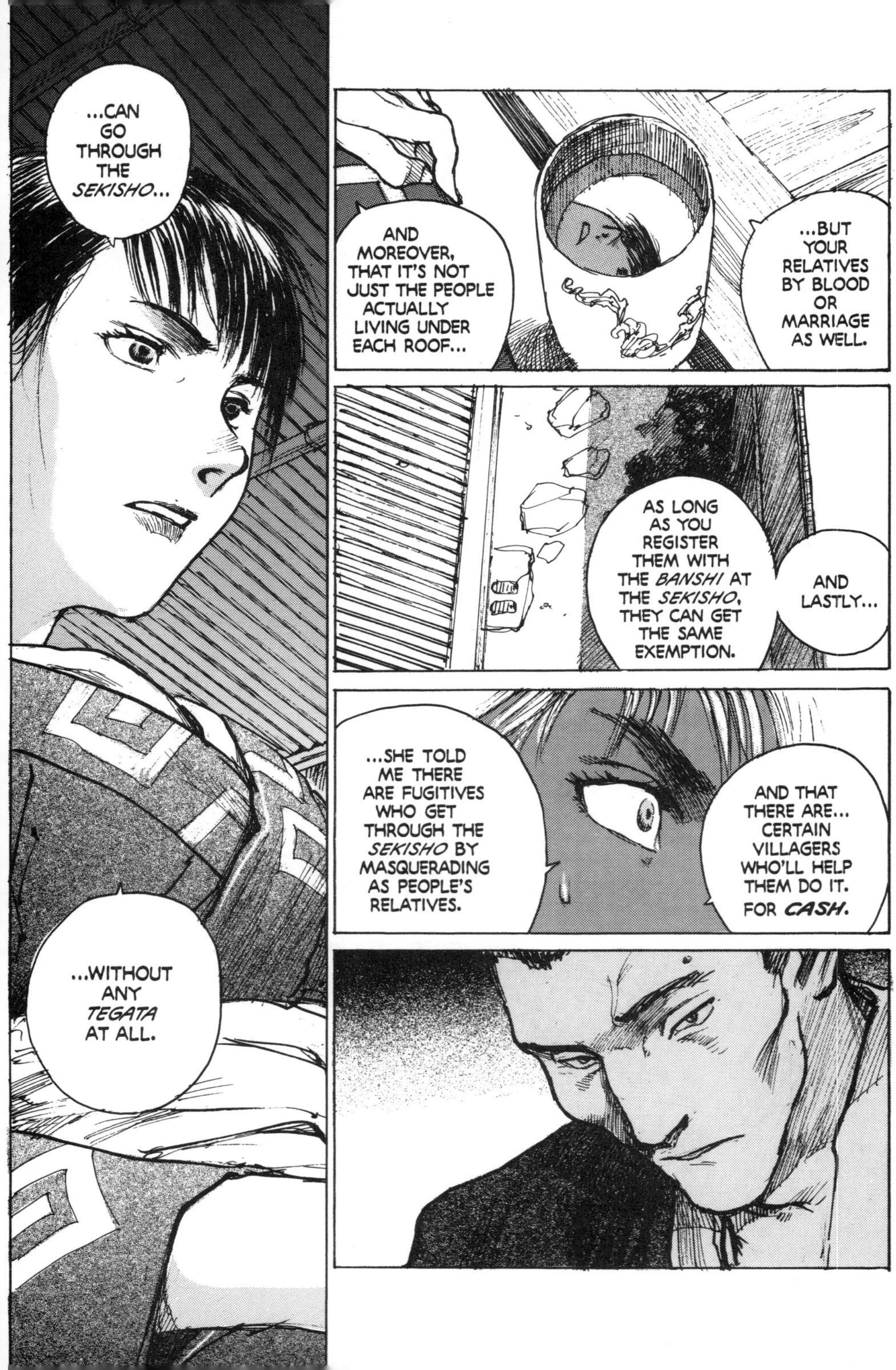
...CAN GO THROUGH THE *SEKISHO*...
...WITHOUT ANY *TEGATA* AT ALL.
AND MOREOVER, THAT IT'S NOT JUST THE PEOPLE ACTUALLY LIVING UNDER EACH ROOF...
...BUT YOUR RELATIVES BY BLOOD OR MARRIAGE AS WELL.
AS LONG AS YOU REGISTER THEM WITH THE *BANSHI* AT THE *SEKISHO*, THEY CAN GET THE SAME EXEMPTION.
AND LASTLY...
...SHE TOLD ME THERE ARE FUGITIVES WHO GET THROUGH THE *SEKISHO* BY MASQUERADING AS PEOPLE'S RELATIVES.
AND THAT THERE ARE... CERTAIN VILLAGERS WHO'LL HELP THEM DO IT. FOR ***CASH***.

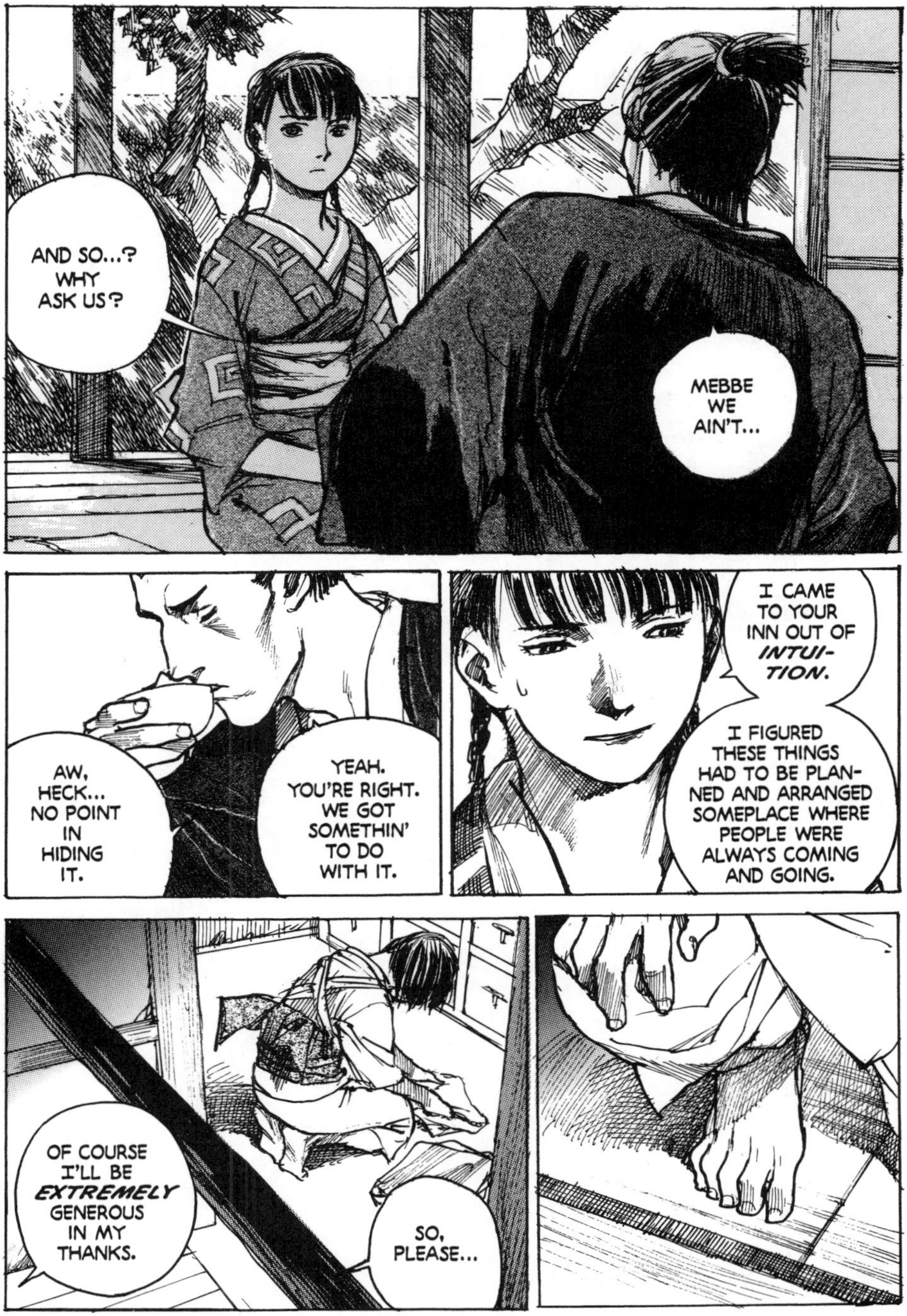
AND SO...? WHY ASK US?
MEBBE WE AIN'T...
AW, HECK... NO POINT IN HIDING IT.
YEAH. YOU'RE RIGHT. WE GOT SOMETHIN' TO DO WITH IT.
I CAME TO YOUR INN OUT OF *INTUITION*.
I FIGURED THESE THINGS HAD TO BE PLANNED AND ARRANGED SOMEPLACE WHERE PEOPLE WERE ALWAYS COMING AND GOING.
OF COURSE I'LL BE *EXTREMELY* GENEROUS IN MY THANKS.
SO, PLEASE...

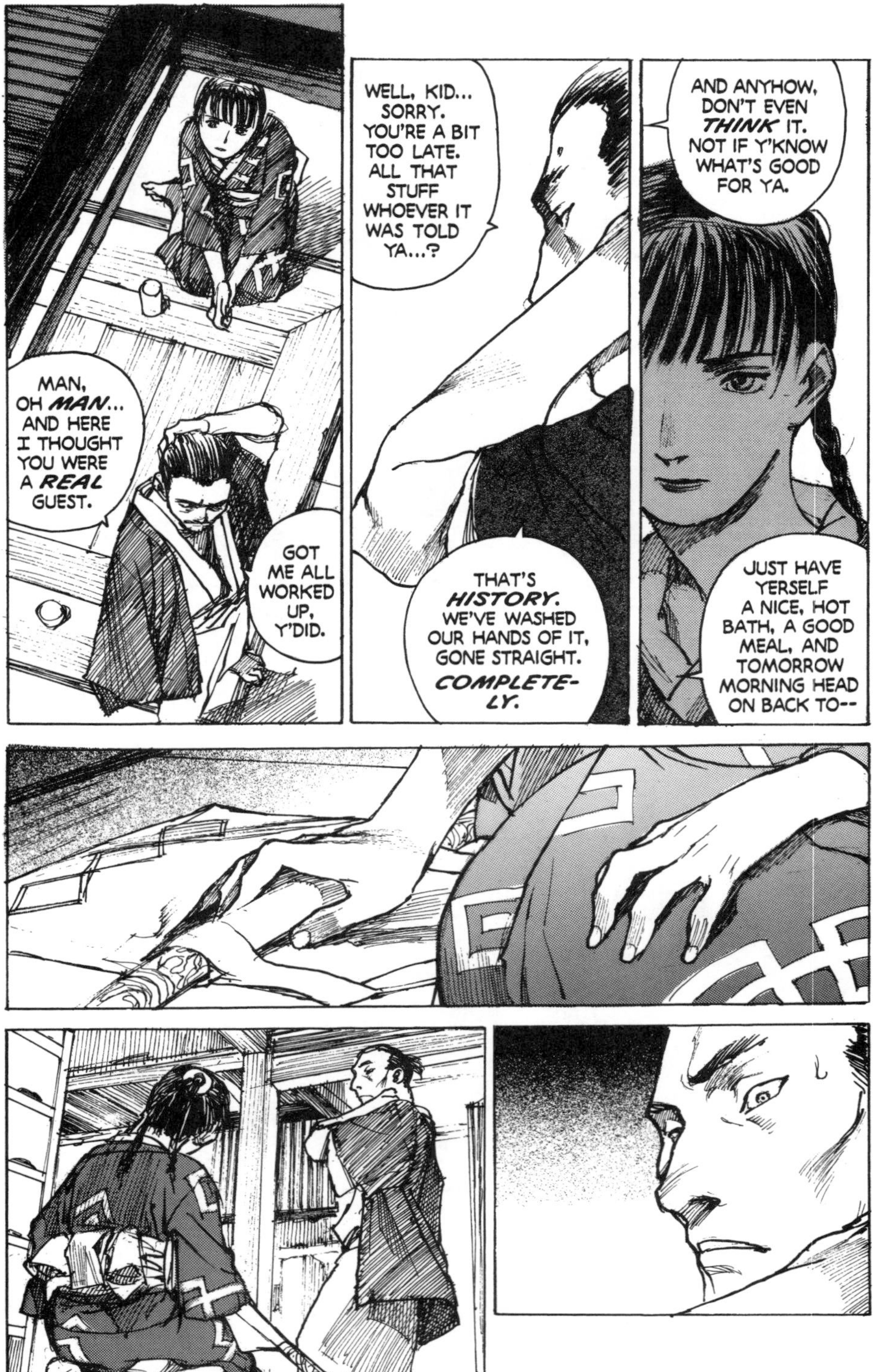
MAN, OH MAN... AND HERE I THOUGHT YOU WERE A REAL GUEST.
GOT ME ALL WORKED UP, Y'DID.
WELL, KID... SORRY. YOU'RE A BIT TOO LATE. ALL THAT STUFF WHOEVER IT WAS TOLD YA...?
THAT'S HISTORY. WE'VE WASHED OUR HANDS OF IT, GONE STRAIGHT. COMPLETE-LY.
AND ANYHOW, DON'T EVEN THINK IT. NOT IF Y'KNOW WHAT'S GOOD FOR YA.
JUST HAVE YERSELF A NICE, HOT BATH, A GOOD MEAL, AND TOMORROW MORNING HEAD ON BACK TO--

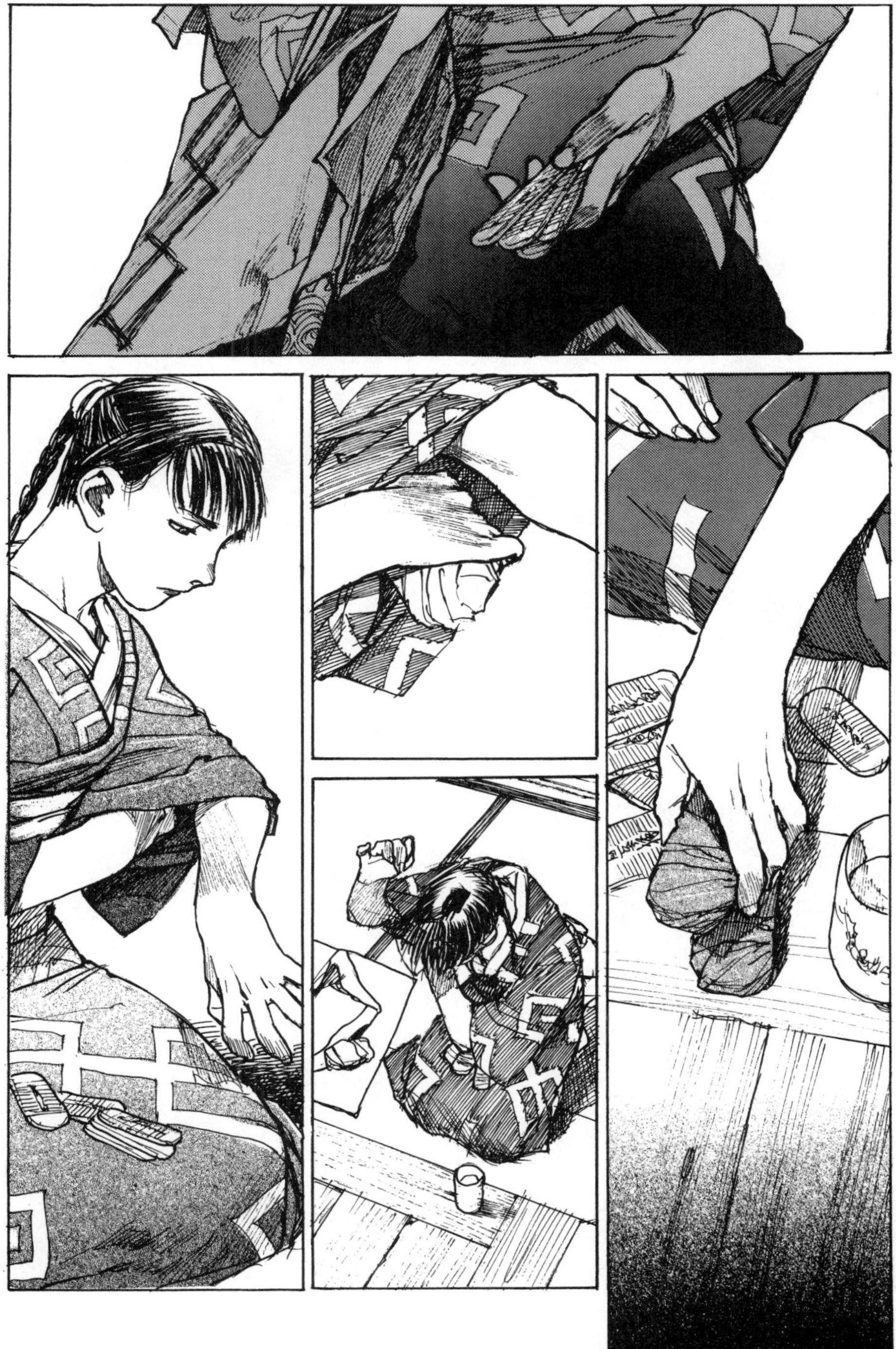

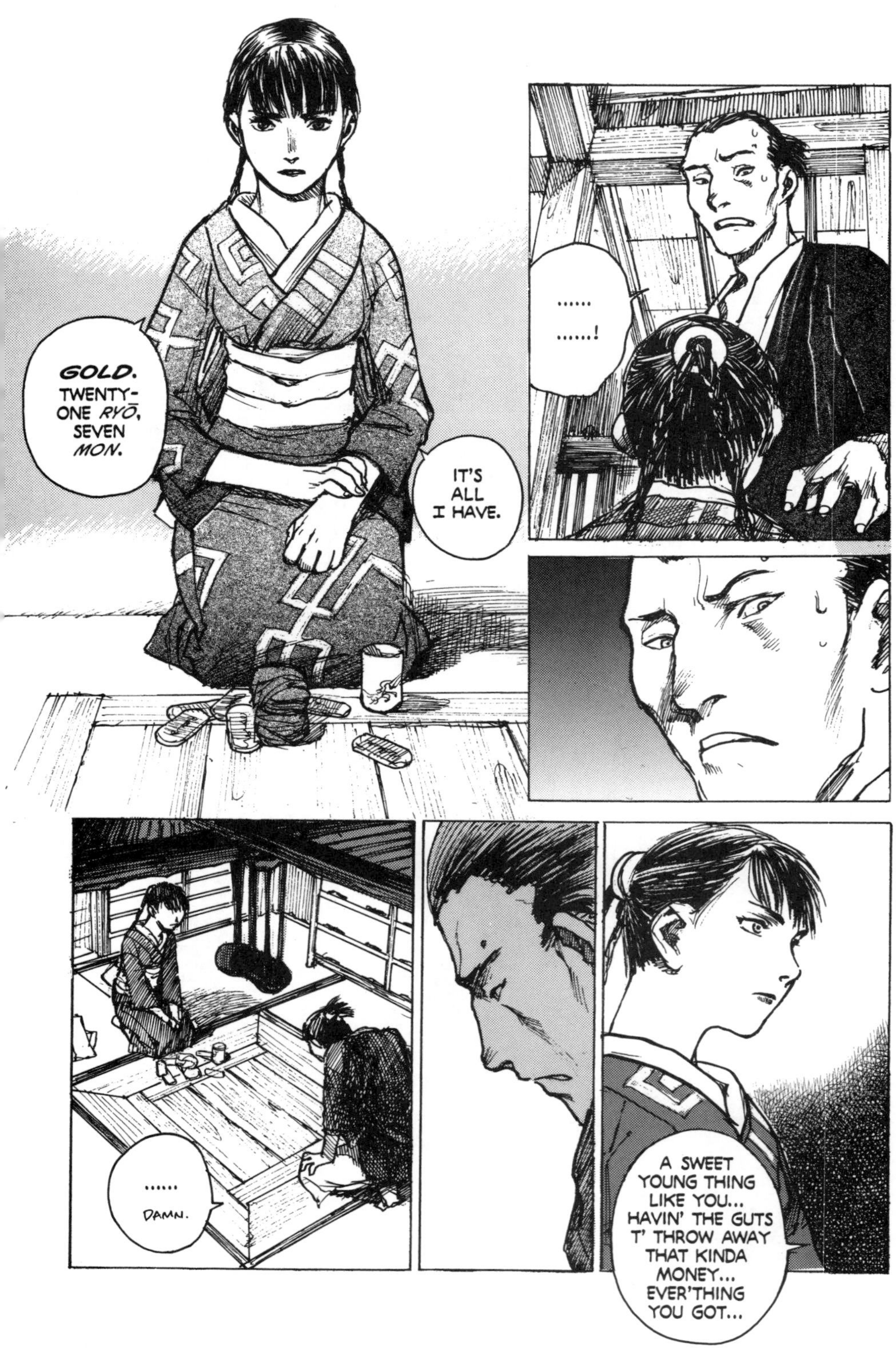
**GOLD.** TWENTY-ONE *RYŌ*, SEVEN *MON*.
IT'S ALL I HAVE.
......
......!
...... DAMN.
A SWEET YOUNG THING LIKE YOU... HAVIN' THE GUTS T' THROW AWAY THAT KINDA MONEY... EVER'THING YOU GOT...

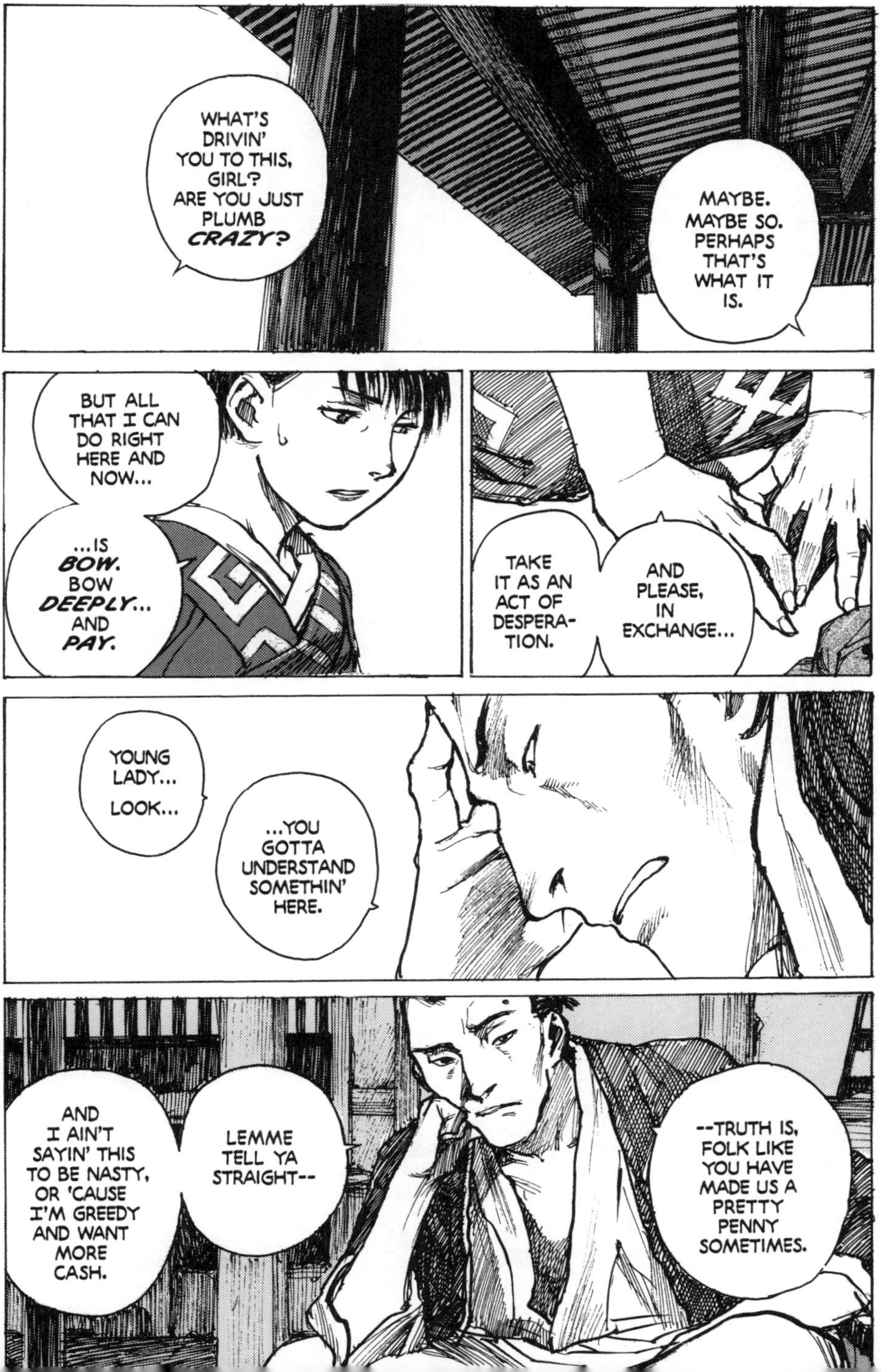
WHAT'S DRIVIN' YOU TO THIS, GIRL? ARE YOU JUST PLUMB *CRAZY?*
MAYBE. MAYBE SO. PERHAPS THAT'S WHAT IT IS.
BUT ALL THAT I CAN DO RIGHT HERE AND NOW...
...IS ***BOW.*** BOW ***DEEPLY...*** AND ***PAY.***
TAKE IT AS AN ACT OF DESPERA-TION.
AND PLEASE, IN EXCHANGE...
YOUNG LADY... LOOK...
...YOU GOTTA UNDERSTAND SOMETHIN' HERE.
AND I AIN'T SAYIN' THIS TO BE NASTY, OR 'CAUSE I'M GREEDY AND WANT MORE CASH.
LEMME TELL YA STRAIGHT--
--TRUTH IS, FOLK LIKE YOU HAVE MADE US A PRETTY PENNY SOMETIMES.

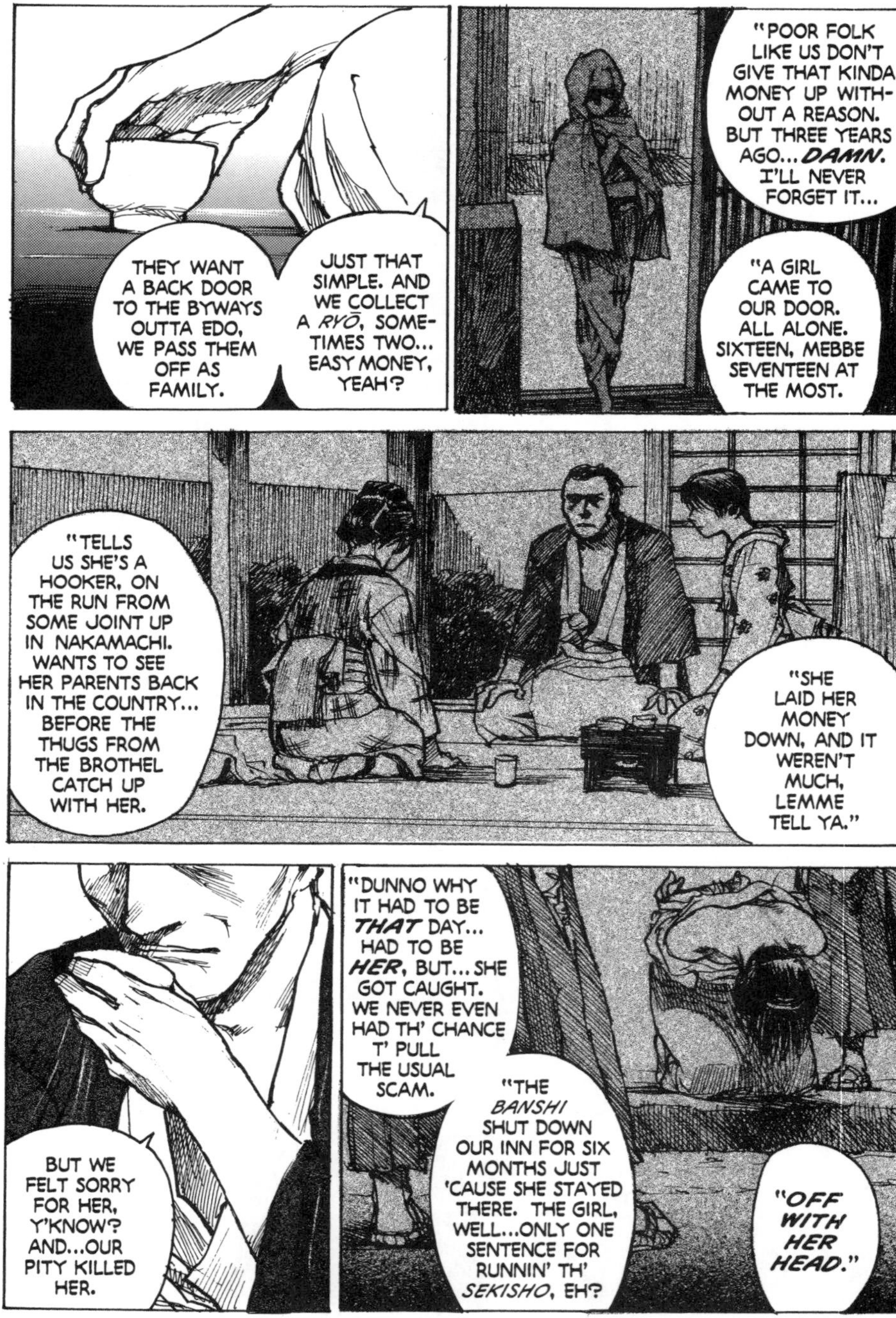
THEY WANT A BACK DOOR TO THE BYWAYS OUTTA EDO, WE PASS THEM OFF AS FAMILY.
JUST THAT SIMPLE. AND WE COLLECT A *RYŌ*, SOMETIMES TWO... EASY MONEY, YEAH?
"POOR FOLK LIKE US DON'T GIVE THAT KINDA MONEY UP WITHOUT A REASON. BUT THREE YEARS AGO... ***DAMN.*** I'LL NEVER FORGET IT...
"A GIRL CAME TO OUR DOOR. ALL ALONE. SIXTEEN, MEBBE SEVENTEEN AT THE MOST.
"TELLS US SHE'S A HOOKER, ON THE RUN FROM SOME JOINT UP IN NAKAMACHI. WANTS TO SEE HER PARENTS BACK IN THE COUNTRY... BEFORE THE THUGS FROM THE BROTHEL CATCH UP WITH HER.
"SHE LAID HER MONEY DOWN, AND IT WEREN'T MUCH, LEMME TELL YA."
BUT WE FELT SORRY FOR HER, Y'KNOW? AND...OUR PITY KILLED HER.
"DUNNO WHY IT HAD TO BE ***THAT*** DAY... HAD TO BE ***HER***, BUT... SHE GOT CAUGHT. WE NEVER EVEN HAD TH' CHANCE T' PULL THE USUAL SCAM.
"THE *BANSHI* SHUT DOWN OUR INN FOR SIX MONTHS JUST 'CAUSE SHE STAYED THERE. THE GIRL, WELL...ONLY ONE SENTENCE FOR RUNNIN' TH' *SEKISHO*, EH?
"***OFF WITH HER HEAD.***"

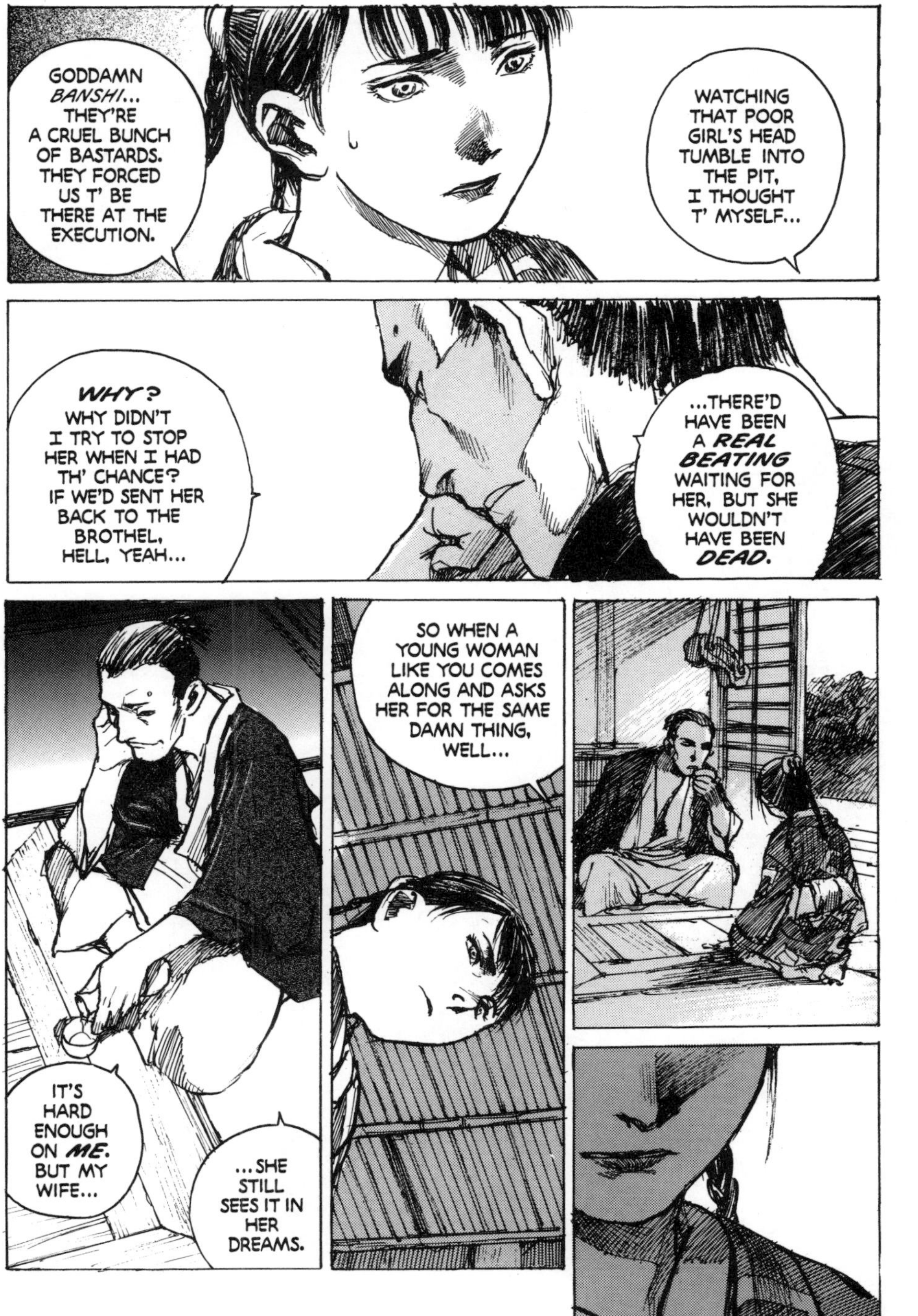
GODDAMN *BANSHI*... THEY'RE A CRUEL BUNCH OF BASTARDS. THEY FORCED US T' BE THERE AT THE EXECUTION.
WATCHING THAT POOR GIRL'S HEAD TUMBLE INTO THE PIT, I THOUGHT T' MYSELF...
*WHY?* WHY DIDN'T I TRY TO STOP HER WHEN I HAD TH' CHANCE? IF WE'D SENT HER BACK TO THE BROTHEL, HELL, YEAH...
...THERE'D HAVE BEEN A *REAL BEATING* WAITING FOR HER, BUT SHE WOULDN'T HAVE BEEN *DEAD*.
IT'S HARD ENOUGH ON *ME*. BUT MY WIFE...
...SHE STILL SEES IT IN HER DREAMS.
SO WHEN A YOUNG WOMAN LIKE YOU COMES ALONG AND ASKS HER FOR THE SAME DAMN THING, WELL...

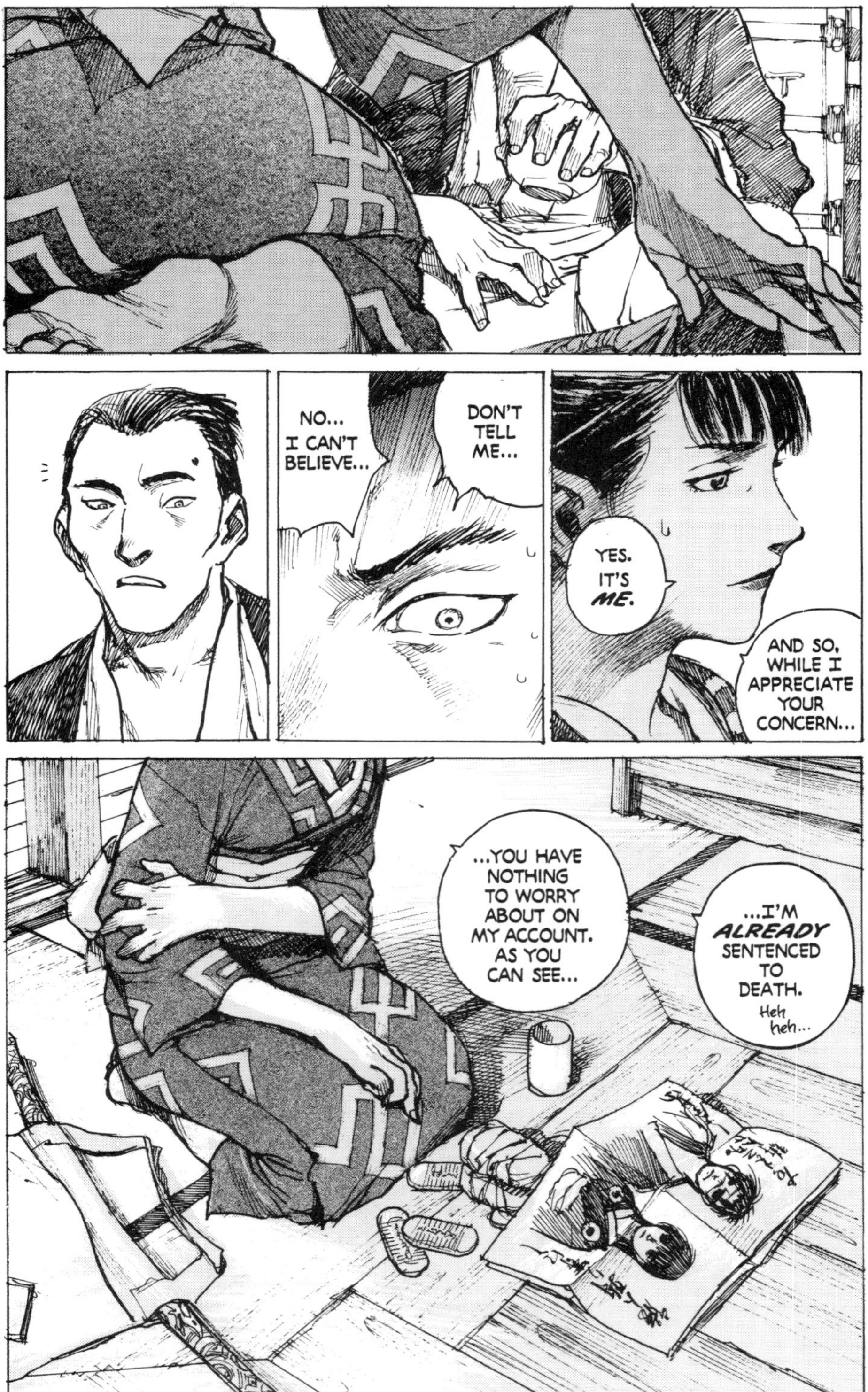
NO... I CAN'T BELIEVE...
DON'T TELL ME...
YES. IT'S *ME*.
AND SO, WHILE I APPRECIATE YOUR CONCERN...
...YOU HAVE NOTHING TO WORRY ABOUT ON MY ACCOUNT. AS YOU CAN SEE...
...I'M *ALREADY* SENTENCED TO DEATH.
Heh heh...

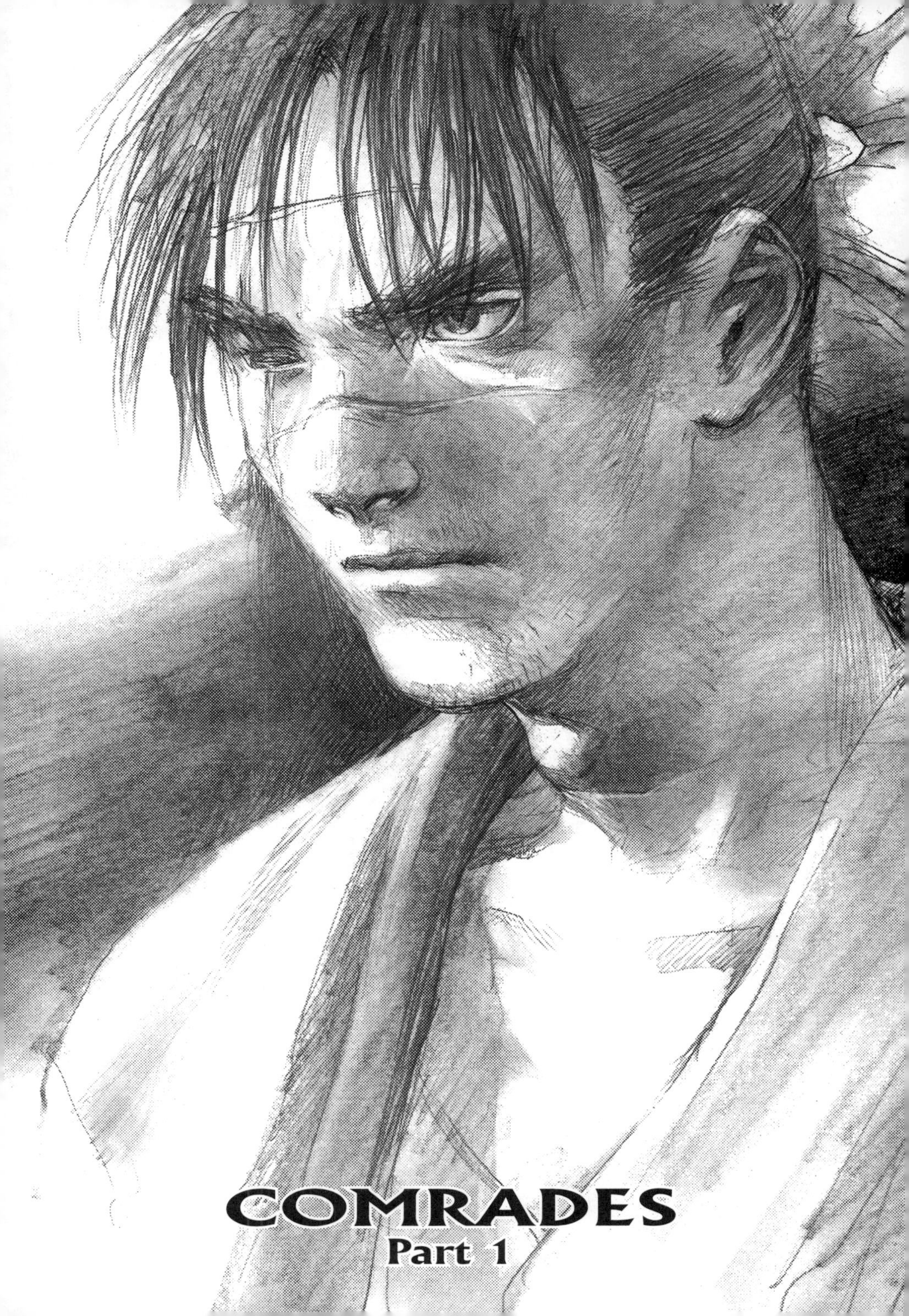

# COMRADES
## Part 1

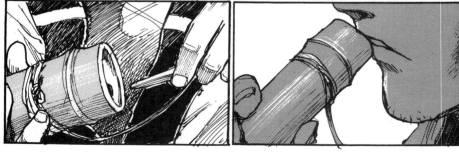

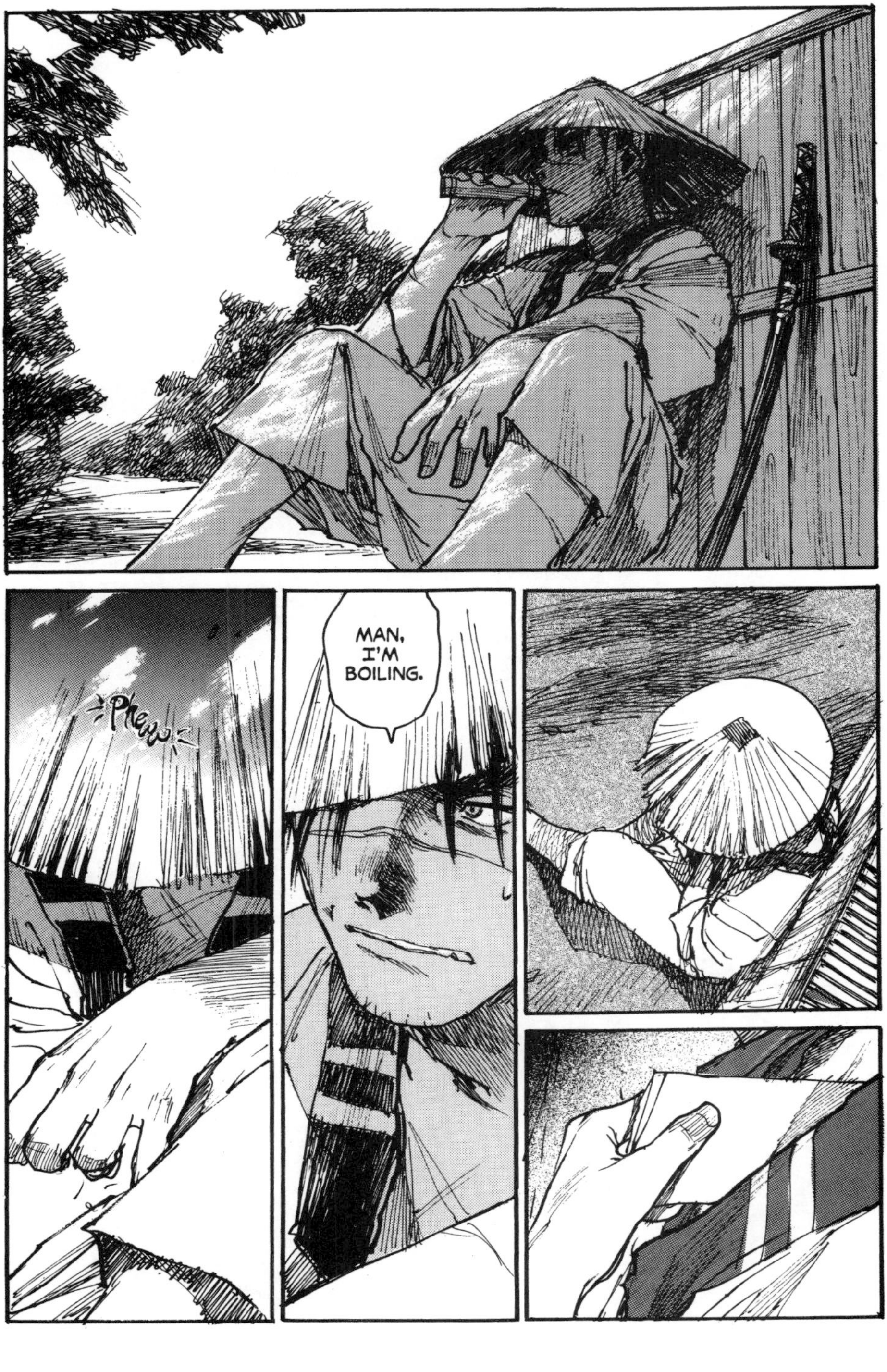

Phew
MAN, I'M BOILING.

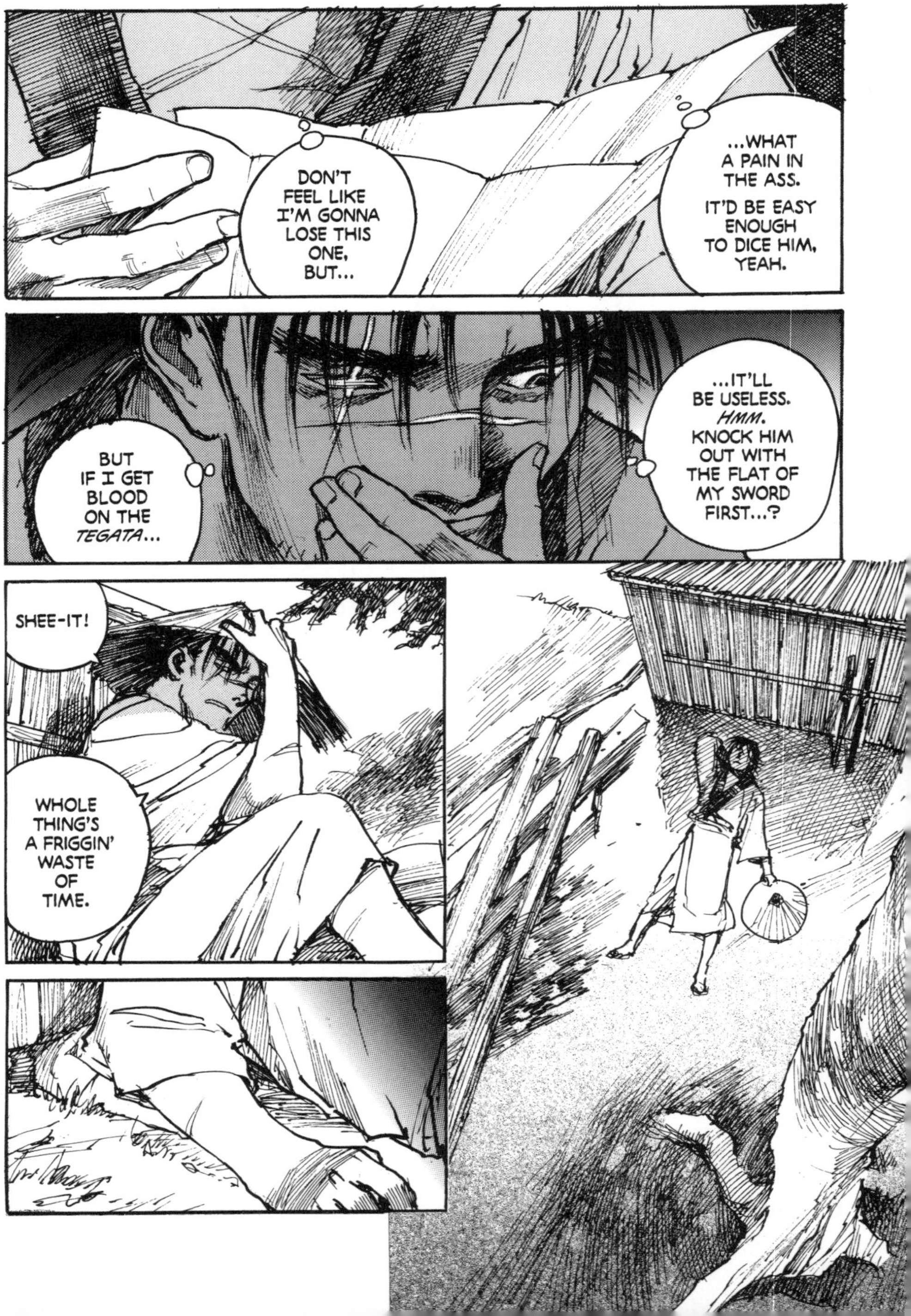
DON'T FEEL LIKE I'M GONNA LOSE THIS ONE, BUT...
...WHAT A PAIN IN THE ASS.
IT'D BE EASY ENOUGH TO DICE HIM, YEAH.
BUT IF I GET BLOOD ON THE *TEGATA*...
...IT'LL BE USELESS. *HMM.* KNOCK HIM OUT WITH THE FLAT OF MY SWORD FIRST...?
SHEE-IT!
WHOLE THING'S A FRIGGIN' WASTE OF TIME.

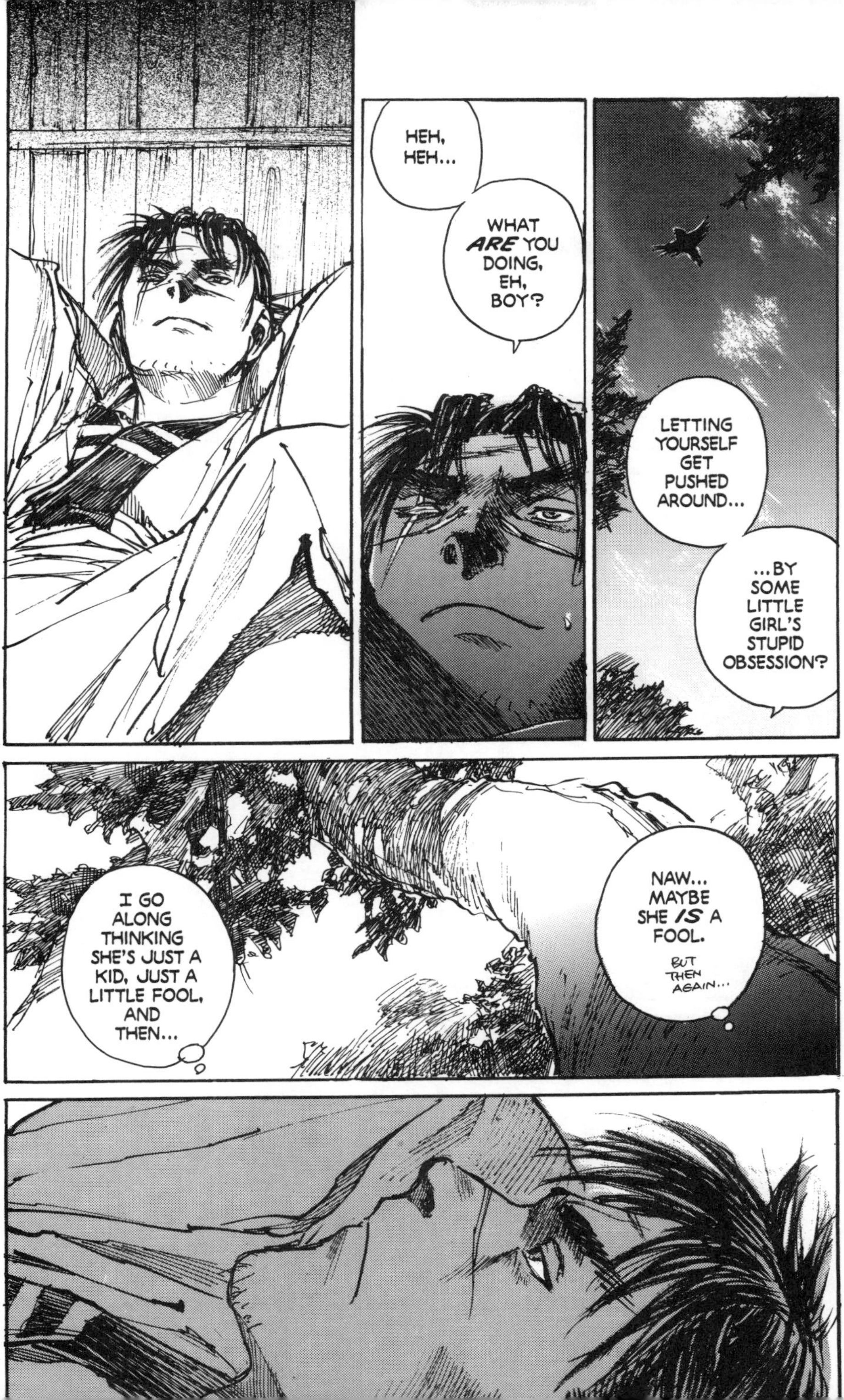
HEH, HEH...
WHAT ARE YOU DOING, EH, BOY?
LETTING YOURSELF GET PUSHED AROUND...
...BY SOME LITTLE GIRL'S STUPID OBSESSION?
I GO ALONG THINKING SHE'S JUST A KID, JUST A LITTLE FOOL, AND THEN...
NAW... MAYBE SHE IS A FOOL.
BUT THEN AGAIN...

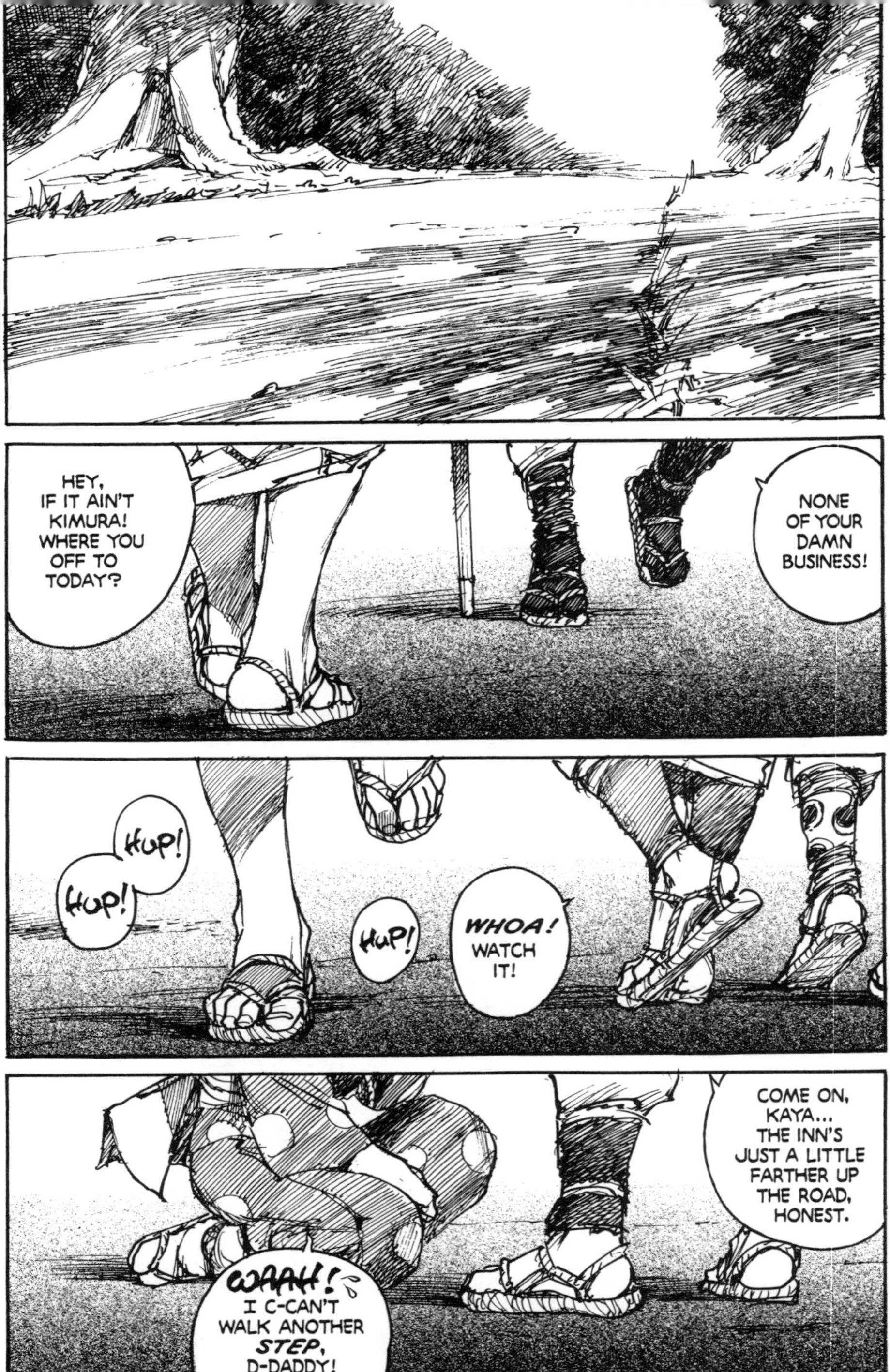
HEY, IF IT AIN'T KIMURA! WHERE YOU OFF TO TODAY?
NONE OF YOUR DAMN BUSINESS!
HUP!
HUP!
HUP!
WHOA! WATCH IT!
COME ON, KAYA... THE INN'S JUST A LITTLE FARTHER UP THE ROAD, HONEST.
WAAH! I C-CAN'T WALK ANOTHER STEP, D-DADDY!

HUH? YOU GOTTA TAKE A LEAK? SO JUST GO OFF INTO THOSE BUSHES!
SHH!! GEEZ, TELL EVERYONE, WHY DON'T YOU?!
LOOK, SIR! WE CAN ALREADY SEE MOUNT FUJI!
HOH! WE'VE MADE GOOD TIME, THEN.

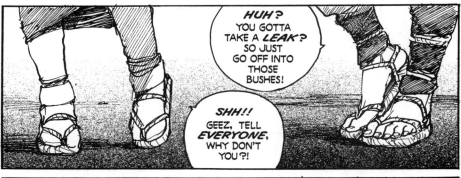

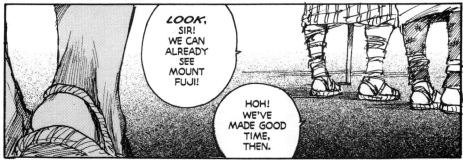

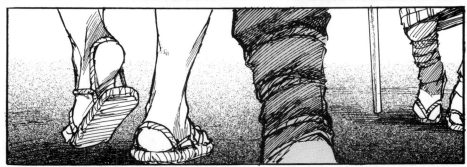

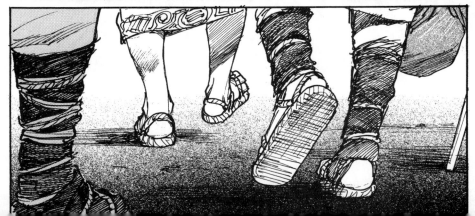

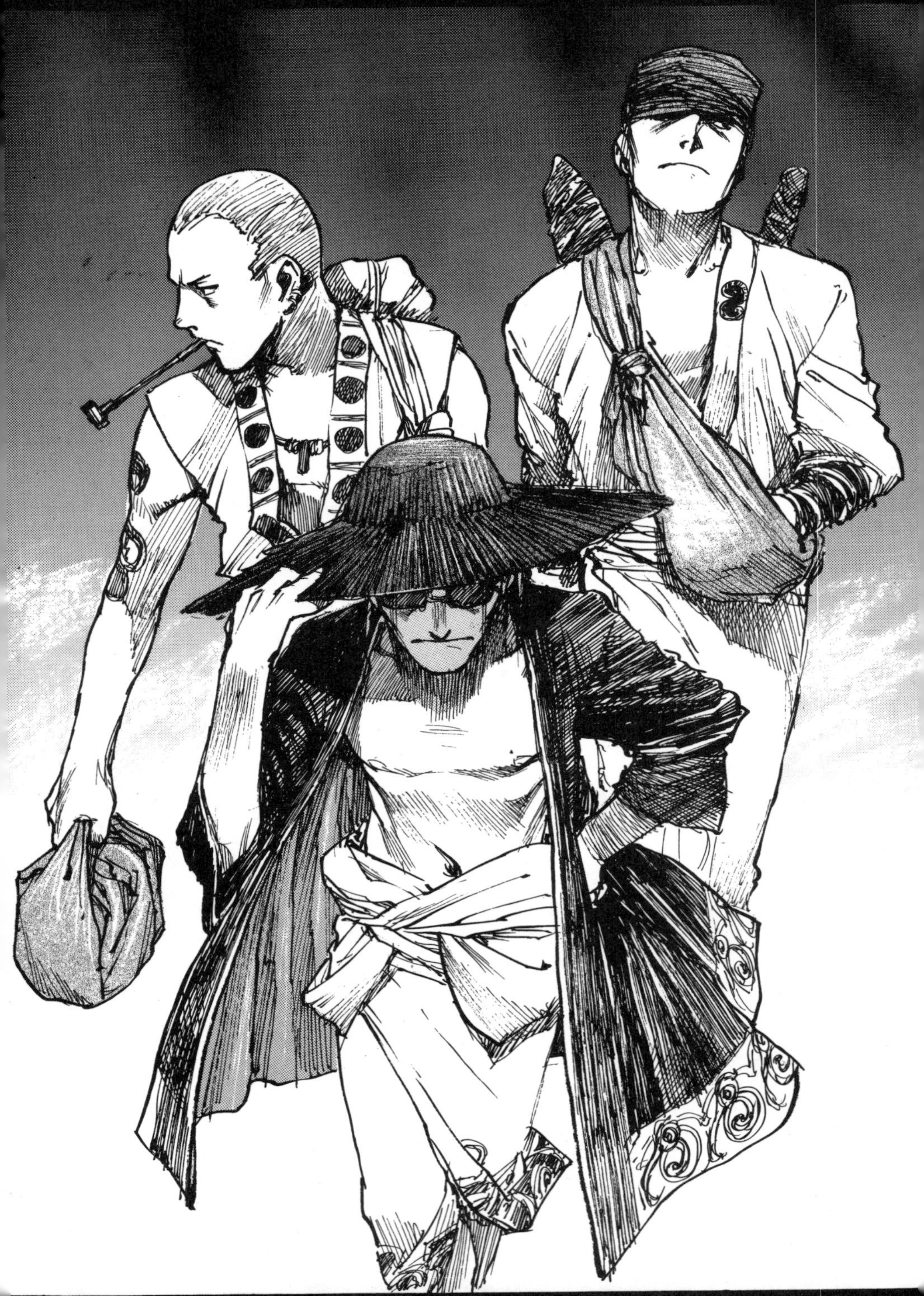

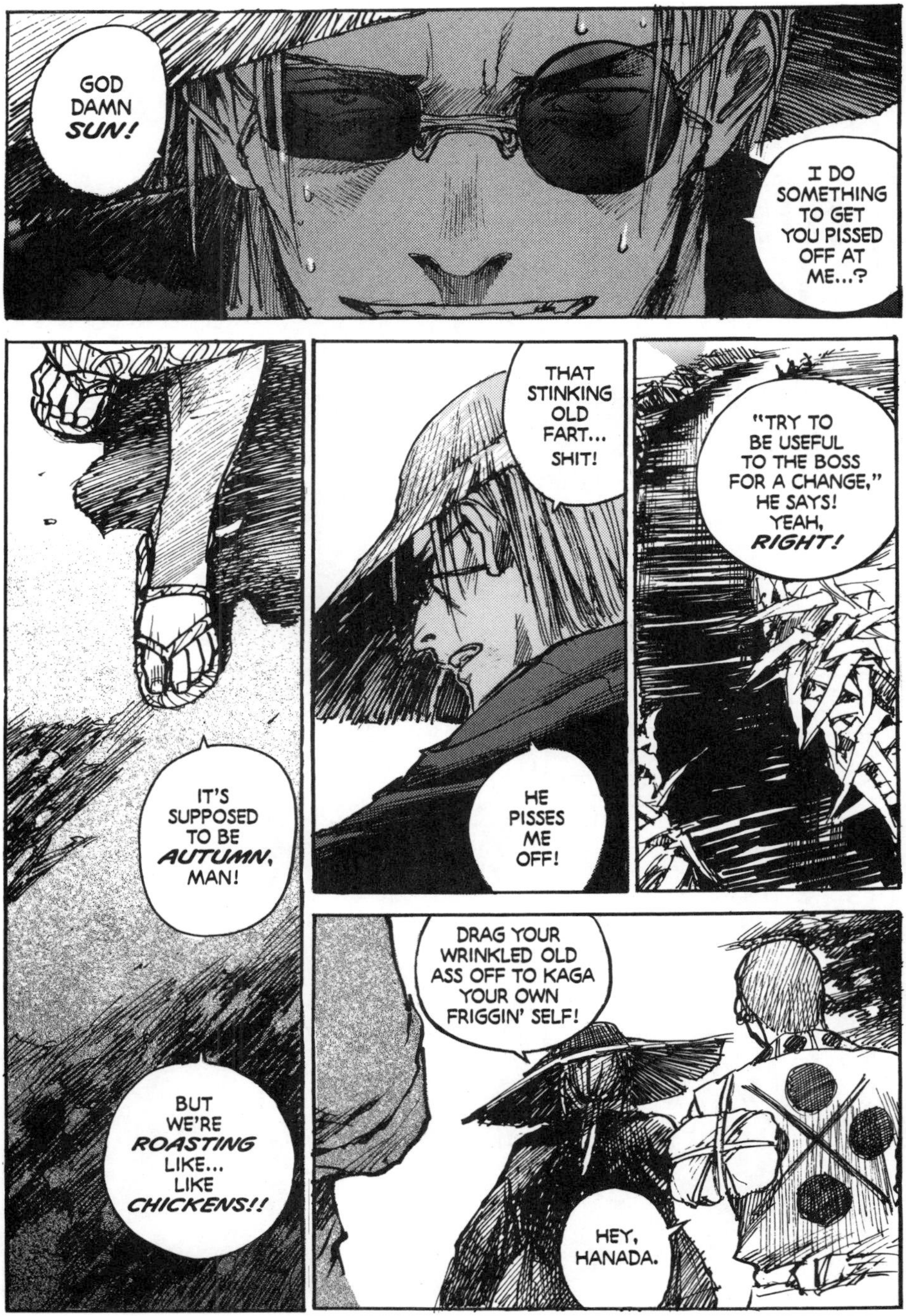
GOD DAMN *SUN!*
I DO SOMETHING TO GET YOU PISSED OFF AT ME...?
IT'S SUPPOSED TO BE *AUTUMN*, MAN!
BUT WE'RE *ROASTING* LIKE... LIKE *CHICKENS!!*
THAT STINKING OLD FART... SHIT!
HE PISSES ME OFF!
"TRY TO BE USEFUL TO THE BOSS FOR A CHANGE," HE SAYS! YEAH, *RIGHT!*
DRAG YOUR WRINKLED OLD ASS OFF TO KAGA YOUR OWN FRIGGIN' SELF!
HEY, HANADA.

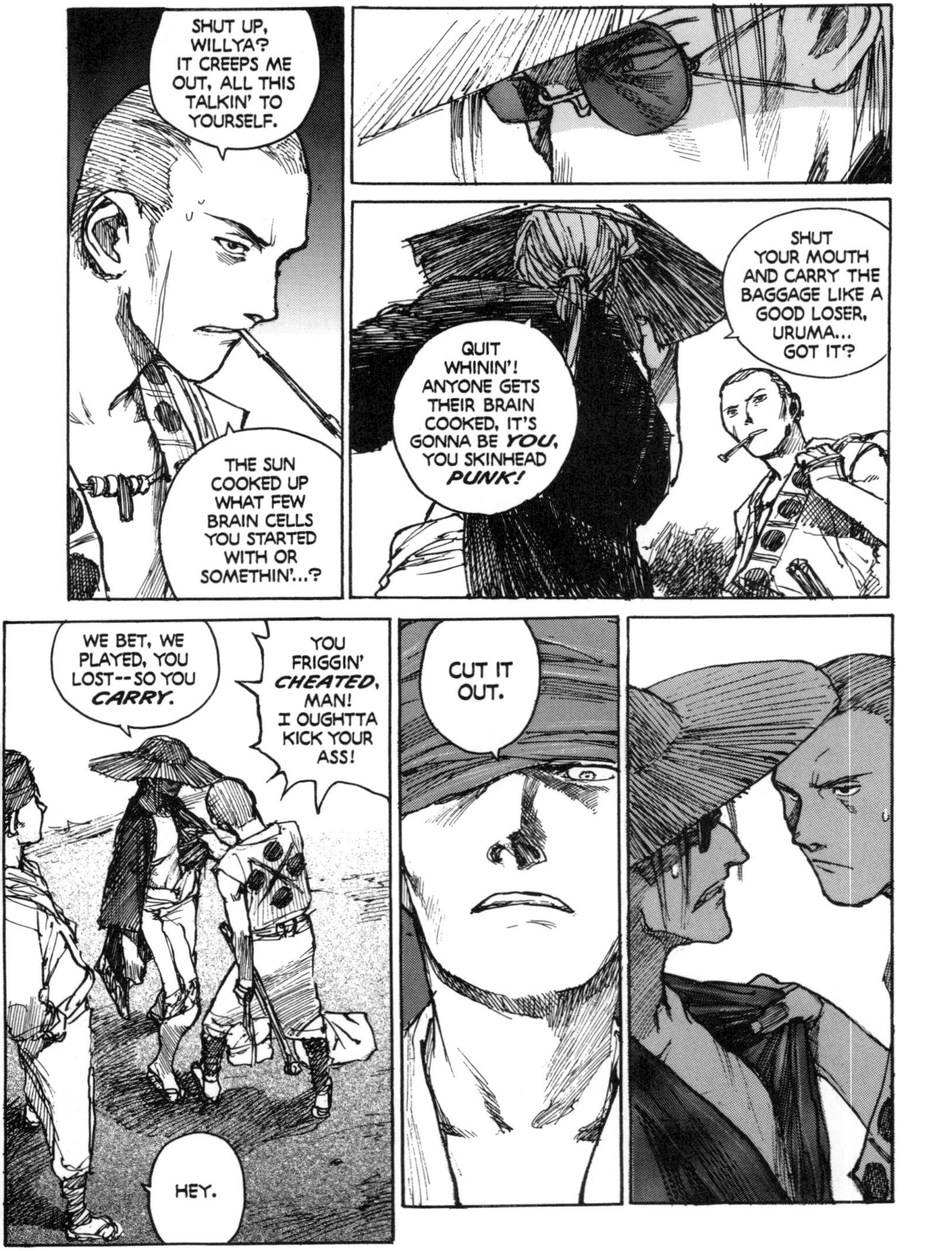
SHUT UP, WILLYA? IT CREEPS ME OUT, ALL THIS TALKIN' TO YOURSELF.
THE SUN COOKED UP WHAT FEW BRAIN CELLS YOU STARTED WITH OR SOMETHIN'...?
QUIT WHININ'! ANYONE GETS THEIR BRAIN COOKED, IT'S GONNA BE *YOU*, YOU SKINHEAD *PUNK!*
SHUT YOUR MOUTH AND CARRY THE BAGGAGE LIKE A GOOD LOSER, URUMA... GOT IT?
WE BET, WE PLAYED, YOU LOST--SO YOU *CARRY*.
YOU FRIGGIN' *CHEATED*, MAN! I OUGHTTA KICK YOUR ASS!
HEY.
CUT IT OUT.

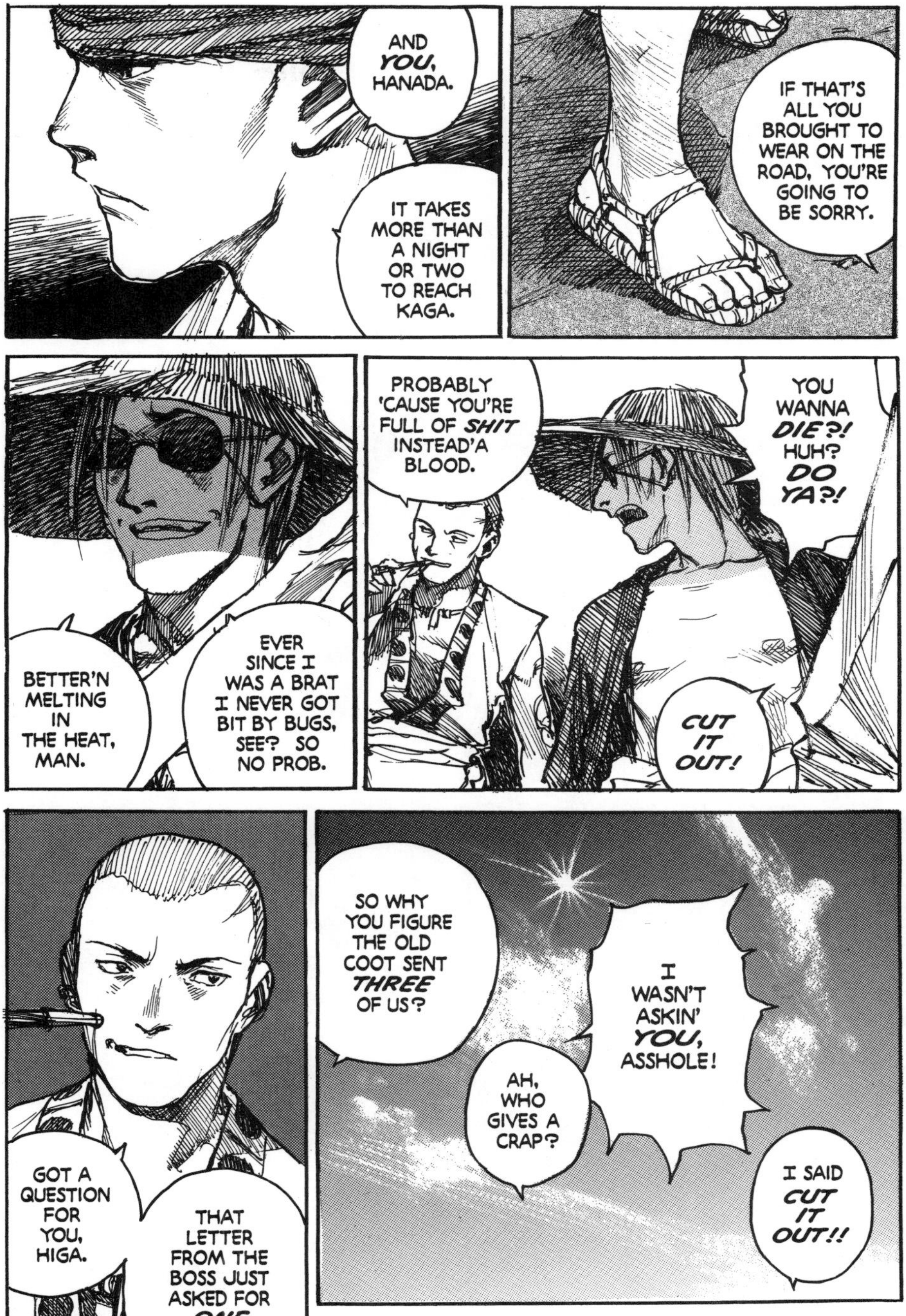
AND YOU, HANADA.
IT TAKES MORE THAN A NIGHT OR TWO TO REACH KAGA.
IF THAT'S ALL YOU BROUGHT TO WEAR ON THE ROAD, YOU'RE GOING TO BE SORRY.
BETTER'N MELTING IN THE HEAT, MAN.
EVER SINCE I WAS A BRAT I NEVER GOT BIT BY BUGS, SEE? SO NO PROB.
PROBABLY 'CAUSE YOU'RE FULL OF SHIT INSTEAD'A BLOOD.
YOU WANNA DIE?! HUH? DO YA?!
CUT IT OUT!
GOT A QUESTION FOR YOU, HIGA.
THAT LETTER FROM THE BOSS JUST ASKED FOR ONE GUY.
SO WHY YOU FIGURE THE OLD COOT SENT THREE OF US?
I WASN'T ASKIN' YOU, ASSHOLE!
AH, WHO GIVES A CRAP?
I SAID CUT IT OUT!!

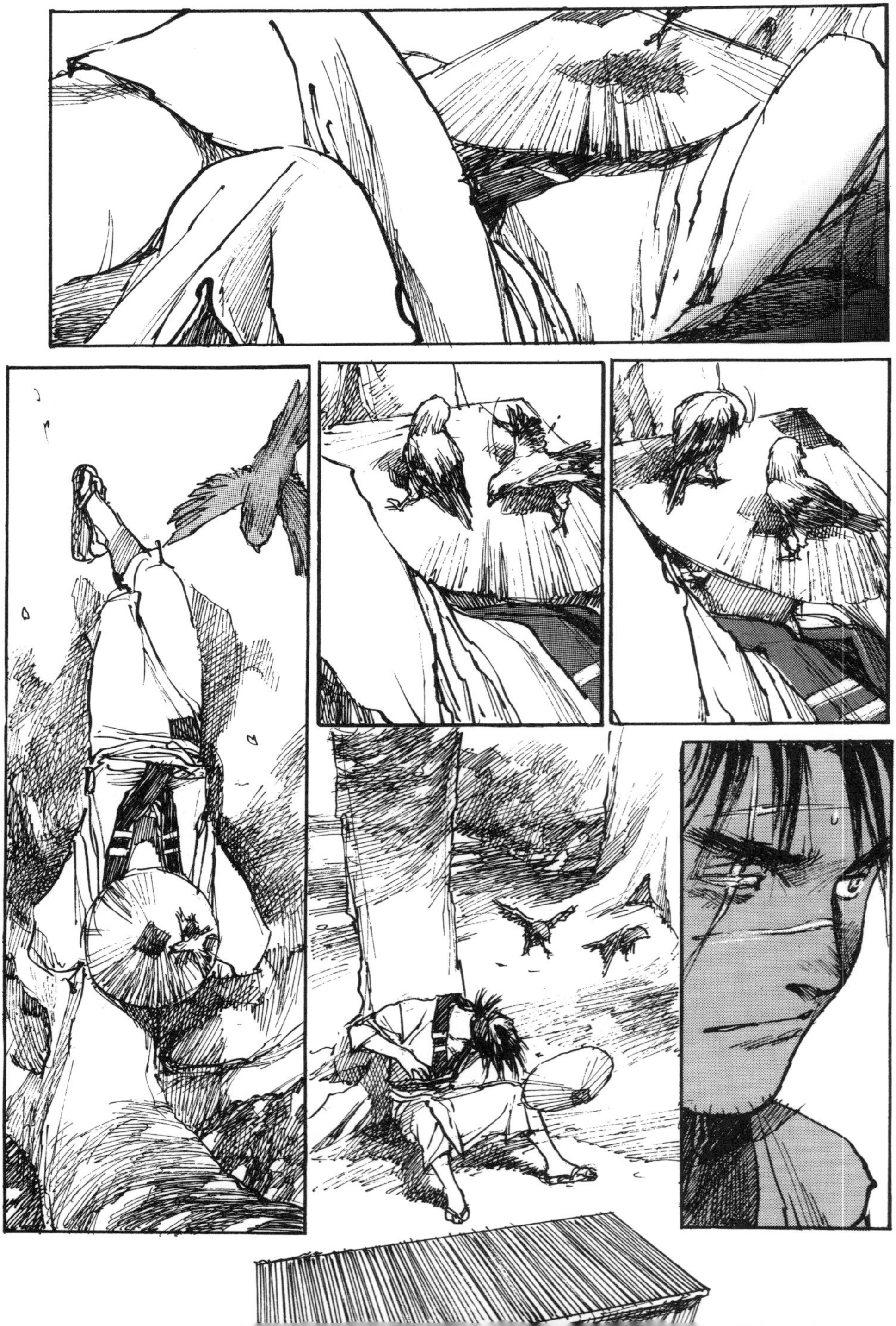

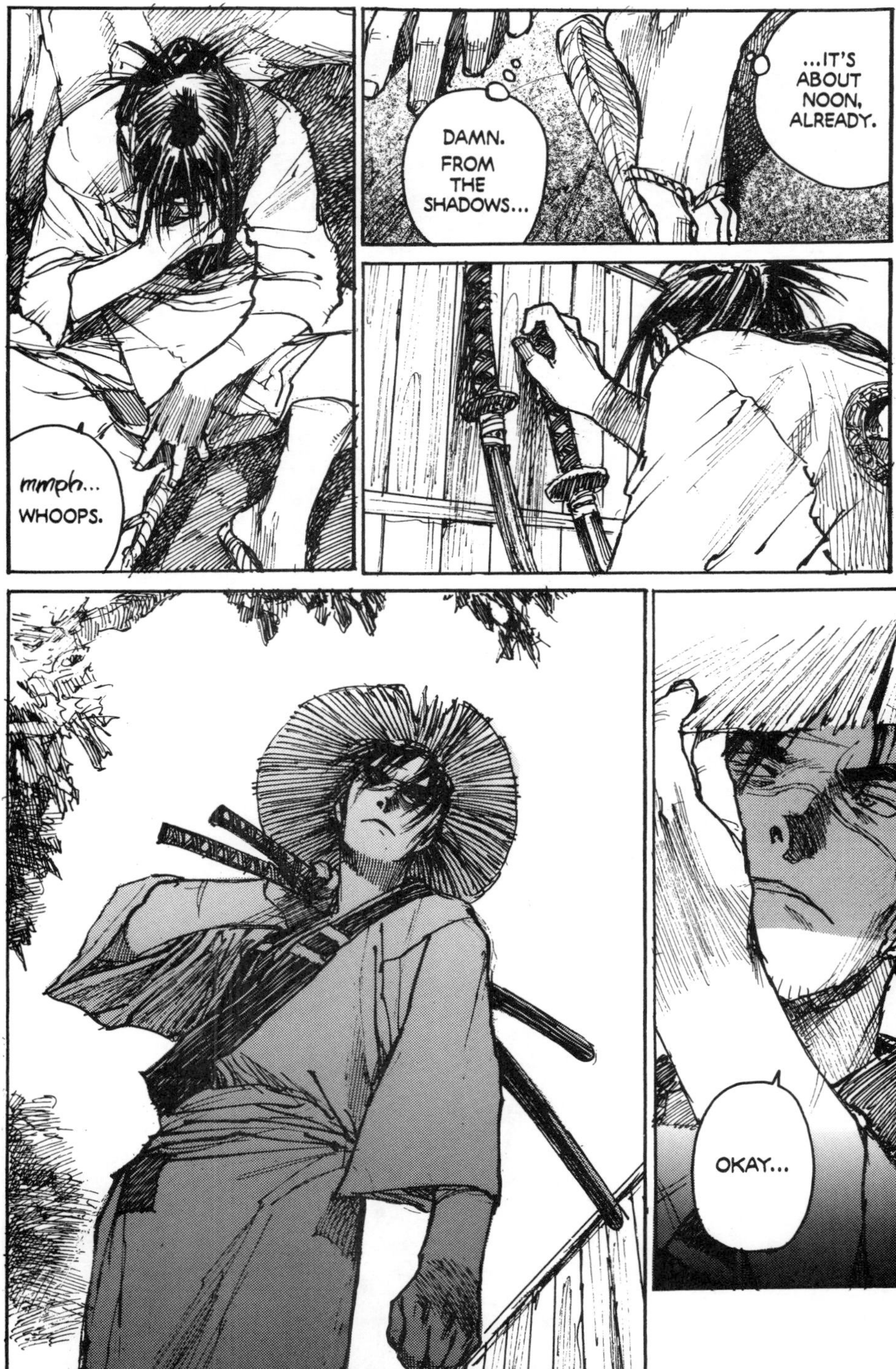
mmph... WHOOPS.
DAMN. FROM THE SHADOWS...
...IT'S ABOUT NOON, ALREADY.
OKAY...

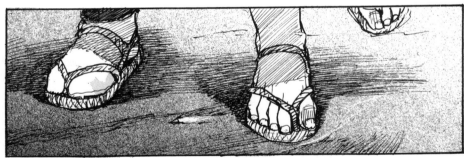

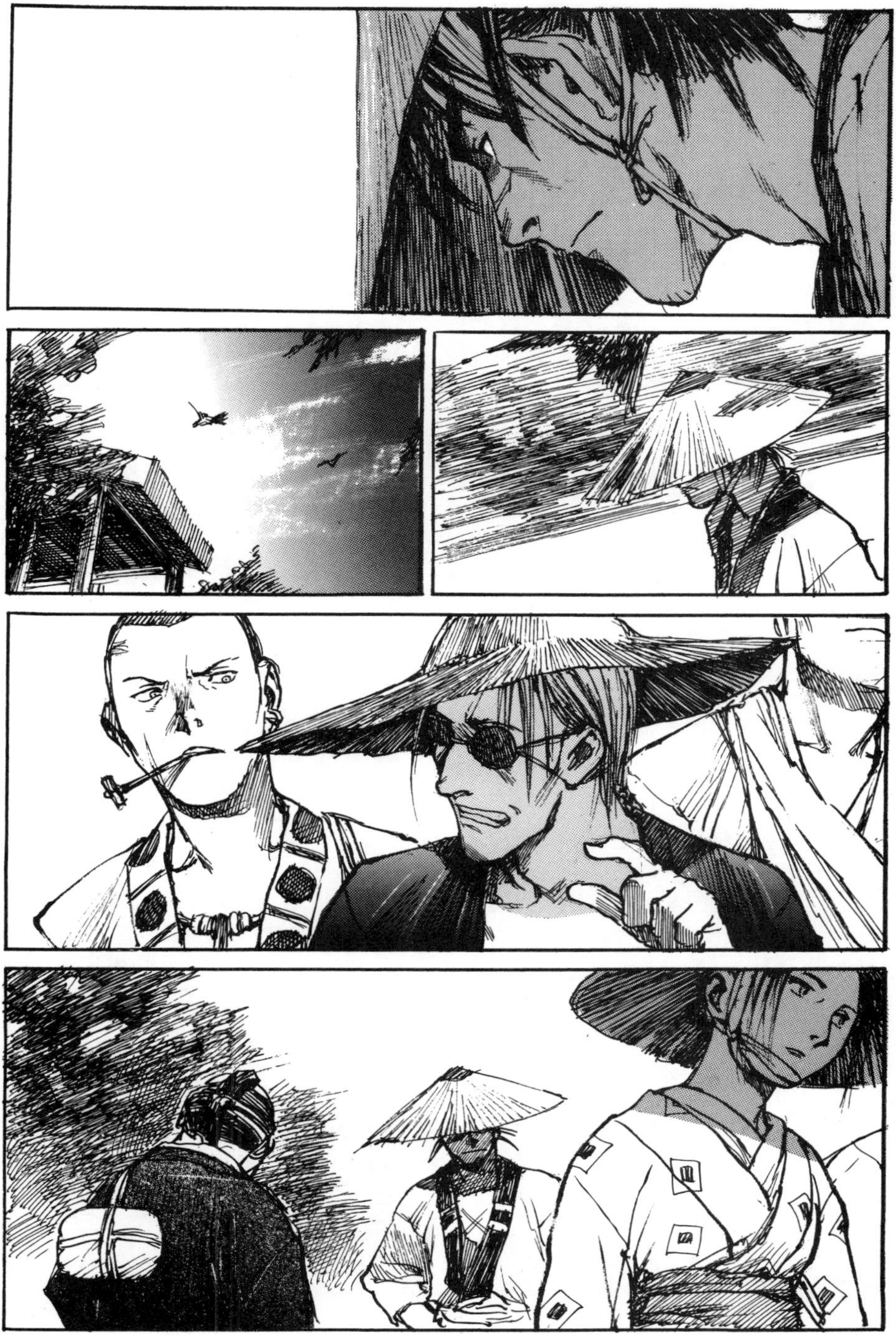

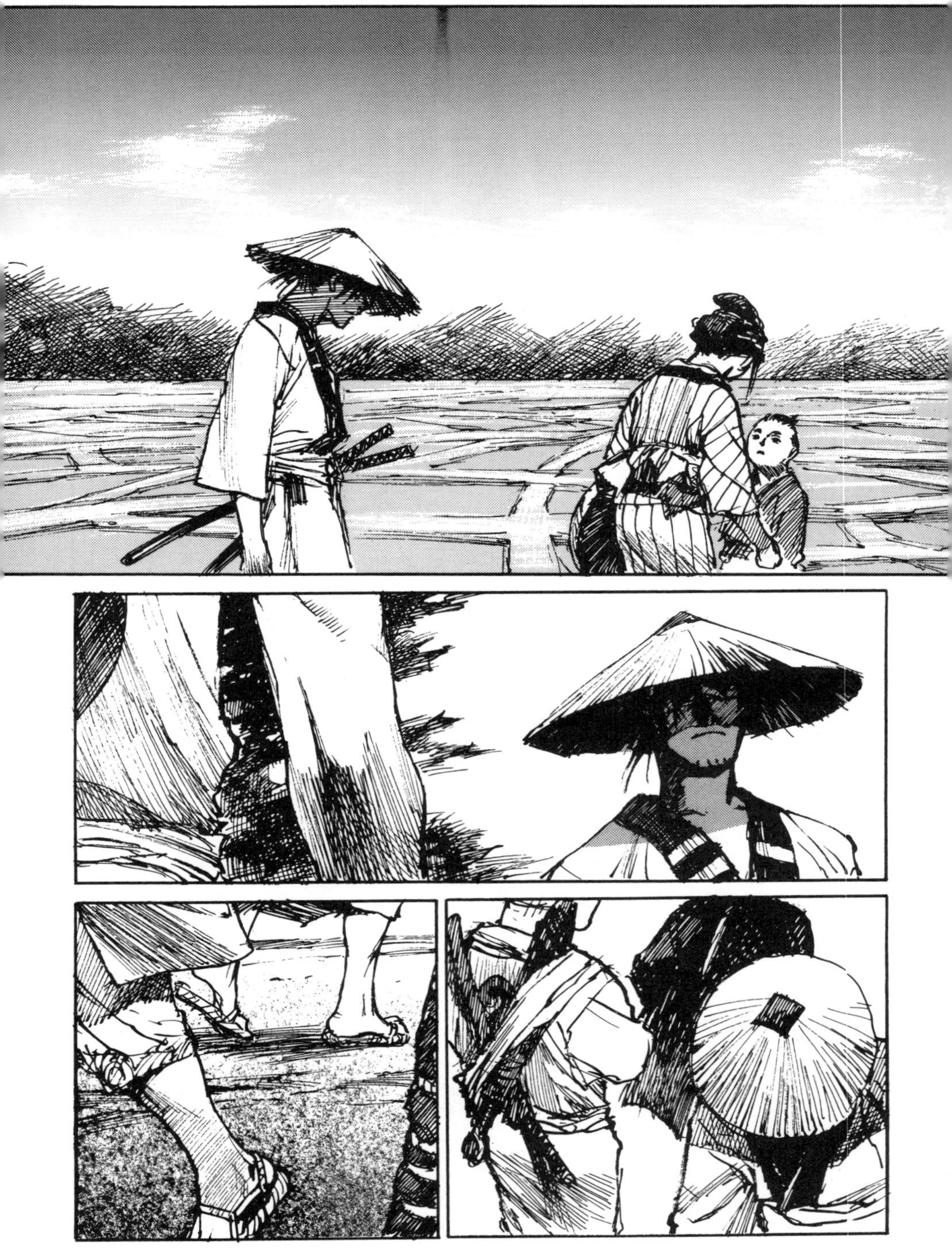

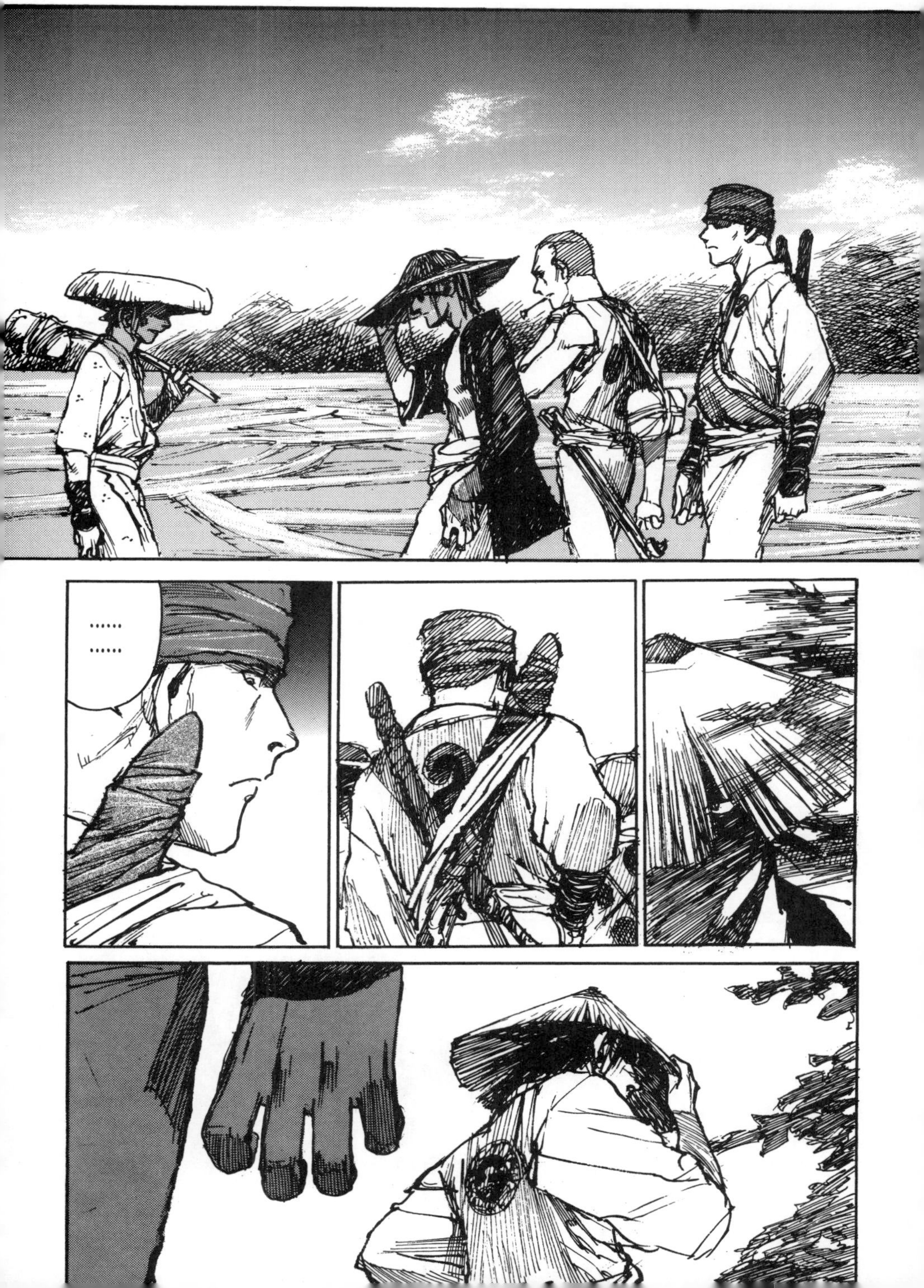
......
......

HYAKURIN, YOU DEVIOUS BITCH!

HEH... ONE GUY, OKAY... *THREE GUYS* IS A DIFFERENT STORY, GIRL!

FROM THOSE CRAZY GET-UPS...

HELL. GUESS I DON'T NEED TO ASK.

*HMM...* WAIT A SEC.

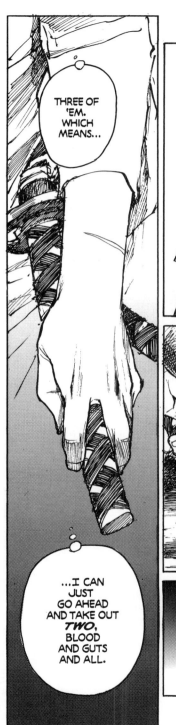

THREE OF
'EM.
WHICH
MEANS...

...I CAN
JUST
GO AHEAD
AND TAKE OUT
*TWO*,
BLOOD
AND GUTS
AND ALL.

HEH,
HEH.
YEAH...

...BE
NICE TO
HAVE
A LITTLE
*FUN.*

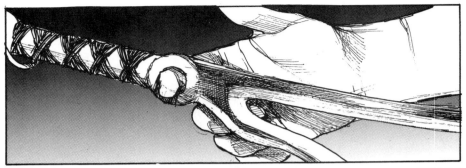

=huffh=

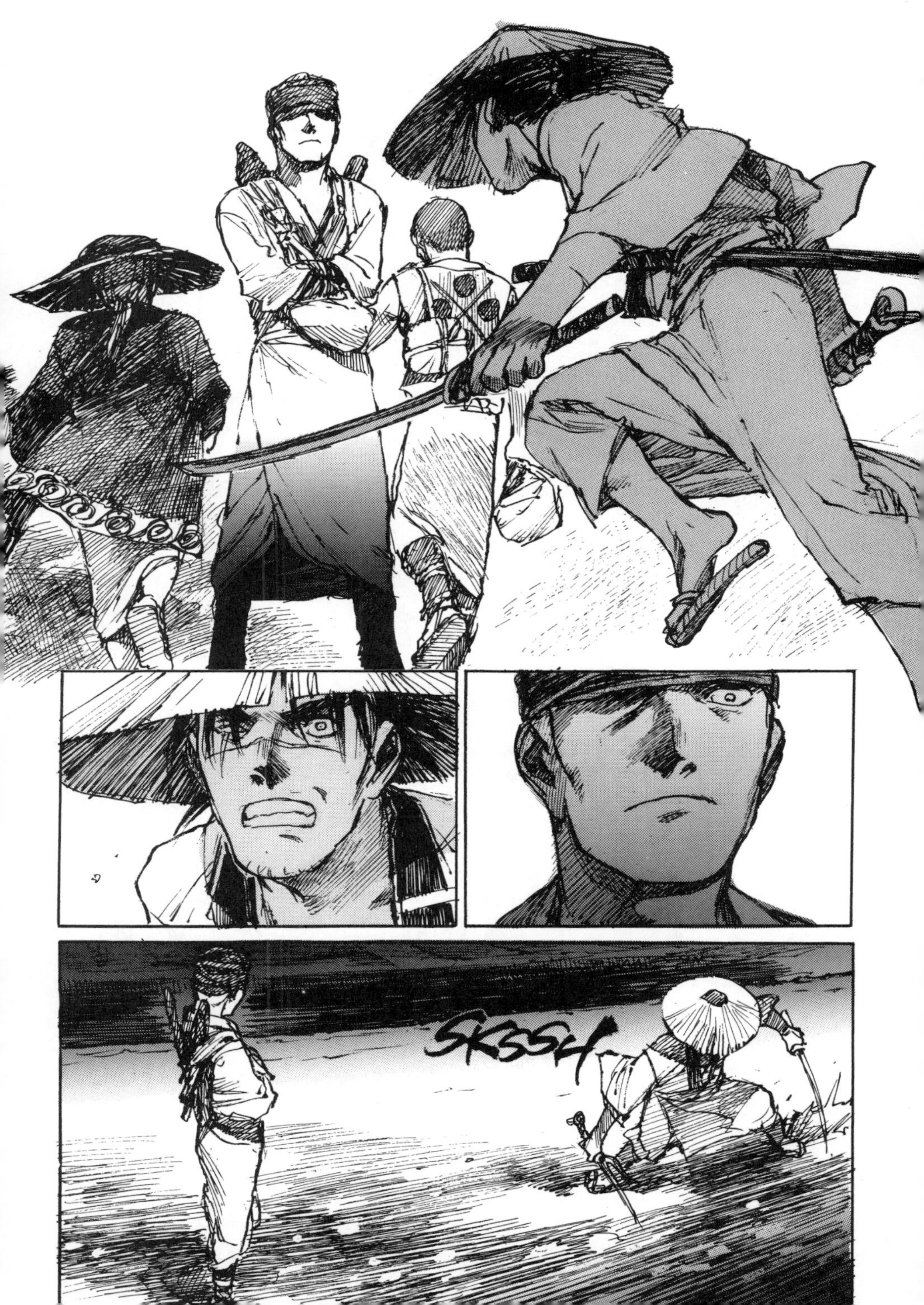
SKSSH

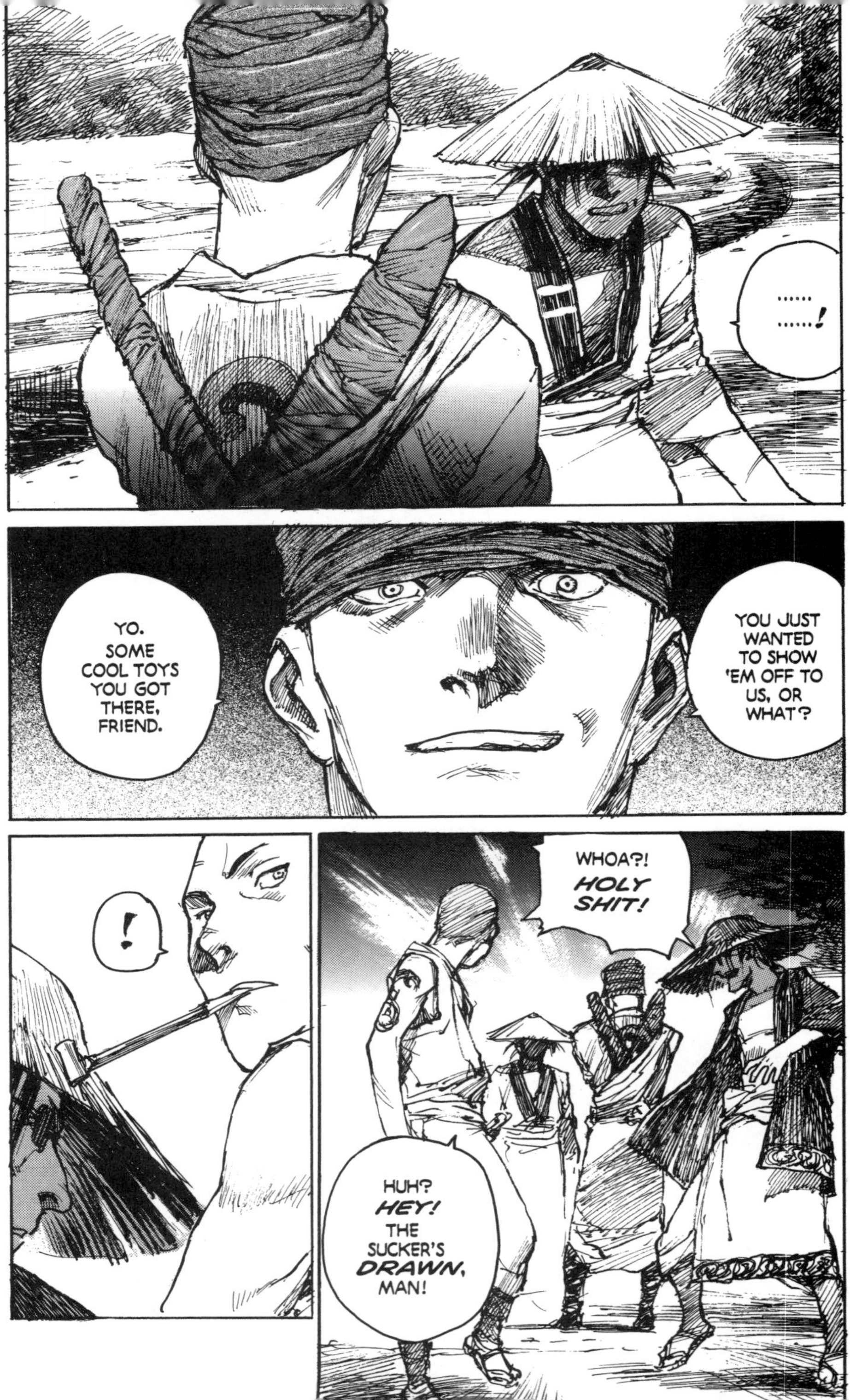
......
......!
YO. SOME COOL TOYS YOU GOT THERE, FRIEND.
YOU JUST WANTED TO SHOW 'EM OFF TO US, OR WHAT?
!
WHOA?! HOLY SHIT!
HUH? HEY! THE SUCKER'S DRAWN, MAN!

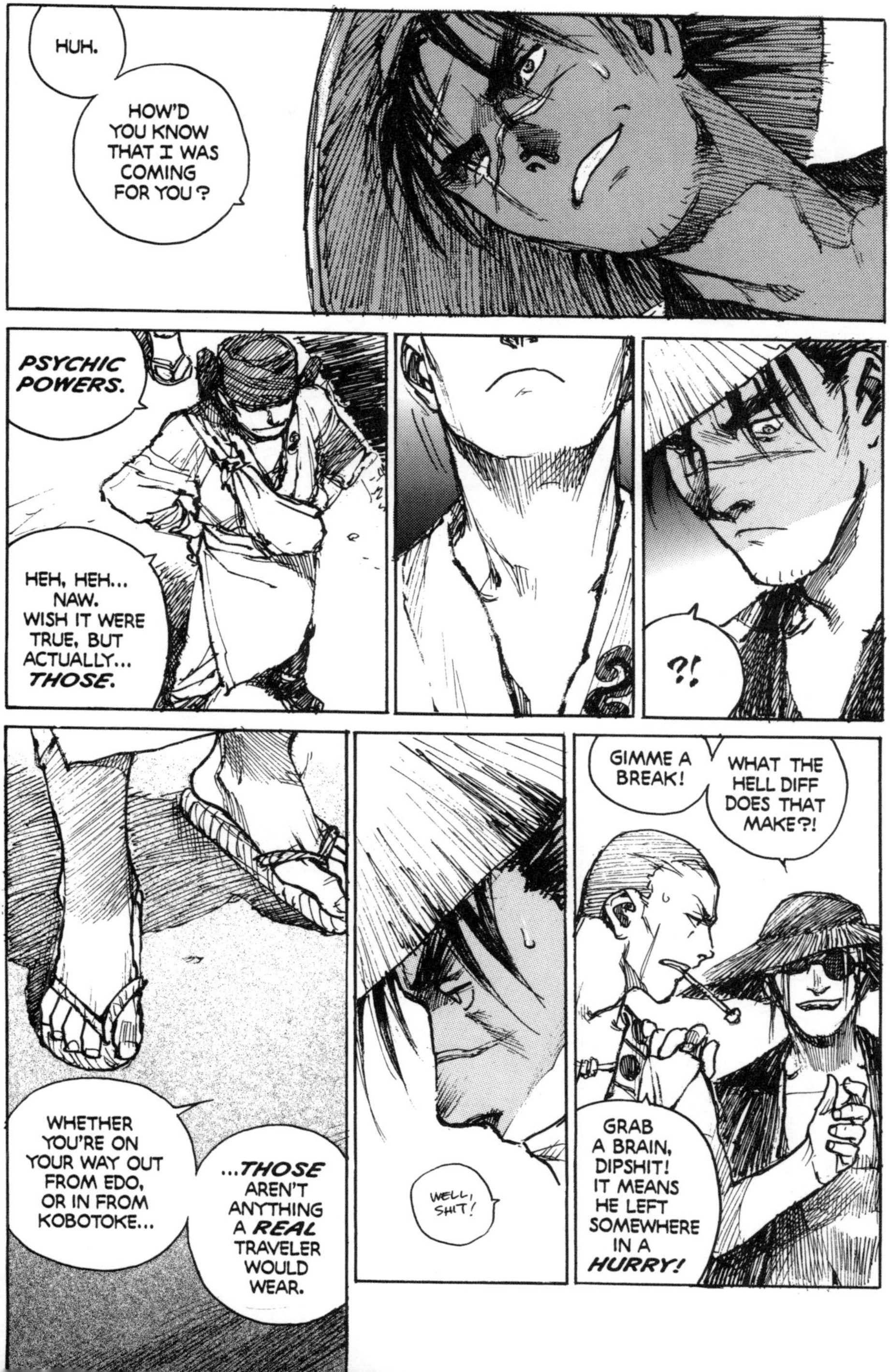
HUH.
HOW'D YOU KNOW THAT I WAS COMING FOR YOU?
PSYCHIC POWERS.
HEH, HEH... NAW. WISH IT WERE TRUE, BUT ACTUALLY... THOSE.
?!
WHETHER YOU'RE ON YOUR WAY OUT FROM EDO, OR IN FROM KOBOTOKE...
...THOSE AREN'T ANYTHING A REAL TRAVELER WOULD WEAR.
WELL, SHIT!
GIMME A BREAK!
WHAT THE HELL DIFF DOES THAT MAKE?!
GRAB A BRAIN, DIPSHIT! IT MEANS HE LEFT SOMEWHERE IN A HURRY!

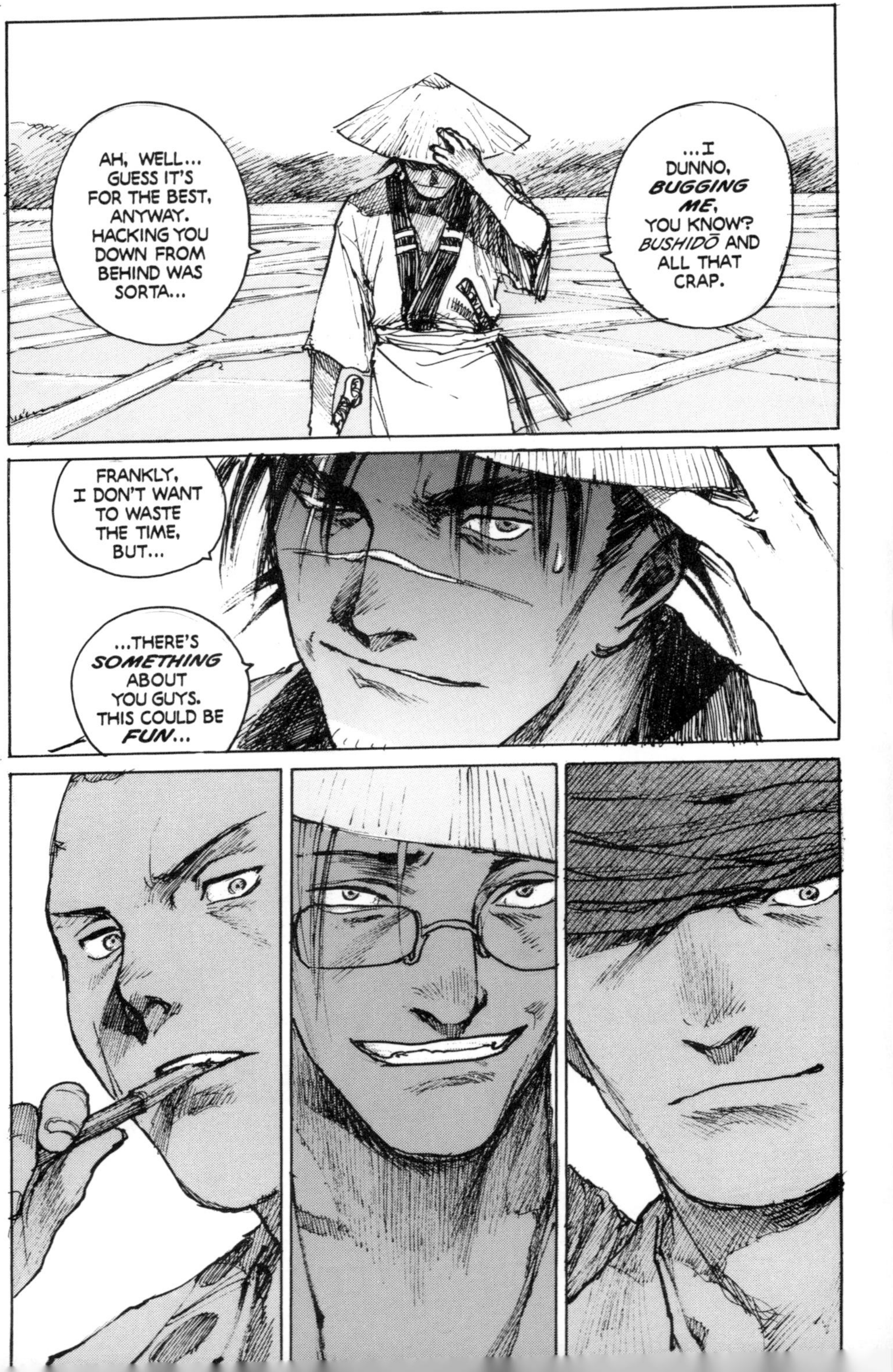
AH, WELL... GUESS IT'S FOR THE BEST, ANYWAY. HACKING YOU DOWN FROM BEHIND WAS SORTA...
...I DUNNO, BUGGING ME, YOU KNOW? BUSHIDŌ AND ALL THAT CRAP.
FRANKLY, I DON'T WANT TO WASTE THE TIME, BUT...
...THERE'S SOMETHING ABOUT YOU GUYS. THIS COULD BE FUN...

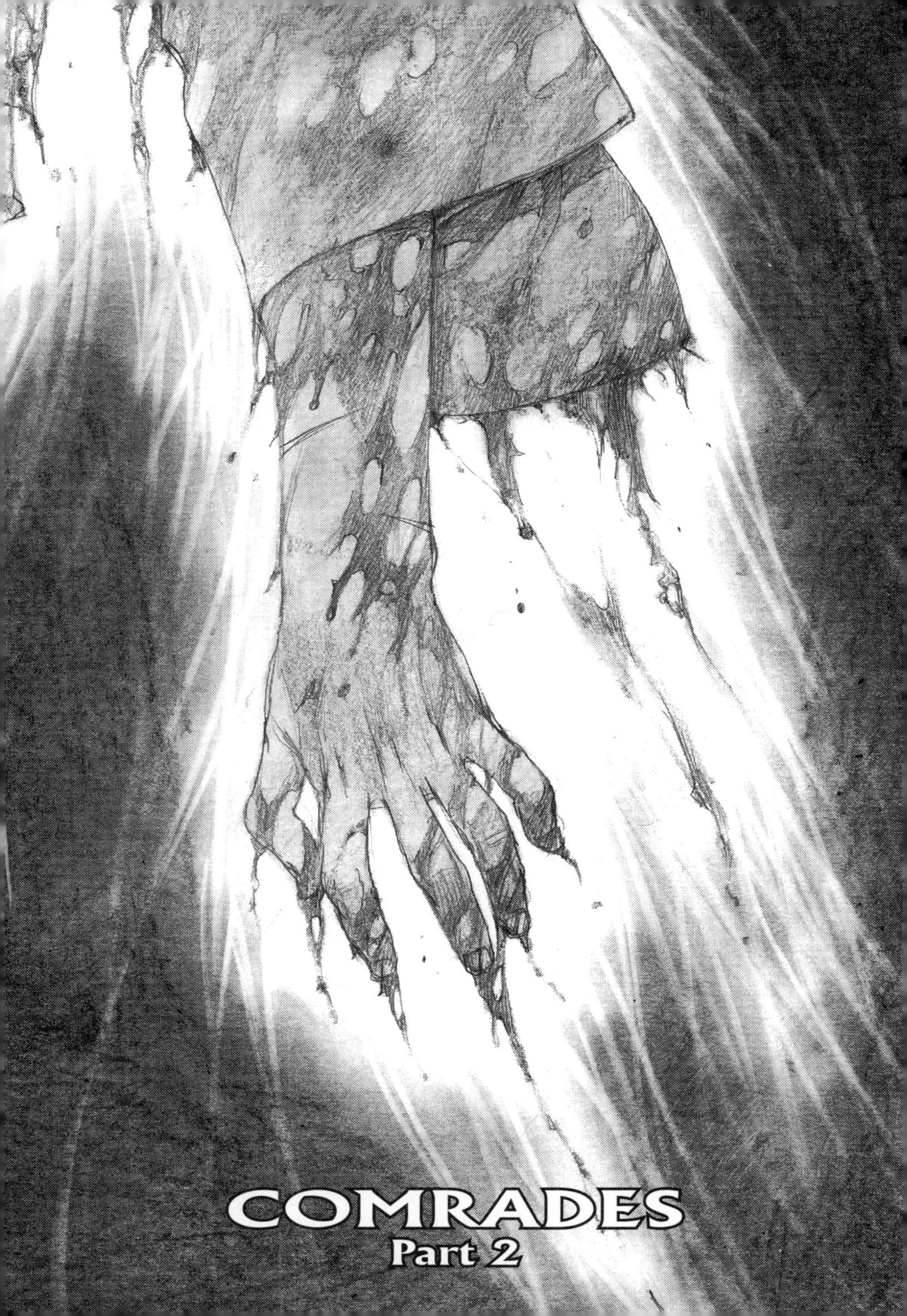

# COMRADES
## Part 2

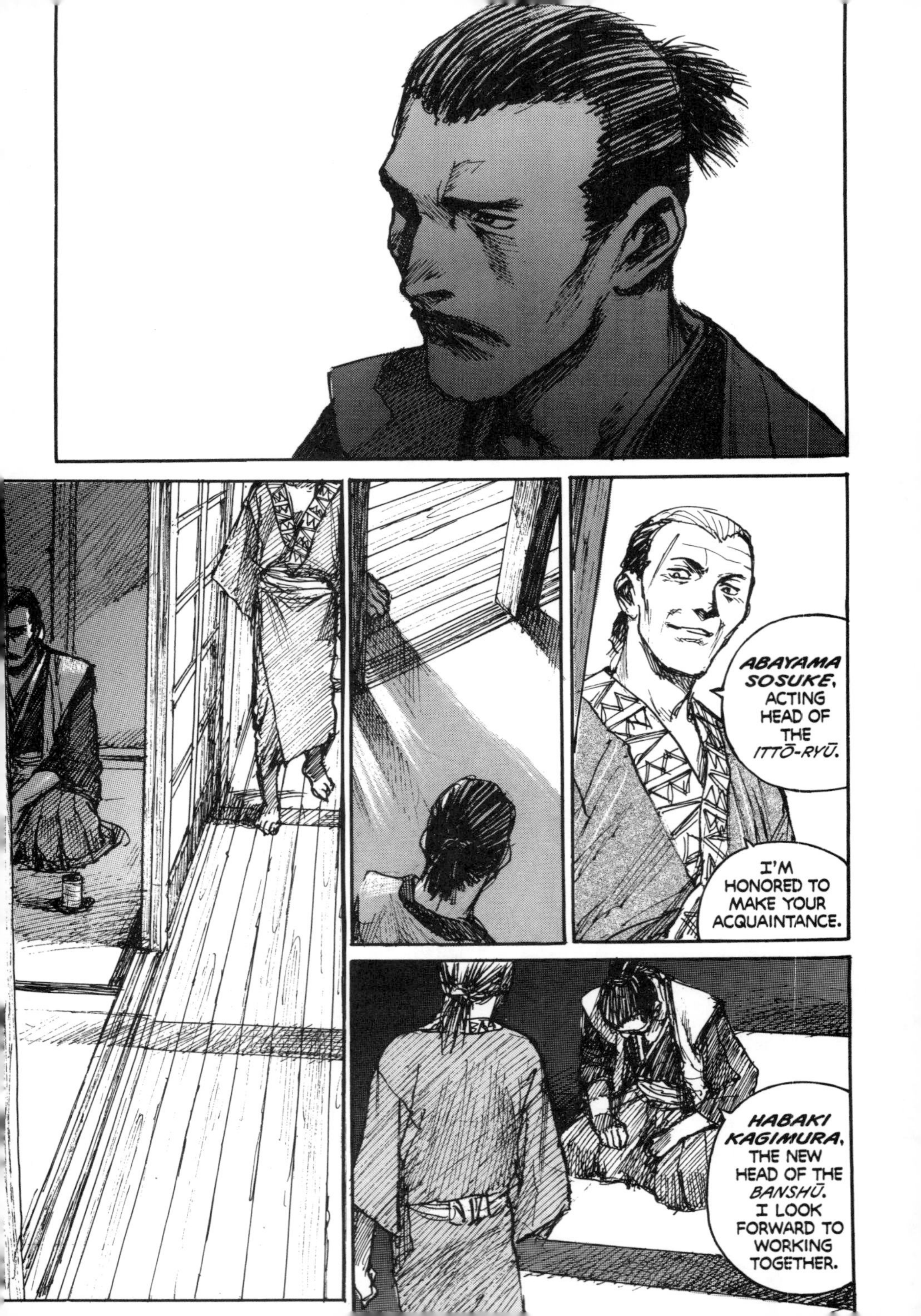
ABAYAMA SOSUKE, ACTING HEAD OF THE ITTŌ-RYŪ.
I'M HONORED TO MAKE YOUR ACQUAINTANCE.
HABAKI KAGIMURA, THE NEW HEAD OF THE BANSHŪ. I LOOK FORWARD TO WORKING TOGETHER.

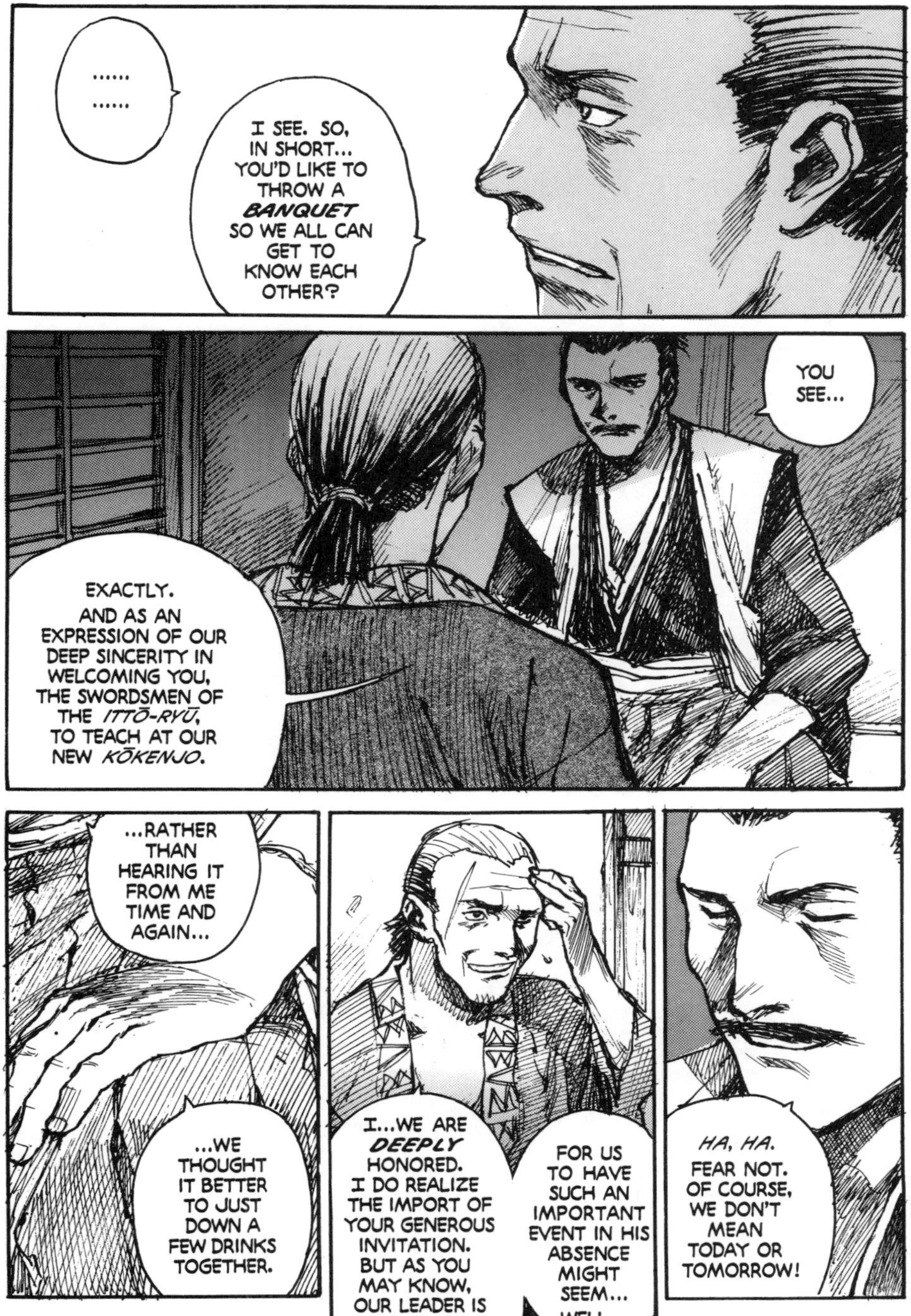
......
......
I SEE. SO, IN SHORT... YOU'D LIKE TO THROW A *BANQUET* SO WE ALL CAN GET TO KNOW EACH OTHER?
EXACTLY. AND AS AN EXPRESSION OF OUR DEEP SINCERITY IN WELCOMING YOU, THE SWORDSMEN OF THE *ITTŌ-RYŪ*, TO TEACH AT OUR NEW *KŌKENJO*.
YOU SEE...
...RATHER THAN HEARING IT FROM ME TIME AND AGAIN...
...WE THOUGHT IT BETTER TO JUST DOWN A FEW DRINKS TOGETHER.
I...WE ARE *DEEPLY* HONORED. I DO REALIZE THE IMPORT OF YOUR GENEROUS INVITATION. BUT AS YOU MAY KNOW, OUR LEADER IS CURRENTLY AWAY ON A JOURNEY.
FOR US TO HAVE SUCH AN IMPORTANT EVENT IN HIS ABSENCE MIGHT SEEM... WELL...
*HA, HA.* FEAR NOT. OF COURSE, WE DON'T MEAN TODAY OR TOMORROW!

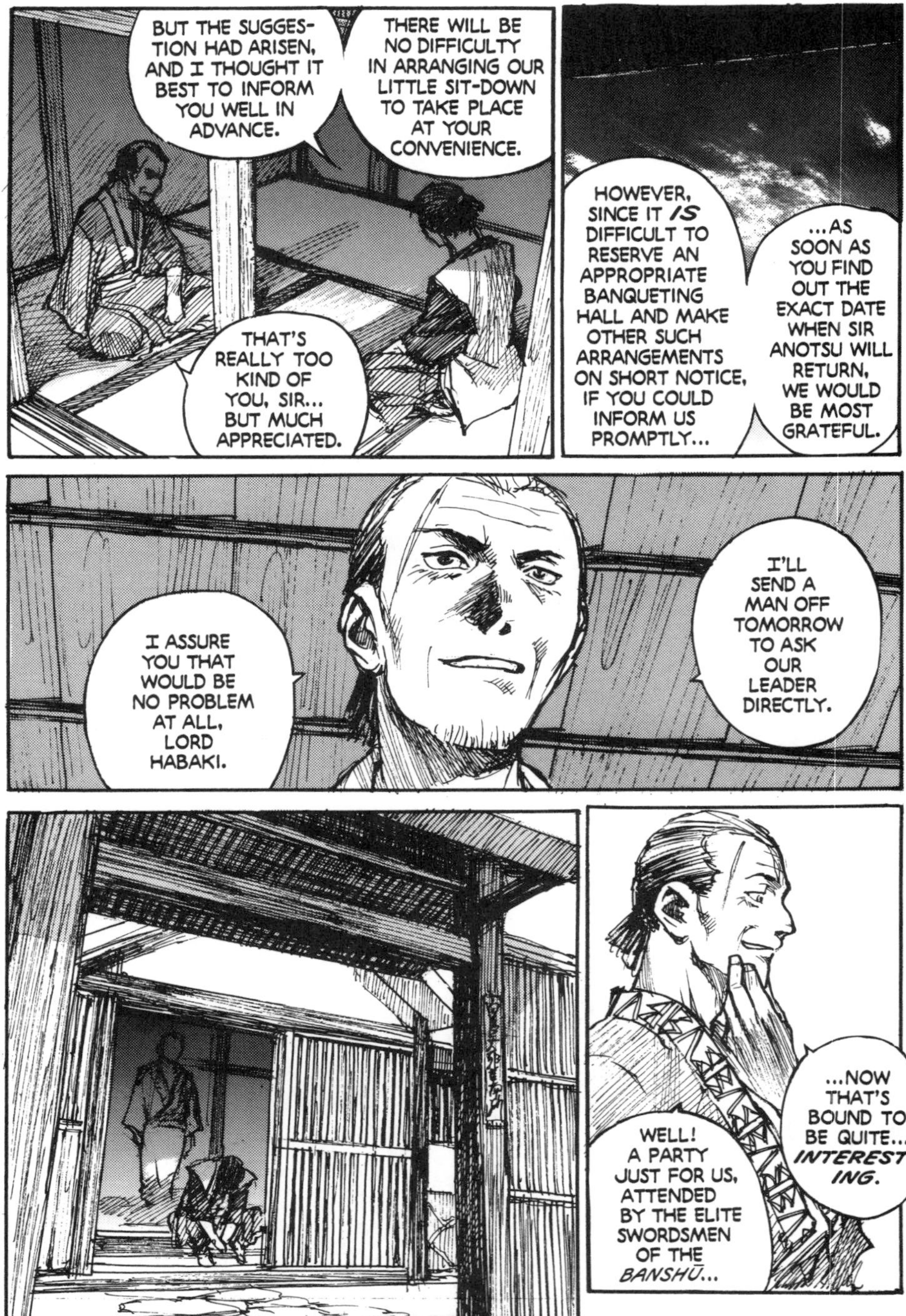
BUT THE SUGGES-TION HAD ARISEN, AND I THOUGHT IT BEST TO INFORM YOU WELL IN ADVANCE.
THERE WILL BE NO DIFFICULTY IN ARRANGING OUR LITTLE SIT-DOWN TO TAKE PLACE AT YOUR CONVENIENCE.
THAT'S REALLY TOO KIND OF YOU, SIR... BUT MUCH APPRECIATED.
HOWEVER, SINCE IT *IS* DIFFICULT TO RESERVE AN APPROPRIATE BANQUETING HALL AND MAKE OTHER SUCH ARRANGEMENTS ON SHORT NOTICE, IF YOU COULD INFORM US PROMPTLY...
...AS SOON AS YOU FIND OUT THE EXACT DATE WHEN SIR ANOTSU WILL RETURN, WE WOULD BE MOST GRATEFUL.
I ASSURE YOU THAT WOULD BE NO PROBLEM AT ALL, LORD HABAKI.
I'LL SEND A MAN OFF TOMORROW TO ASK OUR LEADER DIRECTLY.
WELL! A PARTY JUST FOR US, ATTENDED BY THE ELITE SWORDSMEN OF THE *BANSHŪ*...
...NOW THAT'S BOUND TO BE QUITE... ***INTEREST-ING.***

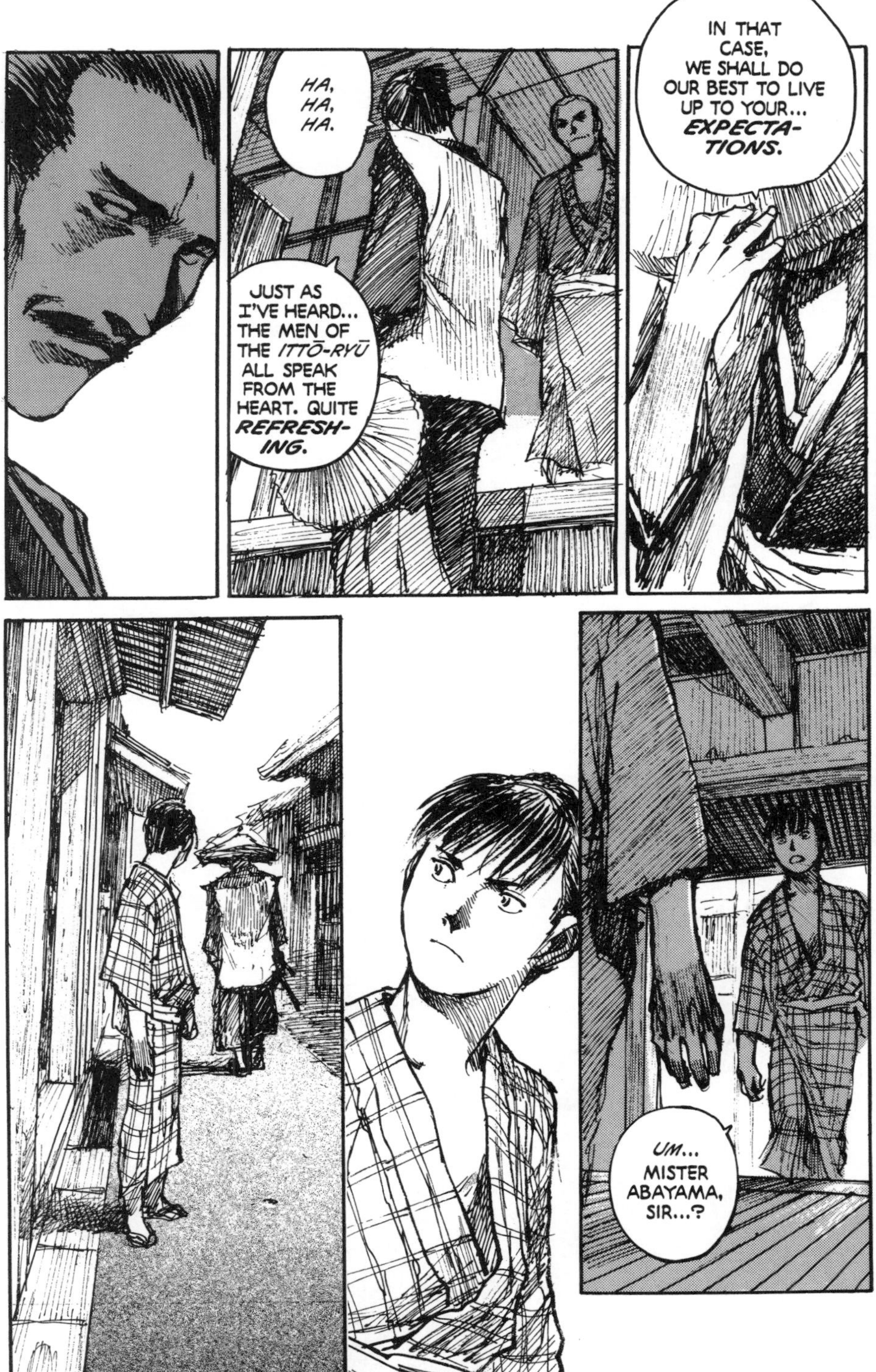
HA, HA, HA.
JUST AS I'VE HEARD... THE MEN OF THE ITTŌ-RYŪ ALL SPEAK FROM THE HEART. QUITE REFRESHING.
IN THAT CASE, WE SHALL DO OUR BEST TO LIVE UP TO YOUR... EXPECTATIONS.
UM... MISTER ABAYAMA, SIR...?

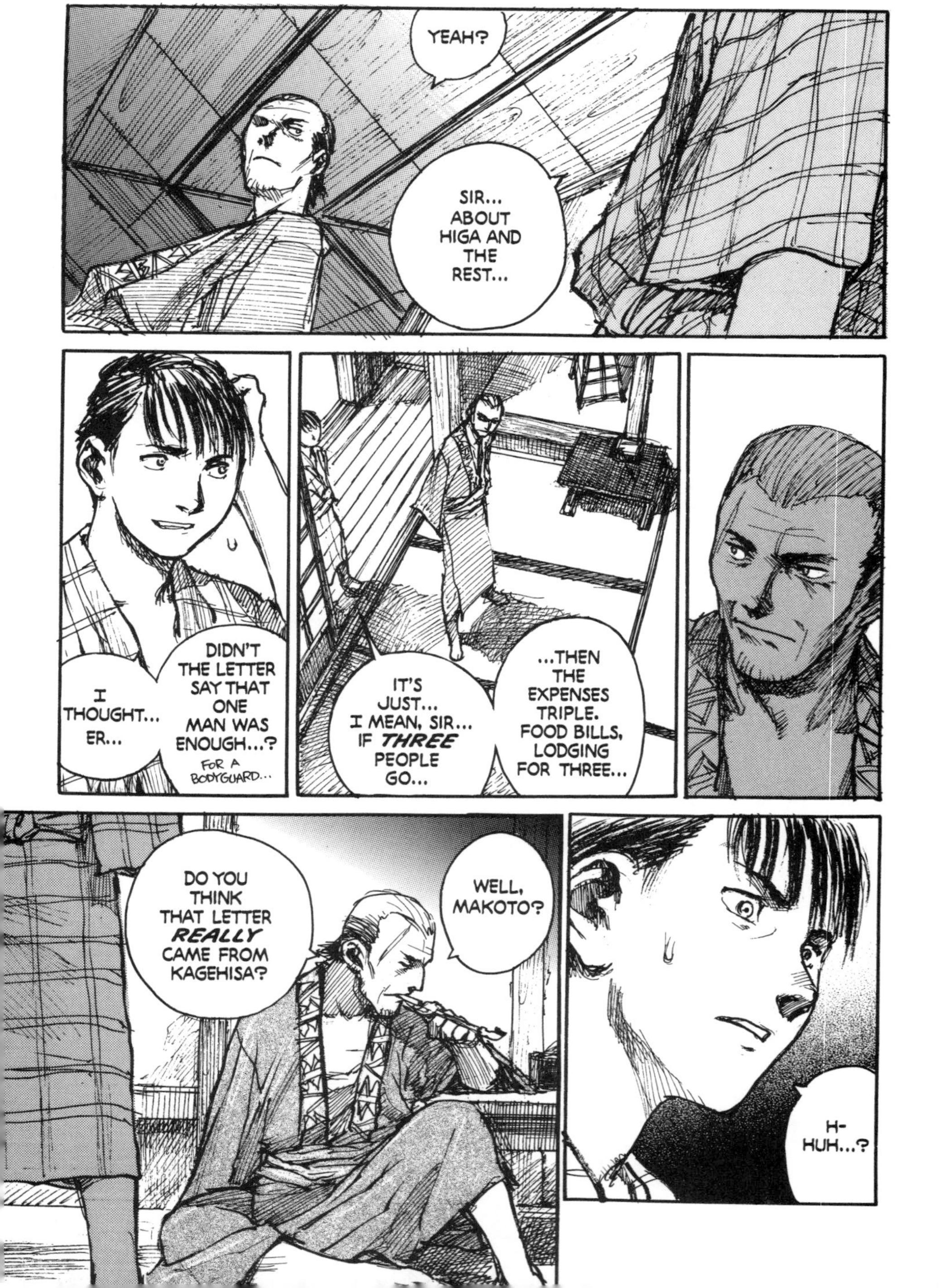
YEAH?
SIR... ABOUT HIGA AND THE REST...
I THOUGHT... ER...
DIDN'T THE LETTER SAY THAT ONE MAN WAS ENOUGH...?
FOR A BODYGUARD...
IT'S JUST... I MEAN, SIR... IF *THREE* PEOPLE GO...
...THEN THE EXPENSES TRIPLE. FOOD BILLS, LODGING FOR THREE...
DO YOU THINK THAT LETTER *REALLY* CAME FROM KAGEHISA?
WELL, MAKOTO?
H-HUH...?

WHAT DO YOU MEAN, SIR? I'M NOT SURE I UNDERSTAND...

MAYBE NOTHING.

JUST... IT SEEMED TO ME THE HANDWRITING WAS A TAD *DIFFERENT* FROM HOW I REMEMBER HIS BEING.

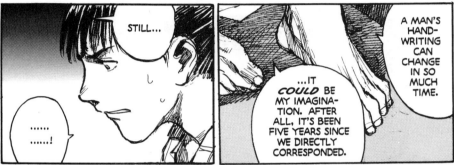

STILL...

......
......!

...IT *COULD* BE MY IMAGINATION. AFTER ALL, IT'S BEEN FIVE YEARS SINCE WE DIRECTLY CORRESPONDED.

A MAN'S HANDWRITING CAN CHANGE IN SO MUCH TIME.

HOWEVER, IN THE WORST CASE, WE HAVE TO BE PREPARED FOR A TRAP!

RIGHT...?

SO, I TOOK CARE OF EITHER EVENTUALITY, MY BOY.

THAT'S WHY I SENT THREE OF 'EM.

*HEH... AN EYE FOR AN EYE... A LIE FOR A LIE.*

YOU SEE...?

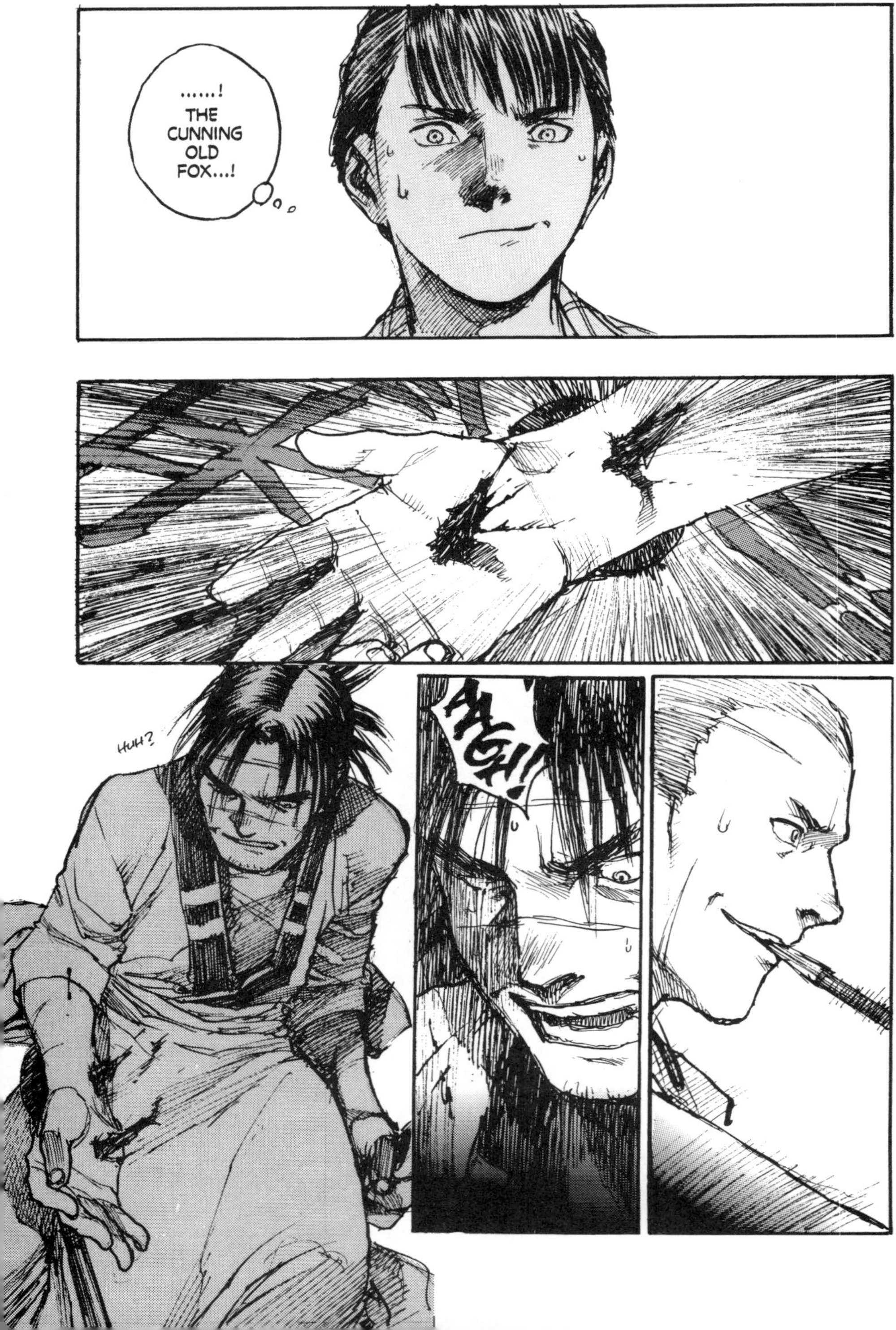
......! THE CUNNING OLD FOX...!
HUH?
AAGH!!

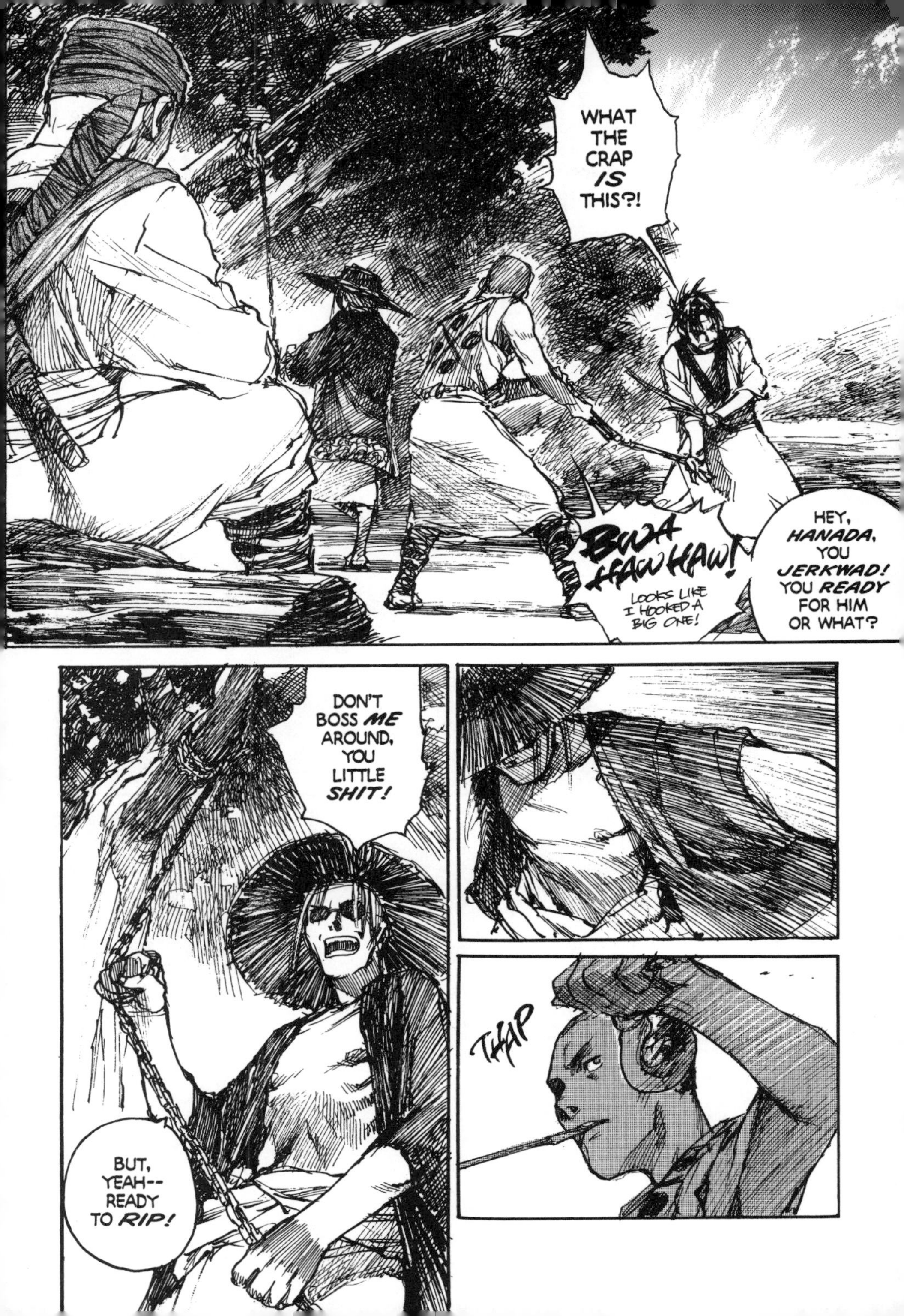
WHAT THE CRAP *IS* THIS?!
BWA HAW HAW!
LOOKS LIKE I HOOKED A BIG ONE!
HEY, *HANADA,* YOU *JERKWAD!* YOU *READY* FOR HIM OR WHAT?
DON'T BOSS *ME* AROUND, YOU LITTLE *SHIT!*
BUT, YEAH-- READY TO *RIP!*
THAP

GOD *DAMN,* THAT *HURTS!*

WHAT TH-?! CAN'T GET 'EM OUT!

DAMN *RIGHT* YOU CAN'T--

TAKE A *GOOD LOOK* AT THOSE SUCKERS, PAL!

AND BY THE WAY...

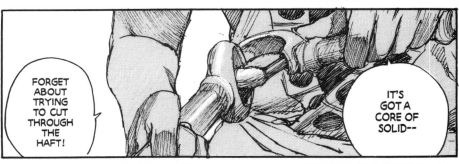

FORGET ABOUT TRYING TO CUT THROUGH THE HAFT!

IT'S GOT A CORE OF SOLID--

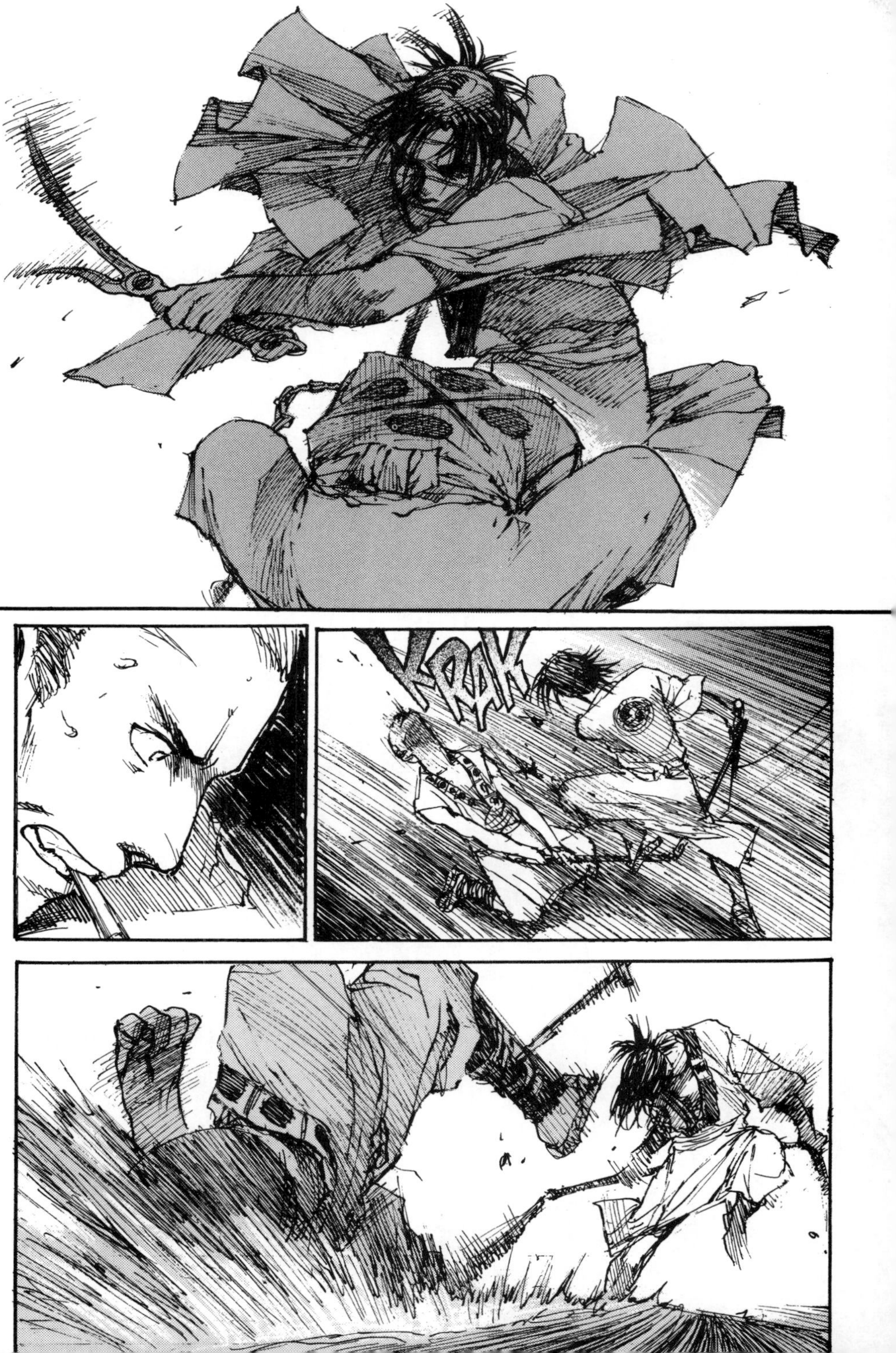
KRAK

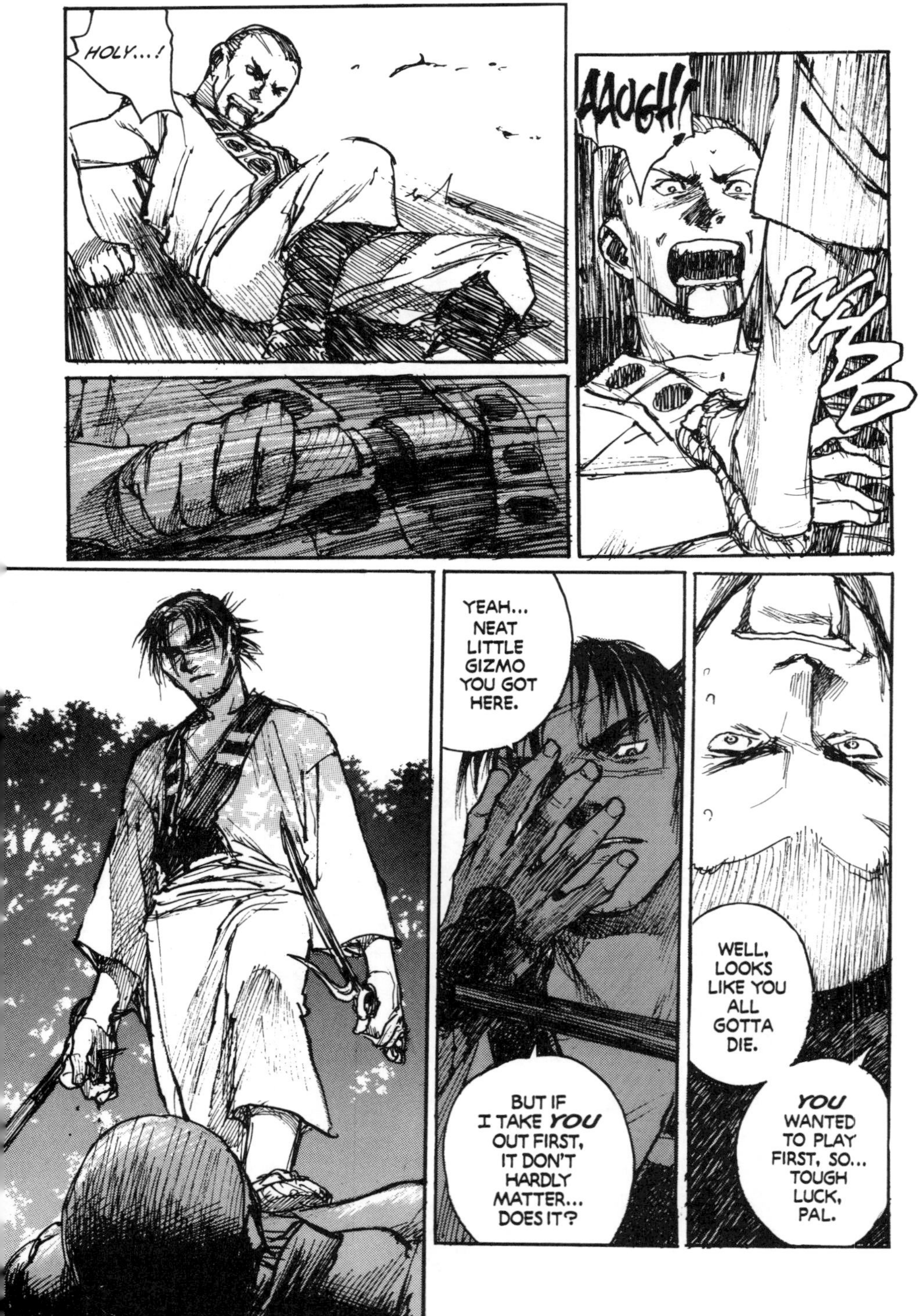
HOLY...!
AAOGH!
YEAH... NEAT LITTLE GIZMO YOU GOT HERE.
BUT IF I TAKE *YOU* OUT FIRST, IT DON'T HARDLY MATTER... DOES IT?
WELL, LOOKS LIKE YOU ALL GOTTA DIE.
*YOU* WANTED TO PLAY FIRST, SO... TOUGH LUCK, PAL.

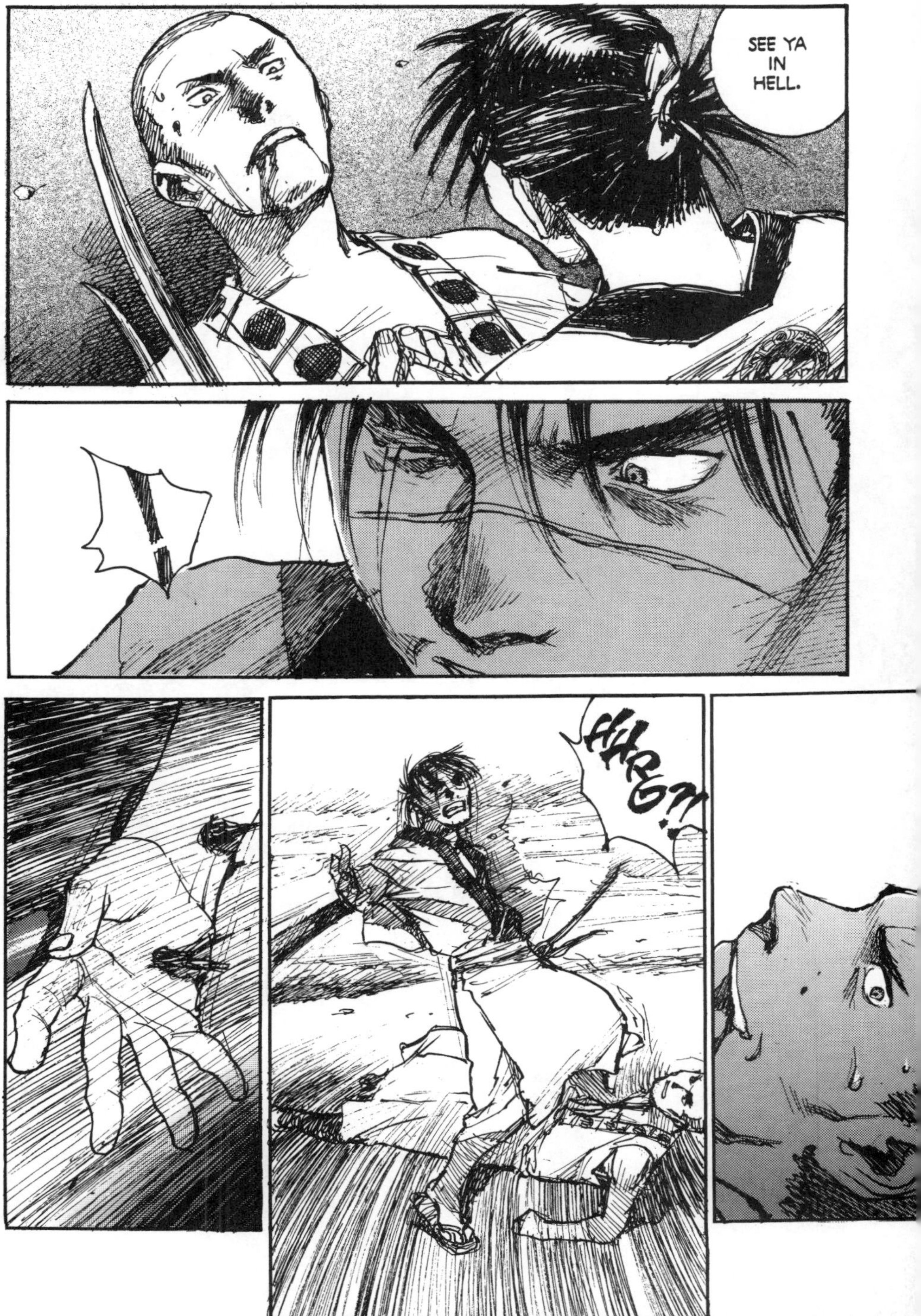
SEE YA IN HELL.
!
HURG!!

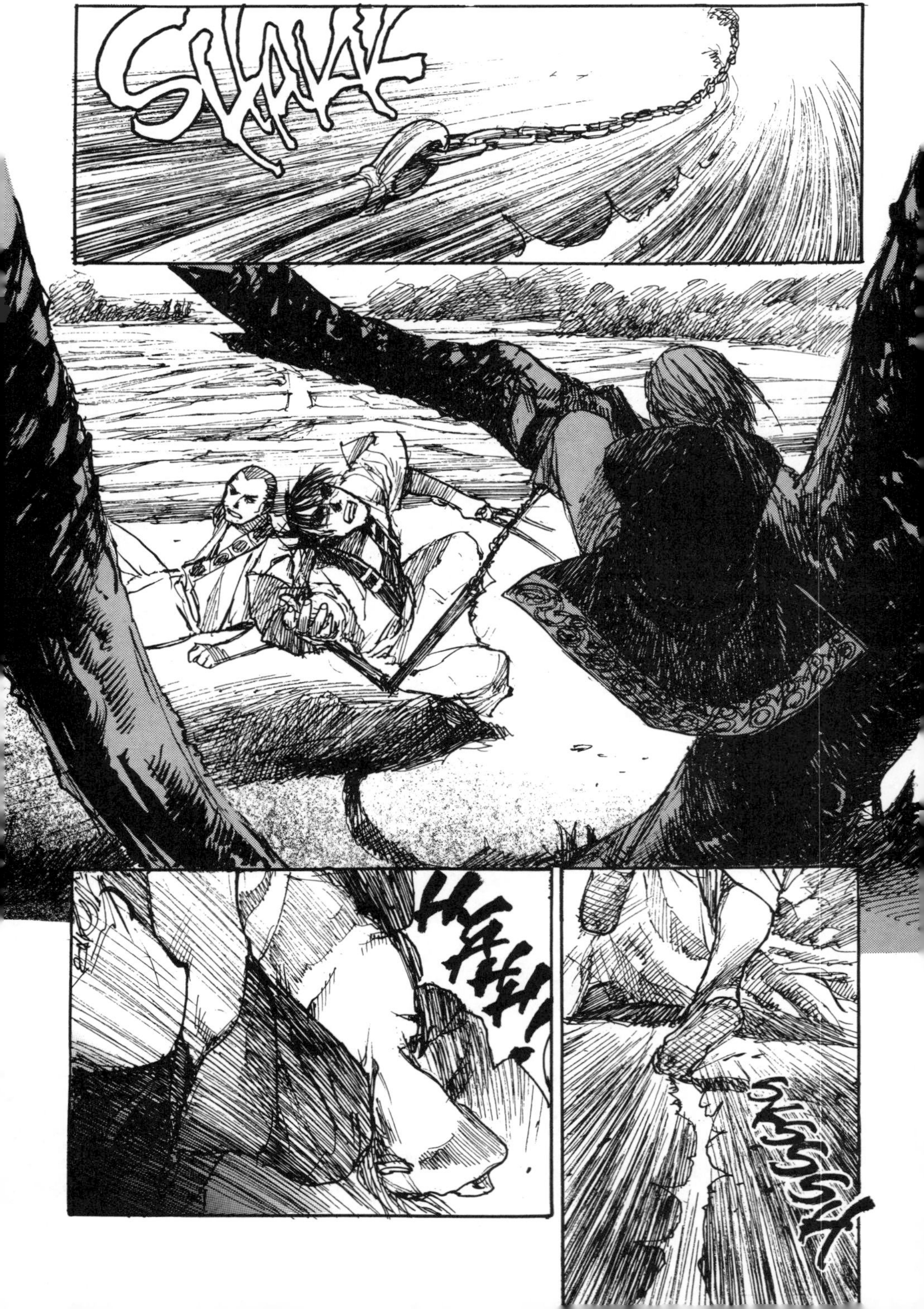

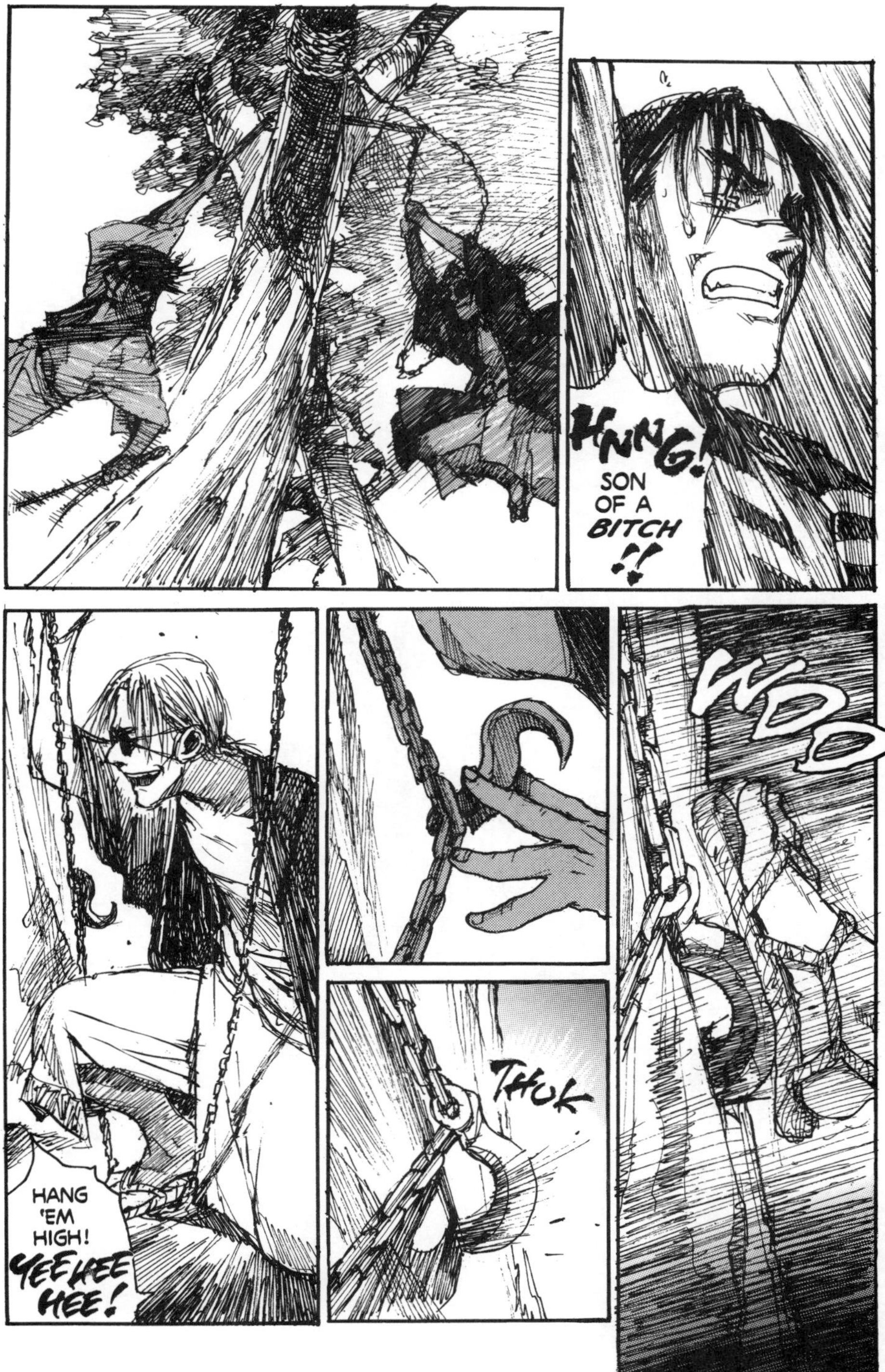
HNNG! SON OF A BITCH!!
HANG 'EM HIGH! YEE HEE HEE!
THUK
WOO

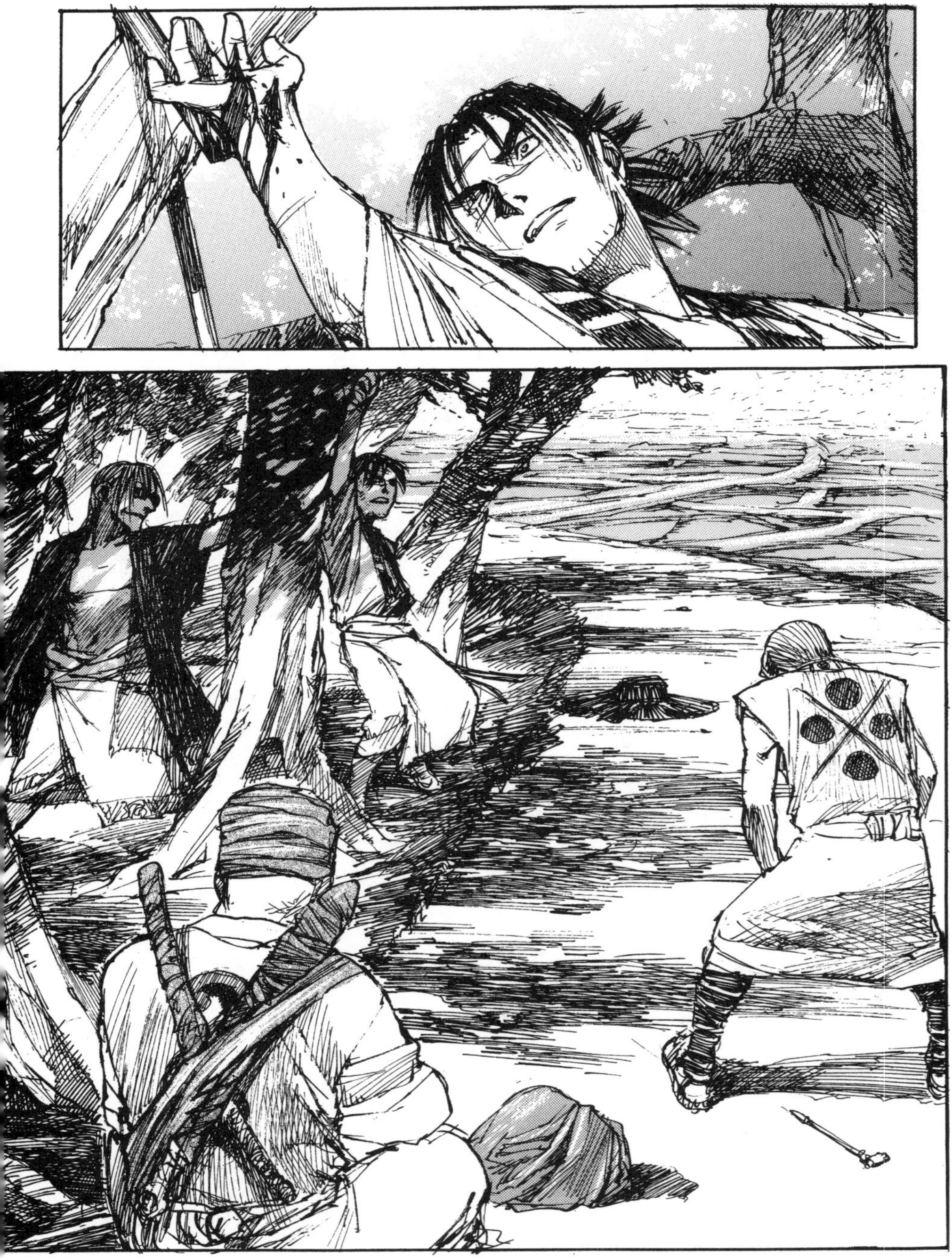

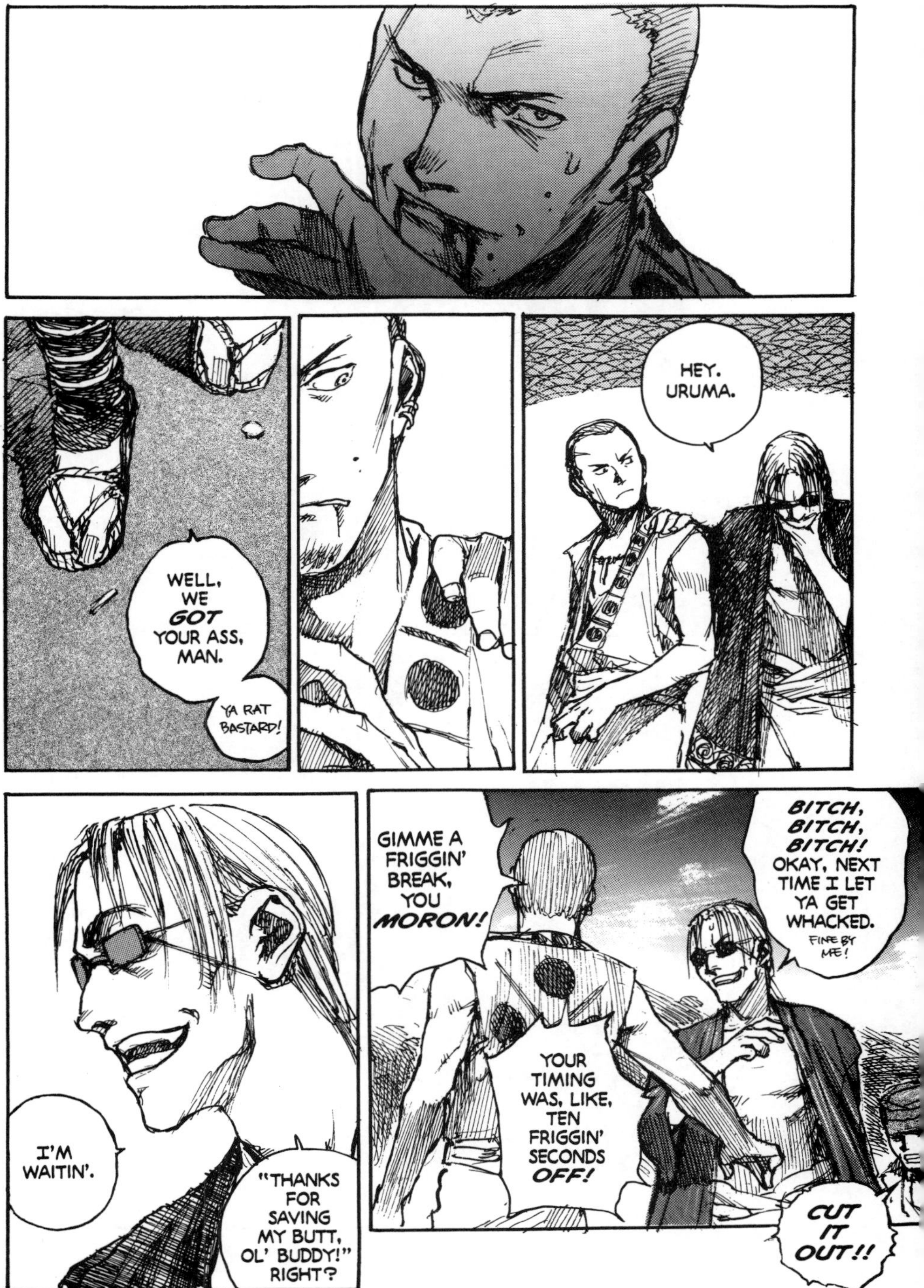
WELL, WE GOT YOUR ASS, MAN.
YA RAT BASTARD!
HEY. URUMA.
I'M WAITIN'.
"THANKS FOR SAVING MY BUTT, OL' BUDDY!" RIGHT?
GIMME A FRIGGIN' BREAK, YOU MORON!
YOUR TIMING WAS, LIKE, TEN FRIGGIN' SECONDS OFF!
BITCH, BITCH, BITCH! OKAY, NEXT TIME I LET YA GET WHACKED.
FINE BY ME!
CUT IT OUT!!

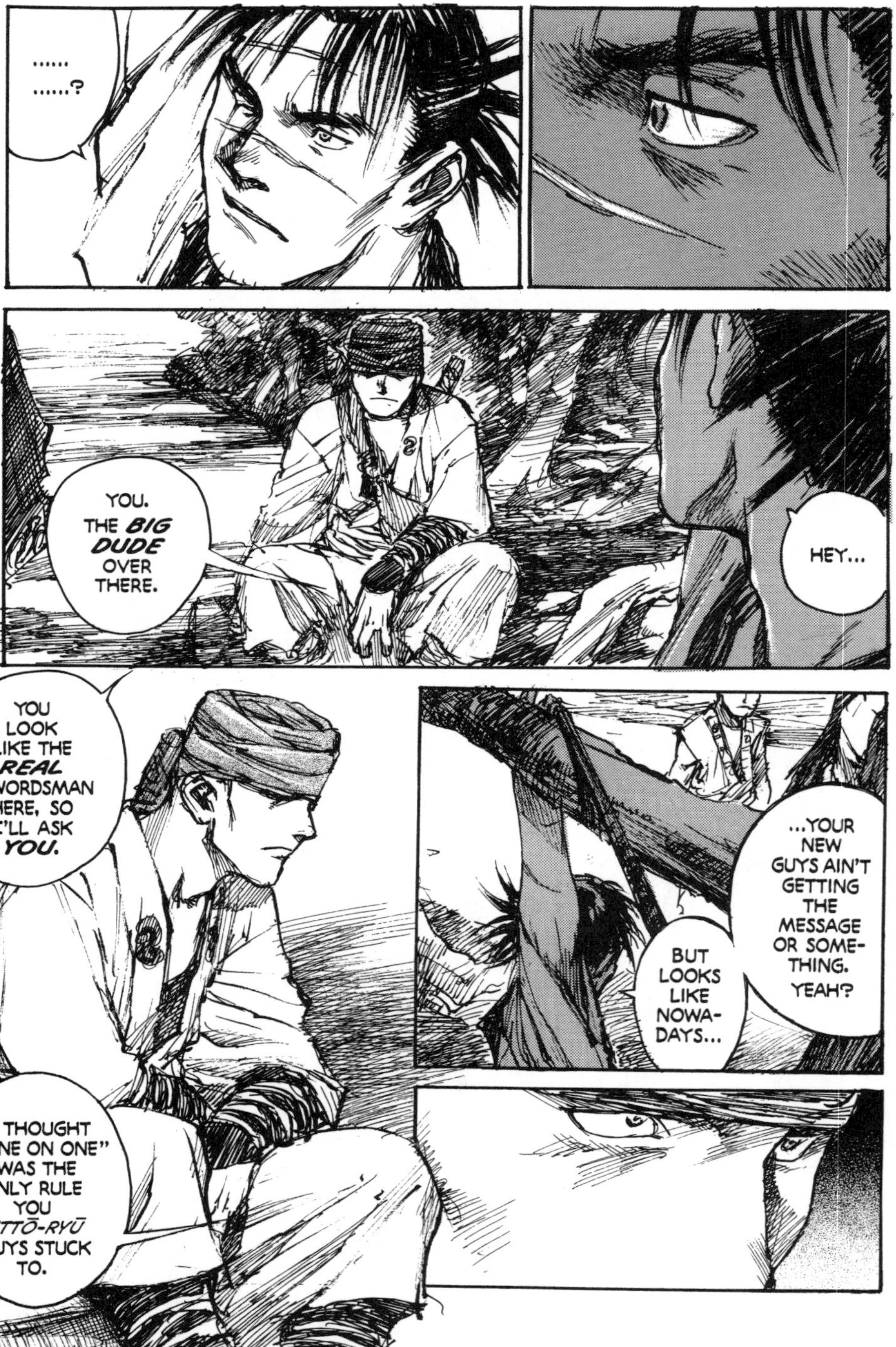

...... ......?
YOU. THE *BIG DUDE* OVER THERE.
HEY...
YOU LOOK LIKE THE *REAL* SWORDSMAN HERE, SO I'LL ASK *YOU*.
I THOUGHT "ONE ON ONE" WAS THE ONLY RULE YOU *ITTŌ-RYŪ* GUYS STUCK TO.
BUT LOOKS LIKE NOWA-DAYS...
...YOUR NEW GUYS AIN'T GETTING THE MESSAGE OR SOME-THING. YEAH?

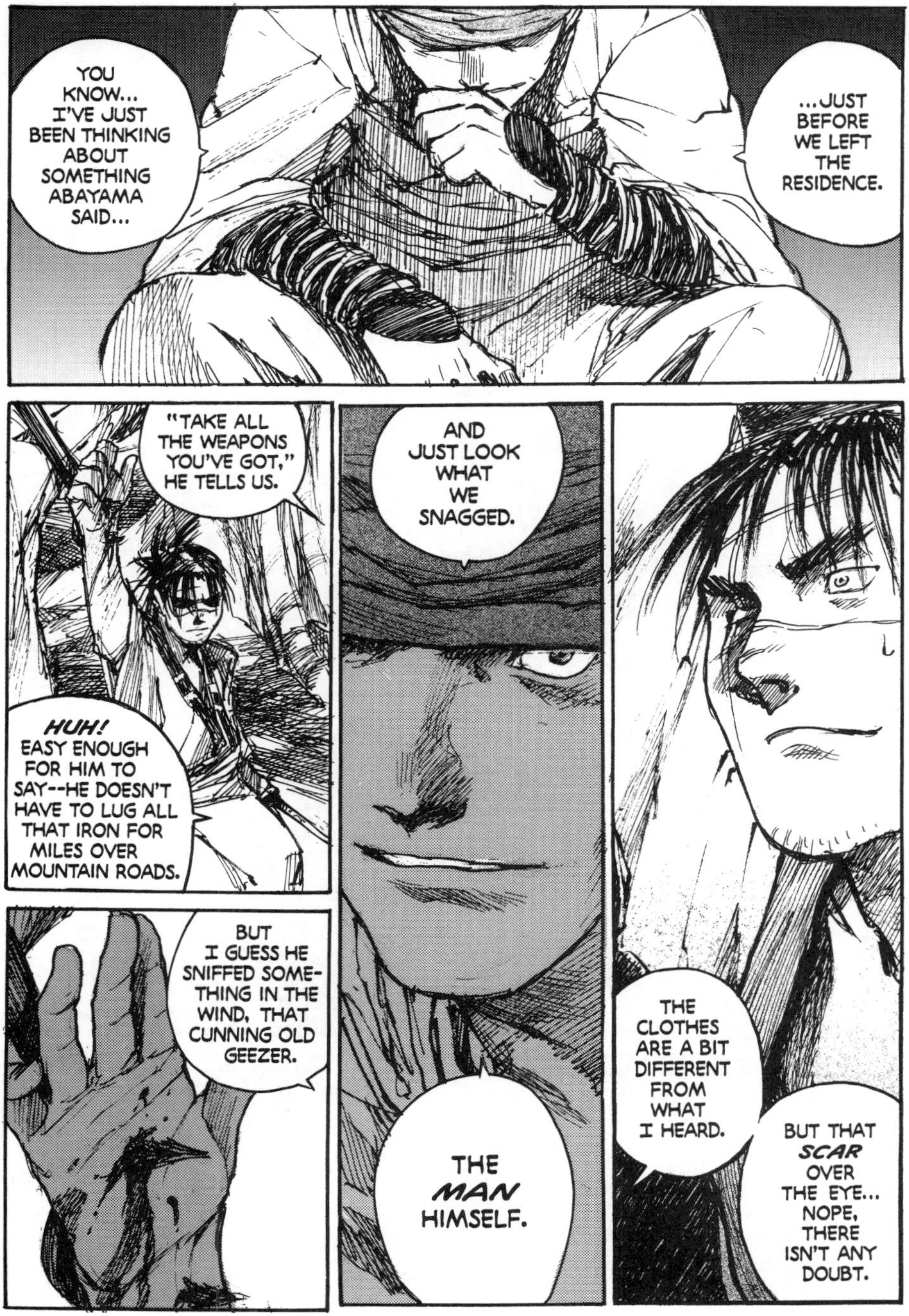
YOU KNOW... I'VE JUST BEEN THINKING ABOUT SOMETHING ABAYAMA SAID...
...JUST BEFORE WE LEFT THE RESIDENCE.
"TAKE ALL THE WEAPONS YOU'VE GOT," HE TELLS US.
*HUH!* EASY ENOUGH FOR HIM TO SAY--HE DOESN'T HAVE TO LUG ALL THAT IRON FOR MILES OVER MOUNTAIN ROADS.
BUT I GUESS HE SNIFFED SOME-THING IN THE WIND, THAT CUNNING OLD GEEZER.
AND JUST LOOK WHAT WE SNAGGED.
THE *MAN* HIMSELF.
THE CLOTHES ARE A BIT DIFFERENT FROM WHAT I HEARD.
BUT THAT *SCAR* OVER THE EYE... NOPE, THERE ISN'T ANY DOUBT.

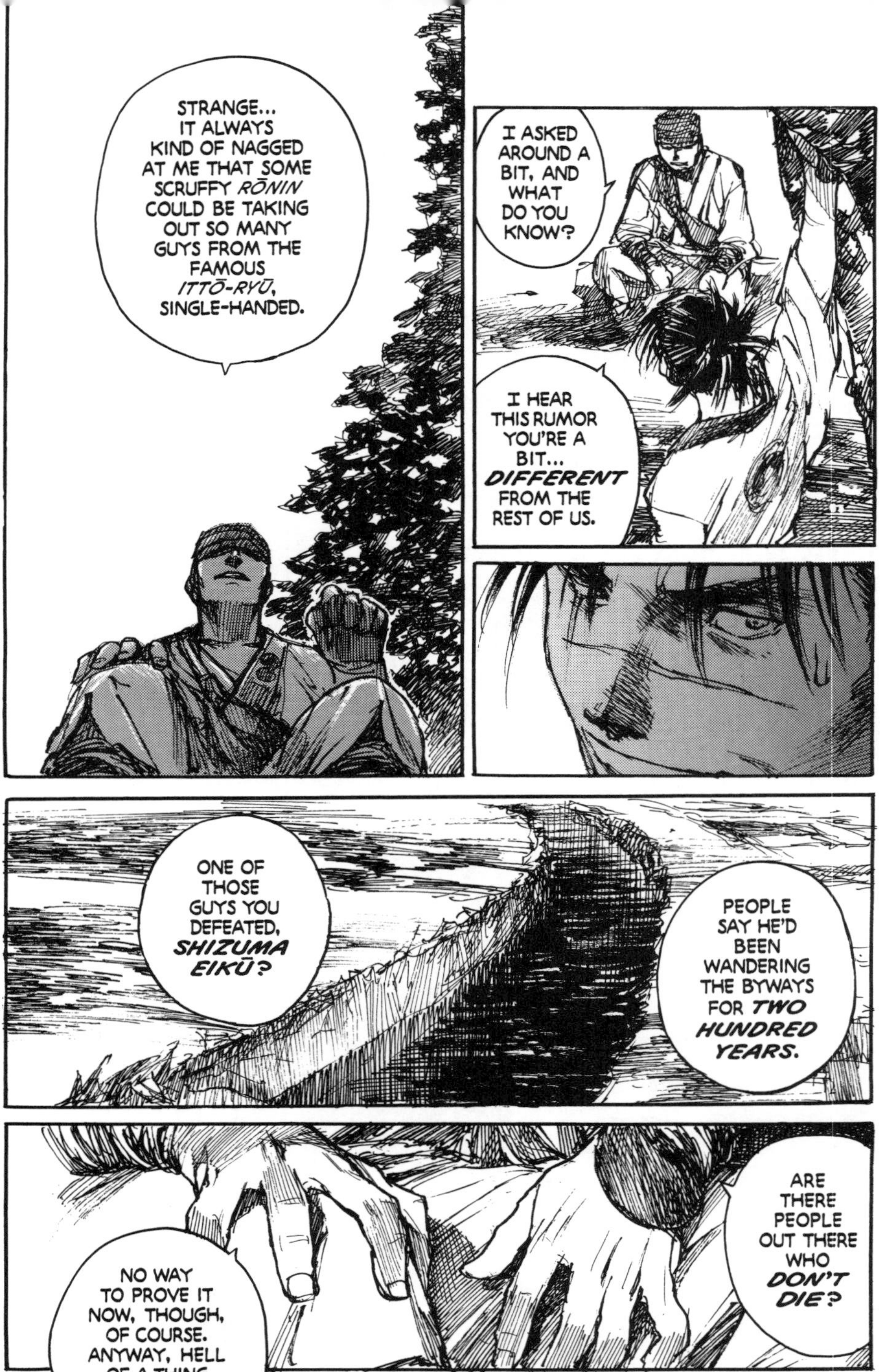
STRANGE... IT ALWAYS KIND OF NAGGED AT ME THAT SOME SCRUFFY *RŌNIN* COULD BE TAKING OUT SO MANY GUYS FROM THE FAMOUS *ITTŌ-RYŪ*, SINGLE-HANDED.
I ASKED AROUND A BIT, AND WHAT DO YOU KNOW?
I HEAR THIS RUMOR YOU'RE A BIT... ***DIFFERENT*** FROM THE REST OF US.
ONE OF THOSE GUYS YOU DEFEATED, ***SHIZUMA EIKŪ***?
PEOPLE SAY HE'D BEEN WANDERING THE BYWAYS FOR ***TWO HUNDRED YEARS***.
NO WAY TO PROVE IT NOW, THOUGH, OF COURSE. ANYWAY, HELL OF A THING TO THINK ABOUT.
ARE THERE PEOPLE OUT THERE WHO ***DON'T DIE***?

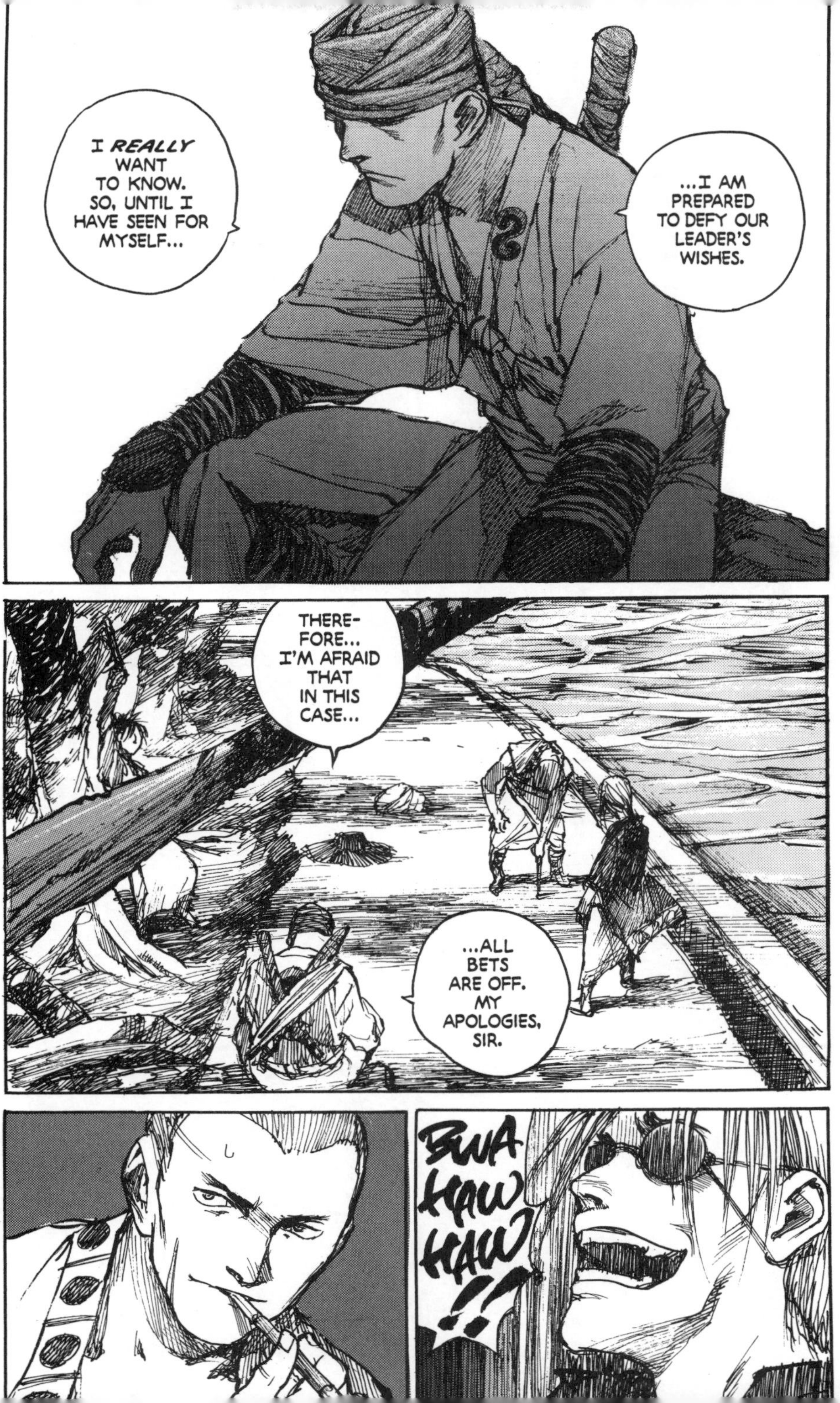
I *REALLY* WANT TO KNOW. SO, UNTIL I HAVE SEEN FOR MYSELF...
...I AM PREPARED TO DEFY OUR LEADER'S WISHES.
THERE-FORE... I'M AFRAID THAT IN THIS CASE...
...ALL BETS ARE OFF. MY APOLOGIES, SIR.
BWA HAW HAW HAW!!

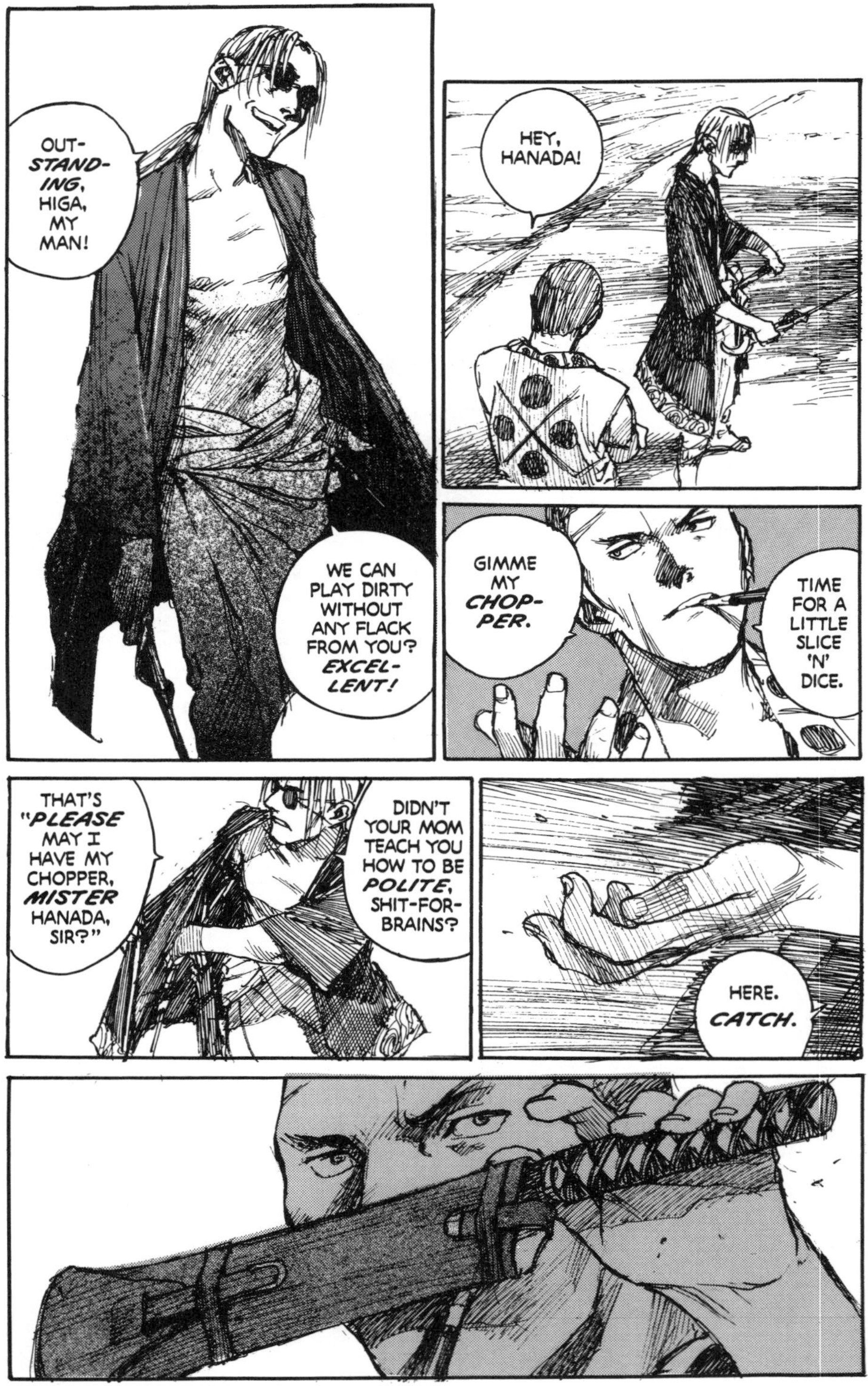
OUT-*STANDING-ING*, HIGA, MY MAN!
WE CAN PLAY DIRTY WITHOUT ANY FLACK FROM YOU? *EXCEL-LENT!*
HEY, HANADA!
GIMME MY *CHOP-PER*.
TIME FOR A LITTLE SLICE 'N' DICE.
THAT'S "*PLEASE* MAY I HAVE MY CHOPPER, *MISTER* HANADA, SIR?"
DIDN'T YOUR MOM TEACH YOU HOW TO BE *POLITE*, SHIT-FOR-BRAINS?
HERE. *CATCH*.

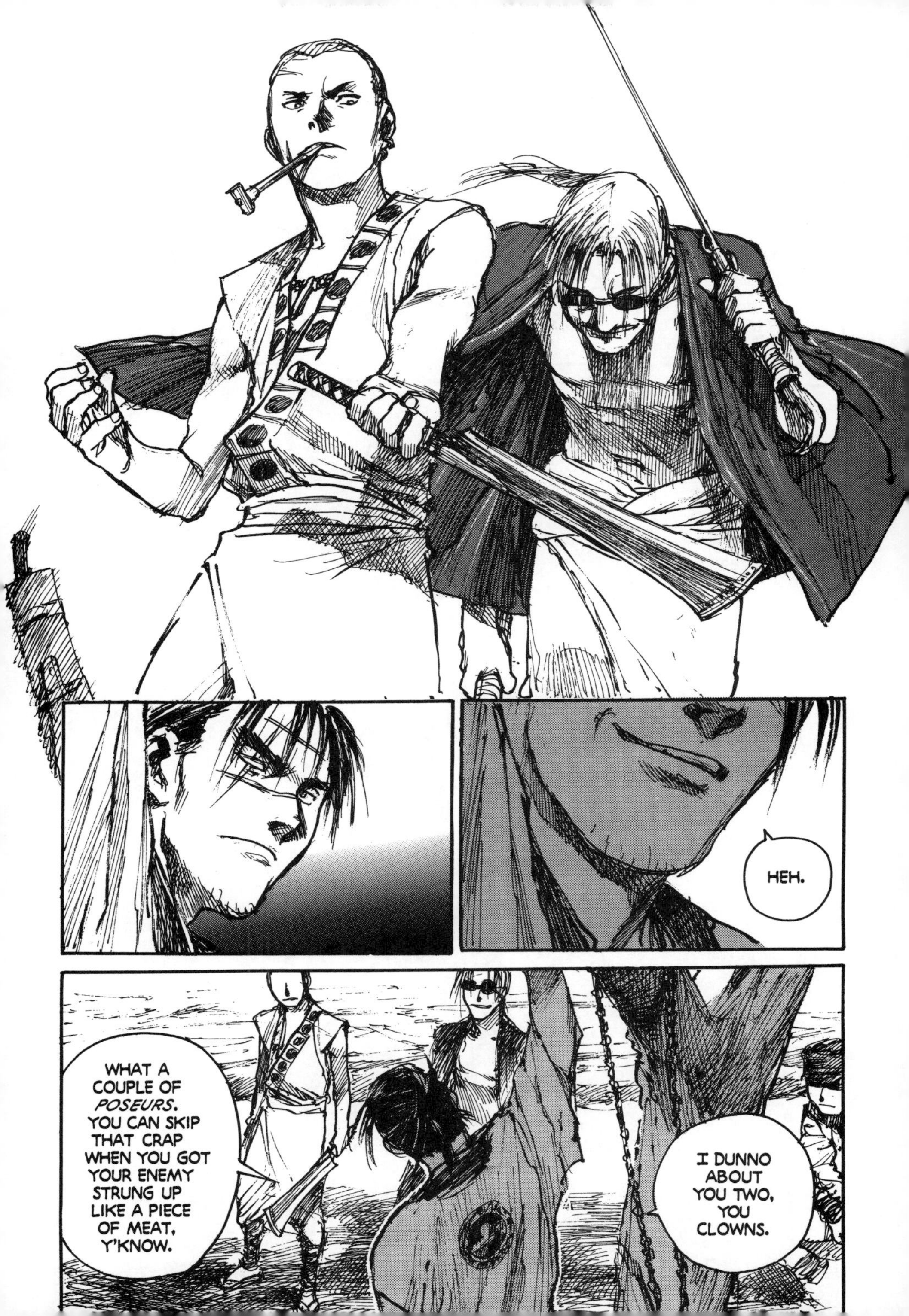
HEH.
WHAT A COUPLE OF *POSEURS*. YOU CAN SKIP THAT CRAP WHEN YOU GOT YOUR ENEMY STRUNG UP LIKE A PIECE OF MEAT, Y'KNOW.
I DUNNO ABOUT YOU TWO, YOU CLOWNS.

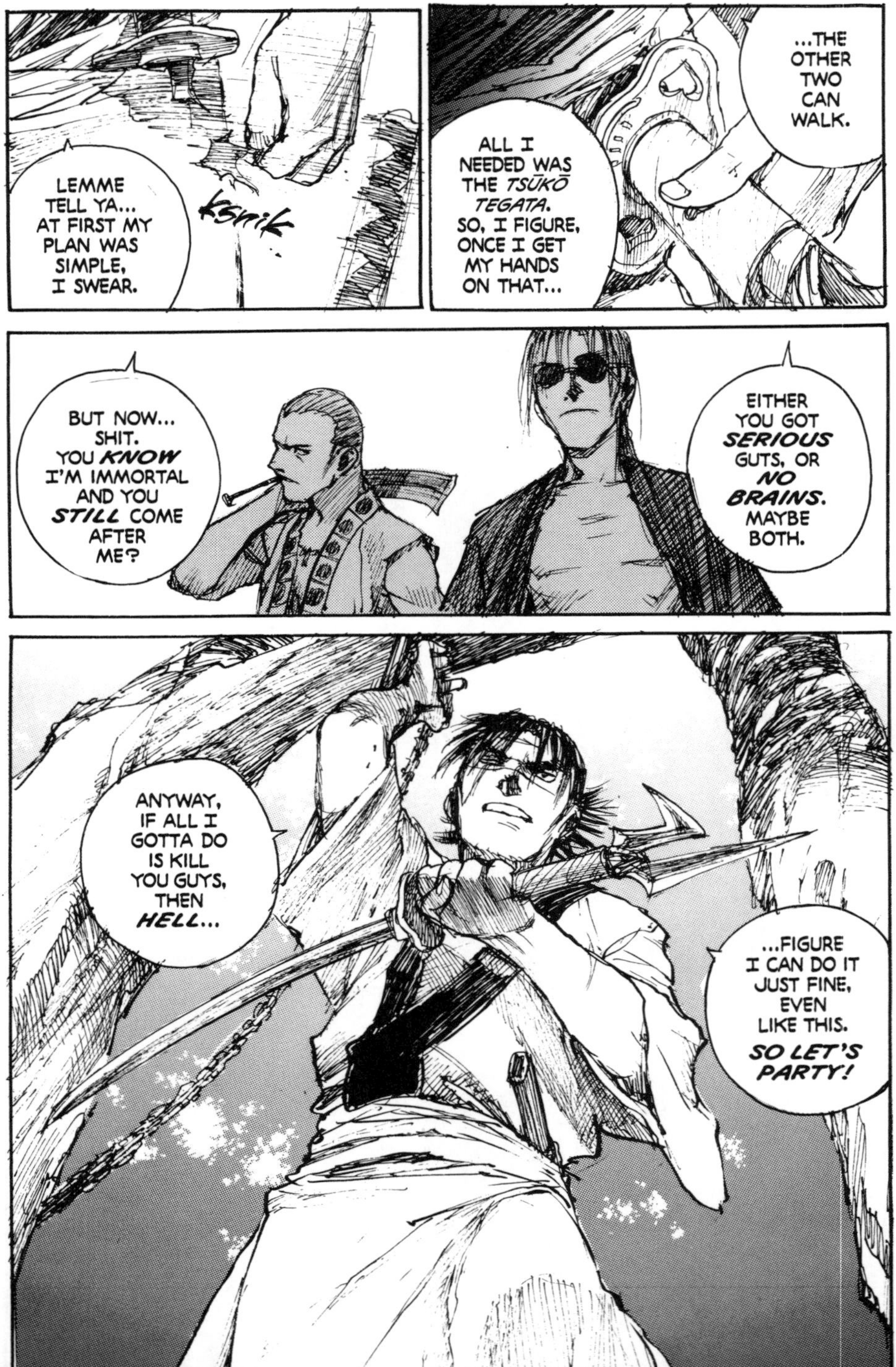
LEMME TELL YA... AT FIRST MY PLAN WAS SIMPLE, I SWEAR.
ksnik
ALL I NEEDED WAS THE TSŪKŌ TEGATA. SO, I FIGURE, ONCE I GET MY HANDS ON THAT...
...THE OTHER TWO CAN WALK.
BUT NOW... SHIT. YOU KNOW I'M IMMORTAL AND YOU STILL COME AFTER ME?
EITHER YOU GOT SERIOUS GUTS, OR NO BRAINS. MAYBE BOTH.
ANYWAY, IF ALL I GOTTA DO IS KILL YOU GUYS, THEN HELL...
...FIGURE I CAN DO IT JUST FINE, EVEN LIKE THIS. SO LET'S PARTY!

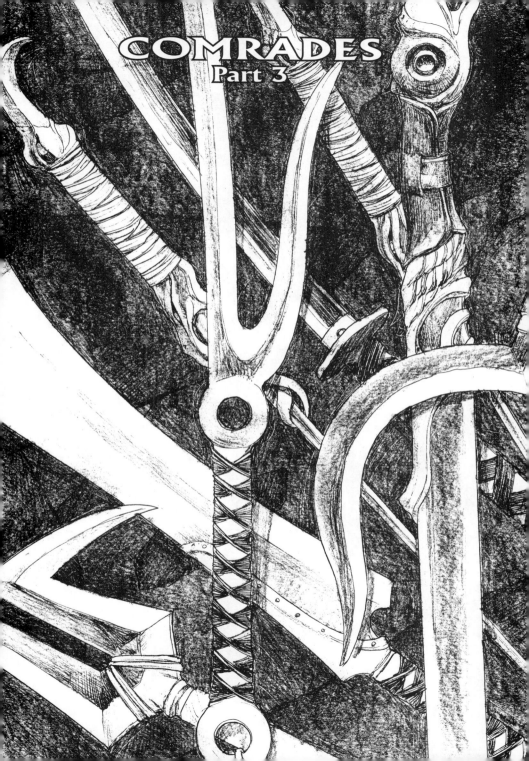

# COMRADES
## Part 3

HEH
HEH
HEH ...

GYA HA
HA HA!

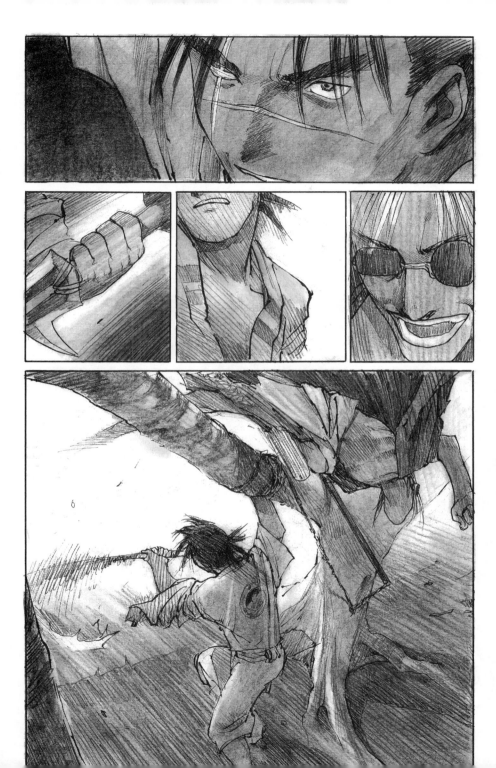

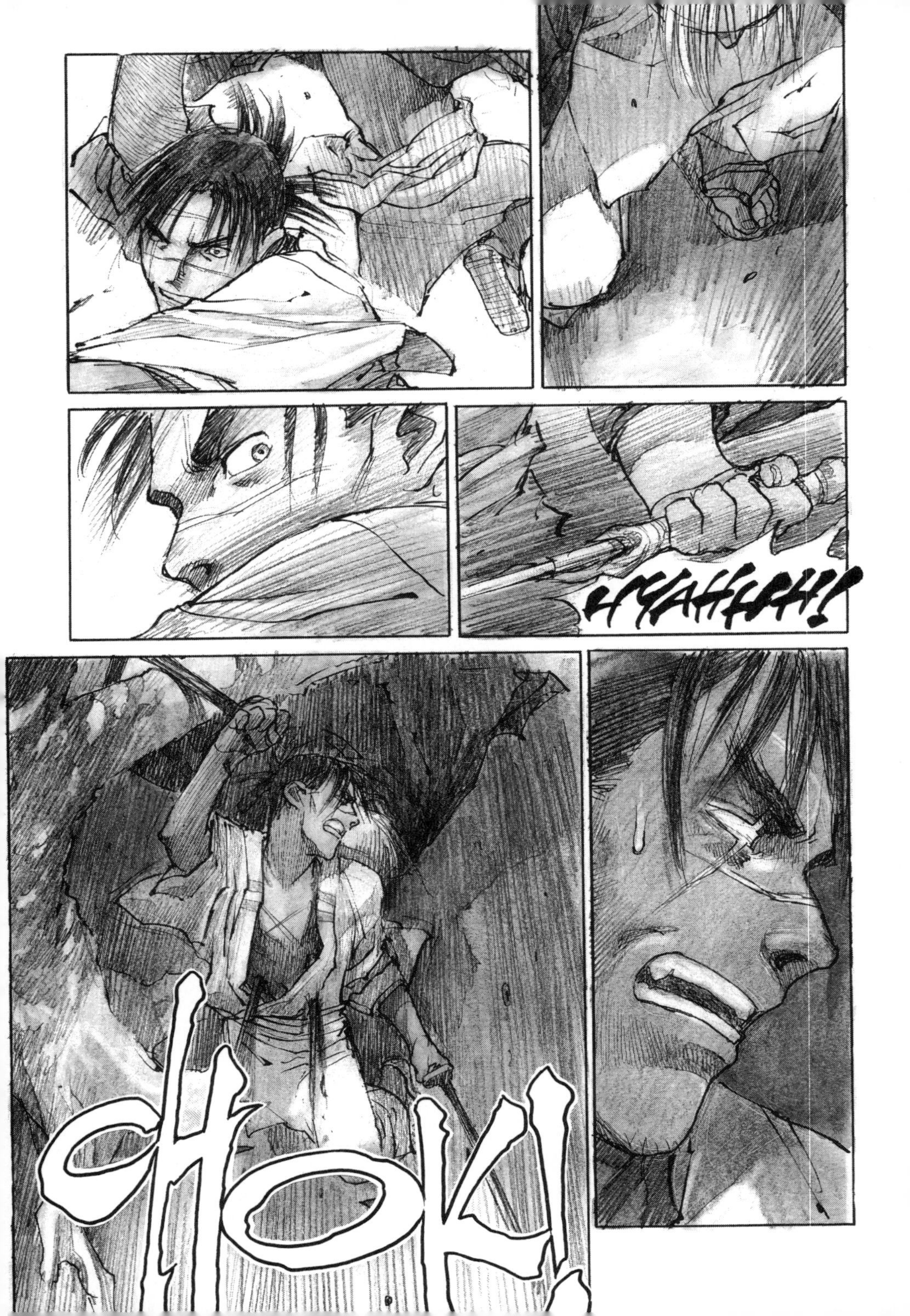
HYAHHHH!
CHOK!

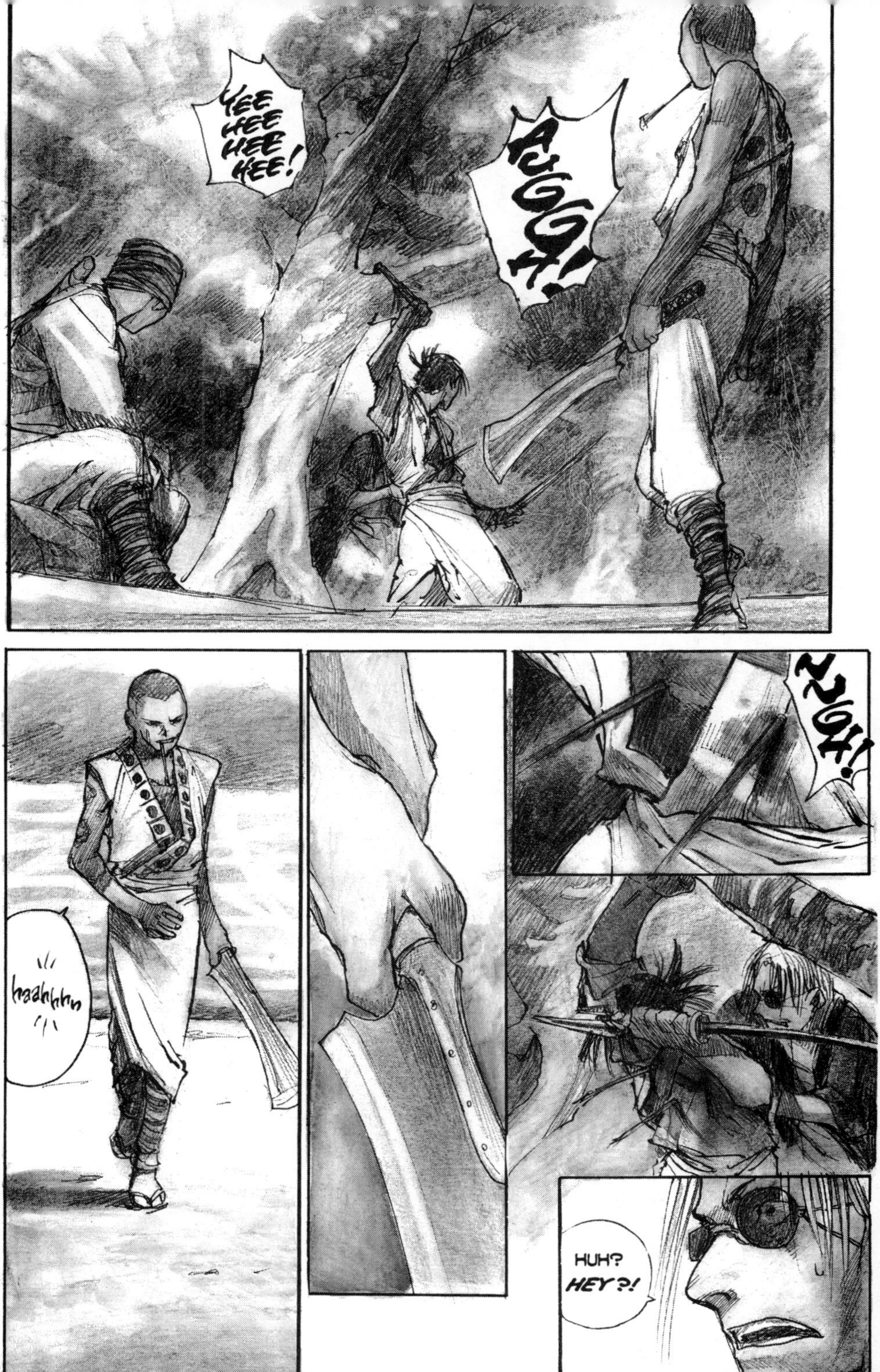
YEE HEE HEE HEE!
AUGGH!
haahhhn
NNGH!
HUH? HEY?!

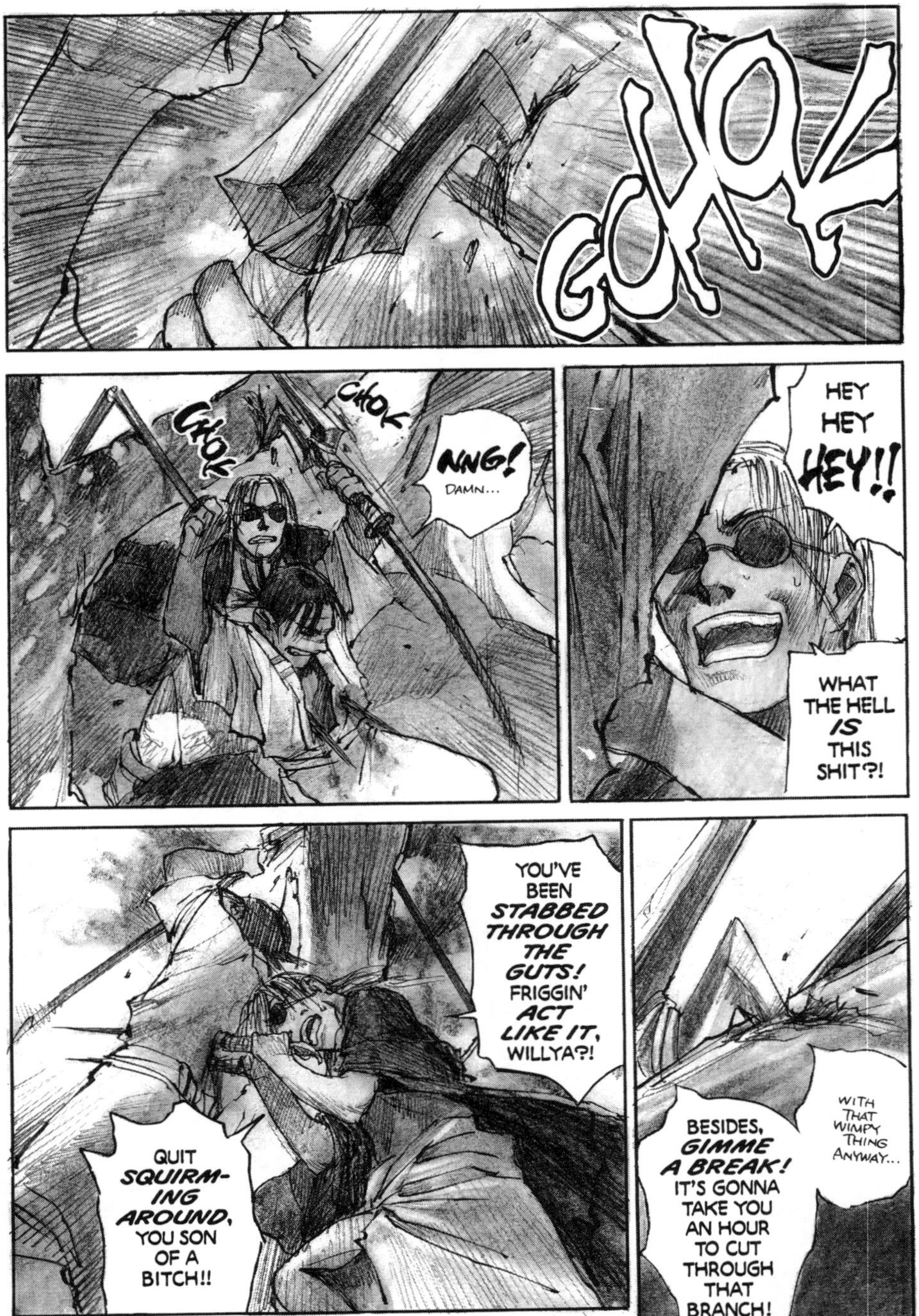
GOKK
CHOK
CHOK
NNG! DAMN...
HEY HEY HEY!!
WHAT THE HELL IS THIS SHIT?!
YOU'VE BEEN STABBED THROUGH THE GUTS! FRIGGIN' ACT LIKE IT, WILLYA?!
QUIT SQUIRMING AROUND, YOU SON OF A BITCH!!
BESIDES, GIMME A BREAK! IT'S GONNA TAKE YOU AN HOUR TO CUT THROUGH THAT BRANCH!
WITH THAT WIMPY THING ANYWAY...

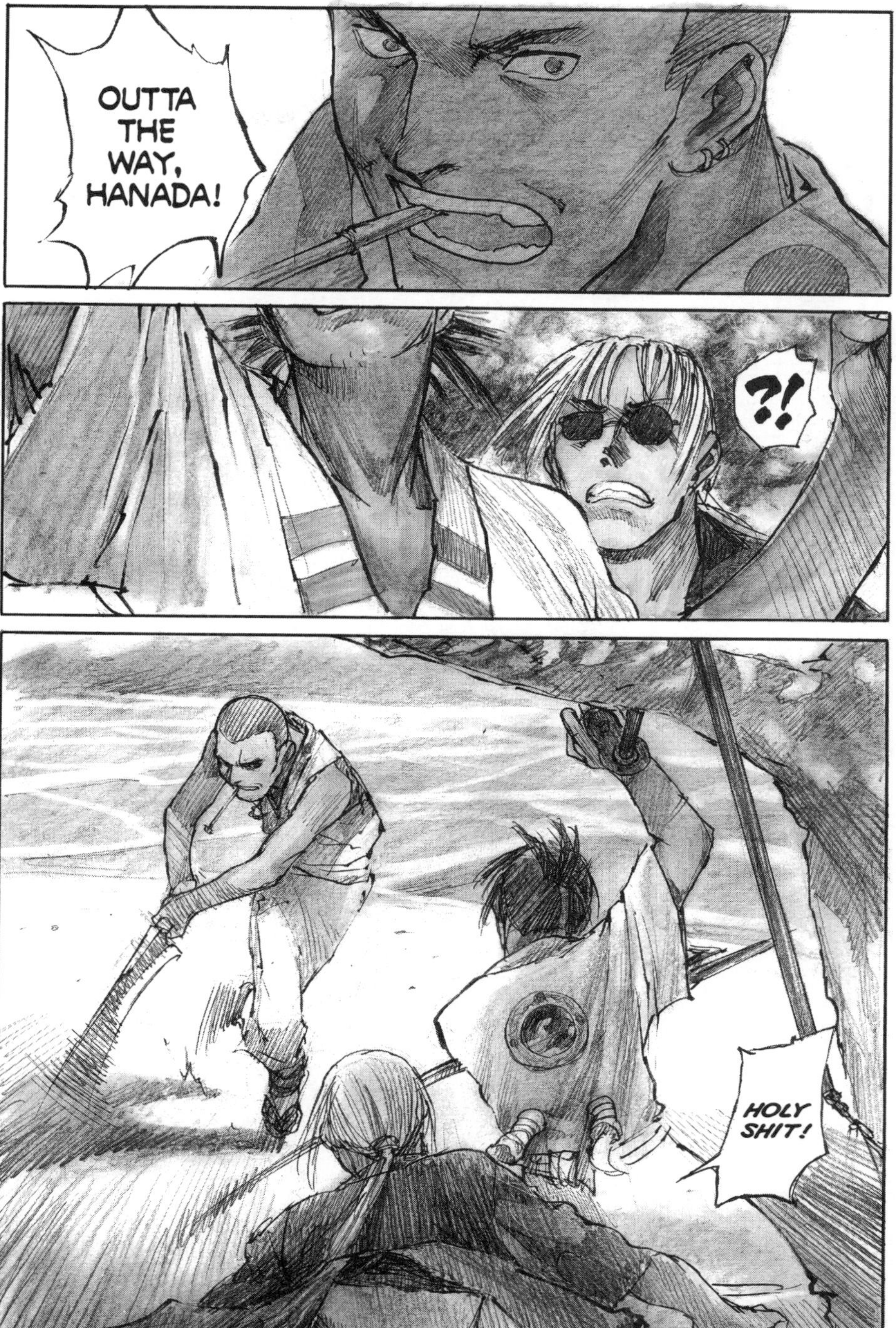
OUTTA THE WAY, HANADA!
?!
HOLY SHIT!

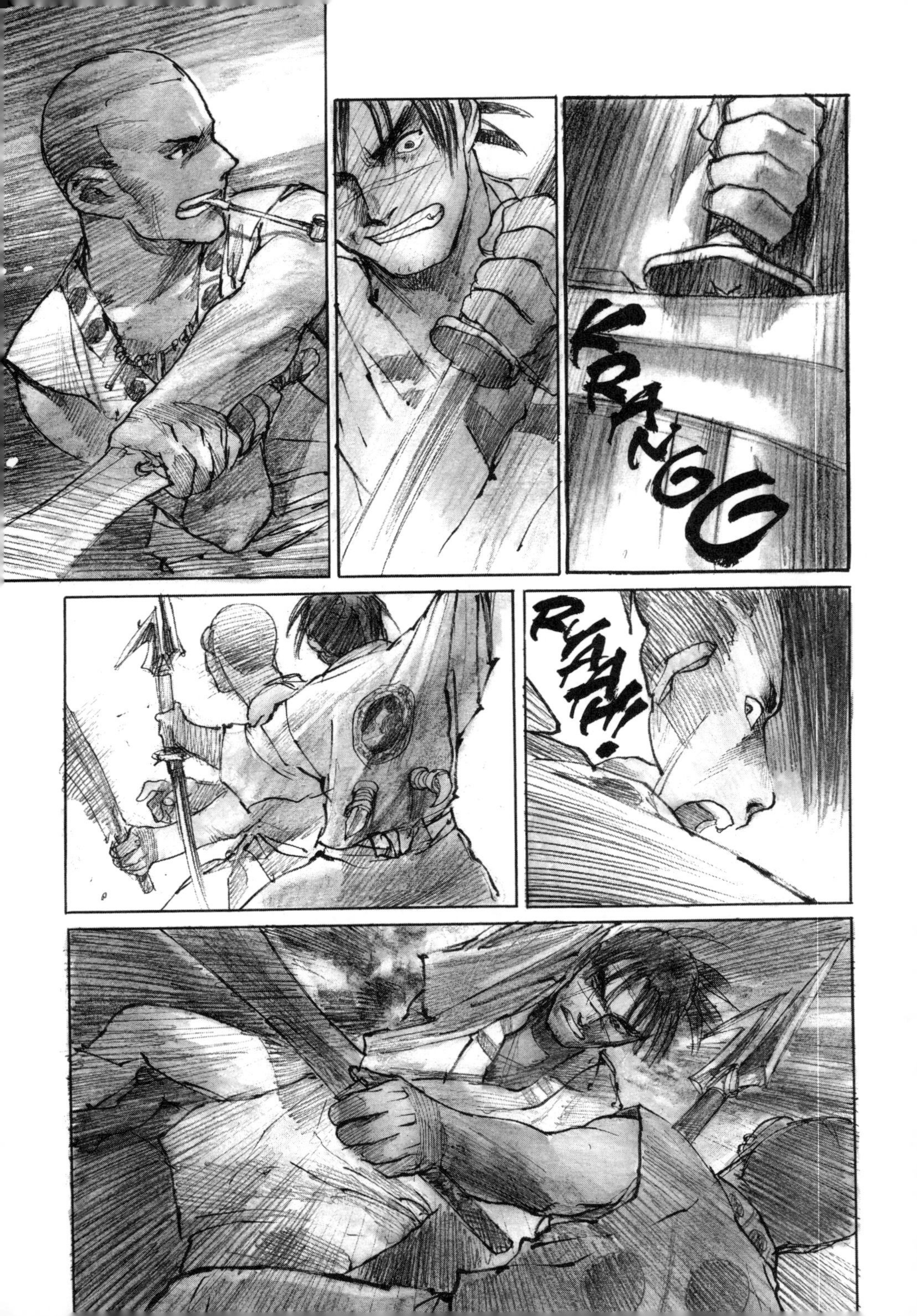

KRANGG
RUMM!

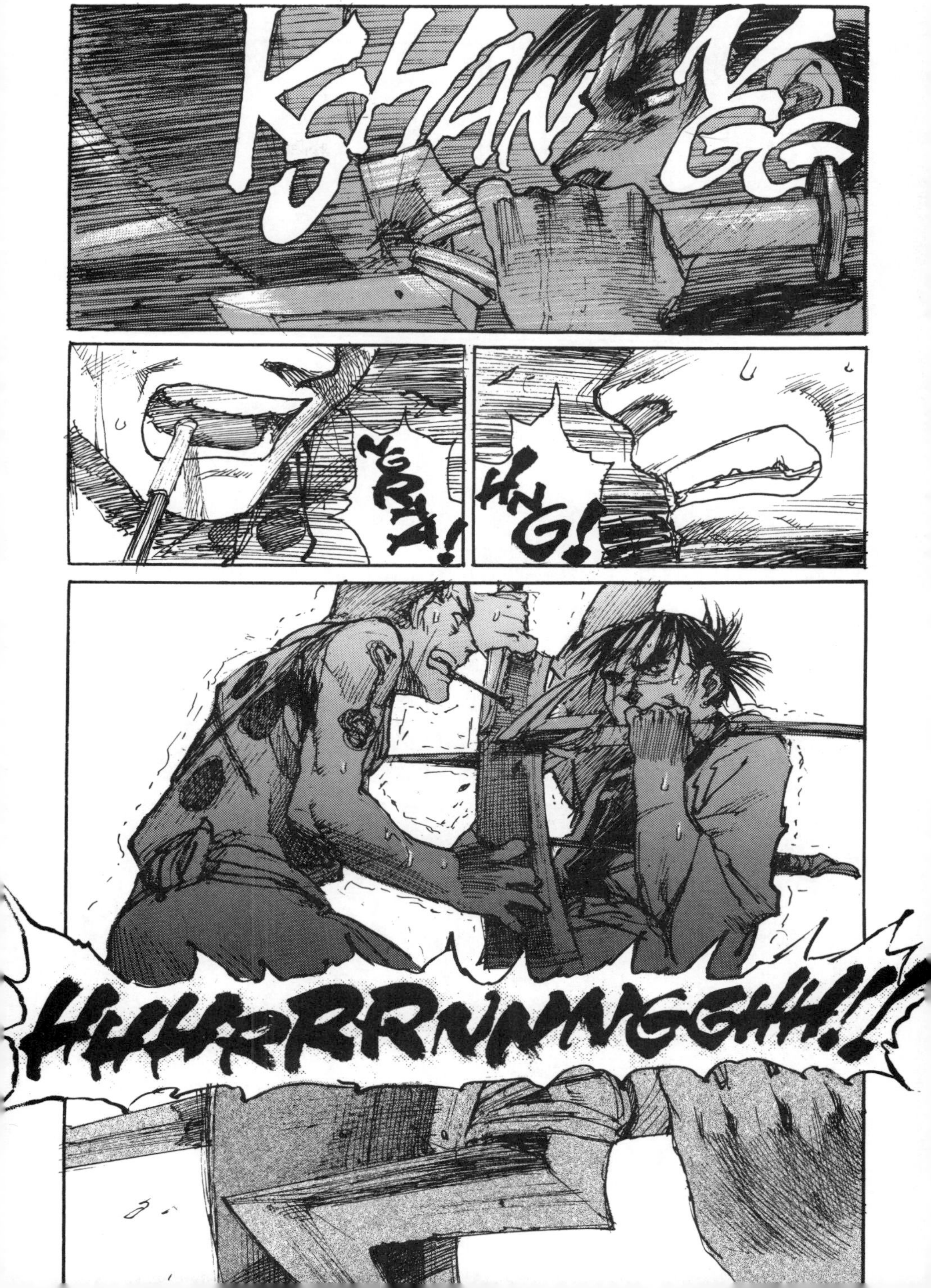
KSHANNGG
NGRAH!
HNG!
HHURRRNNNGGHH!!

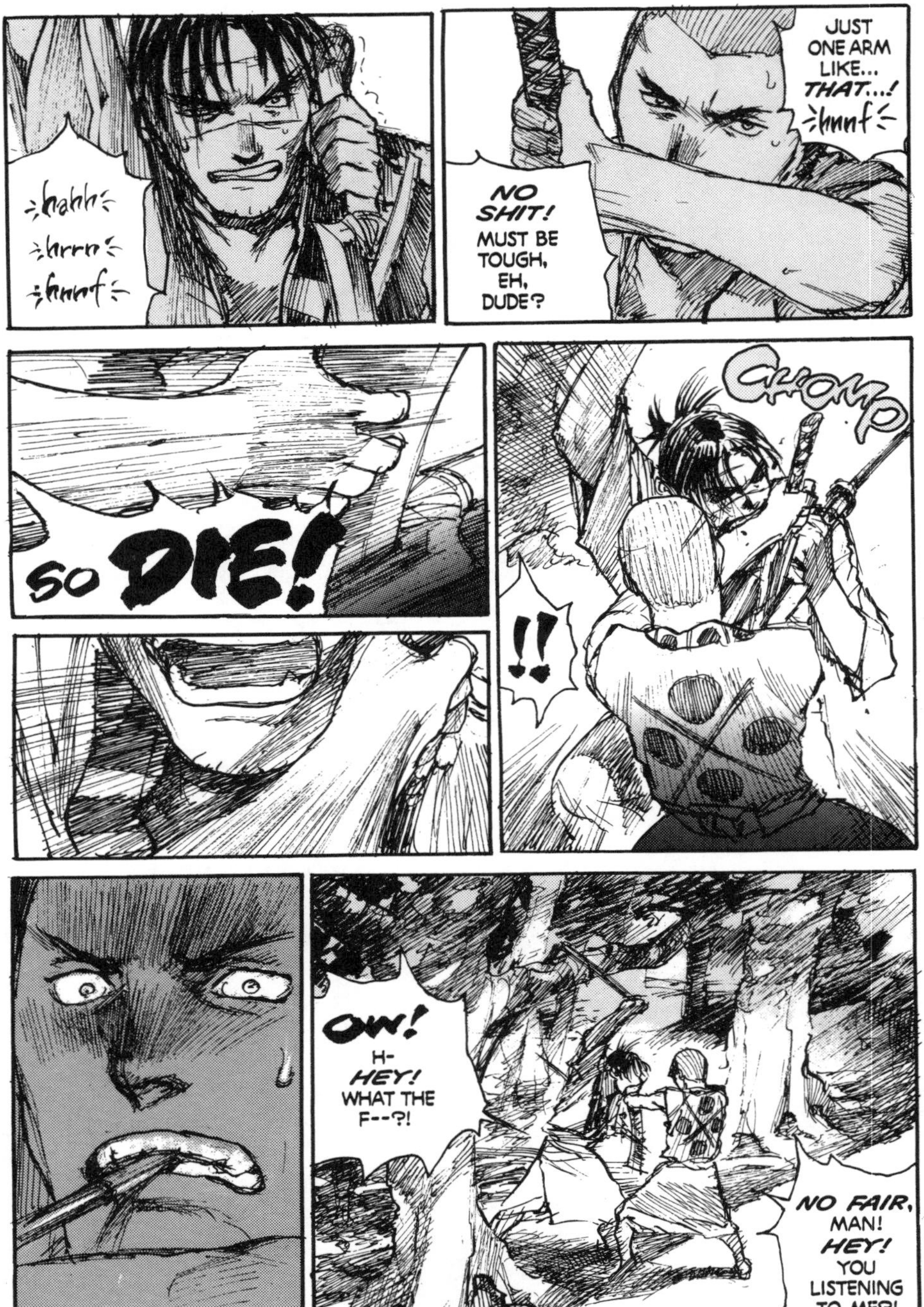

hahh
hrrn
hnnf
NO SHIT! MUST BE TOUGH, EH, DUDE?
JUST ONE ARM LIKE... THAT...!
hnnf
SO DIE!
CHOMP
!!
OW!
H-HEY! WHAT THE F--?!
NO FAIR, MAN! HEY! YOU LISTENING TO ME?!

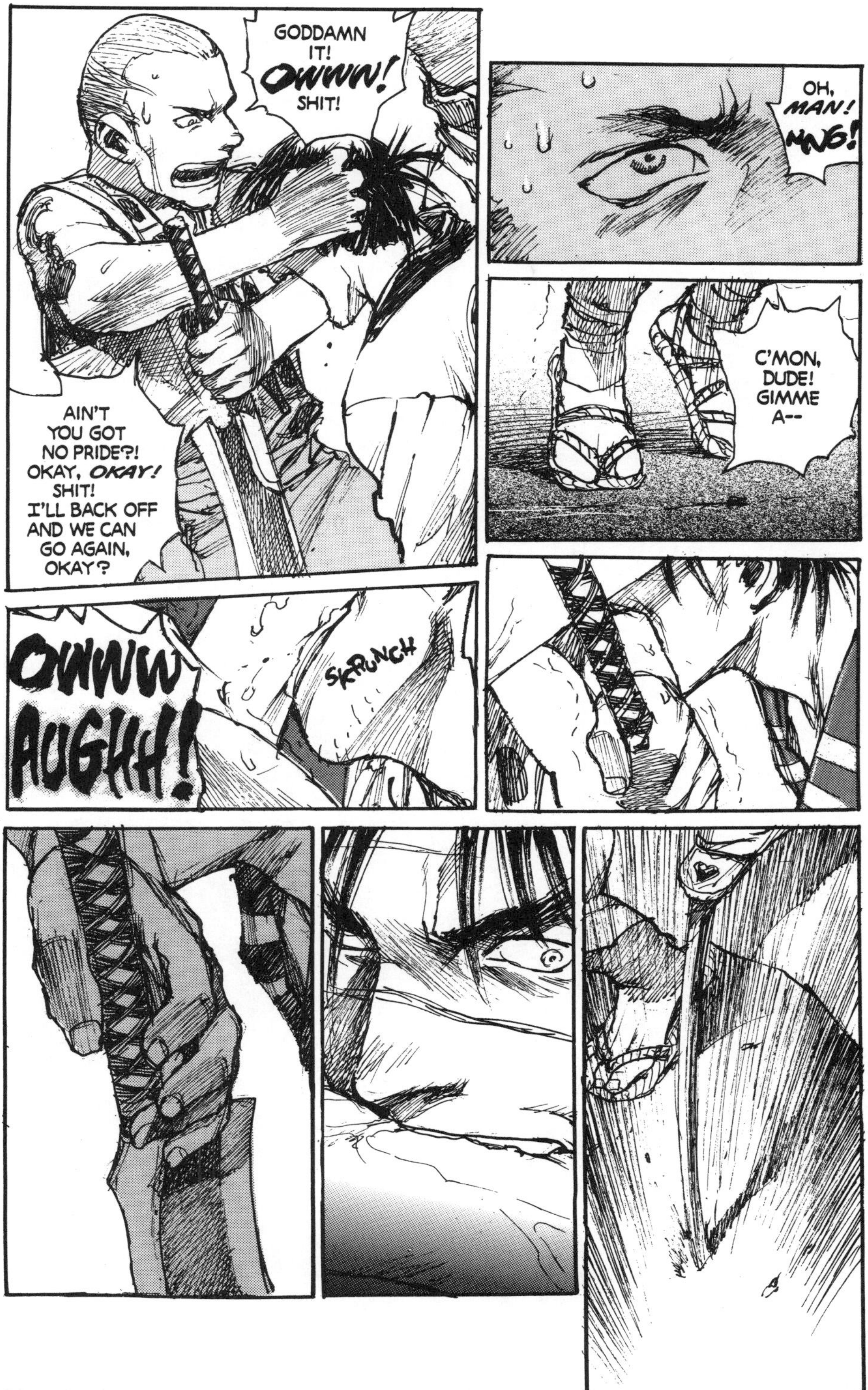
GODDAMN IT! OWWW! SHIT!
AIN'T YOU GOT NO PRIDE?! OKAY, OKAY! SHIT! I'LL BACK OFF AND WE CAN GO AGAIN, OKAY?
OH, MAN! MNG!
C'MON, DUDE! GIMME A--
OWWW AUGHH!
SKRUNCH

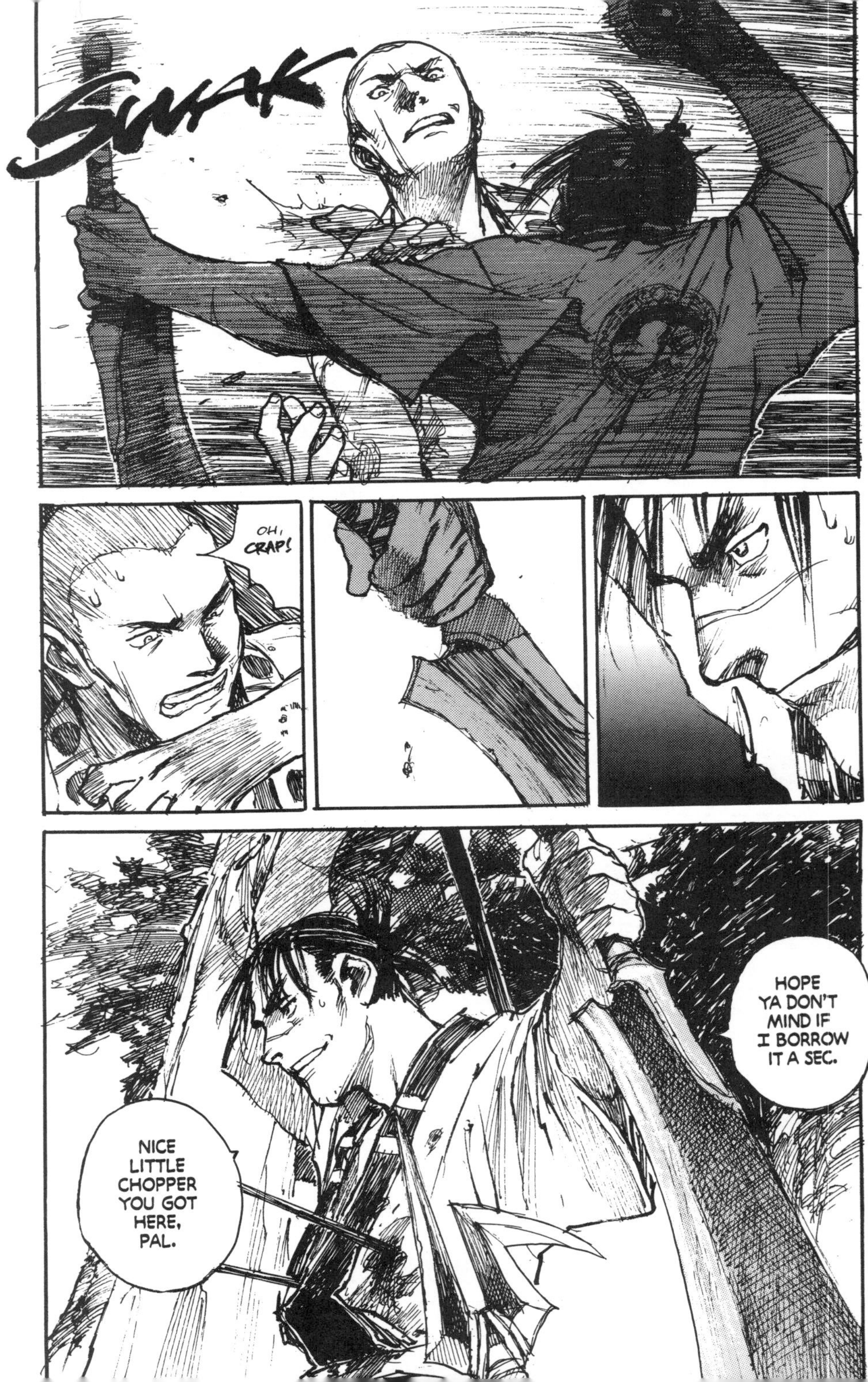
SWAK
OH, CRAP!
HOPE YA DON'T MIND IF I BORROW IT A SEC.
NICE LITTLE CHOPPER YOU GOT HERE, PAL.

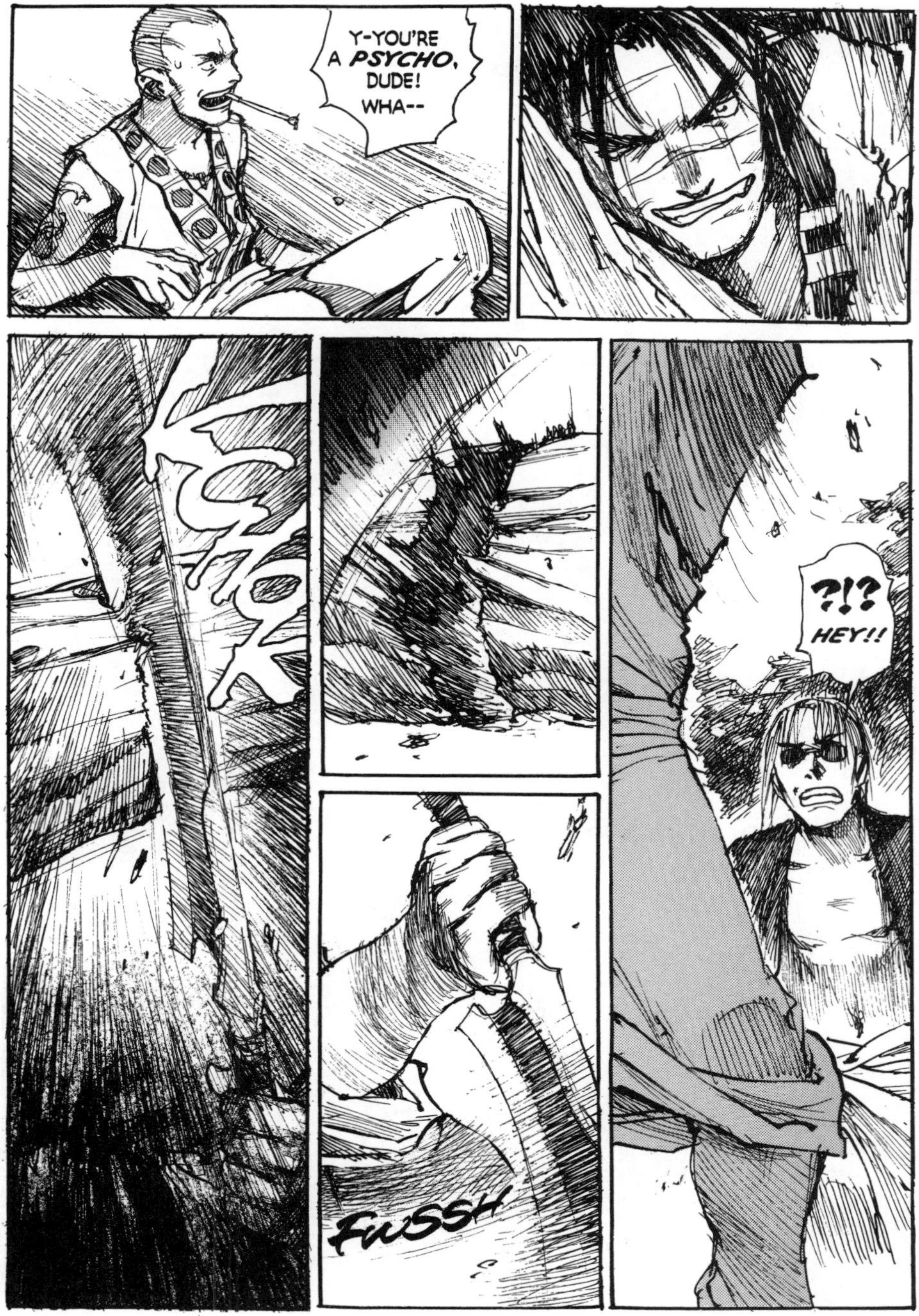
Y-YOU'RE A *PSYCHO*, DUDE!
WHA--
CHOK
FWSSH
?!?
HEY!!

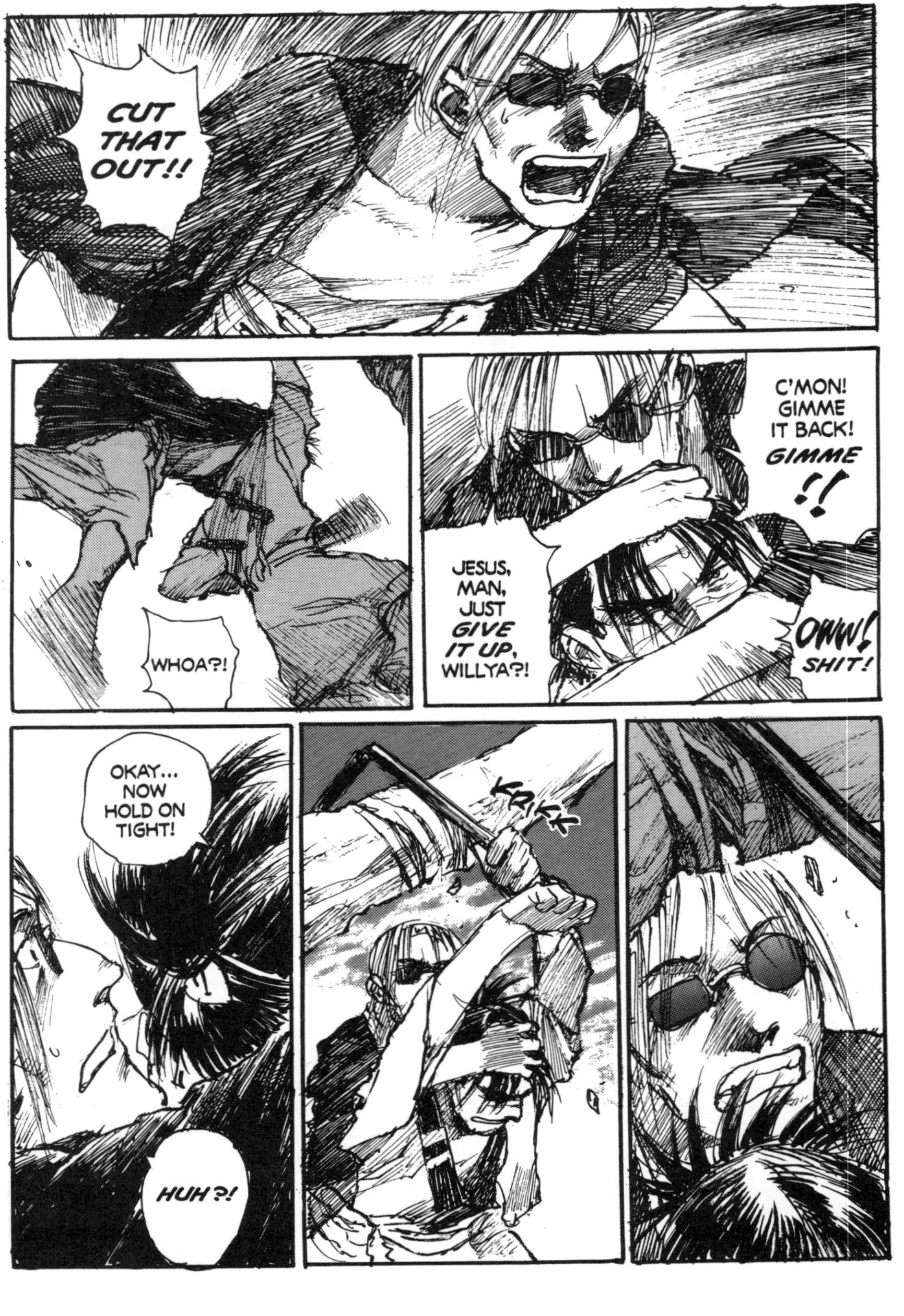
CUT THAT OUT!!
WHOA?!
C'MON! GIMME IT BACK! GIMME !!
JESUS, MAN, JUST GIVE IT UP, WILLYA?!
OWW! SHIT!
OKAY... NOW HOLD ON TIGHT!
HUH?!
KRIKK

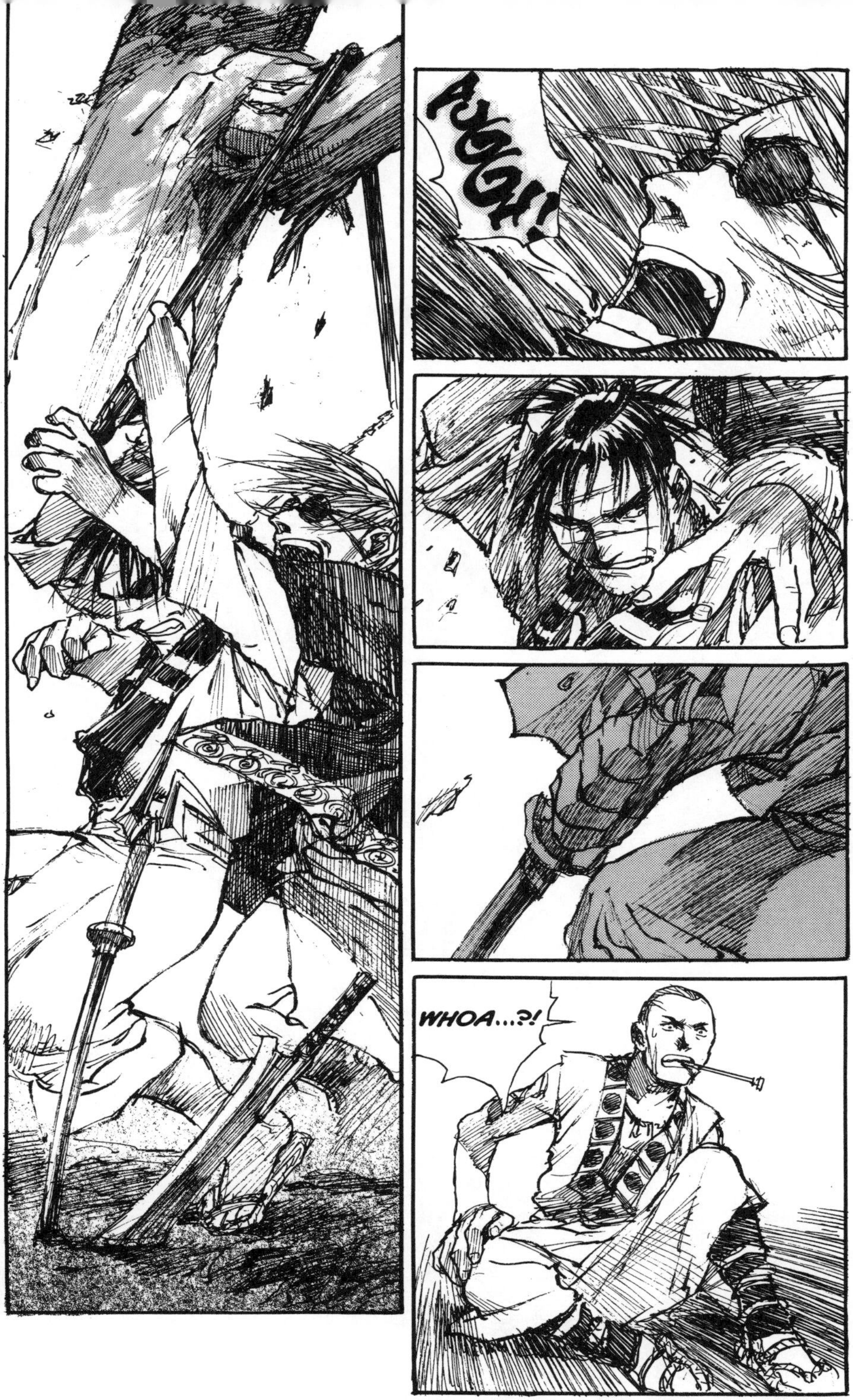
AUGGH!!
WHOA...?!

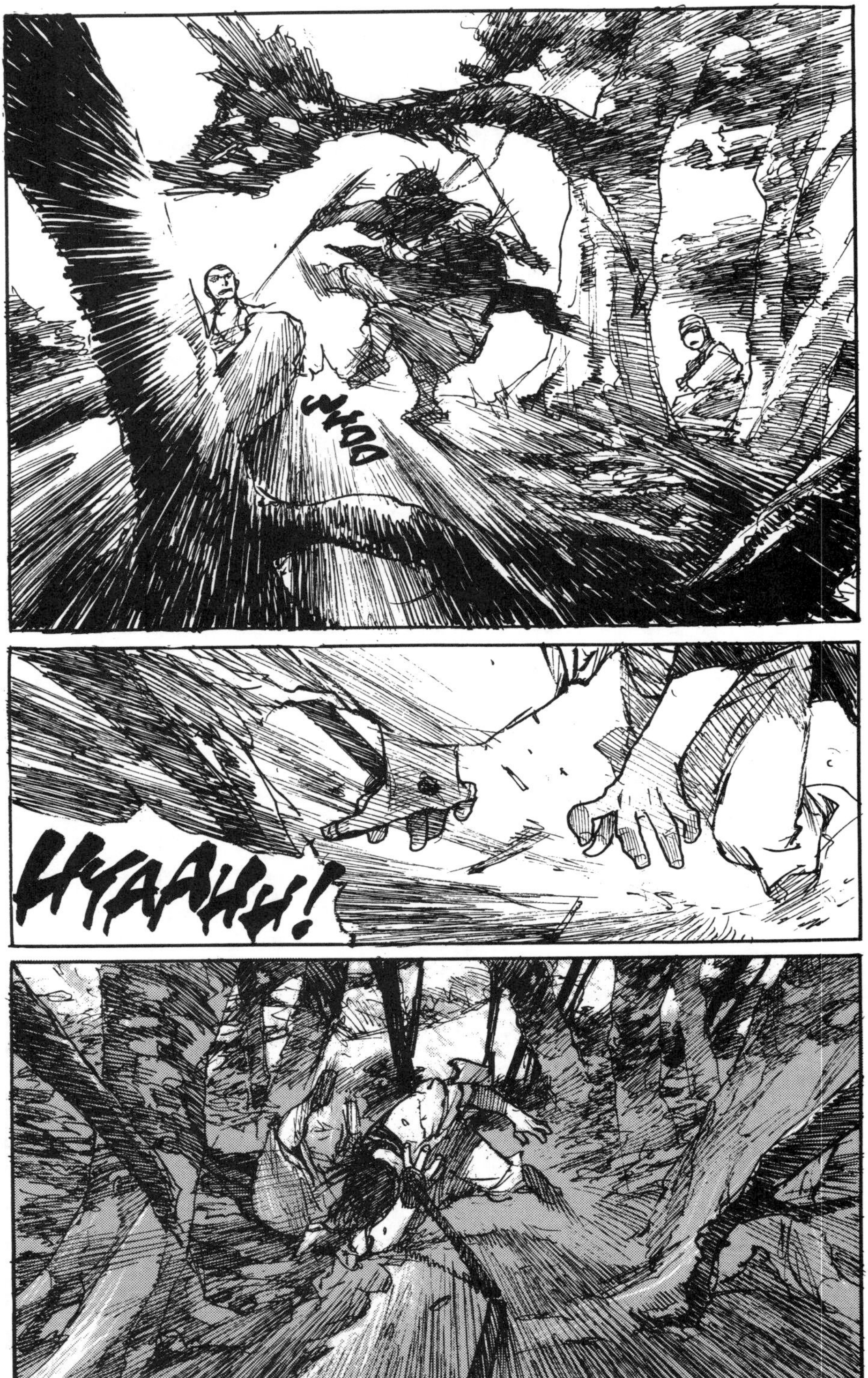
HYAAHH!

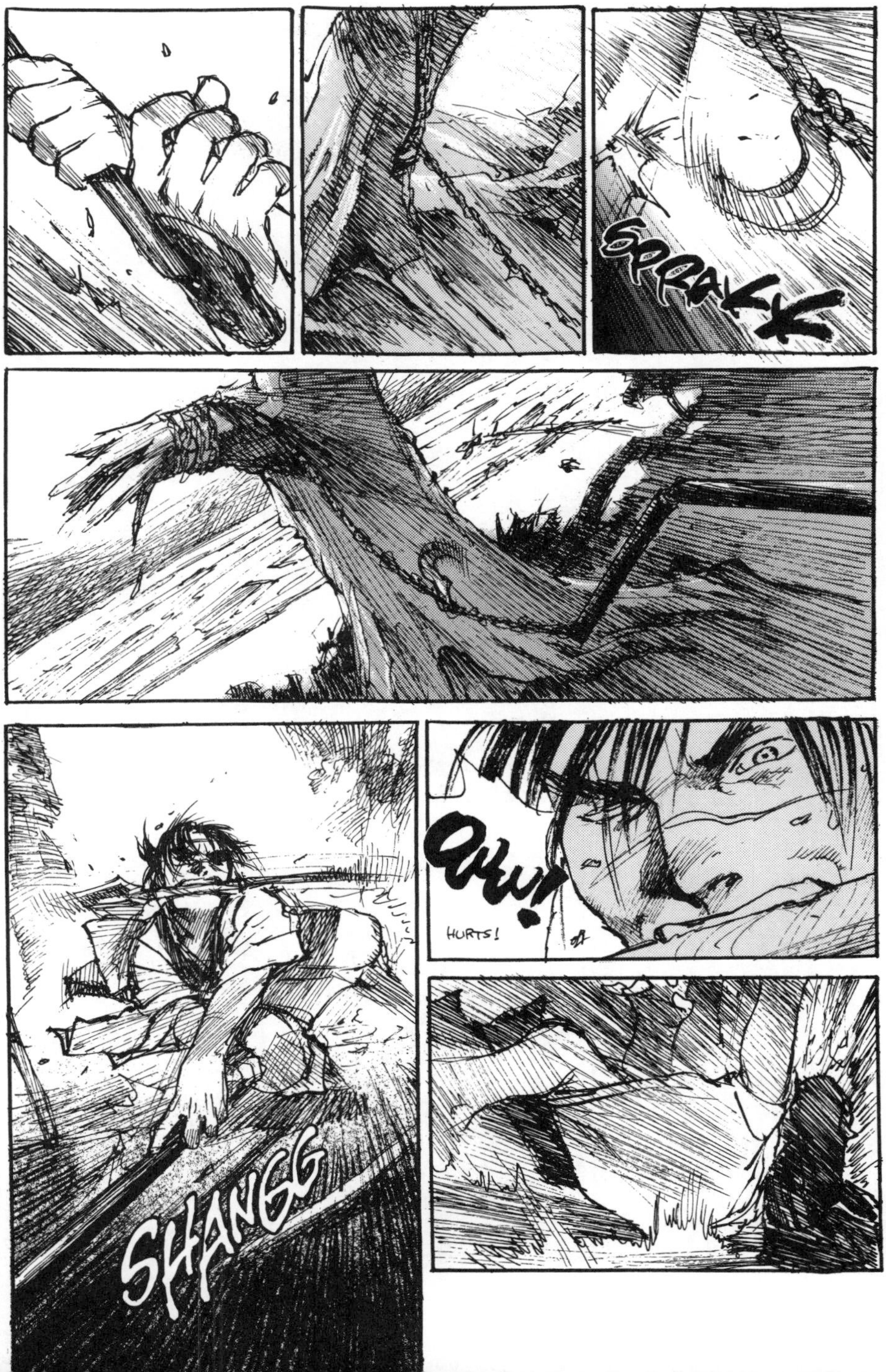
SPRAKK
SHANGG
OWW!
HURTS!

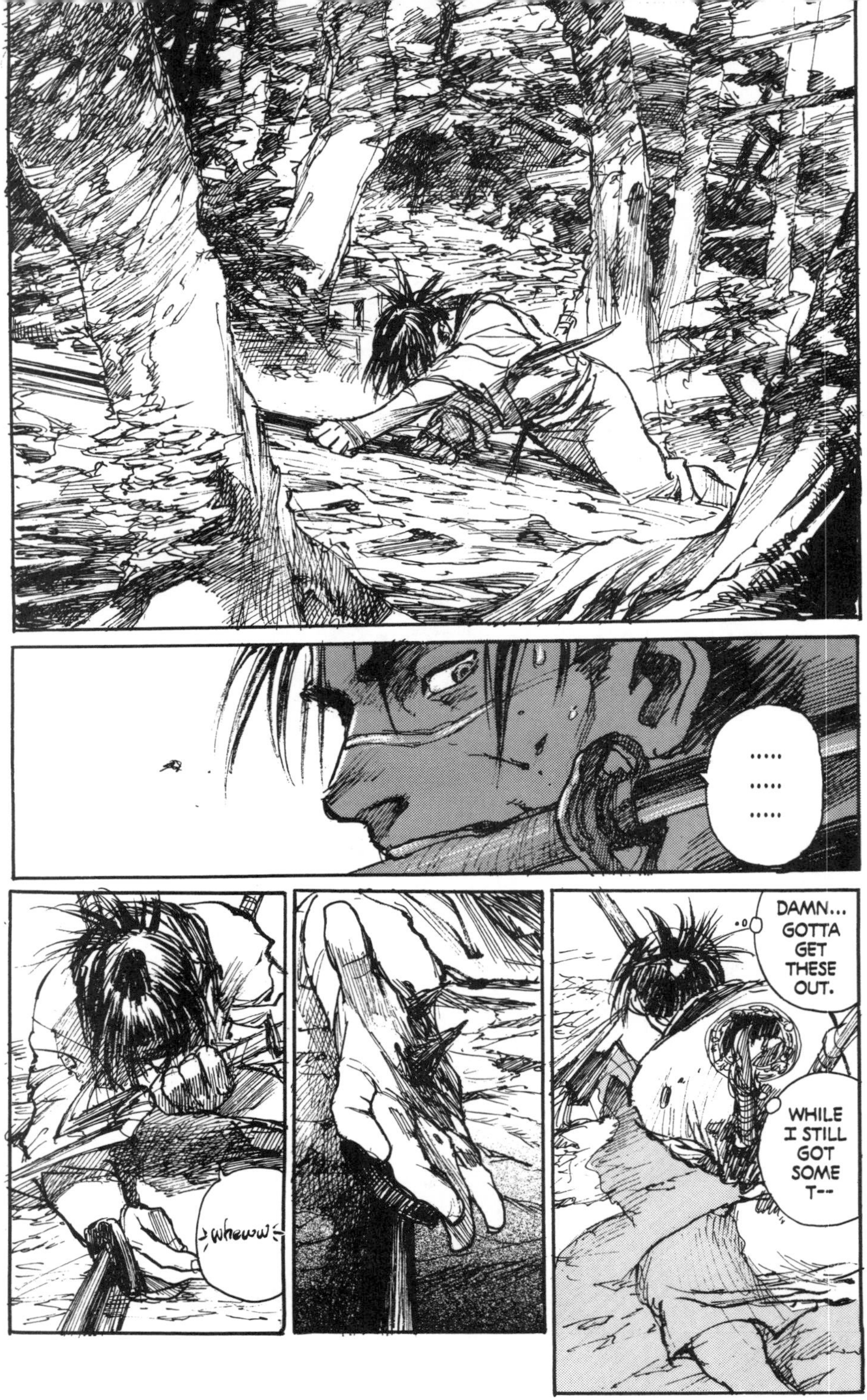
.....
.....
.....
whewww
DAMN... GOTTA GET THESE OUT.
WHILE I STILL GOT SOME T--

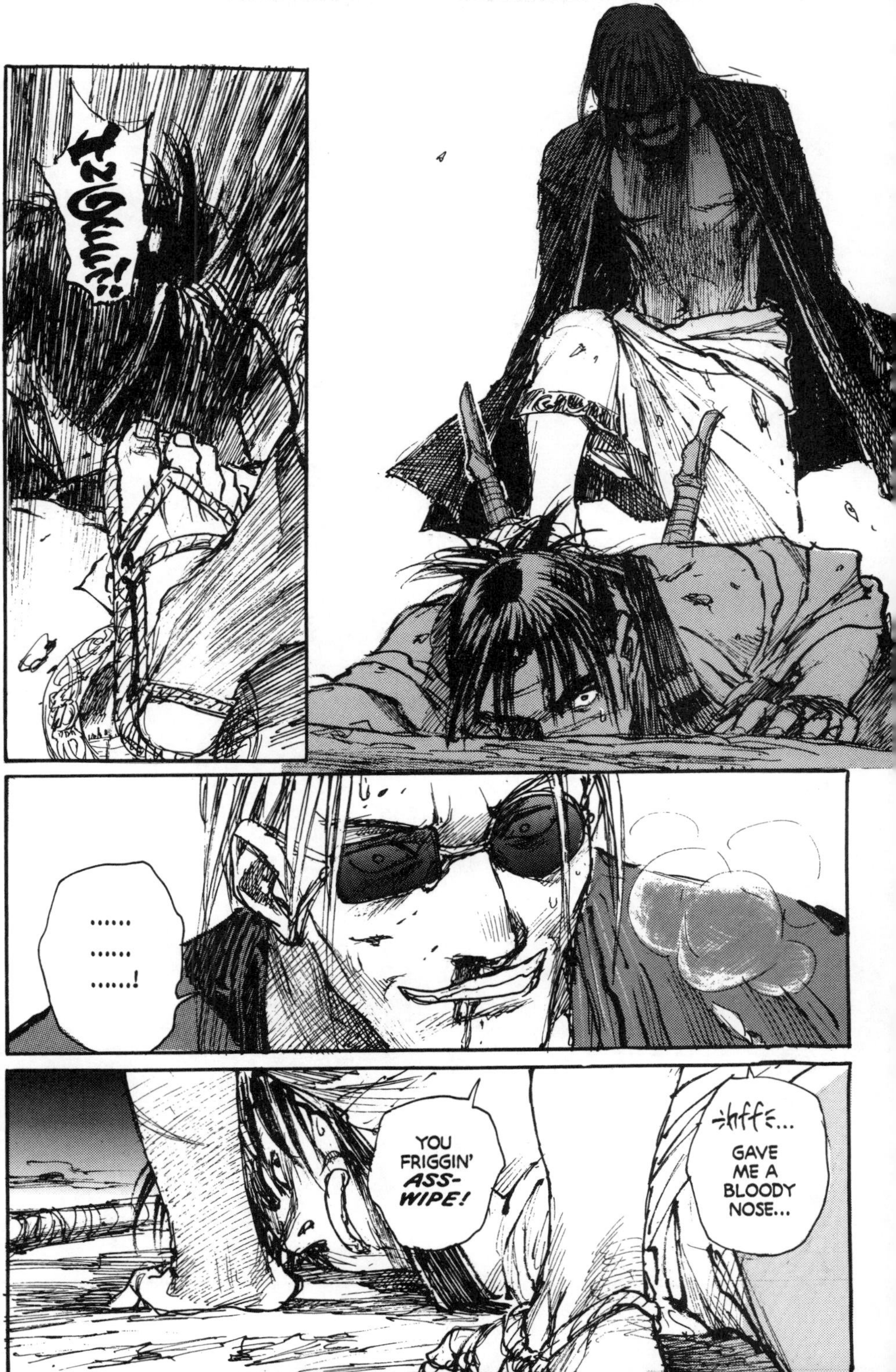
......
......
......!
YOU FRIGGIN' ***ASS-WIPE!***
snff...
GAVE ME A BLOODY NOSE...

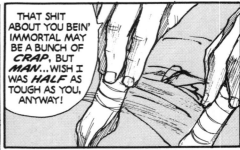

THAT SHIT ABOUT YOU BEIN' IMMORTAL MAY BE A BUNCH OF *CRAP*, BUT *MAN*...WISH I WAS *HALF* AS TOUGH AS YOU, ANYWAY!

YOU ARE *SOME-THIN' ELSE*, DUDE.

YOU ACT LIKE YOU DON'T EVEN GOT MY TWO STICKERS THROUGH YOUR GUTS!

*SLCCH*

*UNNG!*

BUT IT BLOWS MY MIND THAT YA SEEM TO THINK YOU CAN TURN YOUR BACK ON YOUR OPPONENT...

...JUST 'CAUSE YOU KNOCKED HIM DOWN FOR A SEC!

WELL, DUDE... YOU CAN TAKE THAT LITTLE LESSON WITH YA TO *HELL!*

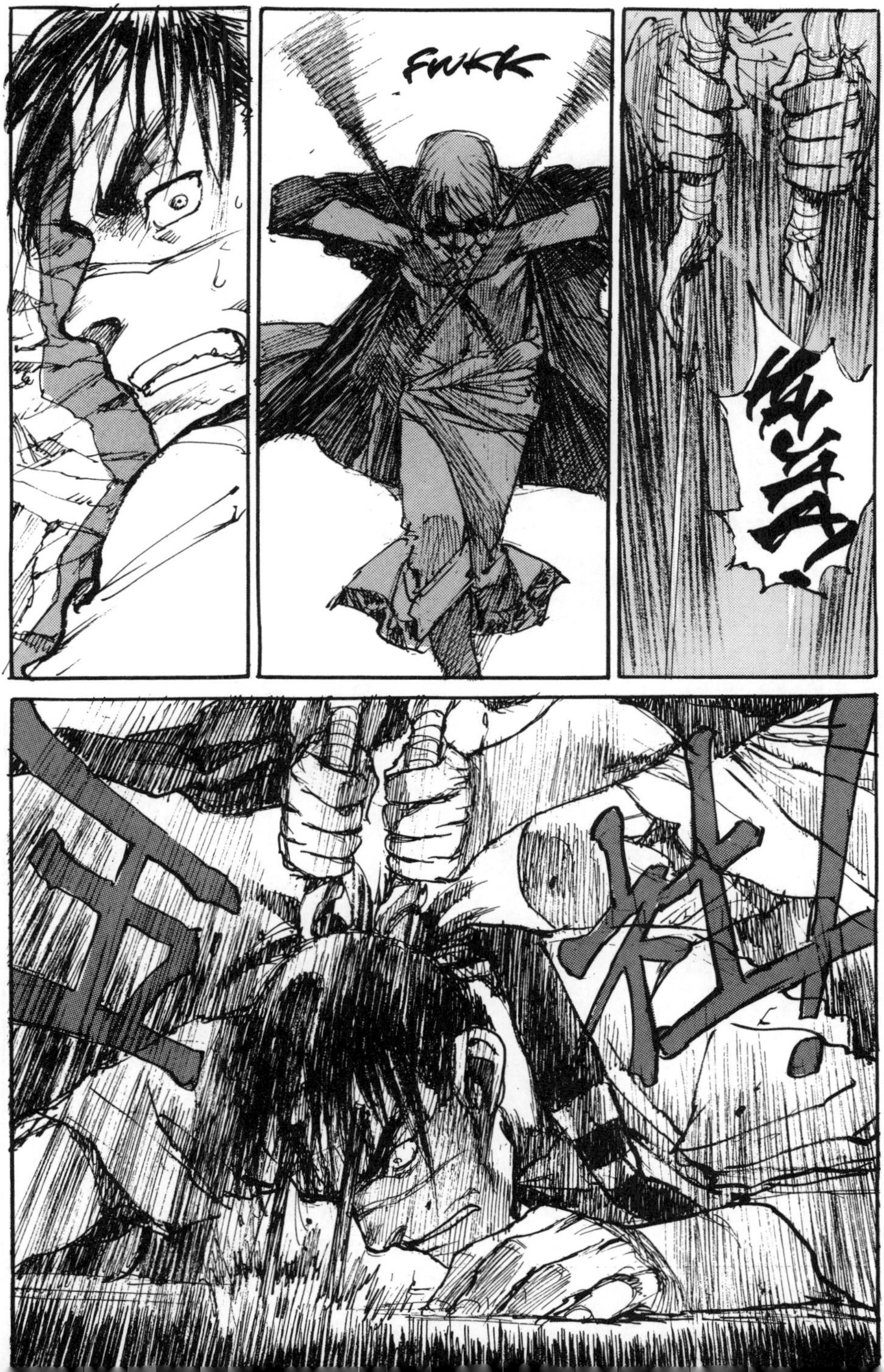
FWKK

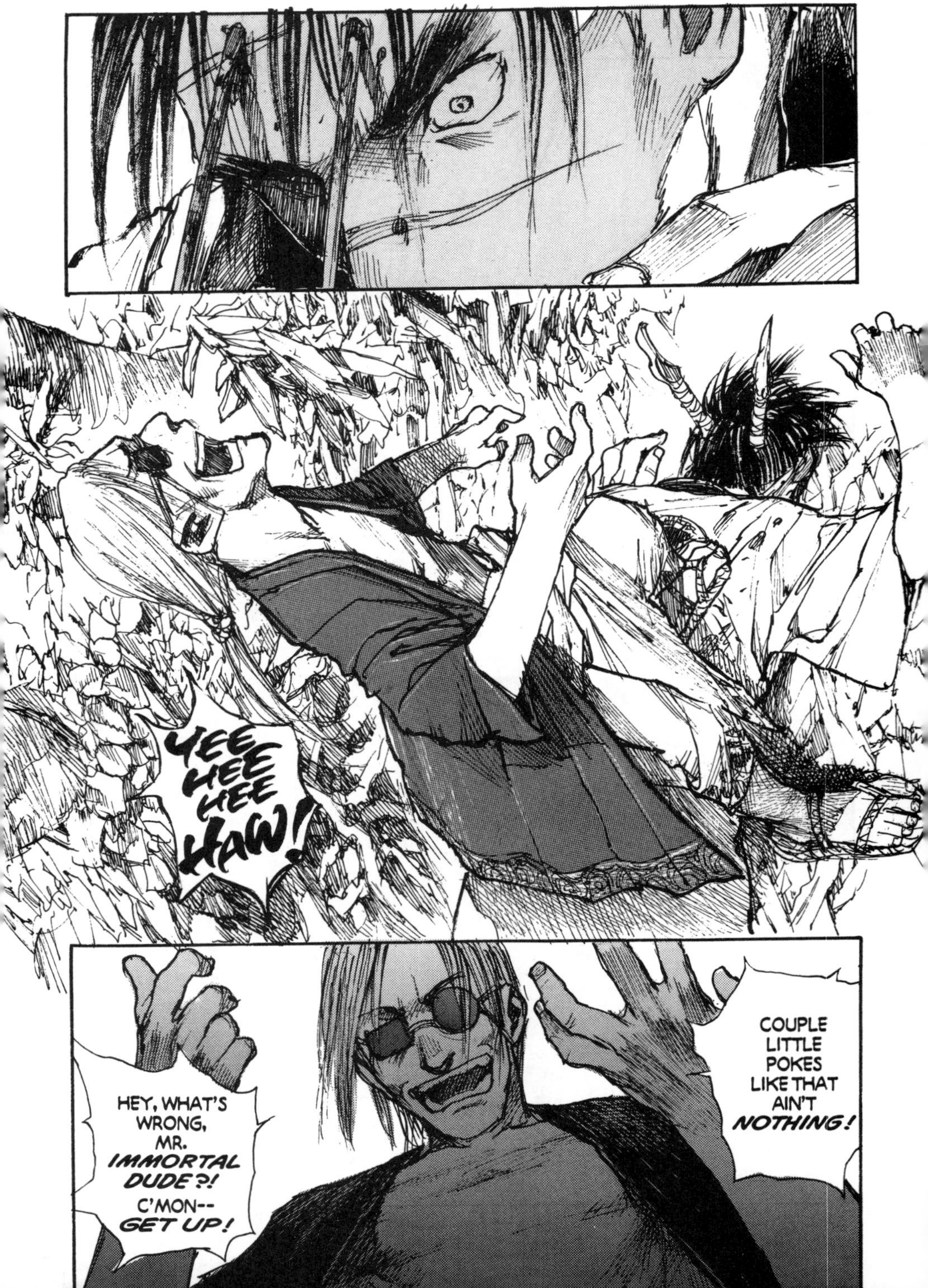
YEE HEE HEE HAW!
HEY, WHAT'S WRONG, MR. IMMORTAL DUDE?! C'MON-- GET UP!
COUPLE LITTLE POKES LIKE THAT AIN'T NOTHING!

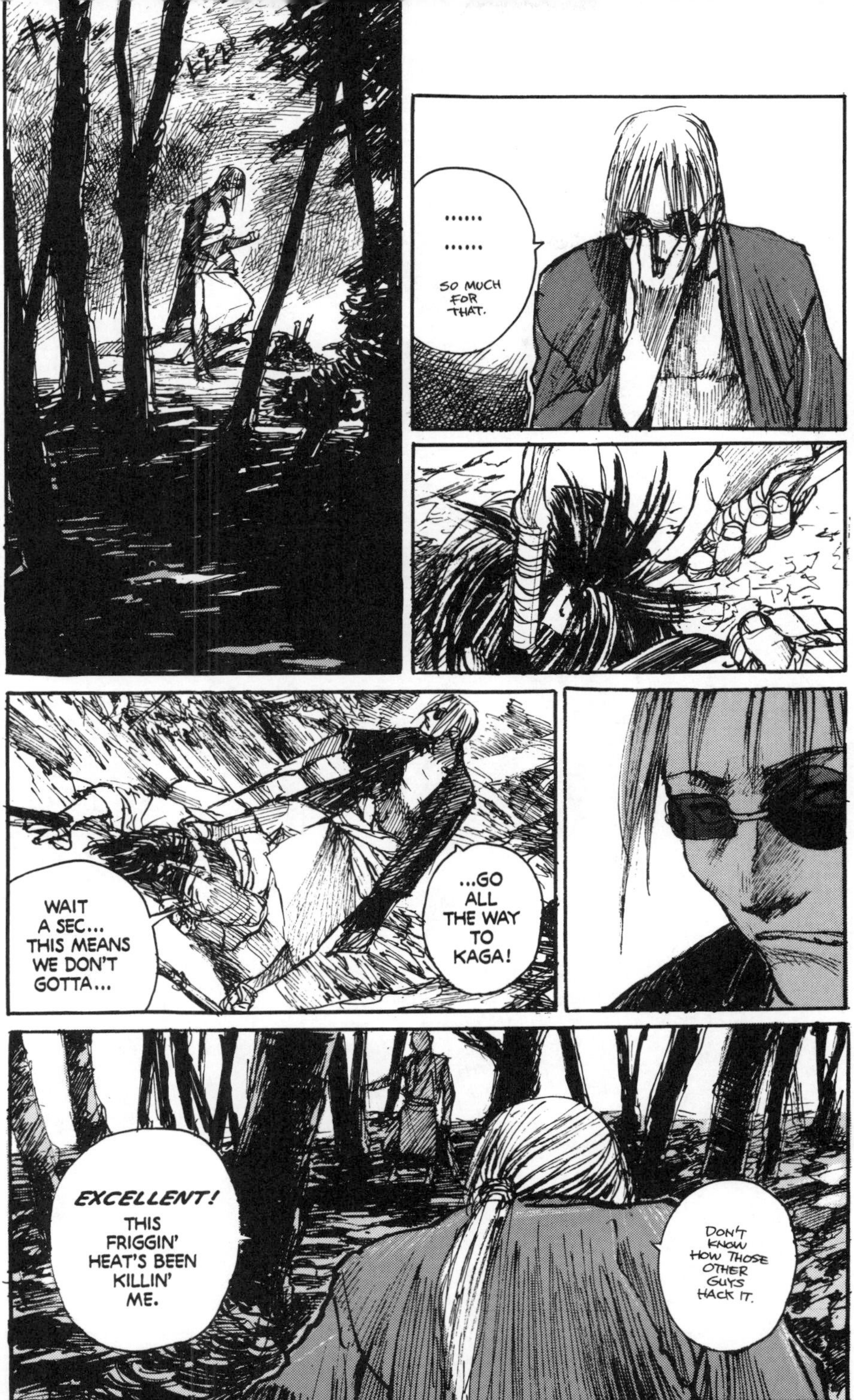

...... ...... SO MUCH FOR THAT.
WAIT A SEC... THIS MEANS WE DON'T GOTTA...
...GO ALL THE WAY TO KAGA!
*EXCELLENT!* THIS FRIGGIN' HEAT'S BEEN KILLIN' ME.
DON'T KNOW HOW THOSE OTHER GUYS HACK IT.

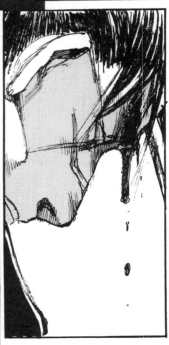

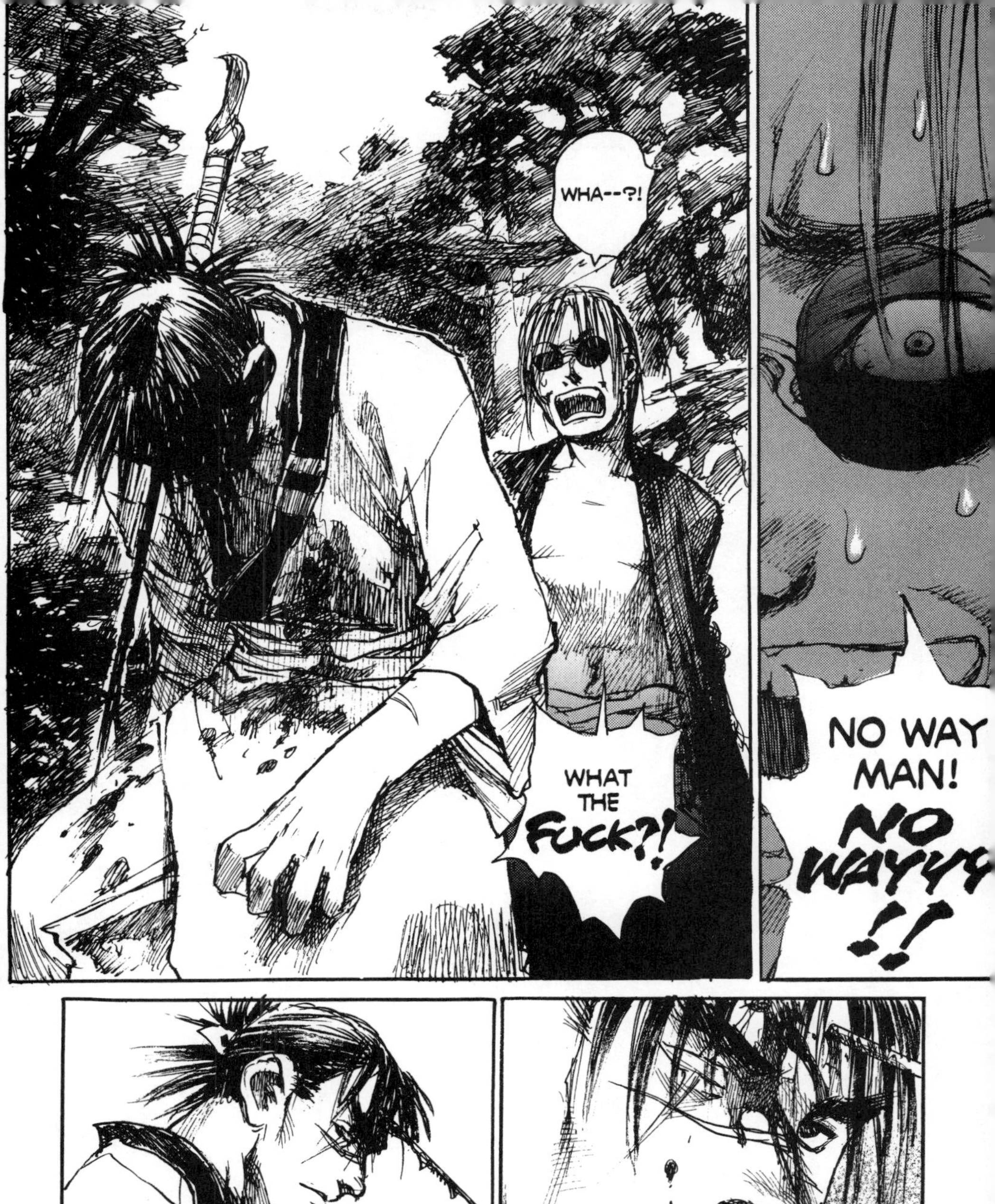
WHA--?!
WHAT THE FUCK?!
NO WAY MAN! NO WAYYY!!

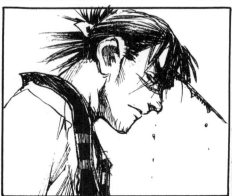

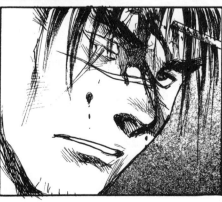

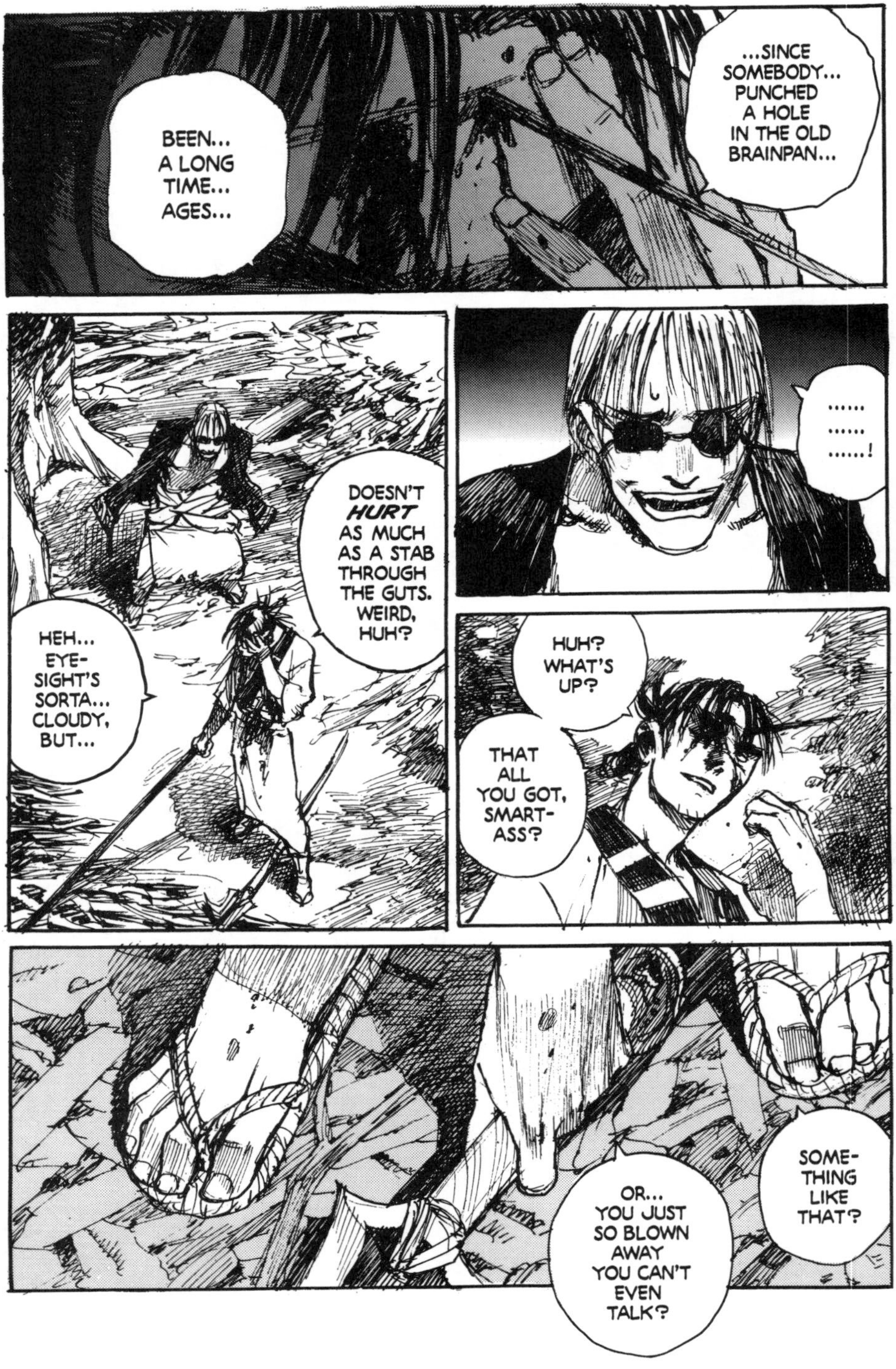
BEEN... A LONG TIME... AGES...
...SINCE SOMEBODY... PUNCHED A HOLE IN THE OLD BRAINPAN...
HEH... EYE-SIGHT'S SORTA... CLOUDY, BUT...
DOESN'T *HURT* AS MUCH AS A STAB THROUGH THE GUTS. WEIRD, HUH?
...... ...... ......!
HUH? WHAT'S UP?
THAT ALL YOU GOT, SMART-ASS?
OR... YOU JUST SO BLOWN AWAY YOU CAN'T EVEN TALK?
SOME-THING LIKE THAT?

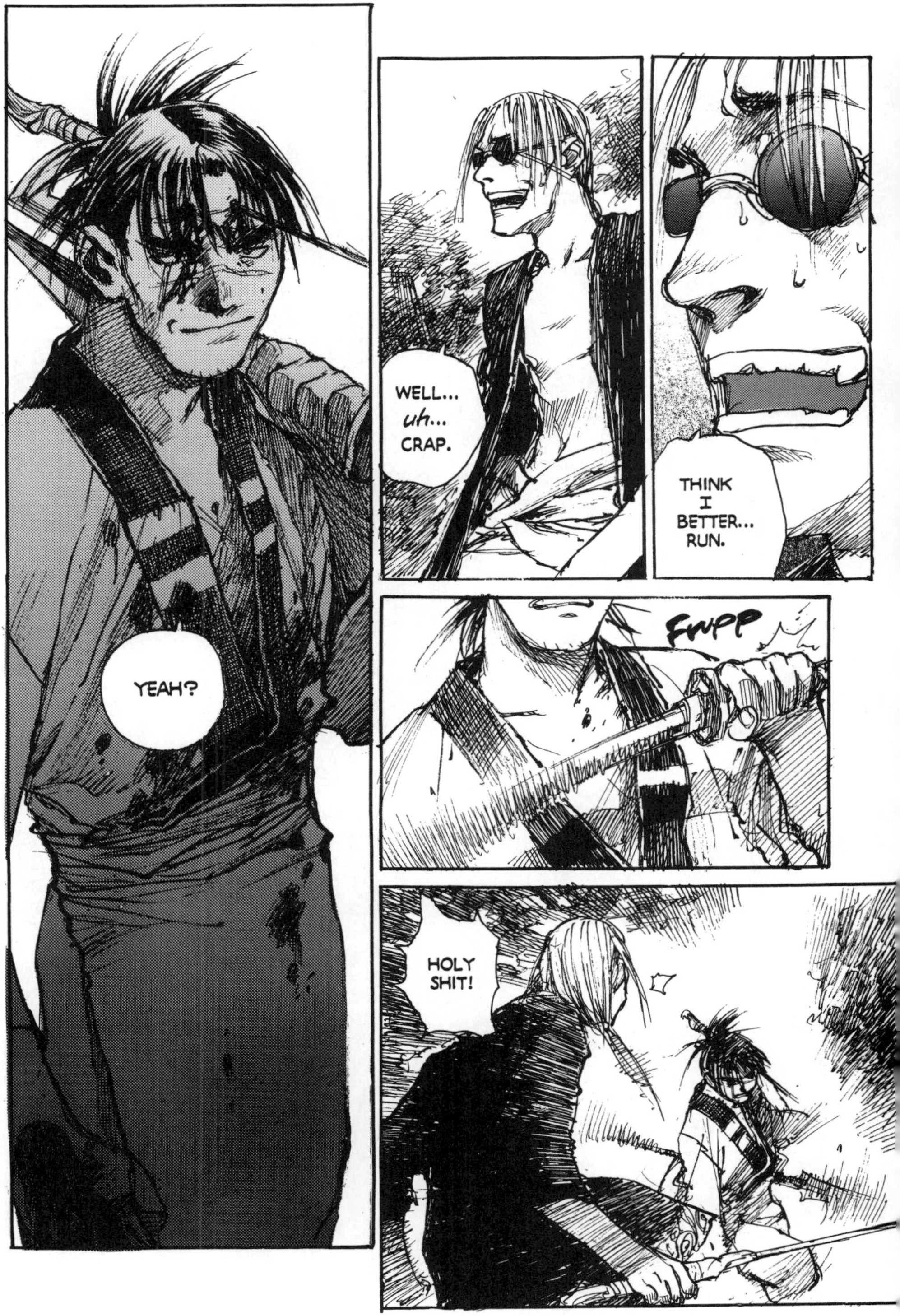
YEAH?
WELL... uh... CRAP.
THINK I BETTER... RUN.
FWPP
HOLY SHIT!

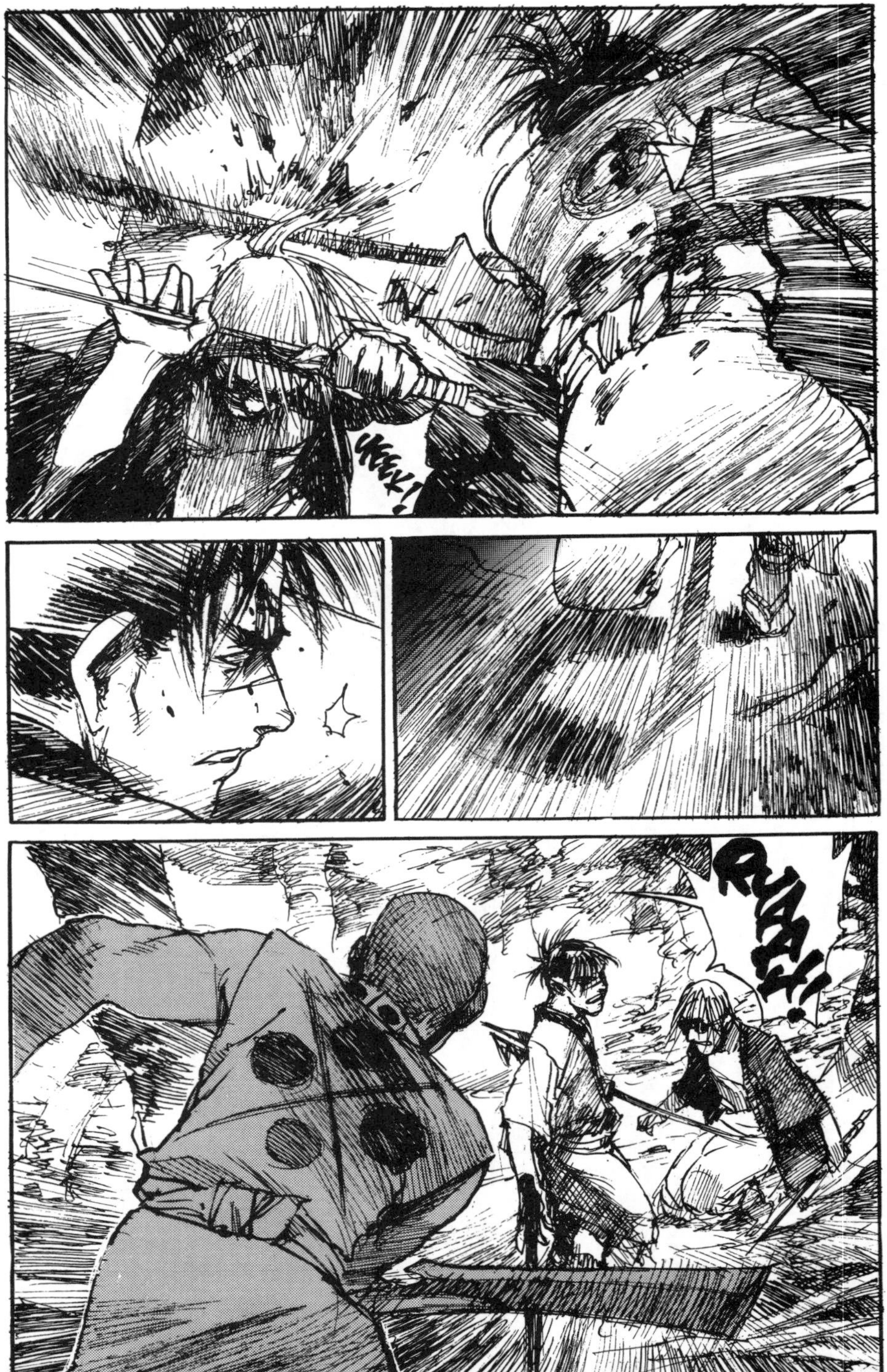
SEEK!
RYAAAH!!

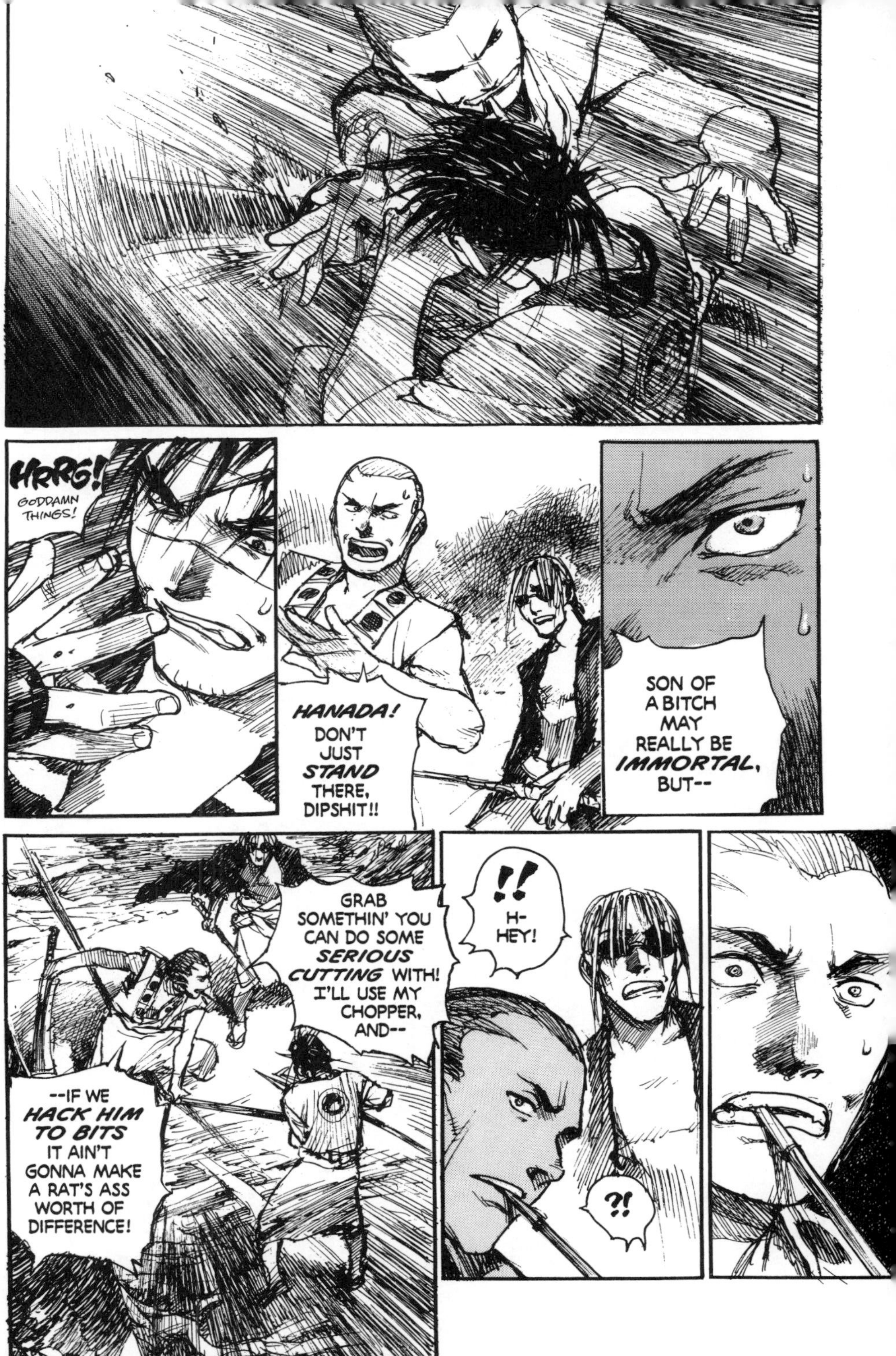
HRRG!
GODDAMN THINGS!
HANADA! DON'T JUST STAND THERE, DIPSHIT!!
SON OF A BITCH MAY REALLY BE IMMORTAL, BUT--
GRAB SOMETHIN' YOU CAN DO SOME SERIOUS CUTTING WITH! I'LL USE MY CHOPPER, AND--
--IF WE HACK HIM TO BITS IT AIN'T GONNA MAKE A RAT'S ASS WORTH OF DIFFERENCE!
!!
H-HEY!
?!

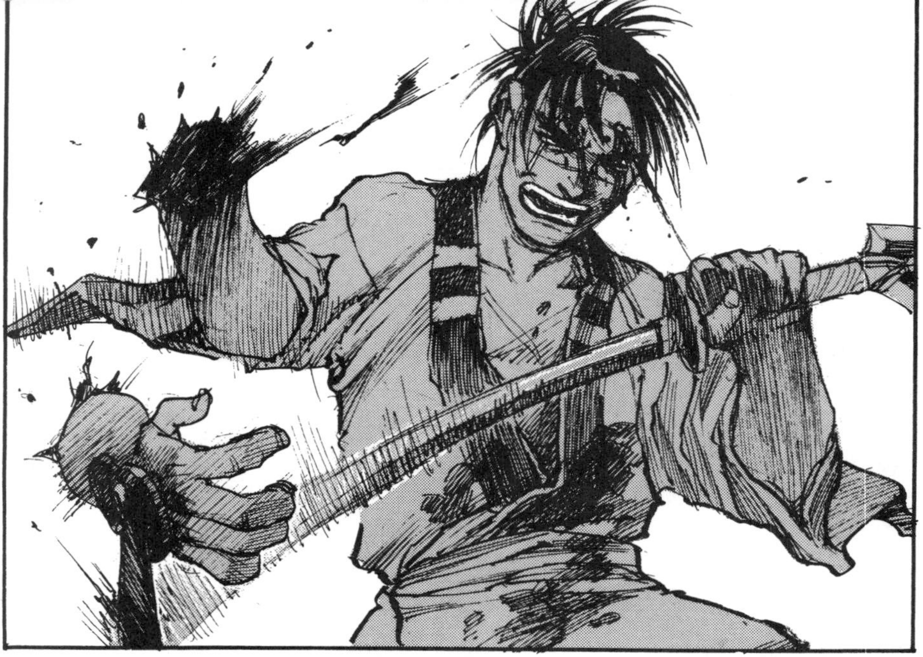

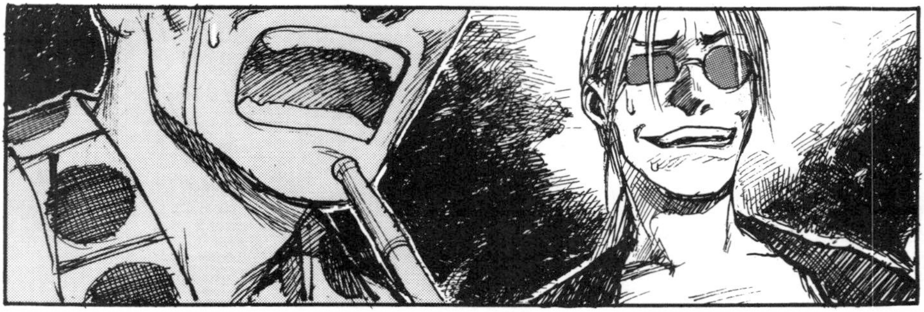

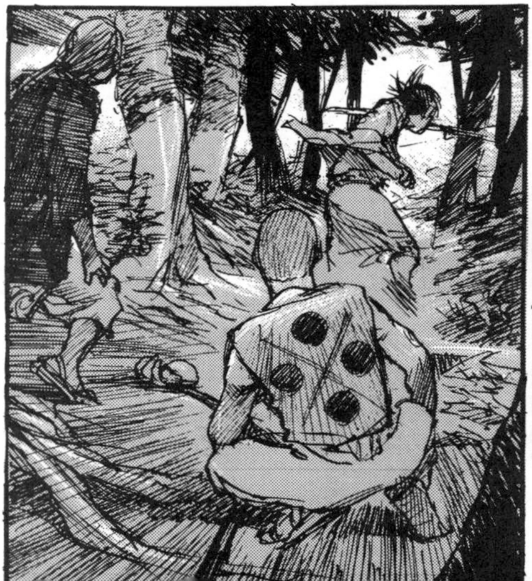

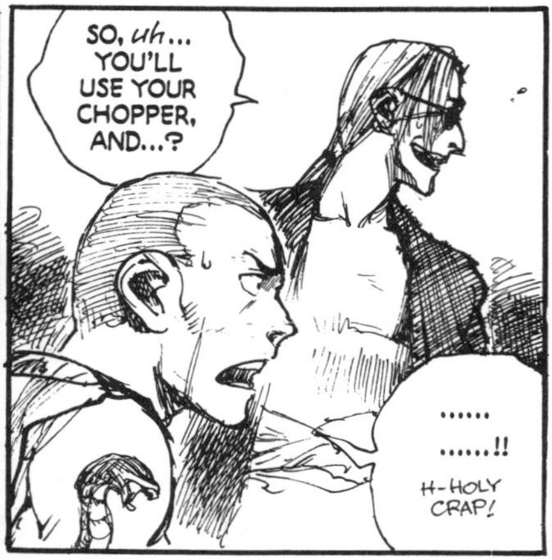
SO, *uh*... YOU'LL USE YOUR CHOPPER, AND...?
......
......!!
H-HOLY CRAP!

**TO BE CONTINUED...!**

# GLOSSARY

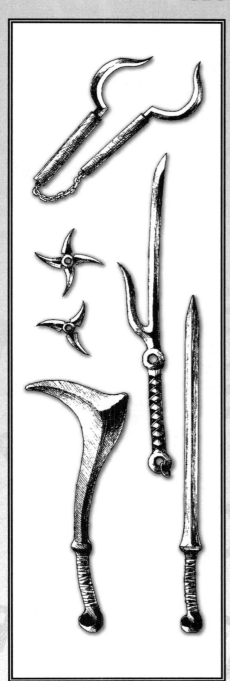

**banshi:** samurai manning a *sekisho* (checkpoint)

**banshu:** officers serving under the Shogun, usually assigned to Edo Castle to defend the Shogun himself

**dōjō:** a hall for martial arts training; here, centers for swordsmanship

**han:** a feudal domain

**Ittō-ryū:** the radical sword school of Anotsu Kagehisa

**kōkenjo:** sword school established by the Shogunate

**mon:** a small coin

**Mugai-ryū:** alleged sword school of Hyakurin and the Akagi assassins; literally, "without form"

**Mŭko-jima:** a district in Edo and also in present-day Tokyo

**musubi:** a hand-molded rice ball, often with a filling of fish or vegetables

**Mutenichi-ryū:** sword school inherited by Rin's father

**ochazuke:** a soupy mix of rice and green tea, flavored with various garnishes

**ri:** old Japanese unit of measurement equivalent to 2.44 miles

**rōnin:** a masterless samurai

**ryō:** a gold piece

**sekisho:** checkpoint. The central government strictly regulated travel, and all travelers had to submit papers at official checkpoints along the main highways into and out of Edo.

**Shi-shuku:** four areas of old Edo best known as unofficial red-light districts

**tegata:** travel pass

**yukimachi:** brothel favored by the Ittō-ryū

TAKE IT OR LEAVE IT...

SPECIAL "PAD OUT THE END OF THE BOOK" SPECIAL!

# SAMURA'S WEAPON SHOP OPEN 24 HOURS

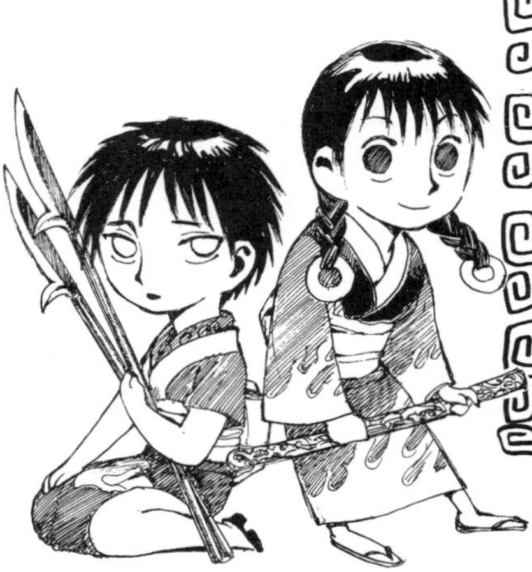

萬次 MANJI

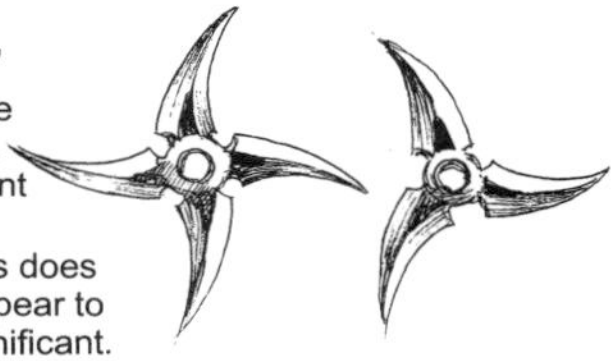

**鳥 KARASU: "The Crow"**

These weapons were originally used by Sabato Kuroi. The number of blades is different for the left and right hands, but this does not appear to be significant.

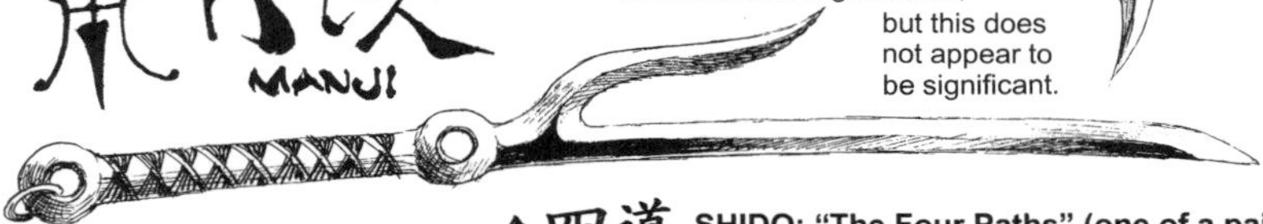

**▲四道 SHIDO: "The Four Paths" (one of a pair)**

MANJI'S BEEN RUN THROUGH BY THIS ONE.

Manji has a tendency to name his weapons after their former owners, and this is no exception. This is a relatively short sword, but even so, no normal person would hide this in his clothes.

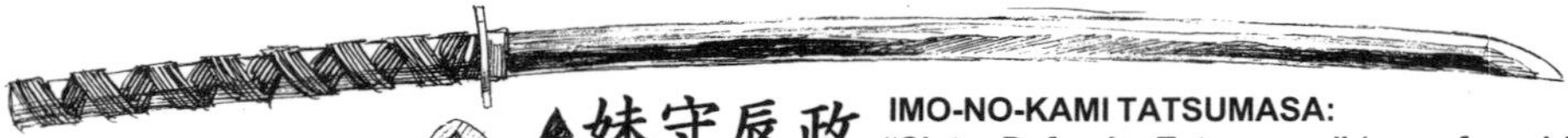

**▲妹守辰政 IMO-NO-KAMI TATSUMASA: "Sister Defender Tatsumasa" (one of a pair)**

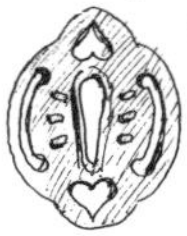

MANJI'S BEEN SLICED UP BY THIS ONE.

According to my notes to myself back at the time of my debut, this is apparently the work of "famed swordsmith Toratoru Kotetsu." But there doesn't seem to be anything particularly special about it. It's an okay sword by itself, but there's no reason to get *two* of them.

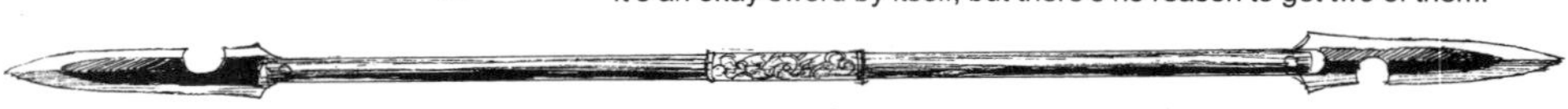

**▲阿吽 AUN:**

Usually this is folded up as shown on the right. ➜ It's only assembled for combat. It can also be used as a two-part spear.

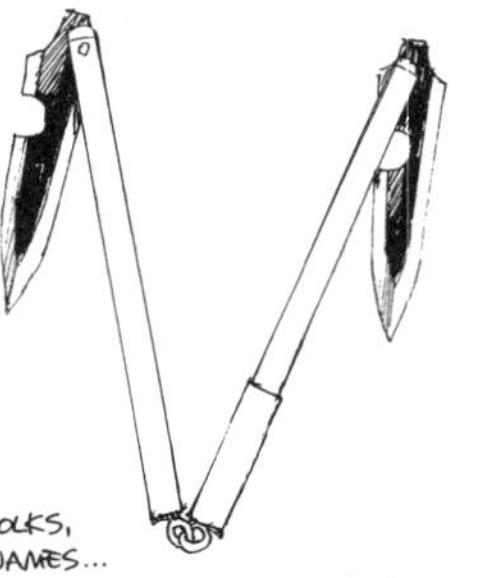

**(無銘) (NO NAME)**

These are different from the similar weapons in the first episode.

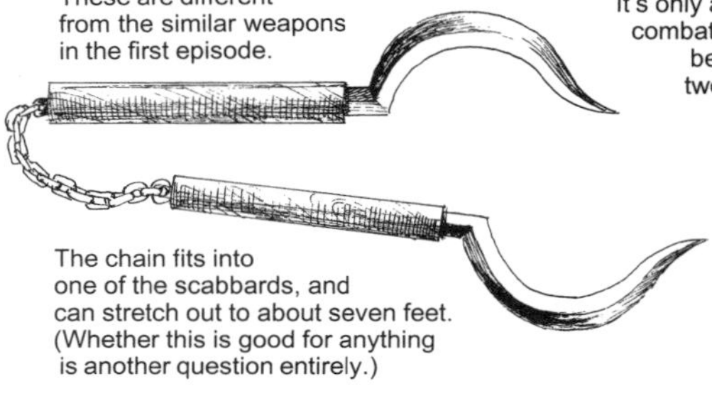

The chain fits into one of the scabbards, and can stretch out to about seven feet. (Whether this is good for anything is another question entirely.)

HERE THEY ARE, FOLKS, THE WEAPON NAMES... AS REQUESTED IN YOUR MANY POSTCARDS. BUT I'M BEGGING YOU... DON'T MAKE ME TRY TO COME UP WITH A BUNCH OF DOPEY NAMES FOR EVERYONE'S "SPECIAL SWORD TECHNIQUES"...!

## RIN

### ▼クトネシリカ KUTONESHIRIKA:

"Kutoneshirika" is the name of a spirit sword that appears in an Ainu myth cycle. Since the sword came from Ezo (the northern island now known as Hokkaidō), Rin probably just named it on a whim. It's not very sharp.

### 刀綬 TŌJU: (back view)

Rin's handmade special. It doubles as a carry-all pouch. It's the same problem Makie deals with by a special *shamisen*. Women couldn't wear swords tucked into their sash like the men, so when they did carry swords, they had to come up with their own solutions.

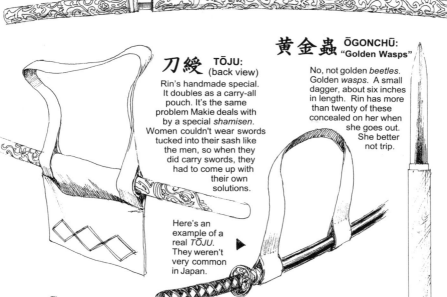

### 黄金蟲 ŌGONCHŪ: "Golden Wasps"

No, not golden *beetles*. Golden *wasps*. A small dagger, about six inches in length. Rin has more than twenty of these concealed on her when she goes out. She better not trip.

Here's an example of a real *TŌJU*. They weren't very common in Japan. ▶

## ANOTSU

### 頭椎（斧）KABUTSUCHI: "Head Hammer" (Axe)

A blunt axe. It's small, but has quite a bit of mass. Battle axes weren't very popular weapons in Japan; this one is modeled on an example from Nepal. It appears in the story *Rin's Bane*.

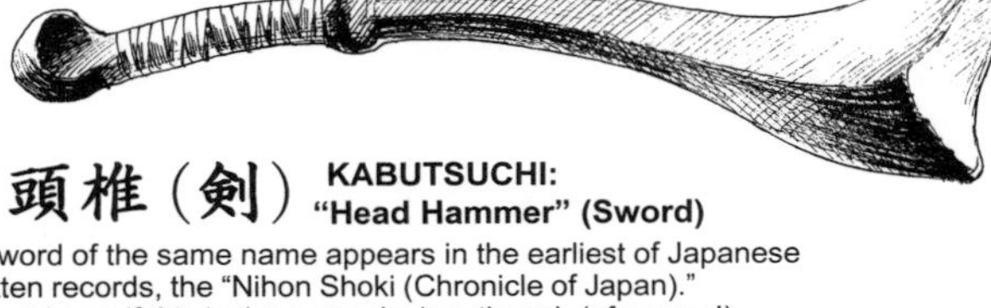

### 頭椎（剣）KABUTSUCHI: "Head Hammer" (Sword)

A sword of the same name appears in the earliest of Japanese written records, the "Nihon Shoki (Chronicle of Japan)."
I don't know if this is the same design, though (of course!).
I might mention here that Anotsu's name, clothing, and even his weapons all still show the mark of the "ethnic-flavored" universe I'd been planning to set the story in until just before I began the series.

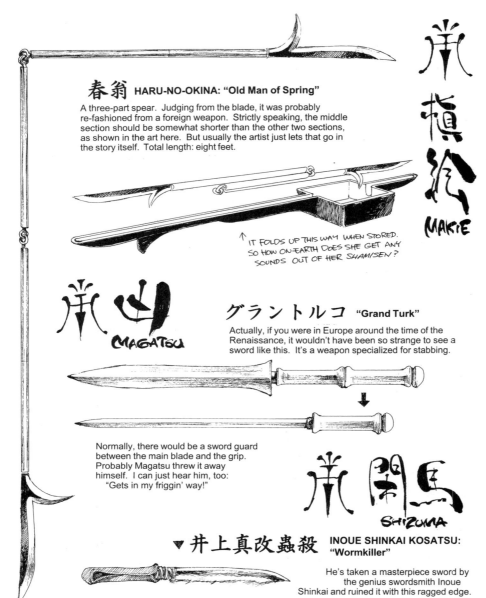

春翁 **HARU-NO-OKINA: "Old Man of Spring"**

A three-part spear. Judging from the blade, it was probably re-fashioned from a foreign weapon. Strictly speaking, the middle section should be somewhat shorter than the other two sections, as shown in the art here. But usually the artist just lets that go in the story itself. Total length: eight feet.

*MAKIE*

↑ IT FOLDS UP THIS WAY WHEN STORED. SO HOW ON-EARTH DOES SHE GET ANY SOUNDS OUT OF HER *SHAMISEN*?

*MAGATSU*

グラントルコ "Grand Turk"

Actually, if you were in Europe around the time of the Renaissance, it wouldn't have been so strange to see a sword like this. It's a weapon specialized for stabbing.

Normally, there would be a sword guard between the main blade and the grip. Probably Magatsu threw it away himself. I can just hear him, too: "Gets in my friggin' way!"

*SHIZUMA*

▼ 井上真改蟲殺 **INOUE SHINKAI KOSATSU: "Wormkiller"**

He's taken a masterpiece sword by the genius swordsmith Inoue Shinkai and ruined it with this ragged edge.

What's more frightening than the cutting edge itself is the poison that's supposed to trickle down those slivers. It's a horrible weapon, truly made to "kill with one blow."